ḤESED AND THE NEW TESTAMENT

Ḥesed and the New Testament

An Intertextual Categorization Study

KAREN NELSON

EISENBRAUNS | University Park, Pennsylvania

Library of Congress Cataloging-in-Publication Data

Names: Nelson, Karen (Presbyterian minister), author.
Title: Ḥesed and the New Testament : an intertextual categorization study / Karen Nelson.
Description: University Park, Pennsylvania : Eisenbrauns, [2023] | Includes bibliographical references and index.
Summary: "Investigates the relationship between the concept of ḥesed—often translated as steadfast love, loyalty, and devotion—and the New Testament through a category analysis of ḥesed in the Hebrew Bible and an intertextual examination of New Testament text for corresponding concepts"—Provided by publisher.
Identifiers: LCCN 2023005044 | ISBN 9781646022427 (paperback)
Subjects: LCSH: Bible. New Testament—Criticism, interpretation, etc. | Ḥesed (The Hebrew word) | Intertextuality in the Bible.
Classification: LCC BS2385 .N45 2023 | DDC 225.6/6—dc23/eng/20230411
LC record available at https://lccn.loc.gov/2023005044

Printed in the United States of America
Published by The Pennsylvania State University Press,
University Park, PA 16802-1003

Eisenbrauns is an imprint of The Pennsylvania State University Press.

The Pennsylvania State University Press is a member of the Association of University Presses.

It is the policy of The Pennsylvania State University Press to use acid-free paper. Publications on uncoated stock satisfy the minimum requirements of American National Standard for Information Sciences—Permanence of Paper for Printed Library Material, ANSI Z39.48–1992.

CONTENTS

List of Tables xi
Preface xiii
Acknowledgments xv
List of Abbreviations xvii
Typographical Conventions for Intertextual Categorization xxiii

CHAPTER 1. *Ḥesed* and the New Testament: Goal, Obstacles, and Responses. 1
1.1 Recovering *Ḥesed* 1
1.2 Obstacles and Responses 2

CHAPTER 2. An Intertextual Categorization Study: Methodological Approaches 7
2.1 Intertextuality 8
2.2 Categorization 11
2.3 Intertextual Categorization and *Ḥesed* 18

CHAPTER 3. Interpersonal Relationships in Ancient Israel: The Domain of *Ḥesed* 19

CHAPTER 4. *Ḥsd* in the Hebrew Bible and Other Literature of the Second Temple Period 22
4.1 *Ḥsd* in the Hebrew Bible 22
4.2 *Ḥsd* in Other Literature of the Second Temple Period 44

CHAPTER 5. *Ḥsyd* in the Hebrew Bible and Other Literature of the Second Temple Period 47
5.1 *Ḥsyd* in the Hebrew Bible 47
5.2 *Ḥsyd* in Other Literature of the Second Temple Period 52

CHAPTER 6. Greek Words That Evoke *Ḥsd* or *Ḥsyd* 55
6.1 *Eleos* 55
6.2 *Hosios* 58
6.3 New Testament Occurrences of *Eleos* and *Hosios* 61

CHAPTER 7. *Eleos* in Matthew's Gospel: A Weighty Matter of the Law 62
7.1 Intertextual Connections Between *Eleos* in Matthew's Gospel and *Ḥsd* in the Hebrew Bible 62
7.2 The Category *ḤSD* in Matthew's Gospel 66
7.3 Exegetical Value of Recognizing Engagement with the Category *ḤSD* in Matthew's Gospel 70
7.4 Conclusions 77

CHAPTER 8. *Eleos* in Paul's Letters: The Reason for Gentiles Glorifying God. 78
8.1 Intertextual Connections Between *Eleos* in Paul's Letters and *Ḥsd* in the Hebrew Bible 79
8.2 The Category *ḤSD* in Romans and Galatians 91
8.3 Exegetical Value of Recognizing Engagement with the Category *ḤSD* in Romans and Galatians 95
8.4 Conclusions 98

CHAPTER 9. *Eleos* in Luke's Gospel: A Basis for Remembered Promises and Neighborly Actions 100
9.1 Intertextual Connections Between *Eleos* in Luke's Gospel and *Ḥsd* in the Hebrew Bible 100
9.2 The Category *ḤSD* in Luke's Gospel 108
9.3 Exegetical Value of Recognizing Engagement with the Category *ḤSD* in Luke's Gospel 113
9.4 Conclusions 117

CHAPTER 10. *Eleos* in Other New Testament Books: Characteristic of God, Reason for Hope 119
10.1 Intertextual Connections Between *Eleos* in Hebrews, James, First Peter, Second John, and Jude and *Ḥsd* in the Hebrew Bible 119
10.2 The Category *ḤSD* in First Peter 1:3–2:10 128
10.3 Exegetical Value of Recognizing Engagement with the Category *ḤSD* in First Peter 1:3–2:10 129
10.4 Conclusions 134

CHAPTER 11. *Hosios* in Acts: A Gift and Promises Concerning David and His Descendant 136
11.1 Intertextual Connections Between *Hosios* in Acts and *Ḥsd* or *Ḥsyd* in the Hebrew Bible 136
11.2 The Categories ḤSD and ḤSYD in Acts 144
11.3 Exegetical Value of Recognizing Engagement with the Categories ḤSD and ḤSYD in Acts 149
11.4 Conclusions 153

CHAPTER 12. *Hosios* in Other New Testament Books: A Description of the One Who Makes Faithful and Righteous Judgments 155
12.1 Intertextual Connections Between *Hosios* in First Timothy, Titus, Hebrews, and Revelation and *Ḥsyd* in the Hebrew Bible 155
12.2 The Category ḤSYD in Revelation 15–16 163
12.3 Exegetical Value of Recognizing Engagement with the Category ḤSYD in Revelation 15–16 165
12.4 Conclusions 167

CHAPTER 13. ḤSD, ḤSYD, *Eleos*, and *Hosios* in the New Testament 169
13.1 The Categories ḤSD and ḤSYD in the New Testament 169
13.2 *Eleos* in the New Testament 175
13.3 *Hosios* in the New Testament 177

CHAPTER 14. *Ḥesed* and the New Testament: Conclusions and Outlook 179
14.1 Evidence of New Testament Engagement with the Concept Corresponding to *Ḥesed* 179
14.2 Aspects of New Testament Engagement with the Concept Corresponding to *Ḥesed* 181
14.3 Exegetical Value of Recognizing New Testament Engagement with the Concept Corresponding to *Ḥesed* 184
14.4 Conclusion 187
14.5 Limitations and Implications 188

APPENDIXES 193
1. Hebrew Bible Occurrences of חסד and חסיד 193
2. LXX Occurrences of ἔλεος, ἐλεέω, and ὅσιος 229
3. Occurrences of חסד and חסיד in the Dead Sea Scrolls and Sirach 235

Bibliography 245
Index 261

TABLES

PREFACE

As a pastor, I note the struggles that some people have with trying to reconcile the portrayal of God in the Old Testament with the portrayal of God in the New Testament and/or perceiving that they have been let down, perhaps even by God. Having heard comments about *agapē*-love being the New Testament equivalent of Old Testament *ḥesed*-love, I thought I could use verses in which those terms occur to demonstrate that love is a consistent aspect of God's character throughout the Bible. As I began investigating the terms, however, I discovered more than I had anticipated: God's character is consistent, but comparing *ḥesed* and *agapē* may not be the best way to show this. "Love" may not even be the best English translation for *ḥesed*, partly because it does not highlight explicitly the aspects of loyalty, faithfulness, and dependability involved. And finding evidence of *ḥesed* in the background of experiences described in the New Testament is not a simple task! Nevertheless, this investigation led me to valuable insights, presented here for those still struggling to reconcile the Old and New Testament portrayals of God, for those who perceive that they have been let down or for whom "words like 'faithfulness' and 'loyalty' have lost their power,"[1] for those wanting better understanding of "*ḥesed*-love" or New Testament texts that point to this, and for those seeking to determine the relationship between other Hebrew words and the New Testament. Indeed, the investigation eventually became the basis for this monograph.

1. Sakenfeld, *Faithfulness in Action*, 1.

ACKNOWLEDGMENTS

I acknowledge the contributions of many others who have made this project possible. Special thanks are owing to Dr. Tim Meadowcroft, a trustworthy, conscientious, highly competent, and pastorally sensitive guide; Dr. Philip Church, an unfailingly kind yet meticulous adviser, especially with regard to biblical languages and literature of the Second Temple Period; and Dr. Yael Cameron Klangwisan, who reflected thoughtfully on linguistic issues associated with my methodological approach and cheered me on in the writing process.

I am also grateful for the assistance of Joanna Smith (linguistic advice); Dr. Dianne Scouller (proofreading); Dr. James Harding (assistance with Dead Sea Scrolls research); the Faculty of Culture and Society at Auckland University of Technology (advice and funding); the librarians at Auckland University of Technology, Laidlaw College, Carey Baptist College, and John Kinder Theological Library (accessing resources); Prof. Christo van der Merwe of Stellenbosch University (Department of Ancient Studies) and the staff and research communities of Laidlaw College, the Aotearoa New Zealand Association of Biblical Studies, Tyndale House, and Tyndale Fellowship (subject expertise, presentation feedback, recommending resources); Jim Eisenbraun, Dr. Jen Singletary, Dr. Gabriele Fassbeck, Dr. Alex Ramos, and other staff of Pennsylvania State University Press (guidance on publication matters); friends and family (practical help and support).

The biblical texts to which this monograph refers are *BHS*, Rahlfs edition of "the LXX" (Logos Bible Software),[1] and NA[28]. English translations are my own, unless otherwise stated. However, when translating biblical texts, I consult NRSV, ESV, NETS, *HALOT*, *GELS*, *Brill Dictionary of Ancient Greek*, LEH, and BDAG, and when translating texts from the DSS, I consult James

1. While I use the term "the LXX," I note that other Greek translations of the Hebrew Scriptures from the Hellenistic period are extant.

Charlesworth's Dead Sea Scrolls series, DJD volumes, and *Dead Sea Scrolls Study Edition*. For Hebrew Sirach transcriptions and translations, I consult *Book of Ben Sira* at https://www.bensira.org.

ABBREVIATIONS

Bible Texts and Versions

BHS	*Biblia Hebraica Stuttgartensia*
ESV	English Standard Version
LXX	Septuagint
MT	Masoretic Text
NA^{28}	*Novum Testamentum Graece*, Nestle-Aland, 28th ed.
NETS	Albert Pietersma and Benjamin G. Wright, eds. *A New English Translation of the Septuagint*. New York: Oxford University Press, 2007.
NIV	New International Version
NRSV	New Revised Standard Version

Dead Sea Scrolls (DSS) and Related Ancient Texts

CD	Cairo Genizah copy of the Damascus Document
1QIsa^{a}	Isaiah^{a}
1QpHab	Pesher Habakkuk
1Q16	Pesher Psalms
1QS	Rule of the Community
1QSb	Rule of the Blessings
1QM	War Scroll
1QH^{a}	Hodayot^{a} (Thanksgiving Hymns^{a})
4Q174	Florilegium
4Q175	Testimonia
4Q176	Tanḥumim
4Q185	Sapiential Work
4Q215a	Time of Righteousness
4Q256	Rule of the Community^{b}
4Q258	Rule of the Community^{d}

4Q260	Rule of the Community[f]
4Q286	Berakot[a]
4Q298	Cryptic A, Words of the Maskil to All Sons of Dawn
4Q299	Mysteries[a]
4Q372	Apocryphon of Joseph[b]
4Q377	Apocryphon Pentateuch B
4Q378	Apocryphon of Joshua[a]
4Q380	Non-Canonical Psalms A
4Q381	Non-Canonical Psalms B
4Q385	Pseudo-Ezekiel[a]
4Q385a	Apocryphon of Jeremiah C[a]
4Q386	Pseudo-Ezekiel[b]
4Q388	Pseudo-Ezekiel[d]
4Q393	Communal Confession
4Q398	Miqṣat Maʿaśê ha-Torah[e] (Some of the Torah Observations)
4Q400	Songs of the Sabbath Sacrifice[a]
4Q403	Songs of the Sabbath Sacrifice[d]
4Q405	Songs of the Sabbath Sacrifice[f]
4Q408	Apocryphon of Moses[c]?
4Q413	Composition Concerning Divine Providence
4Q414	Ritual Purity A
4Q418	Instruction[d]
4Q423	Instruction[g]
4Q427	Hodayot[a]
4Q434	Barkhi Nafshi[a]
4Q437	Barkhi Nafshi[d]
4Q438	Barkhi Nafshi[e]
4Q463	Narrative D
4Q491	War Scroll[a]
4Q502	Ritual of Marriage
4Q504	Words of the Luminaries[a]
4Q509	Festival Prayers[c]
4Q511	Songs of the Sage[b]
4Q512	Ritual Purity B
4Q521	Messianic Apocalypse
4Q525	Beatitudes
5Q13	Rule
11Q5	Psalms Scroll[a]
11Q6	Psalms Scroll[b]
11Q11	Apocryphal Psalms
PAM	Palestine Archaeological Museum

Other Ancient Texts

A.J.	Josephus, *Antiquitates judaicae*
Pss. Sol.	Psalms of Solomon

Secondary Sources

AB	Anchor Bible
ABD	David Noel Freedman, ed. *Anchor Bible Dictionary*. 6 vols. New York: Doubleday, 1992.
ANF	*Ante-Nicene Fathers*
BCOTWP	Baker Commentary on the Old Testament Wisdom and Psalms
BDAG	Frederick W. Danker, Walter Bauer, William F. Arndt, and F. Wilbur Gingrich. *A Greek-English Lexicon of the New Testament and Other Early Christian Literature*. 3rd ed. Chicago: University of Chicago Press, 2000.
BSac	*Bibliotheca Sacra*
CBQ	*Catholic Biblical Quarterly*
DJD	Discoveries in the Judaean Desert
DJG	Joel B. Green, Jeannine K. Brown, and Nicholas Perrin, eds. *Dictionary of Jesus and the Gospels*. 2nd ed. Downers Grove, IL: InterVarsity Press, 2013.
DNTB	Craig A. Evans and Stanley E. Porter, eds. *Dictionary of New Testament Background*. Downers Grove, IL: InterVarsity, 2000.
DOTP	T. Desmond Alexander and David W. Baker, eds. *Dictionary of the Old Testament: Pentateuch*. Downers Grove, IL: InterVarsity Press, 2003.
DOTWPW	Tremper Longman III and Peter Enns, eds. *Dictionary of the Old Testament: Wisdom, Poetry, and Writings*. Downers Grove, IL: IVP Academic; Nottingham: Inter-Varsity Press, 2008.
DPL	Gerald F. Hawthorne and Ralph P. Martin, eds. *Dictionary of Paul and His Letters*. Downers Grove, IL: InterVarsity Press, 1993.
DSSC	Martin G. Abegg Jr., James E. Bowley, and Edward M. Cook. *The Dead Sea Scrolls Concordance*. 3 vols. Leiden: Brill, 2003–10.
GELS	Takamitsu Muraoka. *A Greek-English Lexicon of the Septuagint: Chiefly of the Pentateuch and the Twelve Prophets*. Leuven: Peeters, 2002.
GKC	Emil Kautzsch, ed. *Gesenius' Hebrew Grammar*. Translated by Arther E. Cowley. 2nd English ed. Oxford: Clarendon, 1910.

HALOT	Ludwig Koehler, Walter Baumgartner, and Johann J. Stamm. *The Hebrew and Aramaic Lexicon of the Old Testament*. Translated and edited under the supervision of Mervyn E. J. Richardson. 4 vols. Leiden: Brill, 1994–99. Electronic ed. 1994–2000.
IBC	Interpretation: A Bible Commentary for Teaching and Preaching
ICC	International Critical Commentary
JSNTSup	Journal for the Study of the New Testament Supplement Series
JSOT	*Journal for the Study of the Old Testament*
L&N	Johannes P. Louw and Eugene A. Nida, eds. *Greek-English Lexicon of the New Testament: Based on Semantic Domains*. Electronic ed. of 2nd ed. New York: United Bible Societies, 1989. Logos Bible Software.
LCL	Loeb Classical Library
LEH	Johan Lust, Erik Eynikel, and Katrin Hauspie, eds. *Greek-English Lexicon of the Septuagint*. Rev. ed. Stuttgart: Deutsche Bibelgesellschaft, 2003.
LSJ	Henry George Liddell, Robert Scott, and Henry Stuart Jones. *A Greek-English Lexicon*. 9th ed. with revised supplement. Oxford: Clarendon, 1996.
NIB	Leander E. Keck, ed. *The New Interpreter's Bible*. 12 vols. Nashville: Abingdon, 1994–2004.
NICNT	New International Commentary on the New Testament
NICOT	New International Commentary on the Old Testament
NIDOTTE	Willem A. VanGemeren, ed. *New International Dictionary of Old Testament Theology and Exegesis*. 5 vols. Grand Rapids: Zondervan, 1997.
NIGTC	New International Greek Testament Commentary
NIVAC	New International Version Application Commentary
NovT	*Novum Testamentum*
PG	Patrologia Graeca. Edited by Jacques-Paul Migne. 162 vols. Paris, 1857–86.
SBL	Society of Biblical Literature
SNTSMS	Society for New Testament Studies Monograph Series
SP	Sacra Pagina
TDNT	Gerhard Kittel and Gerhard Friedrich, eds. *Theological Dictionary of the New Testament*. Translated and edited by Geoffrey W. Bromiley. 10 vols. Grand Rapids: Eerdmans, 1964–76.
TDOT	G. Johannes Botterweck and Helmer Ringgren, eds. *Theological Dictionary of the Old Testament*. Translated by John T. Willis et al. 15 vols. Grand Rapids: Eerdmans, 1974–2015.

TLOT	Ernst Jenni, ed. *Theological Lexicon of the Old Testament.* Edited with assistance from Claus Westermann. Translated by Mark E. Biddle. 3 vols. Peabody, MA: Hendrickson, 1997.
TNTC	Tyndale New Testament Commentaries
TynBul	*Tyndale Bulletin*
WBC	Word Biblical Commentary

Grammatical Abbreviations

1/2/3	first, second, and third person
aor.	aorist tense
consec.	consecutive
const.	construct
fut.	future tense
gen.	genitive
impf.	imperfect aspect
inf.	infinitive mood
masc.	masculine
neg.	negated
neut.	neuter
pass.	passive voice
pf.	perfect aspect
pl.	plural
pres.	present tense
ptc.	participle mood
sg.	singular

TYPOGRAPHICAL CONVENTIONS FOR INTERTEXTUAL CATEGORIZATION

Bold	Technical terms needing definition/explanation when introduced (e.g., **transumed**); labels of tests for allusions/echoes
Italics	Linguistic forms (e.g., *school*), including those in foreign languages; emphasis
"Double quotes"	Meanings of linguistic forms (e.g., "explore")
SMALL_CAPITALS	Metaphors; names of categories/subcategories (e.g., CHARACTERISTIC_*ḤSD*)[1]
[SMALL_CAPITALS_IN _SQUARE_BRACKETS]	Category elements (e.g., [MANIFESTATION])[2]
*	Logos Bible Software count
**	My count

Additionally, some linguistic descriptors, such as "Modifier," "Contrastive-Purpose Verbal Clause," and "Obligatory and Optional Clause Elements," are signaled by initial capitals.

1. Note that the name YHWH is also written in small capitals throughout this monograph, except within quotations from secondary sources.

2. These typographical conventions are adapted from Taylor's conventions (*Linguistic Categorization*, ix) to suit the specific needs of this project.

CHAPTER I

Ḥesed and the New Testament: Goal, Obstacles, and Responses

This monograph deals with the relationship between *ḥesed* and the New Testament, a relationship that is not obvious in English translations of the Bible. I focus particularly on *eleos* and *hosios* (commonly rendered "mercy" and "holy"), the most frequent LXX translations of the noun *ḥesed* and the related adjective *ḥāsîd,* respectively, as keys to reveal that relationship.

1.1. Recovering *Ḥesed*

In the Hebrew Bible, *ḥesed* refers to such experiences as Joseph fulfilling his father's request by burying Israel with his ancestors (Gen 47; 50), Ruth accompanying and seeking to provide security for her mother-in-law (Ruth 1; 3), David honoring his prior commitment to his friend Jonathan by restoring land to a member of Saul's household (1 Sam 20; 2 Sam 9), and God choosing to forgive and maintain relationship with the people of Israel, even after they worship a golden calf (Exod 32–34).[1] Thus, *ḥesed* is transacted between two parties in a trusting relationship when the situationally powerful party meets the current essential need of the situationally needy party.[2] It is also the characteristic potential to do so. As the relationship involves mutual obligations, *ḥesed* is expected to be reciprocal.[3]

1. Sakenfeld, *Faithfulness in Action*, 13–15, 28, 32–33, 47–48.

2. Regarding its "secular" usage, Sakenfeld describes *ḥesed* as "an action performed . . . for the situationally inferior party by the situationally superior one." The superior party is usually the only one available to provide for the essential need and has responsibility "because of the relationship in which he stands," but is also free not to act. *Ḥesed* can be a specific act of "deliverance from dire straits" or ongoing protective behavior (*Meaning of Hesed*, 234).

3. Glueck emphasizes the mutual rights and obligations associated with *ḥesed* in "secular" relationships (*Ḥesed in the Bible*, 52, 55). The offended reactions in scenes where *ḥesed* is not reciprocated (e.g., 2 Chr 24:22) support Routledge's conclusion that the expectation to reciprocate is social and moral ("*Ḥesed* as Obligation," 195).

Even though the word *ḥesed* itself cannot be located in texts written in Greek,[4] a significant Hebrew Bible concept such as that denoted by *ḥesed* is still likely to feature in the New Testament because of the shared tradition. But, to date, there has been insufficient clarity on resonances of *ḥesed* in the New Testament, and consequently insufficient emphasis on the importance of these. Therefore, the goal of this study is to recover the relationship between *ḥesed* and the New Testament by establishing (1) *whether* there is evidence of New Testament engagement with the concept corresponding to *ḥesed*, and if so, (2) *how* that engagement occurs and (3) the *exegetical value* of recognizing that engagement.

In keeping with the foundational works about *ḥesed* by Nelson Glueck and Katharine Doob Sakenfeld, both of which include sections on the related adjective *ḥāsîd*,[5] this study also considers *ḥāsîd* under the title "*Ḥesed* and the New Testament." The *ḥāsîd* is one party in a *ḥesed* relationship.[6] Hereafter I use *ḥesed* only when referring to the overarching idea of which *ḥāsîd* is a part, when another author includes vowels in the word, or within the phrase "the concept corresponding to *ḥesed*." Otherwise, I use *ḥsd* referring to the noun and *ḥsyd* when referring to the adjective. This is consistent with my general practice of representing unpointed Hebrew text in transliteration. Asserting that New Testament occurrences of the most frequent LXX renderings of *ḥsd/ḥsyd* are more likely to evoke those terms than are occurrences of previously proposed "equivalents" has proven to be a daring but significant innovation.[7]

1.2. Obstacles and Responses

Several significant obstacles to achieving my goal probably also account for the reluctance of others to address the relationship between *ḥesed* and the New Testament in a comprehensive way. I articulate and address these obstacles in the following.

First, there is an overwhelming range of recorded experiences from which to choose New Testament resonances of *ḥesed*. Sakenfeld, who uses "loyalty" to render *ḥesed* and whose brief attempt at identifying New Testament resonances of "loyalty" became an inspiration for my own research,[8] selects those

4. Thus, the monograph is not entitled "*Ḥesed in* the New Testament."

5. Glueck, *Das Wort ḥesed*, 31–34, and Sakenfeld, *Meaning of Hesed*, 241–45.

6. I treat the genuine *ḥsyd* as equivalent to *ʾyš ḥsd* ("person of *ḥsd*"). See Glueck, *Ḥesed in the Bible*, 67. The *hithpael* impf. of the verb *ḥsd* occurs in 2 Sam 22:26 // Ps 18:26 MT, but the LXX translation of *htḥsd* (*hosioō*) does not occur in the New Testament, so this verb is not considered.

7. *Ḥsd*, *ḥsyd*, *eleos*, and *hosios* are usually left untranslated to avoid confusion and distortion. I also leave *npš* untranslated.

8. Sakenfeld acknowledges the shortcomings of her choice of translation (*Faithfulness in Action*, 2–3).

resonances from "any number of New Testament texts" or events, including "all the acts of Jesus' earthly life."[9] It appears that Sakenfeld's main control for identifying resonances is a list of features included in what she calls "the basic meaning of loyalty."[10] However, my treatment of the relationship between *ḥesed* and the New Testament is bound by additional methodological controls that further limit the scope of the investigation.

Second, the assumption that one might find direct correspondence between one word and one concept generates concern. There is the issue of whether each word denotes one particular concept, and if so, whether all that can be derived from every occurrence of the word in the literature concerned should be read into any individual use of that word.[11] There is also a more complex question for this study: how much of the concept corresponding to *ḥesed* formed by examining Hebrew Bible occurrences of *ḥsd* and *ḥsyd* can be legitimately read into New Testament occurrences of "equivalent" Greek terms? Related considerations include: (1) how much weight should be given to LXX translations when determining whether a Greek word in the New Testament evokes the concept corresponding to a word from the Hebrew Bible; (2) whether the connection between biblical language and theology can be located in a single word or should be limited to sentences or larger complexes;[12] and specifically for this study, (3) whether the use in a New Testament text of a word also used in the LXX to translate *ḥsd* or *ḥsyd* necessarily indicates that the word in the New Testament context evokes one of those terms.

Regarding word–concept correspondence, it is in light of the semitechnical nature of *ḥsd/ḥsyd* and the relatively consistent set of ideas and situations associated with *ḥsd/ḥsyd* in the Hebrew Bible that I proceed. The phrase "the concept corresponding to *ḥesed*" labels a "mental entity" that mediates the range of entities, experiences, and individuals to which *ḥsd/ḥsyd* refer in the Hebrew Bible and distinguishes it from that which does not match the scriptural

9. Sakenfeld provides examples of resonances, such as the responsibility demonstrated in the Good Samaritan parable and "Jesus as expression of God's continuing but transformed loyalty to the Davidic line" (ibid., 133–36).

10. This meaning is summarized, though not tightly defined, as "a freely undertaken carrying through of an existing commitment to another who is now in a situation of need." Ibid., 131–32, 136.

11. Barr highlights the error of what he labels "illegitimate totality transfer." *Semantics of Biblical Language*, 209, 218. Mitrović raises issues regarding use of the label "*the* concept," as opposed to "*a* concept" ("Attribution of Concepts," 314; emphasis original).

12. See Barr, *Semantics of Biblical Language*, 249, 263. Without denying that word uses can become "specially stamped by . . . frequent recurrence in sentences of a particular kind," Barr thinks that this connection "must be made in the first place at the level of the larger linguistic complexes such as the sentences" (263). On the other hand, Poirier writes, "To say meaning resides in the sentence rather than the word is like saying flavor resides in the recipe rather than in the ingredients" ("Case for Italics," 215).

evidence.[13] I consider which aspects of this concept are both highlighted by particular intertextual links and relevant to a particular New Testament context before using understandings about *ḥesed* to enhance my reading of the text concerned.

Regarding the influence of LXX translations, it would be inappropriate to ignore the two-way impact of the translation process or to claim that a Greek word has "the same semantic value" as the Hebrew word it usually renders.[14] Nevertheless, I am not alone in giving considerable weight to the influence of LXX translations on New Testament vocabulary.[15] The LXX translations and contexts can highlight the particular areas in which the meanings of Hebrew Bible and New Testament terms intersect.[16] For instance, *nomos* ("law") is commonly used in the New Testament to refer specifically to the Mosaic law (e.g., Heb 10:1, 8, 28).[17] This search for the concept corresponding to *ḥesed* thus *begins* by identifying in the New Testament words also used in the LXX to translate *ḥsd* or *ḥsyd.*

As for word or sentence locations of the connection between biblical language and theology, I note texts such as Col 1:17, where, according to Gerald Janzen, "every word carries a great freight of meaning and connotation."[18] On the other hand, my study indicates that, although the meanings and respective LXX translations for *ḥsd* and *ḥsyd* remain relatively consistent, there is still a degree of overlap with the semantic fields and LXX translations of related Hebrew terms. Therefore, evidence in the sentence or larger unit of accompanying intertextual connections to verses that contain *ḥsd* or *ḥsyd* in the Hebrew Bible is necessary for determining whether the concept corresponding to *ḥesed* is evoked when a particular word or group of words occurs in the New Testament. In seeking such evidence, I adopt what John Poirier describes as "a middle position" on where meaning resides: It is "mapped through the give-and-take between words and the sentences they comprise."[19]

Third, *ḥsd* is difficult to translate into other languages and, consequently, difficult to track in biblical translations. For instance, there are fifteen** different

13. A concept mediates "a word and the range of entities to which it may refer." Taylor, *Linguistic Categorization*, xiii. Croft and Cruse use phrases such as "words and their corresponding concepts" and "*The* concept of RESTAURANT" (*Cognitive Linguistics*, 7; emphasis in italics mine).

14. That would amount to what Barr calls "illegitimate identity transfer" (*Semantics of Biblical Language*, 217–18). Moreover, there has been strong critique of the claim that the Hebrew and Greek languages involve two different kinds of thought. As per Boman, *Hebrew Thought*, 17. Contra Barr, *Semantics of Biblical Language*, 21, 23.

15. See, e.g., Bauer, "Introduction," xxii.

16. Hill, *Greek Words and Hebrew Meanings*, 19–20.

17. Silva, *Biblical Words and Their Meaning*, 94.

18. Janzen discusses the connotations of *synestēken* in Col 1:17 (*When Prayer Takes Place*, 296).

19. Poirier, "Case for Italics," 215.

words used in the LXX to translate *ḥsd*,[20] and even for its most frequent rendering, *eleos*, the overlap in meaning between the Hebrew term and its rendering is limited (see §6.1.2). Similarly, many different alternatives have been used to translate or to describe *ḥsd* in English. Having struggled to find one suitable noun to render *ḥsd*,[21] those translating the Revised Standard Version of the Old Testament most often use a two-word phrase: "steadfast love." But alternative translations emphasize kindness, love, loyalty, faithfulness, mercy, devotion, godliness, goodness, righteousness, or favor, depending on the context and/or the words with which *ḥsd* is combined.[22]

The depth of trusting relationship established between parties (cf. "loyalty" against "devotion") and the amount of emphasis placed on demonstration or precondition (cf. "mercy" against "commitment") are factors to consider when choosing a fitting translation for *ḥsd* in each context.[23] However, using different translations in different contexts would be confusing for identifying *ḥsd* within the analysis of this study. For this reason, I usually leave *ḥsd* untranslated. When translation is unavoidable, I use "devotion," which communicates the relationship, precondition, and demonstration of *ḥsd* but seems more appropriate in the context of close relationships than in formal or recently formed relationships.

Probably owing to these complex challenges, study of the relationship between *ḥesed* and the New Testament thus far generally has been limited to proposing various "equivalents" between *ḥsd* and individual Greek words (e.g., *agapē*)[24] and identifying specific New Testament quotations of or allusions to Hebrew Bible texts containing *ḥsd* or *ḥsyd*.[25] Focused, thorough, and rigorous consideration of the relationship between *ḥesed* and the New Testament has been largely avoided. But that is my task, the approach and findings of which are outlined in the remaining chapters.

In chapter 2, I articulate the methodological tools used to complete the project. Chapters 3–6 introduce the domain of *ḥesed*, present summaries of the findings from my category analyses of all occurrences of *ḥsd* and *ḥsyd* respectively within the Hebrew Bible and other literature of the Second Temple period (and

20. See table A1.3. This count includes *polyeleos* with *eleos*.

21. Kuyper, "Grace and Truth," 8–9.

22. In addition, "rock" (Ps 144:2) and "beauty" (Isa 40:6) both render *ḥsd*.

23. "Demonstration" and "precondition": Stoebe, "חֶסֶד *ḥesed*," 2:453.

24. So Goldingay, *Psalms 90–150*, 753.

25. E.g., Bultmann attributes to *eleos* in Matt 9:13; 12:7; and 23:23 "the original OT sense of the kindness which we owe one another in mutual relationships," because of what he calls an allusion to Hos 6:6. Bultmann actually points out several connections between New Testament occurrences of *eleos* and Hebrew Bible occurrences of *ḥesed*, or LXX renderings of phrases to which *ḥesed* belongs ("ἔλεος, ἐλεέω," 2:482–84). See also Dickey's discussion about "the ḥesed idea" and the New Testament ("Development of the Hebrew Idea," 5, 93–106). However, neither author makes a clear distinction between the senses of *eleos* and *eleeō*.

their LXX translations, where appropriate), and introduce the most likely Greek terms to evoke *ḥsd* or *ḥsyd* in the New Testament, *eleos* and *hosios*.

Chapters 7–13 consider the New Testament occurrences of *eleos* and *hosios*, as potentially denoting instances of the categories *ḤSD* and *ḤSYD*. My focus on these terms does not imply that they are the *only* words with the potential to signal instances of those categories, but rather the *most likely* words to do so. The New Testament occurrences of *eleos* and then *hosios* are ordered according to the strength of intertextual connection with *ḥsd* or *ḥsyd*. Chapter titles reflect the particular nature of *eleos* (cf. *ḥsd*) or *hosios* (cf. *ḥsd* or *ḥsyd*) within the texts discussed. For example, in Matthew's Gospel, *eleos* is "A Weighty Matter of the Law." Three respective sections in each of chapters 7–12 are devoted to the three key issues of this study outlined in section 1.1.

In chapter 14, I compare the Hebrew Bible and New Testament data, present my conclusions about *ḥesed* and the New Testament, and discuss the limitations and implications of this research.

CHAPTER 2

An Intertextual Categorization Study: Methodological Approaches

Describing *ḥesed* is a slippery, demanding endeavor, for propositions about it refuse "to stay put."[1] But describing the relationship between *ḥesed* and the New Testament is more complex, because translation from one language to another and movement from one context to a later, culturally distinct context are introduced.

Part of the challenge in achieving this goal is that there are few methodological models for the research involved. Theories about intertextuality have already been well utilized in biblical studies. But the focus of intertextuality in *this* study is narrowed from the common concern with how one biblical text quotes, alludes to, or echoes another to New Testament engagement in *Koine* Greek with one concept originally denoted by a term in the Hebrew Bible. For that, I have found few models of methodological strategy articulated in succinct and accessible ways.[2]

Therefore, for the purpose of completing this investigation and to provide further direction for those attempting a similar task in the future, I have devised a hybrid of two methodological approaches and called it **Intertextual Categorization**. The first "approach" is **intertextuality**, although intertextuality is more accurately described as a phenomenon than as a methodology.[3] It occurs wherever "texts draw upon, incorporate, recontextualize, [or] dialogue with other texts."[4] But, in this study, intertextuality usually refers to New

1. This description is used of any proposition about piety in Plato's *Euthyphro* 11c (as cited in Plato, "Euthyphro," 95).

2. Park identifies four "categories of חרם" in order to find "the concept of חרם" in Luke-Acts, but his methodological framework focuses more on intertextuality than explaining how the **word** (linguistic unit) *ḥrm* is distinguished from the **concept** (mental entity) it denotes/symbolizes or articulating other issues pertaining to categorization (*Finding Herem?*, 4–6, 53, 53n2, 115, 167–68). For these linguistic definitions, I depend on Croft and Cruse, *Cognitive Linguistics*, 7, 14, and Taylor, *Linguistic Categorization*, xiii, 202.

3. Hays, *Echoes of Scripture in the Letters*, 14–15, and Wakefield, *Where to Live*, 63.

4. "Recontextualize" is bold type in the original. Fairclough, *Analysing Discourse*, 17.

Testament appropriation of scriptural texts, or more specifically, appropriation of a particular concept to which those texts point.

The second approach is **categorization**, an activity that occurs when an individual entity or experience is taken as an instance of a class of related entities or experiences. This "class" is "an abstract mental construct" known as a **category**. For example, the category *ḤSD* is the class of entities or experiences to which the word *ḥsd* can be applied. When individual entities or experiences that belong to the category *ḤSD* are distinguished from that which is non-*ḤSD*, categorization takes place.[5]

As biblical scholars have made considerable use of intertextuality already, I introduce that briefly before explaining categorization in more detail.

2.1. Intertextuality

Determining where (and whether) the concept corresponding to *ḥesed* is evoked in the New Testament certainly involves intertextuality, because quotations, allusions, and echoes of texts that originally contained *ḥsd* or *ḥsyd* (i.e., in the Hebrew Bible) are the most reliable indicators of engagement with that concept. While the term "inter-textuality" was coined by Julia Kristeva to denote the "transposition of one (or several) sign-system(s) into another,"[6] this study draws more from John Hollander's insights about **metalepsis**, and especially Richard Hays's illustrations of biblical metalepsis.

Metalēpsis is a Greek term,[7] used in this context to refer to "a kind of intermediate step" of transition.[8] One text is linked to an earlier text by means of a literary echo, but resonances between the two are "unstated or suppressed (transumed)" in the transition.[9] Therefore, in order to interpret the metaleptic echo, the **transumed** material must be recovered.[10]

The echo both values the tradition by continuing it and revises the tradition by distorting the "original voice" and producing "new figuration." Thus, interpreting such echoes involves bringing them to the attention of others and

5. These definitions and examples are based on ideas and statements from Croft and Cruse, *Cognitive Linguistics*, 54–55, 74 (including the quoted phrase), and Taylor, *Linguistic Categorization*, xi. See also §2.2.

6. Kristeva, *Revolution in Poetic Language*, 59–60.

7. Cf., e.g., Philo, *De plantatione* 74.

8. Hollander, *Figure of Echo*, 114, 133–35, and Quintilian, *Institutio oratoria* 8.6.37–38 (Butler, LCL).

9. Hays, *Echoes of Scripture in the Letters*, 20.

10. Hollander, *Figure of Echo*, 115, and Hays, "*Echoes of Scripture in the Letters of Paul*: Abstract," 43. There will probably also be "echoes of *interpreted* Scripture" (Evans, "Listening for Echoes," 51), as per the "inner-biblical exegesis" tradition (Fishbane, *Biblical Interpretation*, 6–12, and parts 1–4).

accounting for that which is distorted or produced.[11] For example, when Paul uses a clause from Job 13:16 LXX ("this will turn out for my salvation/deliverance") in Phil 1:19, he does not make explicit the ways in which he resembles Job, nor how his "rivals" resemble "Job's interlocutors." Understanding the correspondences requires "an imaginative act."[12] On the other hand, the Gospel writers perceive Jeṣus's life, death, and resurrection as holding "the key to understanding all that had gone before."[13]

While authorial intention is an important aspect of allusion, readers may also perceive meanings that the author did not intend. Indeed, what Hays labels the "hermeneutical event" or "intertextual fusion" may be located in the interaction between the author's mind,[14] the original readers, the text itself, an individual's reading of the text, and the "community of interpretation." Hays's seven criteria, suitable for determining and/or interpreting scriptural echoes, emphasize different aspects of the hermeneutical event:[15] **availability** (to this author and his original audience), **volume** (e.g., amount of explicit/verbatim repetition, prominence of the "precursor text"), **recurrence/clustering** (multiple echoes from the same passage), **thematic coherence** (how well an "alleged echo" fits into the argument), **historical plausibility** (whether the "alleged meaning" could have been intended by the author and understood by the first-century audience), **history of interpretation** (whether earlier interpreters have heard the same echoes), and **satisfaction** (whether a proposed reading interprets the result of the "intertextual relation" in a satisfying way).[16]

2.1.1. *Intertextuality and* Ḥesed

In this study, metaleptic interpretation pertains to the transition from Old Testament texts (in this case, containing *ḥsd* or *ḥsyd* in the Hebrew Bible) to New Testament appropriations of those texts.

The most reliable evidence that the concept corresponding to *ḥesed* is evoked in the New Testament is quotations of texts that originally contained *ḥsd* or *ḥsyd*. There are six such quotations: Hos 6:6 in Matt 9:13 and 12:7; Ps 16:10 (15:10 LXX)

11. Hays, *Echoes of Scripture in the Letters*, 19, including Hays's quotations from Hollander, *Figure of Echo*, ix, 111. Hays distinguishes "echo" from "allusion" only by degree of subtlety (*Echoes of Scripture in the Letters*, 29). However, in this study, "allusion" usually refers to a group of words in the New Testament that evokes a specific Old Testament text. In contrast, "echo" refers to a group of words that resonates with a familiar grammatical construction containing *ḥsd* when there is no certainty about which specific text is evoked. Cf. Porter's distinction between allusion and echo ("Allusions and Echoes," 40).

12. Hays, *Echoes of Scripture in the Letters*, 21, 23.

13. I.e., "*revelatory*" events (emphasis original). Hays, *Echoes of Scripture in the Gospels*, 358.

14. Hays refers specifically to Paul's mind.

15. Hays, *Echoes of Scripture in the Letters*, 26–27, 29, 33, and Porter, *Sacred Tradition*, 9–10.

16. Hays, *Echoes of Scripture in the Letters*, 29–32, and *Conversion of the Imagination*, 34–45.

in Acts 2:27 and 13:35; Isa 40:6 in 1 Pet 1:24; and Isa 55:3b in Acts 13:34.[17] Hosea 6:6 LXX contains one of the many LXX occurrences of *eleos* that render *ḥsd*. Thus, the quotations of Hos 6:6 form the core of my discussion about New Testament occurrences of *eleos* as potentially denoting instances of the category *ḤSD* (chs. 7–10). Most LXX occurrences of *hosios* render *ḥsyd*. Therefore, the two quotations of Ps 16:10 (15:10 LXX), where *hosios* renders *ḥsyd*, form the core of my discussion about New Testament occurrences of *hosios* as potentially denoting instances of the category *ḤSYD* (chs. 11–12). But I also consider the Acts 13:34 quotation of Isa 55:3, the only text where *hosios* in the LXX renders *ḥsd*. The quotation in 1 Pet 1:24 of Isa 40:6, the only text where *doxa* in the LXX renders *ḥsd*, is another special case. In addition, the occurrence of *eleos* in Rom 15:9a is associated with quotations of verses from Pss 18 (17 LXX) and 117 (116 LXX) that, in their MT contexts, are immediately followed by verses containing *ḥsd*.

I also identify intertextual connections between other occurrences of *eleos* and *hosios* in the New Testament and *ḥsd* and/or *ḥsyd* in the Hebrew Bible. Some occurrences of *eleos* or *hosios* and their literary contexts feature allusions to verses that contain *ḥsd/ḥsyd* in the Hebrew Bible (Luke 1:50, 54, 58, 72, 78; Rev 15:4) or resemble a phrase containing *ḥsd* (1 Pet 1:3). I consider others (Matt 23:23; Luke 10:37; Rom 9:23; 11:31; Gal 6:16; Rev 16:5) as corollaries of intertextual connections already established. However, with the exception of *doxa* in 1 Pet 1:24, I do not consider in detail other words used in the LXX to render *ḥsd* or *ḥsyd*,[18] since they are *less likely* to evoke those Hebrew terms.[19]

But metaleptic interpretation does not end with identification of quotations, allusions, and echoes. Recovery of transumed material (i.e., "aspects of the original context" not made explicit in the New Testament[20]) and observation of "the revisionary power" of appropriation (e.g., new interpretations of Old Testament texts) also enhance my reading of selected New Testament texts.[21]

In addition, Hays's criteria provide helpful constraints for identifying in the New Testament both allusions to and echoes of Hebrew Bible texts involving *ḥsd* or *ḥsyd*. With respect to the **availability** and **historical plausibility** tests, I note the assumption inherent in the key issues of this study (see §1.1) that the concept corresponding to *ḥesed* was familiar and important to New Testament authors and their original audiences. Given the frequency of *ḥsd* and *ḥsyd*,[22]

17. In addition, 1 Cor 1:9, 31; 10:13; and 2 Cor 3:3; 10:17 quote from passages that contain *ḥsd* in the Hebrew Bible, although the LXX word that renders *ḥsd* in each instance is not included in the New Testament quotation or elsewhere in the pericope (see §8.1).

18. I comment briefly on *charis* in John 1:14 (§§6.1.1 and 14.5).

19. See, e.g., §6.1.1, n. 3 on *charis* and n. 6 on *dikaiosynē*.

20. Hays, "*Echoes of Scripture in the Letters of Paul*: Abstract," 43.

21. Cf. Hollander, *Figure of Echo*, ix, 114, and Hays, *Echoes of Scripture in the Letters*, 19, 23.

22. *Ḥsd* and *ḥsyd* occur a total of 277** times (table A1.2).

if these texts were known to New Testament authors, it is likely that the concept corresponding to *ḥesed* was also familiar to them. Evidence of such knowledge is documented in chapters 7–10 and 11–12, in the sections dealing with intertextual connections.[23] In addition, the frequency of these terms suggests the importance of that concept within the tradition that New Testament authors considered authoritative, and its suitability for signaling that the New Testament story is continuous with the Hebrew Bible story.[24]

2.2. Categorization

Categorization is a basic, necessary, and efficient activity of all living creatures whereby individual entities or situations of the same kind are grouped together and distinguished from other kinds. Human beings often name these groups or categories by words. Knowledge that an individual item belongs within a particular category provides access to a range of stored information about that item.[25] For example, if I know the word "tree," I may apply that word accurately to "anything that can be categorized as a tree."[26] In addition, knowledge that an individual belongs to the category TREE provides me access to a range of information about that tree. But what happens when I bring my knowledge of the category TREE into a context where people communicate using a different language? Can I say, for example, that "individuals" named by the words *ʿṣ* and *dendron* also belong in my category TREE?

A key task in this study is locating in the New Testament entities, experiences, or individuals to which *ḥsd* or *ḥsyd* can be applied, even though those entities, experiences, and individuals are described in Greek and I speak English. The only way of knowing that to which I *can* apply *ḥsd* or *ḥsyd* is to note that to which each of these terms *has already* been applied. By observing and analyzing all the Hebrew Bible occurrences of *ḥsd* and *ḥsyd* in their contexts, I see the kind of entities, experiences, or individuals that belong in the categories *ḤSD* and *ḤSYD*. I note that there is not always one-to-one correspondence between the categories of one language and those of another language.[27] However, when I see a particular entity, experience, or individual in the New Testament of the same "kind" as those to which *ḥsd* or *ḥsyd* has already been applied,

23. It is more difficult to make assertions about the extent to which members of each original audience were likely to have been exposed to the Hebrew language and/or to have noticed and understood *ḥesed* resonances, especially considering their varied relative proximity to Judea and Judaic roots.

24. Cf. Luke's deliberate use of biblical semitisms. Munck, *Acts of the Apostles*, xxviii.

25. Croft and Cruse, *Cognitive Linguistics*, 74, and Taylor, *Linguistic Categorization*, xi.

26. Taylor, *Linguistic Categorization*, xi–xii.

27. Ibid., xiii.

I include it in my category ḤSD or my category ḤSYD.[28] In so doing, I can also read the relevant New Testament text in light of what I know about *ḥsd* or *ḥsyd*. But I take care not to read *all* that I know about every instance of *ḥsd* or *ḥsyd* into that specific new context.

2.2.1. A Prototype Model of Categorization

Of the three main views about conceptual categories—the classical and prototype models and the dynamic construal approach—the **prototype model** is the most useful approach for *finding* New Testament instances of the categories ḤSD and ḤSYD.[29] Unlike the **classical model**, it accounts for the intuitive sense that some category members represent the category better than others ("graded centrality"),[30] and it allows for categories whose boundaries are characteristically vague or "fuzzy."[31] But, unlike the **dynamic construal approach**, it also assumes a degree of underlying constancy.[32]

The following outline of terms, conventions, and principles utilized in a prototype model of categorization draws on insights from several authors, especially those of John Taylor, who considers what "the notion of prototype categories" implies for linguistic categorization.[33]

2.2.1.1. Family Resemblances

In a set characterized by **family resemblances**, there are not necessarily any elements common to all items. (For example, there are different types of games, such as board games and ball games.) Instead, there are various overlapping similarities between items, and each item resembles at least one other item in the set in some aspect/s.[34]

28. I do not translate these terms into English because that would add yet another layer of complexity to the task.

29. Main views per Croft and Cruse, *Cognitive Linguistics*, 76–97. They also discuss shortcomings of Prototype Theory (87–91).

30. E.g., CARROT might be rated as a better example of VEGETABLE than might be LEMON. According to the classical model, each category has a clear boundary, an entity either belongs to it (displaying the "necessary and sufficient features") or not, and all its members have equal status. Ibid., 76–78, and Taylor, *Linguistic Categorization*, 21.

31. E.g., RED has "fuzzy" boundaries. Croft and Cruse, *Cognitive Linguistics*, 77, and Taylor, *Linguistic Categorization*, 53, 69.

32. In the dynamic construal approach, categories and the systems to which they belong are thought to be inherently variable. Category boundaries can change according to how a word is construed in different contexts. Croft and Cruse, *Cognitive Linguistics*, 92–96.

33. Taylor, *Linguistic Categorization*, xiv.

34. Rosch and Mervis, "Family Resemblances," 575; Taylor, *Linguistic Categorization*, 42–43; Wittgenstein, *Philosophical Investigations*, 27, 27e, 28e.

2.2.1.2. Levels of Categorization

There are different levels of categorization. The **basic level** is associated with what things are named for everyday reference (e.g., CHAIR, not PIECE_OF_FURNITURE), and it includes characteristic patterns of behavior (e.g., it is easier to mime behavior toward a chair than toward furniture).[35] **Superordinate level** categories (e.g., FURNITURE) have fewer distinguishing attributes than those at the basic level, while **subordinate level** categories differ from the basic level by one property/specificity (e.g., ROCKING_CHAIR).[36]

2.2.1.3. Prototypes

Prototypes are typical members of the categories to which they belong, those items to which words primarily refer. For example, *furniture* is applied more characteristically to chairs than to lamps.[37] In more exacting terms, Eleanor Rosch indicates that prototypical instances of a category "contain the attributes most representative of items inside and least representative of items outside the category."[38] We may select items to incorporate into a category according to how closely they resemble the prototype, because that shares more attributes with items in its category than a peripheral member.[39]

There are several ways of understanding "prototype." For example, a specific chair exemplar may be considered the prototype of CHAIR, the entities of a specific subcategory (like WOODEN_DINING_CHAIR) may be considered the prototypical members of CHAIR, or an abstract notion that brings together a specific "set of typical attributes," such as shape, size, and materials, may capture "the conceptual 'centre'" of CHAIR. Preferred use of individual approaches may depend on the nature of the category.[40]

2.2.1.4. Linguistic and Encyclopaedic Knowledge

A person's knowledge of the language (**linguistic knowledge**) should not be strictly distinguished from her background/world knowledge (**encyclopaedic knowledge**) about the entity that a word designates. Taylor explains that

35. Adapted from Taylor, *Linguistic Categorization*, 48–53, and Croft and Cruse, *Cognitive Linguistics*, 82–84.

36. Croft and Cruse, *Cognitive Linguistics*, 84–86.

37. Langacker, *Theoretical Prerequisites*, 371, and Taylor, *Linguistic Categorization*, 50, 53, 69.

38. Rosch, "Principles of Categorization," 30.

39. Langacker, *Theoretical Prerequisites*, 371; Rosch and Mervis, "Family Resemblances," 575–76, 589, 591, 596, 598–99, 602; Taylor, *Linguistic Categorization*, 52, 57, 69.

40. Taylor rejects the prototype-as-exemplar approach (*Linguistic Categorization*, 63–64). The subcategory and abstraction exemplars are mine.

a person's "dog concept" and "mental representation of the prototypical dog" are dependent on his knowledge and beliefs about dogs as an animal species, dog breeds, characteristic behaviors of dogs, and so on. Future new knowledge about these aspects must also be accommodated.[41]

2.2.1.5. Domains

Words and concepts also need to be understood against relevant contexts or **domains**. For example, *mother* could be characterized against "genetic," "birth," "nurturance," "genealogical," or "marital" domains. Together, those domains form a structured "knowledge network" that Taylor calls the "mother frame," and a prototypical mother may be characterized against the idealized scenario where the other five domains come together.[42]

A domain may also be prototypical. Kjell Magne Yri explains that when translators render religious texts in other languages, they choose domains from everyday life to structure the new ideas for speakers of those languages, the first choice of domain for interpreting a word in each language being its central/prototypical domain. For example, SALVATION originates from the MILITARY domain (VICTORY) in Hebrew but from the HEALTH domain (HEALING) in Greek.[43] While there is inevitably some change or loss of meaning in the translation process,[44] the aim is to find sufficient overlap between the domains in the source and target languages to communicate the religion of the translator in the translated text.[45] Yri sums up this phenomenon well: "The history of concepts wandering across cultural and linguistic borders is a history of words wandering from one domain to another."[46]

2.2.1.6. Scripts

Scripts are associated with basic-level events, where the subordinate events follow predictable sequences. For example, Zoltán Kövecses describes five stages

41. Ibid., 84–87.

42. Ibid., 88–91. Lakoff identified the domains of "the concept *mother*" as "models" (*Women, Fire, and Dangerous Things*, 74).

43. Translators also change metaphors to be in line with the domains they choose in the target language. For example, the "warlike expression" *Rock of salvation*, from the Hebrew text, is replaced by *God Savior* in the LXX (RELIGION and HEALTH domains). Yri, *My Father Taught Me*, 29, 41–42, 134–45, 170. Yri is critical of aspects of the prototype theory, including a possible confusion between conceptual and real-world entities (150–51).

44. Yri notes the disillusionment of the translator of "Sirak" (i.e., Sirach), citing from Sirach's preface (ibid., 57).

45. Ibid., 142, 145, 170.

46. Ibid., 155.

in the scenario associated with a "prototypical cognitive model of anger": "Offending Event," "Anger," "Attempt at Control," "Loss of [C]ontrol," and "Act of Retribution." Descriptions of these events combine to form the anger "script" or "prototype scenario."[47]

For a biblical example, Ellen van Wolde identifies a series of four steps in which *ṭimmēʾ* (*piel*: "[DEFILE]") figures: "state of separation," "contact with impure entity," "contamination by impurity" (*ṭimmēʾ*), and "punishment or purification." She explains how those steps are worked out in some of the cognitive domains associated with the word (e.g., sexuality, idolatry, disease). For instance, in the idolatry domain, the third step in the Lev 20:1–4 scenario might involve "Molek's impurity [being] transferred to YHWH's sanctuary." Van Wolde calls the knowledge structure for a representative and recurring sequence of events like this a **prototypical scenario.**[48]

2.2.1.7. Semantic Change and Metonymic/Metaphorical Extension

Semantic change may occur when a word is translated into a new domain, its range of reference narrows or broadens, and/or the meaning of a word shifts from concrete to abstract, among other developments.[49]

Distinct meanings may become associated by metonymic or metaphorical extension. One type of **metonymic extension** (synecdoche) occurs when a person refers to a prominent/significant part in place of the whole (e.g., "*We need some new faces around here*"). **Metaphorical extension** occurs when elements usually associated with a concrete "**source domain**" are used to conceptualize an abstract "**target domain.**"[50] For example, in the metaphor ARGUMENT IS WAR, "war" is the source domain and "argument" is the target domain. Intellectual argument is described using military language.[51] A prototype provides the "*experiential basis*" for a metonymic/metaphorical extension, as distinct from a **schema**, which is a notion abstracted from the physical experiences and applied to nonphysical domains.[52]

Regarding biblical examples, Stephen Shead explains the metaphor "THINKING IS EXPLORING" and applies it to the use of *ḥqr* ("explore") in Job 5:27. [EXPLORE] involves the elements "EXPLORER," "AREA," and "PURPOSE," but in

47. Kövecses, *Metaphors*, 28–29, and Taylor, *Linguistic Categorization*, 91–92.

48. Van Wolde, *Reframing Biblical Studies*, 59, 207, 210–11, 259, 261–63. YHWH's response is expanded in Lev 20:5.

49. Riemer, *Introducing Semantics*, 373–74; Van der Merwe, "Challenge of Better Understanding Discourse Particles," 134; Yri, *My Father Taught Me*, 142.

50. Taylor, *Linguistic Categorization*, 124–25, 134–35, 138.

51. Ibid., 134–35. This metaphor comes from Lakoff and Johnson, *Metaphors We Live By*, 4–6.

52. Shead, *Radical Frame Semantics*, 157–59 (including fig. 6.1), referring to Taylor's "Categorization Triangle" (*Cognitive Grammar*, 522, fig. 26.1).

the mapping [EXPLORE] > [INVESTIGATE], "an abstract TOPIC is 'imagined' as a physical AREA." For *ḥqr* in Job 5:27 then, the "TOPIC/AREA" is Eliphaz's series of statements about God and the one whom God chastens.[53] In other religious texts, metaphorical extension is often from concrete everyday domains (e.g., MILITARY [VICTORY]) to abstract religious domains (e.g., RELIGION [SALVATION]).[54]

As abstractions and other shifts in meaning occur, sometimes it can be difficult to decide whether a lexical item is **polysemous**, having two or more related senses (e.g., *school* as a place of education or "an intellectual trend"), or **monosemous**, having only one sense with exemplars that are more or less central. In a sentence, polysemous lexical items can create ambiguity (i.e., more than one possible reading), as distinct from vagueness.[55]

2.2.2. Categorization and **Ḥesed**

Given that this project is primarily concerned with how a single Hebrew Bible concept is evoked within the New Testament, categorization is the particular "lens" through which intertextuality is focused here. Thus, the results of my *ḥsd*/*ḥsyd* analyses are presented using language and structures that reflect the terminology, conventions, and principles of categorization outlined above.

2.2.2.1. Levels of Categorization, Family Resemblances, and Prototypes

I divide the basic-level categories *ḤSD* and *ḤSYD* into subordinate categories. For each subcategory, the analysis focuses on the grammatical constructions to which *ḥsd* or *ḥsyd* belongs, the grammatical and syntactic roles/relations within the clauses in which these terms occur (e.g., *ḥsyd* as the Direct Object of a particular verb), and the Obligatory/Optional Elements included in those clauses: that is, the types of semantic "participants" that are always/sometimes (respectively) included in descriptions of interactions involving *ḥesed* (e.g., [AGENT], [MANIFESTATION] of *ḥsd*).[56]

There are family resemblances between the subcategories of *ḤSD* and *ḤSYD*. For example, while *ḥsd* is prototypically an article transacted by parties in relationship,[57] some occurrences of *ḥsd* are not necessarily associated with a

53. Shead, *Radical Frame Semantics*, 210–19 (including fig. 9.6). Shead uses "SMALL CAPITALS for conceptual structures and entities," and [square brackets] for "the name of a frame," where "frame" refers to "a rich, *structured* conceptual framework, arising from life experience" (5, 49).

54. Yri, *My Father Taught Me*, 11–12, §6, and 134–38.

55. Taylor, *Linguistic Categorization*, 102–6.

56. See §§4.1 and 5.1. The semantics terminology here is adapted from Shead's usage in *Radical Frame Semantics* (chs. 4, 5, and 9).

57. Sakenfeld's version of the "basic meaning of loyalty" could be considered the *ḤSD* prototype abstraction (see §1.2, n. 10).

reported transaction involving *ḥsd*, but the expectation that *ḥsd* should be outworked in such a transaction is often still communicated. Nevertheless, a few *ḥsd* experiences could be considered more peripheral members of the category ḤSD.[58]

The subcategories, elements, and findings of the Hebrew Bible analysis provide foundational information for locating and analyzing New Testament instances of the same categories. Comparing New Testament instances with generalizations about Hebrew Bible instances from the same subcategories highlights continuity with or development of the tradition. Generalizing across the subcategories provides a basis for conclusions about New Testament engagement with the concept corresponding to *ḥesed*.

2.2.2.2. *Knowledge and Domains*

Ḥsd and *ḥsyd* are characterized against the "Interpersonal Relationships" domain, so I introduce the findings from my analyses of these terms with a discussion about interpersonal relationships in ancient Israel, especially beliefs and practices associated with kinship and covenant relationships (ch. 3). Identifying New Testament instances for the categories ḤSD and ḤSYD gives access to a wider range of information for interpreting the passages where those instances are denoted.

2.2.2.3. *Scripts*

Scripts are recorded within the subcategory summaries (§§4.1 and 5.1), whenever there are predictable stages in the events associated with *ḥsd* or *ḥsyd*. However, unlike TMʾ, the subcategories of ḤSD and ḤSYD all relate to one main domain. Where a script is recorded, I also provide a prototypical exemplar, the associated events and Obligatory Elements of which form a clear and basic match to the script. Prototypical scripts and LXX translations of common grammatical constructions involving *ḥsd* or *ḥsyd* provide additional controls for discerning which New Testament entities, experiences, or individuals belong to the categories ḤSD and ḤSYD.

2.2.2.4. *Semantic Change and Metonymic/Metaphorical Extension*

Overlap between the subcategory elements and scripts for the categories ḤSD and ḤSYD creates vagueness rather than ambiguity. Indeed, some occurrences of *ḥsd* could be incorporated in more than one subcategory. Thus, these

58. E.g., Sakenfeld understands *ḥesed* in Esth 2:9, 17a in relation to physical appearance rather than taking responsibility for an essential need (*Meaning of Hesed*, 159–61).

subcategories represent different extensions of the same core sense, rather than distinct senses. In fact, the success of my approach depends on the largely monosemous nature of ḤSD and ḤSYD.

The extensions include occurrences of *ḥsd* that profile specific demonstrations of *ḥsd* (an example of metonymy). In addition, elements from some clauses containing *ḥsd* or *ḥsyd* have been "imagined" figuratively,[59] and there are developments in the conceptualization of *ḥsd* within the Hebrew Bible (e.g., increasing abstraction). I also consider the extent of overlap between the domains/senses of *ḥsd*, *ḥsyd*, and their Greek equivalents, along with any semantic development resulting from translation.

2.3. Intertextual Categorization and *Ḥesed*

This task is intertextual and diachronic to the extent that it concerns the dependence of one corpus of texts (the New Testament) on another earlier corpus of texts (the Hebrew Bible), and categorization to the extent that it involves identifying entities, experiences, and individuals that can be incorporated into the conceptual categories ḤSD and ḤSYD.

Intertextuality and categorization are both at work throughout the project, but each is emphasized at different stages. The findings from my analysis of Hebrew Bible occurrences (§§4.1 and 5.1) highlight prototypical aspects of the categories ḤSD and ḤSYD (including the frequent LXX translations *eleos* and *hosios*). Intertextual connections are the key control when identifying New Testament instances of those categories, but information about prototypes is also useful for that task. Chapters 7–10 deal with occurrences of *eleos,* and chapters 11–12 deal with occurrences of *hosios*, both generally in the order of probability that they denote instances of the category ḤSD or the category ḤSYD.[60] Those occurrences are analyzed according to the same criteria and within the same subcategories as Hebrew Bible occurrences of *ḥsd* or *ḥsyd.* Insights transumed in the New Testament use of texts that originally contained *ḥsd* and *ḥsyd* are recovered to enhance the reading of the New Testament passages concerned.

This combination of approaches could form a methodological model for other studies of Hebrew Bible words and their relationship with the New Testament, as long as the word–concept links are sufficiently secure.

59. Based on Shead, *Radical Frame Semantics*, 211–20. The verb "profile" is used here to highlight how the word form relates to its meaning. Croft and Cruse, *Cognitive Linguistics*, 15. Profiling is the process by which a linguistic form designates a particular region of a relevant domain. Taylor, *Cognitive Grammar*, 193–94, and *Linguistic Categorization*, 88.

60. Occurrences with highest probability are presented first, except within §§10.1 and 12.1.

CHAPTER 3

Interpersonal Relationships in Ancient Israel: The Domain of *Ḥesed*

Ḥsd takes place within trusting interpersonal relationships, and the *ḥsyd* is one party in a *ḥsd* relationship. The relationship usually exists prior to a *ḥsd* event. Often, the relationship is between YHWH and YHWH's people, but that is described like an anthropomorphic interpersonal relationship. Therefore, I introduce the findings of my analyses of these terms with a discussion about interpersonal relationships in ancient Israel.

In the ancient world, social units were formed to provide food and protection for their members and to distribute power.[1] Various levels of community existed, from the extended family or household (*byt ʾb*) to the clan (*mšpḥh*), the village (*kpr*), and the tribe (*šbṭ*, *ʾlp*, or *mṭh*).[2] The perception was that each member of a kinship group was of one blood, one flesh, and one bone. However, kinship was associated not only with family blood relationships[3] but also with economic and political relationships.[4] Nonkin could be included in kinship groups by legal devices such as marriage and adoption.[5] Thus, relational terms like "son" or "brother" had legal as well as biological connotations.[6] In fact, hosts and their guests, friends, allies, and those who helped one another were all understood to have the mutual rights and obligations of blood relatives.[7] *Ḥsd* expresses the commitment between two parties in such a relationship.[8] The common

1. Matthews and Benjamin, *Social World*, 159.
2. Ibid., 7, 9; McNutt, *Reconstructing the Society*, 88; Meyers, "Family in Early Israel," 37.
3. Cross, *From Epic to Canon*, 3, 7–8.
4. Those with "shared blood" were expected to provide mutual aid. Meyers, "Family in Early Israel," 37. Marriage was often for economic or political reasons. Matthews and Benjamin, *Social World*, 13. Cf. Matthews, "Family Relationships," 294–95, and Blenkinsopp, "Family in First Temple Israel," 58–59.
5. Cross, *From Epic to Canon*, 7–8.
6. Matthews and Benjamin, *Social World*, 7–8.
7. Glueck, *Ḥesed in the Bible*, 38, 43, 46, 49, 52–53.
8. See the six relational contexts in which *ḥesed* is practiced as human conduct, identified by Glueck (ibid., 35–37).

grammatical construction *ʿśh ḥsd ʿm*[9] (lit. "do *ḥsd* with") even seems to reflect the expectation of mutual and reciprocal rights and responsibilities.[10]

With regard to hospitality, the father of a household would "treat travelers properly," providing the best of what was available, if he wished to be treated similarly when traveling elsewhere. While being shown hospitality, strangers were treated as adopted members of a community.[11] A related phenomenon is evident in Abimelech's request of Abraham: "According to the *ḥsd* that I have done with you, you will do with me and with the land in which you have dwelt as an alien [*gwr*]" (Gen 21:23).

Kinship relationships were ratified by covenants.[12] The idea of covenant and its obligations may even have been shaped in the household.[13] The pattern and language of international treaties, specifying rights and responsibilities for each party, also have parallels in the biblical genre of covenant.[14] Rulers or monarchs negotiated covenants to exercise power across the borders of their states for military or trade purposes.[15] Glueck's description of *ḥesed* as representing the "essence" of a covenant seems fitting in exchanges like that between Abraham and Abimelech (above).[16] Furthermore, YHWH is portrayed as "keeper" (*nṣr/šmr*) of the covenant and *ḥsd*, and YHWH's covenant people are responsible for "keeping" (*šmr*) the commandments (e.g., Deut 7:9). In Hosea, the anthropomorphic covenant relationship is even described using marriage imagery, with *ḥsd* as one of the betrothal gifts (2:19–20 [2:21–22 MT]).[17]

In addition, *ḥsd* is "done" in relationships between rulers and their subjects. The king is meant to distribute God's justice on earth (e.g., Isa 11:1–10;

9. Gesenius translates *ʿm* as simply "with" (*GKC* §103b2), and all of the translation alternatives presented in *HALOT* except "as good as" and "even as" include "with" (s.v. "עִם").

10. This is one example where language appears to follow custom. This does not, however, necessarily imply general "peculiarity of Hebrew thinking" (Boman's expression in *Hebrew Thought*, 25). *Ḥsd* also occurs in directional constructions, such as "*ḥsd* to/toward."

11. Hospitality included a minimum of food, water, and shelter, but Abraham provided a calf from his herd (a financial sacrifice) for his guests (Gen 18:7). Cf. Matthews and Benjamin, *Social World*, 82–85.

12. Ibid., 8.

13. Perdue, "Household, Old Testament Theology," 240.

14. With regard to this, Matthews and Benjamin draw attention to the Hittite treaty (*Social World*, 164). Cross notes "the formulary [and kinship language] of West Semitic international treaties" (*From Epic to Canon*, 19).

15. Villages and cities formed into states with centralized power, sometimes in response to crises. Matthews and Benjamin, *Social World*, 159–60, 164.

16. Glueck, *Ḥesed in the Bible*, 45.

17. Instone-Brewer highlights the later prophets' use of a marriage covenant to express God's covenant with Israel, noting the three rights referred to in Exod 21:10–11 (cf. "food, clothing, and love"; Ps 132:13–16) ("Three Weddings and a Divorce," 3, 7–9; referring to Friedman, *Ketubba Traditions of Eretz Israel*, esp. 174–76, 343). Contra Greenberg, who finds no text expressly labeling marriage as a covenant (*Ezekiel, 1–20*, 278).

16:5), shepherd the nation (e.g., 2 Sam 5:2), and give life.[18] But the king must be shown the greatest respect (e.g., in 2 Sam 9:8, the speaker calls himself "your servant" and "dead dog").[19] Language and themes like those associated with rulers and their interactions with subjects are evident in *ḥsd* discourse,[20] especially appeals made on the basis of *ḥsd*. For example, the servants of Ben-Hadad of Aram have heard that the kings of Israel are kings of *ḥsd*, so they go, in sackcloth, to the current king of Israel and deliver Ben-Hadad's plea for his life to be spared (1 Kgs 20:31–32). In a similar vein, some psalms include appeals to YHWH on the basis of YHWH's *ḥsd* (esp. Ps 33:13–14 [where YHWH "sits enthroned," NRSV], 18–19, 22).

In each of these contexts, the relationships that feature *ḥsd* involve responsibilities for both parties. Often there is a sense of mutuality and reciprocity, or a recognition of power imbalance. The findings from the analysis of occurrences of *ḥsd* and *ḥsyd* that follow may be read in light of the relational contexts described here.

18. Deist, *Material Culture*, 272–73.

19. Cf. Prov 20:2; 24:21–22; 30:29–31. Ibid., 272. This example follows David's promise to Mephibosheth that he would do *ḥsd* with him for the sake of Jonathan.

20. E.g., the king's throne and conduct were to be established in *ḥsd* (cf. Isa 16:5; Prov 20:28). Glueck, *Ḥesed in the Bible*, 65.

CHAPTER 4

Ḥsd in the Hebrew Bible and Other Literature of the Second Temple Period

Findings from my category analysis of the Hebrew Bible (*BHS*) occurrences of the noun *ḥsd* indicate that there are four main subcategories of *ḤSD*: ARTICLE_OF_TRANSACTION_*ḤSD*, CHARACTERISTIC_*ḤSD*, SPECIFIC_DEMONSTRATION_OF_*ḤSD*, and ENTITY_*ḤSD*. I summarize and interpret my findings about the Hebrew Bible instances in each subcategory (and their LXX renderings) (§4.1), and then do the same for instances in other literature of the Second Temple period (§4.2).[1] I highlight trends and developments in the category *ḤSD*, noting how this information forms a basis for the New Testament investigation presented in chapters 7–11.

4.1. *Ḥsd* in the Hebrew Bible

There are 245* Hebrew Bible (*BHS*) occurrences of the noun *ḥsd*.[2] I have sorted these into four main groupings, but as their nuances do not vary greatly, the groupings are not easily labeled by four distinct English words (e.g., SOLIDARITY, MERCY, KINDNESS, PIETY). These groupings are more like subordinate categories distinguished by a single property (cf., e.g., ROCKING_CHAIR, DINING_CHAIR), except that they are distinguished by the extent to which certain semantic roles/participants are reportedly included in a *ḥsd* event or particular grammatical constructions are present. The subcategories

1. Table A1.1 presents definitions of the clause elements included in the analyses on which the data in this chapter is based.

2. This figure includes 127** occurrences in Psalms. The names *bn ḥsd* and *ḥsdyh* in 1 Kgs 4:10 and 1 Chr 3:20, respectively, and the occurrences of *ḥsd* in 11Q5 X, 2 (Ps 119:83) and XV, 11 (Ps 136:8 [1]) (so *DSSC* 3:260) are not included. As the negative sense of *ḥsd* used in Lev 20:17 and Prov 14:34; 25:10 ("shame/disgrace") is not the focus of this study, I put those instances aside. Table A1.2 presents all *BHS* instances of the categories *ḤSD* and *ḤSYD*.

ARTICLE_OF_TRANSACTION_*ḤSD*, CHARACTERISTIC_*ḤSD*, SPECIFIC_DEMONSTRATION_OF_*ḤSD*, and ENTITY_*ḤSD* are distinct,[3] but "not unrelated." ARTICLE_OF_TRANSACTION_*ḤSD* is the "central subcategory," from which the noncentral variants are extended.[4]

I have analyzed members of each subcategory with respect to Obligatory and Optional Clause Elements.[5] Where appropriate, I include a script and a prototypical exemplar[6] in the summary of "Findings from the Analysis" for each subcategory. ARTICLE_OF_TRANSACTION_*ḤSD* includes articles transacted between two parties, described using the most predictable Obligatory Elements: [ARTICLE_OF_TRANSACTION], [AGENT], [AGENT'S_ACTIVITY], [PATIENT]. Instances of CHARACTERISTIC_*ḤSD*, on the other hand, feature an attribute or disposition that is not necessarily demonstrated in any transaction at the time of description but may be appealed to for future assistance.[7] Therefore, its only Obligatory Elements are [CHARACTERISTIC] and [POSSESSOR]. Apart from the [SPECIFIC_DEMONSTRATIONS] and [ENTITIES] themselves, there are no other elements common to all instances of the subcategories SPECIFIC_DEMONSTRATION_OF_*ḤSD* and ENTITY_*ḤSD*. Instead, instances of SPECIFIC_DEMONSTRATION_OF_*ḤSD* are recorded using distinctive grammatical constructions (including plural forms or definite articles), and instances of ENTITY_*ḤSD* lack elements that distinguish other subcategories. In addition, I have taken figurative occurrences from each of the main subcategories and included them in two separate groupings instead: personified uses of *ḥsd* and other figurative occurrences of *ḥsd*.

Some occurrences of *ḥsd* are difficult to place within one particular subcategory. For example, *šmr hbryt whḥsd* (lit. "keeps the covenant and the *ḥsd*") includes a definite article before *ḥsd*, but it does not seem to refer to a [SPECIFIC_DEMONSTRATION] of *ḥsd*, and some uses of [CHARACTERISTIC] *ḥsd* are also [ARTICLES_OF_TRANSACTION]. Therefore, the subcategories overlap, there is some subjectivity in decisions made about the placement of particular instances, and the boundaries between subcategories should not be considered rigid.

3. I referred to the FrameNet index and elements in the labeling process (https://framenet.icsi.berkeley.edu/fndrupal/).

4. These descriptive phrases are adapted from Van der Merwe's description of *hinnēh* ("Cognitive Linguistic Perspective," 105).

5. See my explanations about "elements" in §2.2.2 and the location of elements beyond the clause in the introduction to appendix 1.

6. I.e., a Hebrew Bible text that exemplifies clearly and basically all aspects of the script.

7. The description of God as renowned ([CHARACTERISTIC]) for doing *ḥsd* ([ARTICLE_OF_TRANSACTION]) illustrates the related nature of these two subcategories.

4.1.1. ARTICLE_OF_TRANSACTION_ḤSD

The most clearly defined subcategory of *ḤSD* is ARTICLE_OF_TRANSACTION_*ḤSD*. Prototypically, a situationally more powerful party ([AGENT]) does ([AGENT'S_ACTIVITY]) *ḥsd* ([ARTICLE_OF_TRANSACTION]) with another party ([PATIENT]).

4.1.1.1. Findings from the Analysis

Eleos is the most frequent LXX rendering of the [ARTICLE_OF_TRANSACTION] *ḥsd*. Other renderings may reflect the [MANIFESTATIONS] of *ḥsd* in those particular contexts (e.g., *oiktirēma* ["pity/compassion"] in Jer 38:3 LXX). Common grammatical constructions in this subcategory include *ʿśh ḥsd ʿm* ("do *ḥsd* with") and *nṣr/šmr hbryt whḥsd l* ("keeping the covenant and *ḥsd* to"). Aside from *bryt*, *ḥsd* is most frequently paired with *ʾmt* ("faithfulness";[8] e.g., Gen 24:27). [ARTICLE_OF_TRANSACTION] *ḥsd* is almost always the Direct Object of a Verbal Clause,[9] sometimes occurring in requests, wishes, or blessings.

Concerning Obligatory Elements, YHWH/God is the most frequently named [AGENT] of the [ARTICLE_OF_TRANSACTION] *ḥsd* (e.g., Job 10:12). Fittingly, many instances of this subcategory are communicated in prayed/sung words to YHWH. Human [AGENTS] are often kings (especially David; e.g., 2 Sam 9:1, 3, 7) and their associates. The three women named as [AGENTS] are all foreign to Israel (Rahab [Josh 2:12], Ruth, and Orpah [Ruth 1:8]). The most common [AGENT'S_ACTIVITY] is "doing" (*ʿśh*; e.g., Gen 24:12), followed by "keeping" (esp. *šmr*; e.g., Deut 7:12) and "extending" (*nṭh* or *mšk*; e.g., Jer 31:3). Aside from not "remembering to do" (*zkr*; *ʿśh*; Ps 109:16), negated [AGENTS'_ACTIVITIES] have positive outcomes (e.g., not "forsaking" [*ʿzb*]; Ruth 2:20).[10] YHWH is not mentioned as a [PATIENT] of the [ARTICLE_OF_TRANSACTION] *ḥsd*. The most frequent [PATIENTS] are Israel (esp. the thousands/those who love YHWH and keep his commandments;[11] e.g., Exod 20:6), patriarchs and kings (esp. David; e.g., 2 Chr 1:8), their descendants, and their associates. Female [PATIENTS] of *ḥsd* are Rahab, Ruth, Orpah, and Naomi. The most common relational context for the [ARTICLE_OF_TRANSACTION] *ḥsd* is between YHWH/God and YHWH/God's covenant partners (e.g., Mic 7:20), especially those who are faithful. Human transactions involving *ḥsd* are most frequently between kings and their associates (e.g., 2 Sam 9:1–7) and are often communicated within conversations.

8. In parallel cola or the construction *ḥsd wʾmt*.

9. The verb is sometimes a participle.

10. Another verb with negative connotations is *swr* ("remove").

11. I restrict gendered descriptions of YHWH/God, but where maintaining good sense or accuracy requires the use of pronouns, I select masculine ones in keeping with the biblical tradition.

Regarding Optional Elements, the most frequent [POSSESSOR] of the [ARTICLE_OF_TRANSACTION] *ḥsd* is YHWH/God (e.g., 1 Chr 17:13) and the most frequent [PERCEIVERS] are kings and their officials (e.g., Neh 1:5–11). Common [MANIFESTATIONS] include deliverance, salvation, or preservation of lives (e.g., Gen 19:19; 2 Sam 22:47–51), and an enduring throne (e.g., 1 Kgs 3:6). Demonstrations of the [ARTICLE_OF_TRANSACTION] *ḥsd* are commonly [JUSTIFIED] by relationship with YHWH/God (e.g., Gen 24:12), the recipient's good/faithful conduct (e.g., 1 Kgs 8:23), or mutuality/reciprocity (e.g., Josh 2:12, 14). The only expression of [QUANTITY]/[QUALITY] in this subcategory is the greatness of *ḥsd* done by YHWH/God (1 Kgs 3:6 // 2 Chr 1:8). The [ARTICLE_OF_TRANSACTION] *ḥsd* is most often [LOCATED] in [CONTEXTS] of dislocation, transition, and/or distress (e.g., Gen 40:14), or particular houses/households (e.g., 2 Sam 3:8). Regarding [TIME]/[DURATION], demonstrations of *ḥsd* recorded using perfect or waw-consecutive imperfect forms sometimes result from changes/transitions (e.g., 1 Sam 15:6; when the Israelites "came up out of Egypt").[12] Those recorded in present/continuous time (i.e., participles) are often either immediate (e.g., "this day"; 1 Kgs 8:23–24) or ongoing (e.g., "to the thousandth generation"; Jer 32:18). Those with a future orientation are often requests yet to be carried out, associated with everlasting covenants (e.g., "forever"; Ps 89:28 [89:29 MT]), or reflect ongoing (multigenerational) reciprocity (e.g., 1 Kgs 2:7).

Many of the [RESPONSES] of [PATIENTS] and [SECONDARY_POSSESSORS] are expected/instructed. They include praise/blessing and rejoicing (e.g., Ps 31:21 [31:22 MT]), keeping commands (e.g., Deut 7:9–11), and reciprocity (e.g., Josh 2:12). [PERCEIVERS'_RESPONSES] also include praise of YHWH/God (e.g., 2 Chr 6:14) and reciprocity among associates (e.g., 1 Sam 15:6). Many outcomes from *ḥsd* transactions involve granting requests and carrying out promises (e.g., Judg 1:24–25) or making further requests in light of past demonstrations of *ḥsd* (e.g., Gen 19:19–20). Negative or unexpected outcomes may result from one party not carrying out obligations or not reciprocating *ḥsd* (e.g., Gen 40:14; cf. v. 23). [CONTRASTS] relate to two key issues: contrasting people or types of people and their deeds (e.g., Gideon and the Israelites; Judg 8:35), and YHWH's corresponding contrasting responses (e.g., Jer 32:18). In addition, YHWH Godself is contrasted with others (e.g., 1 Kgs 8:23).

4.1.1.2. Script

A trusting (often covenantal) relationship exists between two parties. The situationally powerful party meets (or commits to meeting) the present essential

12. NRSV; ESV.

need or request of the situationally needy party. Reported outcomes are positive. Where possible, *ḥsd* is expected to be reciprocal.

4.1.1.3. Prototypical Exemplar: Genesis 47:29–31 and 50:4–14

When the time drew near for Israel to die, he asked his son Joseph to do *ḥsd w'mt* with him by carrying him from Egypt and burying him among his ancestors. Joseph agreed to do so, and later carried out his commitment.

*4.1.2. CHARACTERISTIC_*ḤSD

CHARACTERISTIC_*ḤSD* shares many of the same Optional Elements as ARTICLE_OF_TRANSACTION_*ḤSD*, but the Obligatory Elements differ. [CHARACTERISTIC] *ḥsd* is not necessarily associated with a reported transaction involving *ḥsd*, although it is often worked out in action sooner or later.

This is the subcategory to which the first occurrence of *ḥsd* in the Exod 34:6–7 formulaic statement belongs. Verse 6 reads, "YHWH, YHWH, a God, compassionate and gracious, slow to anger, and abounding in *ḥsd* and faithfulness." This and other such lists (e.g., Hos 2:19–20 [2:21–22 MT]) raise the question of what to call items like *ḥsd*, *ʾmt* ("faithfulness"), and *rḥmym* ("compassion"). Of the proposed alternatives, it is debatable whether "virtues" can be applied legitimately to terms like *ḥsd*,[13] and "qualities"[14] does not reflect the outworking of *ḥsd* in practical help. On the other hand, "characteristics,"[15] "traits of character,"[16] and "attributes"[17] could include both this formulaic use of *ḥsd* and the many occurrences of *ḥsd* with a pronominal suffix (e.g., "his *ḥsd*"; Ps 107:8) indicating divine or human possession. In addition, William Propp suggests that the thirty-two words in the Exod 34:6–7 proclamation are "Yahweh's full name," where the word *šēm* bears literal and "extended" meanings, including "reputation."[18] This notion of "reputation" is evident in appeals for *ḥsd* (e.g., Ps 115:1–2; Neh 13:22). Therefore, I use the label CHARACTERISTIC_*ḤSD* to communicate both the personal attribute and the disposition to do *ḥsd*.

13. The use of *aretē* ("virtue") in the LXX to translate *hwd* (e.g., Hab 3:3) or *thlh* (e.g., Isa 42:8) differs from its use in Greek philosophy. See Fitzgerald, "Virtue/Vice Lists," 6:857–58.

14. E.g., Ashby, *Go Out and Meet God*, 135, and Oswalt, "God," 248.

15. E.g., Durham, *Exodus*, 454.

16. Sakenfeld, *Meaning of Hesed*, 116.

17. E.g., Enns, *Exodus*, 585, and Propp, *Exodus 19–40*, 610.

18. Propp, *Exodus 19–40*, 609.

4.1.2.1. Findings from the Analysis

In keeping with the pleas associated with CHARACTERISTIC_*ḤSD*, *ḥsd* is commonly connected to various prepositions (e.g., *kḥsdk* ["according to your *ḥsd*"]; Ps 119:88) and pronominal suffixes (e.g., *ḥsdw* ["his *ḥsd*"]; Ps 59:10 [59:11 MT]). YHWH's *ḥsd* is often described using the constructions *rb ḥsd* ("abounding in *ḥsd*"; e.g., Jonah 4:2) and *ky lʿwlm ḥsdw* ("for his *ḥsd* is forever"; e.g., 1 Chr 16:34). Consequently, *ḥsd* is often the Subject of its clause or part of an Adverbial/Prepositional Phrase modifying a Verbal Clause, and it features in Wishes/Pleas/Demands. The most frequent LXX rendering of [CHARACTERISTIC] *ḥsd* is *eleos*, and *polyeleos* translates *rb ḥsd* in YHWH's attribute formula (e.g., Num 14:18). In this subcategory, *ḥsd* is most commonly paired with *ʾmt* or *ʾmwnh* ("faithfulness"), but the attribute formula (Exod 34:6–7) also includes *rḥwm wḥnwn ʾrk ʾpym* ("compassionate and gracious, slow to anger").[19]

Regarding Obligatory Elements, the most frequent [POSSESSOR] of [CHARACTERISTIC] *ḥsd* is YHWH/God. Human [POSSESSORS] are sometimes referred to by generic terms like "person of *ḥsd*" (e.g., Prov 11:17). Regarding Optional Elements, the most frequent people group featured as a [PATIENT] of [CHARACTERISTIC] *ḥsd* is Israel (e.g., Ezra 3:11), sometimes referred to using phrases like "this people." Many occurrences of [CHARACTERISTIC] *ḥsd* are in psalms, so the most common individual [PATIENTS] are psalmists (e.g., Ps 5:7 [5:8 MT]). Jeremiah 2:2 includes the only instance in this subcategory where YHWH appears to be a [PATIENT] of *ḥsd*.[20] Israel[21] and the psalmists (e.g., Ps 26:3) are also the most commonly identified [PERCEIVERS] of [CHARACTERISTIC] *ḥsd*. The most frequent relational context is between YHWH / the Lord and YHWH / the Lord's people, followed by YHWH / God / the Lord and psalmists.

[MANIFESTATIONS] of [CHARACTERISTIC] *ḥsd* are recalled, predicted/expected, or requested. The varied [MANIFESTATIONS] reflect the presenting needs of [PATIENTS]. They include remembering (*zkr*; e.g., Ps 136:23), answering prayer (*ʿnh*; e.g., Ps 69:13, 16 [69:14, 17 MT]), delivering (*hiphil* of *nṣl*; e.g., Ps 86:13), saving (*hiphil* of *yšʿ*; e.g., Ps 6:4 [6:5 MT]), redeeming (*gʾl* or *pdh*; e.g., Ps 44:26 [44:27 MT]), and preserving life (*ḥyh*; e.g., 1 Kgs 20:31–32). Demonstrations of and appeals to YHWH's *ḥsd* are commonly [JUSTIFIED] by relationship with YHWH/God (e.g., Ps 143:12), YHWH/God's reputation (e.g., Ps 115:1–2), and the (potential) recipient's good/faithful conduct (e.g., Ps

19. In that context, the LXX renders *ḥnwn* by *eleēmōn* (cf. *anēr eleēmōn* for *ʾyš ḥsd* in Prov 11:17; 20:6 LXX).

20. See §4.1.2.4.

21. Including groups such as Levitical singers and "those who wait" (e.g., Ps 33:18).

26:1–3).[22] YHWH's *ḥsd* is described as "abundant" (e.g., Exod 34:6), "great" (e.g., Num 14:19), and "good/better" (Ps 109:21; [QUANTITY]/[QUALITY]). It is often associated with distressing [CONTEXTS], including potential death (e.g., Ps 86:13), or [LOCATIONS] connected with YHWH (e.g., 2 Chr 7:3–6) and YHWH's people, including the exodus from Egypt (e.g., Exod 15:13) and the wilderness wanderings (e.g., Ps 136:16). It endures "forever" (*lʿwlm*; e.g., 1 Chr 16:34; [DURATION]) and is sometimes declared or sung about "in the morning" (e.g., Ps 59:16 [59:17 MT]; [TIME]).[23] Demonstrations of CHARACTERISTIC_*ḤSD* are also associated with important events such as milestones in the building/restoration of the temple (Ezra 3:10–11; 2 Chr 5:13; 7:3–6).

[RESPONSES] to [CHARACTERISTIC] *ḥsd* are most commonly associated with [PERCEIVERS], and then [PATIENTS]. They are usually positive and either cognitive (e.g., trust; Ps 52:8 [52:10 MT]) or vocal (e.g., thanksgiving, sometimes accompanied by music; Ezra 3:10–11). Indeed, certain Israelites are appointed to give thanks to YHWH, declaring, "His *ḥsd* is forever" (e.g., 1 Chr 16:41). The most common outcome is YHWH's intervention (e.g., sending an ambush; 2 Chr 20:21–22). [CONTRASTS] are connected with other elements, including [MANIFESTATIONS] (e.g., compassion in place of grief; Lam 3:32), [RESPONSES] (e.g., fleeing in anger vs. relenting/repenting; Jonah 4:1–2; cf. 3:5–8), and [OUTCOMES] (e.g., good vs. ruin; Prov 11:17). In particular, YHWH is contrasted with others (e.g., those who persecute the psalmist; Ps 119:149–51), and those deserving of *ḥsd* / YHWH's help are contrasted with the undeserving (e.g., Ps 13:4–5 [13:5–6 MT]).

4.1.2.2. Script

A perceiver appeals to someone with the reputation for possessing and demonstrating *ḥsd*, on the basis of that *ḥsd* and the positive standing of their relationship, especially in contrast to that of others. When YHWH's *ḥsd* is demonstrated or observed, the response is thanksgiving and praise.

4.1.2.3. Prototypical Exemplar: Psalm 109

The psalmist complains of evil talk against him, despite his love and prayers. He asks YHWH to help, deliver, and save him, according to / because of YHWH's

22. Generally speaking, [JUSTIFICATIONS] relate to the [PATIENT'S]/[PERCEIVER'S] good deeds, the [POSSESSOR'S] reputation, or the relationship between [PATIENT]/[PERCEIVER] and [POSSESSOR].

23. This may indicate that demonstrations of *ḥsd* are expected to come after nighttime distresses. Cf. Goldingay, *Psalms 42–89*, 222; Tate, *Psalms 51–100*, 98; Job 38:12–13 (dawn shakes the wicked out of the earth).

ḥsd. He asks that the accusers be given the same kind of punishment that they wished upon him.[24] His response will be thanksgiving and praise.

4.1.2.4. God's Role in Ḥsd *Relationships*

The description of YHWH as a patient of *ḥsd* raises a controversial issue: whether humans can, in fact, demonstrate *ḥsd* toward God. For example, defining "patient" as " 'the one for whose benefit' the action is performed," Gordon Clark concludes that the patient of *ḥsd* is "always human but never divine."[25] In contrast, Sakenfeld considers it likely that, in each of the six instances in Hosea, "*ḥesed* is something which Israel should do for God, rather than *vice versa*."[26] Sometimes biblical translations also reflect particular perspectives on this issue.[27] The crux of the issue is that people demonstrate *ḥsd* by emulating God, the key agent and source of *ḥsd*,[28] and in an anthropomorphic sense, God is a party in *ḥsd* relationships, but God is always the more powerful party and never in need.

Jeremiah 2:2, which reports YHWH speaking of Israel's youthful *ḥsd*, is one text on which the debate centers. If Israel did not follow after YHWH of her own free will, 2:2 would not depict a "desert ideal" and *ḥsd nʿwryk* might be compared to an objective genitive interpretation of *ḥsdy dwd* in Isa 55:3: divine *ḥsdym* given to David (see §4.1.3.4 below), or in this case, Israel.[29] That would be consistent with Jer 31:3, where the parallel terms *ḥsd* and *ʾhbh* refer to YHWH's *ḥsd* and love for Israel. However, if Israel's loyalty was not forced, then the immediate context of Jer 2:2b implies that the *ḥsd* in that verse is Israel's faithful response to YHWH.[30]

The construction to which *ḥsd* belongs in Jer 2:2 is another factor to consider: *zkrty lk ḥsd nʿwryk ʾhbt klwltyk* (lit. "I remembered to/for you, the *ḥsd* of your youth, the love of your betrothal time"). When *l* comes after *zkr*, it can give the sense that something is remembered to the credit of (or against) an individual or group of people (e.g., Ps 79:8; Neh 13:22[31]). If that is the sense in Jer

24. See table A1.2, n. 37.

25. Clark, *Word Hesed*, 259.

26. Sakenfeld, "Love (Old Testament)," 4:380. Note the parallel connection between *ḥsd* and *dʿt ʾlhym* ("knowledge of God") and the contrast between *ḥsd* and *zbḥ* ("sacrifice") (Hos 6:6). Sakenfeld, *Meaning of Hesed*, 173.

27. E.g., Mic 7:18 states that God delights in *ḥsd*, not in "showing clemency" (NRSV). YHWH is the perceiver of *ḥsd* here, not necessarily the agent, as the NRSV translation suggests.

28. Clark, *Word Hesed*, 267.

29. So Fox, "Jeremiah 2:2," 441, 444, 446.

30. Holladay, *Jeremiah 1*, 82–83. Holladay concludes that the expression is deliberately ambiguous.

31. Cf. Williamson, *Ezra, Nehemiah*, 391.

2:2, then YHWH remembers *ḥsd* "to the credit of" a feminine singular entity who went after him in the wilderness. This suggests that, at one time, Israel's *ḥsd* was demonstrated in loyal action toward YHWH, regardless of the power imbalance. Nevertheless, YHWH/God is much more frequently an agent of *ḥsd* than a patient.

4.1.3. SPECIFIC_DEMONSTRATION_OF_ḤSD

In Ps 89:49 (89:50 MT), the psalmist appears to be waiting for practical demonstrations of YHWH's *ḥsd.* This and other plural occurrences of *ḥsd* match the *HALOT* description "individual actions resulting from solidarity."[32] However, some singular occurrences of *ḥsd* could also match that description. For example, Boaz speaks of Ruth's latter *ḥsd* being better than her former *ḥsd* (Ruth 3:10). The word "instance," inserted in the NRSV translation of this verse, suggests that Boaz is referring to particular *demonstrations* of *ḥsd* here.

It is likely that the extension of *ḥsd* to refer to acts/demonstrations of *ḥsd* came about by metonymy.[33] Some of these occurrences of *ḥsd* may be accompanied by *ʿśh* ("to do"),[34] but that combination usually refers to ongoing devotion transacted between two parties (e.g., Ruth 1:8), even if specific acts are also mentioned as manifestations of *ḥsd.* Thus, I include in this subcategory only plural occurrences of *ḥsd* and any singular occurrences of *ḥsd* that refer to specifically identified demonstrations, as distinct from ongoing relational devotion. The constructions *ḥsdy dwd* (Isa 55:3) and *lḥsdy dwyd* (2 Chr 6:42) are also discussed separately.

4.1.3.1. Findings from the Analysis

The most frequent LXX translation of *ḥsd* in this subcategory is *eleos*. Isaiah 55:3 LXX contains the only use of *hosios* to render *ḥsd.* [SPECIFIC_DEMONSTRATIONS] of *ḥsd* are identified by grammatical constructions rather than Obligatory Elements. The plural construct form of *ḥsd* is frequent (e.g., 2 Chr 32:32), along with instances where the definite article or demonstrative pronoun ("this") is connected to *ḥsd* (e.g., Gen 20:13). *Ḥsdym* is most commonly paired with *ʾmt* or *ʾmwnh* ("faithfulness"; e.g., Ps 89:1, 49 [89:2, 50 MT]) or *rḥmym* ("compassions"; e.g., Isa 63:7). The clause types in this subcategory are diverse, but *ḥsd* is most often featured as the Direct Object in Verbal Clauses.

32. *HALOT*, s.v. "II חֶסֶד."

33. So Joosten, using the phrase "act of benevolence" ("חסד, 'Benevolence', and ἔλεος, 'Pity'," 97).

34. Joosten notes this as a frequent combination (ibid.).

The most frequent [POSSESSOR] and [AGENT] of [SPECIFIC_DEMONSTRATIONS] of *ḥsd* is YHWH (e.g., Gen 32:10 [32:11 MT]; Ps 106:7), so occurrences of *ḥsd* are often communicated in prayers and psalms. Other [POSSESSORS] include Sarah (Gen 20:13), Ruth (Ruth 3:10), David (Isa 55:3), Hezekiah (2 Chr 32:32), Josiah (2 Chr 35:26), Nehemiah (Neh 13:14), and two general groups of people (Isa 55:3; Jer 16:5). Human [AGENTS] include Sarah (Gen 20:13), Abraham and Abimelech (Gen 21:23), Jehoiada (2 Chr 24:22), Nehemiah (Neh 13:14), and the people of Jabesh-Gilead (2 Sam 2:5). These [POSSESSORS]/[AGENTS] "do" (*'śh*; e.g., Gen 20:13), "wondrously do" (*hiphil* of *pl'*; Ps 17:7), "keep" (*šmr*; 1 Kgs 3:6), "make" (*krt*; Isa 55:3), "remember" (*zkr*; e.g., Ps 25:6), or "withdraw" (*'sp*; Jer 16:5) *ḥsd*. Key [PATIENTS] include patriarchs (e.g., Jacob; Gen 32:10 [32:11 MT]), kings (e.g., Saul; 2 Sam 2:5), and the people of Israel (e.g., Isa 63:7). Thus, the most frequent relational context is between YHWH/God and YHWH/God's covenant partners (e.g., 1 Kgs 3:6), followed by relationships between family members, host and guest, and kings and their associates (e.g., 2 Sam 16:17). The most frequent [PERCEIVERS] of *ḥsd* are psalmists (e.g., Ps 89:1 [89:2 MT]) and other writers of Scripture.

There is a wide range of [MANIFESTATIONS] of *ḥsd* in this subcategory but some emphasis on sustaining a dynasty (e.g., 1 Kgs 3:6) and cultic reforms (e.g., Neh 13:14). [MANIFESTATIONS] are usually [JUSTIFIED] by relationship with / trust in YHWH (e.g., 2 Chr 6:42), or personal goodness / good deeds (e.g., 1 Kgs 3:6). [SPECIFIC_DEMONSTRATIONS] of *ḥsd* are [QUALIFIED]/[QUANTIFIED] by the terms "all" (Gen 32:10 [32:11 MT]), "better" (Ruth 3:10), "great" (1 Kgs 3:6), "abundance of" (Ps 106:7; Isa 63:7), and "faithful" (Isa 55:3). They are [LOCATED] in Israel (e.g., Jerusalem; 2 Sam 16:15–17 [location in v. 15]), away from Israel (e.g., before reaching the Sea of Reeds; Ps 106:7), in situations associated with YHWH/God (e.g., at YHWH's right hand; Ps 17:7), and in negative states (e.g., misery; Ps 107:39–43 [context recorded before v. 43]). The [TIMES]/[DURATIONS] for [SPECIFIC_DEMONSTRATIONS] of *ḥsd* are specific (e.g., "today" [1 Kgs 3:6], "from of old"[35] [Ps 25:6]) or associated with particular events (e.g., news of Saul's burial; 2 Sam 2:4–5). The order of [SPECIFIC_DEMONSTRATIONS] may also be indicated (Ruth 3:10; Ps 89:49 [89:50 MT]).

The range of [RESPONSE] types in this subcategory includes writing (*ktb*) deeds down (e.g., 2 Chr 32:32), remembering (*zkr*; e.g., Isa 63:7) and considering (*hithpolel* of *byn*; Ps 107:43) them, singing (*šyr*; Ps 89:1 [89:2 MT]), feeling insignificant (*qṭn*; Gen 32:10 [32:11 MT]), and so on. There are almost as many negative or unexpected [OUTCOMES] (e.g., Joash killed Jehoiada's son; 2 Chr 24:22) as positive ones (e.g., honor; 2 Chr 32:32–33). [CONTRASTS] relate to

35. NRSV; ESV.

attitudes (Ps 106:7; cf. v. 4), deeds (comparison in Ruth 3:10), people (Isa 16:5, contrast in v. 4), and circumstances (Lam 3:19–24).

4.1.3.2. Script

Within a relationship with mutual obligations, one party addresses, is expected to address, or neglects to address a need by specific deeds. Specific demonstrations of *ḥsd* are or should be remembered, considered, and/or honored to the credit of those who do or possess them.

4.1.3.3. Prototypical Exemplar: 2 Chronicles 35:26

Josiah's *ḥsdym* were in accordance with what is written in the torah of YHWH. The *ḥsdym* are written in the Book of the Kings of Israel and Judah. Josiah's death was mourned by all Judah and Jerusalem.

4.1.3.4. Ḥsdy Dwd

The role of David, as indicated by the grammatical construction *ḥsdy dwd* (Isa 55:3; 2 Chr 6:42), has been the subject of considerable debate. André Caquot's 1965 article challenged the traditional and "almost unanimous"[36] view that *ḥsdy dwd* is an objective genitive expression (i.e., *ḥsdym* for David).[37] Noting "the normal way to construe the bound phrase,"[38] Caquot argued that David was the *auteur*[39] of the *ḥsdym* (i.e., *ḥsdym* by David; subjective genitive).[40] On the other hand, contextual considerations, especially with respect to the Davidic covenant,[41] provide the strongest argument against viewing *ḥsdy dwd* as a subjective genitive.[42] Sakenfeld reads *ḥsdy dwd hnʾmnym* ("the trustworthy *ḥesed*s which were for David"; Isa 55:3) in an elliptical sense, depending on the previous statement: "I will establish with you an everlasting covenant."[43]

Apart from Isa 55:3, the only use of the plural construct form of *ḥsd* in relation to David is in 2 Chr 6:42: "Remember *lḥsdy dwyd* your servant!" Glueck translates *ḥsdy dwd* (*sic*) here as "der Gemeinschaft mit David" ("the covenant with David") or "der . . . David zugeschworenen Treue" ("the loyalty sworn

36. This is Kaiser's description ("Unfailing Kindnesses," 91).
37. Caquot, "Les 'Graces de David,'" 46. Cf. Zobel, "חֶסֶד *ḥeseḏ*," 5:58.
38. Gentry, "Rethinking the 'Sure Mercies of David,'" 279–81, esp. 281.
39. I.e., "'person responsible' for. . . ."
40. Caquot, "Les 'Graces de David,'" 51.
41. Cf. vocabulary shared with the 2 Sam 7 oracle.
42. Kaiser, "Unfailing Kindnesses," 96, and Williamson, "'Sure Mercies of David,'" 43–44, 48–49.
43. Sakenfeld, *Meaning of Hesed*, 201–3.

to . . . David").[44] But it is possible, in light of the mutuality of *ḥsd* interactions (cf. 1 Kgs 3:6)[45] and the emphasis in Chronicles on David's role in the temple planning, that the Chronicler combined a statement about the *ḥsdym* of David with a portion of Ps 132 (2 Chr 6:41–42), in order to convey *both* "David's piety and God's promises."[46] Reading *ḥsdy dwd* in Isa 55:3 / 2 Chr 6:42 as simply "*ḥsdym* of David" preserves the dual responsibility for the *ḥsdym*.

In section II.1.2, I pick up the key issue for this study, which is Luke's interpretation of the Hebrew phrase or its Greek equivalent (Acts 13:34).

4.1.4. ENTITY_ḤSD

Several Hebrew Bible occurrences of *ḥsd* are not associated with the Obligatory Elements or grammatical constructions of the previous subcategories. In the literary contexts of these occurrences, there may be no explicit indication of a transaction between two parties, no possessor of *ḥsd*, nor any typical grammatical constructions involving *ḥsd*. The [ENTITY] *ḥsd* may simply be present or absent. For example, in Ps 101:1a ("I will sing of *ḥsd* and justice"), the celebrated [ENTITY] *ḥsd* is contrasted with the entity "evil," which the psalmist will "not know" (v. 4). This is a more schematic use of the term than in other subcategories.

4.1.4.1. Findings from the Analysis

The [ENTITY] *ḥsd* features most often in the Prophets (esp. Hosea). It is always rendered by *eleos* in the LXX, except in Prov 31:25 LXX (*taxis* ["order"]). There is no typical clause type or grammatical construction, although statements involving *ḥpṣ ḥsd* ("he delights in *ḥsd*"; e.g., Mic 7:18) belong in this subcategory. The [ENTITY] *ḥsd* is paired with *mšpṭ* ("justice") four times, with *ʾmt* ("faithfulness") twice, with *dʿt ʾlhym* ("knowledge of God") twice, and with *ṣdqh* ("righteousness") and *ḥkmh* ("wisdom") once each. It is [CONTRASTED] with *zbḥ* ("sacrifice"), *qṣp* ("wrath"), and *ʾp* ("anger").

The only [POSSESSORS] of the [ENTITY] *ḥsd* are Judah, Jacob, and the worthy woman (Hos 12:6 [12:7 MT]; Prov 31:26). The only [AGENT] is YHWH/God (YHWH "does" [*ʿśh*] *ḥsd*; Jer 9:24 [9:23 MT]). With everlasting *ḥsd* ([DURATION]), YHWH has compassion on the barren one (Isa 54:8; [PATIENT]). YHWH also [PERCEIVES] the presence or absence of the [ENTITY] *ḥsd* more than others,

44. Glueck, *Das Wort ḥesed*, 43; Glueck, *Ḥesed in the Bible*, 78. Cf. Ps 89:50 MT, where the *ḥsdym* are sworn to David.

45. It was on account of David's faithfulness, righteousness, and uprightness of heart that YHWH kept great *ḥsd* for him.

46. Sakenfeld, *Meaning of Hesed*, 157–58.

so perception is often communicated in oracles (e.g., Hos 4:1). The most frequent relational context is between YHWH/God and YHWH/God's people (e.g., Mic 7:18), although there is an additional emphasis on the involvement of all humanity, all the earth, and creation in this subcategory (e.g., Jer 9:24 [9:23 MT]).

Other notable factors include (1) the [MANIFESTATION] compassion (Isa 54:8; Mic 7:18–19) and the contrast with covenant transgressions (Hos 4:1–2; 6:6–10), (2) the impact when *ḥsd* is present or absent (e.g., mourning land or dwindling inhabitants; Hos 4:1–3; [LOCATION]; [OUTCOME]), and (3) YHWH's repeated [RESPONSE] to the [ENTITY] *ḥsd* ("delight" [*ḥpṣ*]).

4.1.4.2. Script

A perceiver observes, predicts, or appreciates the entity *ḥsd* (or critiques its absence) in a particular location/context. That perception is communicated.

4.1.4.3. Prototypical Exemplar: Hosea 4:1

YHWH declares that there is no *ḥsd* in the land.

4.1.5. Personified Uses of Ḥsd

Figurative occurrences of *ḥsd* are especially frequent in the Psalms, Proverbs, and the Prophets. Among these occurrences, *ḥsd* is most often portrayed as a personal helper (e.g., guardian, envoy, personal attendant to the king), whom I label "Personified *Ḥsd*."

Words used to denote the activities of Personified *Ḥsd* (often accompanied by its "partner," *ʾmt*) or YHWH, who commissions *ḥsd* ([AGENTS'_ACTIVITIES]), are sometimes associated with particular roles in Israelite society. For example, *nṣr* is associated with those who keep watch from booths (e.g., Job 27:18) or keep watch over the ramparts (e.g., Nah 2:1 [2:2 MT]). Thus, one might imagine *ḥsd* and *ʾmt* stationed to watch over those in their care (Pss 40:11 [40:12 MT]; 61:7 [61:8 MT]; Prov 20:28). The *piel* of *ṣwh* can have the sense of one in authority commanding or commissioning someone else to do a task (e.g., Gen 50:2). But God can command/commission anything in creation (e.g., Isa 45:12; Amos 9:3), including *ḥsd* (Ps 42:8 [42:9 MT]). The *qal* of *šlḥ* can be used of dispatching someone, especially to deliver a message, instead of going oneself (e.g., 2 Sam 2:5).[47] But YHWH sends forth *ḥsd* and *ʾmt* from heaven to carry

47. Cf. *HALOT*, s.v. "שׁלח."

out works of salvation (Ps 57:3 [57:4 MT]). Personified *Ḥsd* can also "come," "go before," "depart," "forsake," "pursue," "meet," "hold up," "comfort," and "atone" (i.e., "iniquity 'is atoned for' ").

4.1.5.1. Findings from the Analysis

Personified instances of the category *ḤSD* are mostly rendered by *eleos* (2 Kingdoms and Psalms LXX), except in Proverbs, where *eleēmosynē* ("mercy/charity/almsgiving") is used three times (3:3; 15:27a; 20:28 LXX) and *dikaiosynē* ("righteousness") once (20:28 LXX). The most common word pair and grammatical construction (with variations) among the personified instances of *ḤSD* is *ḥsd wʾmt* ("*ḥsd* and faithfulness"; e.g., Ps 61:7 [61:8 MT]). Personified *Ḥsd* often features in a Verbal Clause, usually as a Subject, because it is the active party ([AGENT]). Personified *Ḥsd* performs each of its [MANIFESTATIONS] (e.g., ongoing presence or protection). Therefore, the overarching metaphor is *ḤSD*_IS_A_HELPFUL_PERSON. Relational/Abstract [CHARACTERISTIC], [SPECIFIC_DEMONSTRATION], and [ENTITY] *ḥsd* all function like human [AGENTS].

YHWH is the most frequent [POSSESSOR] of Personified *Ḥsd* (e.g., Ps 40:11 [40:12 MT]), but there is no qualitative or quantitative descriptor of *ḥsd* in these instances. [PATIENTS] of Personified *Ḥsd* include psalmists (e.g., Ps 94:18) and the king (e.g., Ps 61:7 [61:8 MT]). They are [CONTRASTED] with those who work against YHWH's purposes (e.g., Ps 57:3 [57:4 MT]). Common relational contexts feature YHWH/God, YHWH/God's *ḥsd*, and psalmists or kings (esp. David and his offspring). [PERCEIVERS] of Personified *Ḥsd* are psalmists (e.g., Ps 23:6) and teachers of wisdom (e.g., implied in Prov 3:1–3). Likewise, its activity is communicated through psalms, proverbs, and one prophetic word addressed to David. Repeated [MANIFESTATIONS] include watchfulness (*nṣr*; e.g., Prov 20:28), salvation (e.g., *hiphil* of *yšʿ* in Ps 57:3 [57:4 MT]), support (*sʿd*; e.g., Ps 94:18), and comfort (e.g., *piel* of *nḥm* in Ps 119:76). The only justification for this activity is some indication of relationship with YHWH/God (e.g., trusting YHWH's word; Ps 119:41–42). Personified *Ḥsd* is found in diverse [LOCATIONS], from holding up the psalmist whose foot is slipping (Ps 94:18), to near the king (Prov 20:28). The outcomes are positive for those in relationship with YHWH (e.g., Ps 85:10–12 [85:11–13 MT]), but negative for those opposed to YHWH's ways and people (e.g., Ps 94:18–23).

4.1.5.2. Script

YHWH commissions *ḥsd* and *ʾmt* to assist one of YHWH's faithful people when the need arises. The wicked do not receive this assistance.

4.1.5.3. Prototypical Exemplar: Psalm 57:3 (57:4 MT)

YHWH sends forth *ḥsd* and *ʾmt* to save the psalmist, but those who are after the psalmist's life have been put to shame.

4.1.6. Other Figurative Occurrences of Ḥsd

In addition to personified uses, *ḥsd* occurs in other types of figurative expressions, including similes (e.g., "all its [all flesh's] *ḥsd* is as a flower of the field"; Isa 40:6), metaphors (e.g., "all the paths of YHWH are *ḥsd* and faithfulness"; Ps 25:10), and metonymic extensions (e.g., YHWH as "my *ḥsd*"; Ps 144:2). Imagery associated with *ḥsd* sometimes reflects agricultural processes, aspects of creation, or covenantal relationships. For example, Hos 10:12–13 and Prov 14:22 contrast what YHWH's people should or should not be sowing and reaping. YHWH's *ḥsd* is compared to the height of the heavens (e.g., Ps 108:4 [108:5 MT]), the expanse of the earth (Pss 33:5; 119:64), and the stability of the mountains (Isa 54:10), but human *ḥsd* is compared to a fading/withering flower (Isa 40:6–8), a morning cloud, and dew that goes away early (Hos 6:4; cf. 13:3).[48] The [ENTITY] *ḥsd* is also listed among the betrothal (*ʾrś*) gifts that YHWH contributes to his renewed relationship with Israel (Hos 2:19–20 [2:21–22 MT]).[49] In addition, *ḥsd* is associated with the ways of wisdom (Ps 25:10; Prov 21:21), a crown (Ps 103:4), various forms of protection (Pss 32:10; 144:2), and a structure built to last (Ps 89:2 [89:3 MT]).[50]

4.1.6.1. Findings from the Analysis

Figurative *Ḥsd* is usually rendered by *eleos* in the LXX, although the translator/s of Proverbs favor *eleēmosynē*. One occurrence is rendered by *doxa* ("glory";

48. Morning clouds and early dew did not remain for long, just as Israel's "early loyalty" to the covenant with YHWH (cf. Jer 2:2) was short-lived once they were "enticed" by the idolatry of Canaan. Snaith, *Distinctive Ideas*, 105, 112. Cf. Smith, *Hosea, Amos, Micah*, 112, and Stuart, *Hosea—Jonah*, 109.

49. See Clark, *Word Hesed*, 152–53; Dearman, *Book of Hosea*, 127–28; Kelle, *Hosea 2*, 278 (including the citation in n. 213 of Abma, *Bonds of Love*, 192n187); Kidner, *Message of Hosea*, 34; Smith, *Hosea, Amos, Micah*, 63; Stuart, *Hosea—Jonah*, 59; Wolff, *Hosea*, 52, for discussions about the incomplete betrothal metaphor, and whether YHWH betroths his bride with a set of entities that reflect his own character, the entities are simply gifts that YHWH brings to the relationship, or they "accompany the marriage" (Stuart).

50. Goldingay compares "Yhwh's commitment and truthfulness" to "the city and temple in the exile"; each of these requires building up again (*Psalms 42–89*, 668). Proverbs 3:3 (dealt with in §4.1.5) indicates that *ḥsd* and *ʾmt* should also be bound around the neck and written on the heart's tablet.

Isa 40:6) and one by *zōē* ("life"; Hos 10:12). *Ḥsd* is sometimes paired/grouped with other entities, including *ʾmt/ʾmwnh* ("faithfulness"; e.g., Ps 25:10), *ṣdqh* ("righteousness"; e.g., Prov 21:21), *mšpṭ* ("justice"; e.g., Ps 33:4–5), and *rḥmym* ("compassion/s"; Hos 2:19 [2:21 MT]). Figurative *Ḥsd* is most often the Subject of its clause.

The most common elements to be figuratively compared are [QUANTITY]/[QUALITY], [DURATION], and [OUTCOME]. Figurative *Ḥsd* is most often a [CHARACTERISTIC] or an [ENTITY]. The most frequent and reliable [POSSESSOR] of Figurative *Ḥsd* is YHWH (e.g., Ps 108:4 [108:5 MT]), and the most frequent [PERCEIVERS] are psalmists (e.g., Ps 89:2 [89:3 MT]). Apart from psalmists and Israel, the [PATIENTS] are generic groupings of faithful people (they keep YHWH's covenant and trust or fear YHWH [Pss 25:10; 32:10; 103:11]). The range of [MANIFESTATIONS] reflects the presenting needs of [PATIENTS] (e.g., sin; Ps 103:10–12), although, in Hosea, *ḥsd* is contrasted with covenant transgressions (e.g., Hos 6:4–10; 10:12–13). Demonstrations of Figurative *Ḥsd* are commonly [JUSTIFIED] by relationship with YHWH (e.g., Ps 32:10). The principle of reaping according to what one has sown also features (Hos 10:12; Prov 14:22).

Figurative *Ḥsd* is or should be [LOCATED] in contexts associated with YHWH (e.g., YHWH's paths; Ps 25:10), the earth and heaven (e.g., Pss 36:5 [36:6 MT]; 119:64), the ground (Hos 10:12), and Israel/Judah (e.g., Hos 6:4). YHWH's *ḥsd* is vast and great. It fills the earth (Pss 33:5; 119:64) and is compared to the heavens in various ways (e.g., Ps 57:10 [57:11 MT]; [QUALITY]/[QUANTITY]). It endures forever (e.g., Ps 89:2 [89:3 MT]; [DURATION]). In contrast, human *ḥsd* is fleeting (e.g., Hos 6:4).

Common positive [RESPONSES] to Figurative *Ḥsd* are vocal (e.g., Ps 108:3–4 [108:4–5 MT]) or involve seeking relationship with YHWH (e.g., Hos 10:12). [OUTCOMES] are either positive (e.g., finding life, righteousness, and glory; Prov 21:21) or negative (e.g., YHWH having hewn Ephraim and Judah by the prophets; Hos 6:4–5), depending on the extent to which *ḥsd* is pursued/sustained or not. *Ḥsd* itself is the harvest in Hos 10:12. The most frequent [CONTRASTS] are between YHWH and others[51] and between trust/good/righteousness and wickedness/evil.[52]

There is no typical script for Figurative *Ḥsd*, but the imagery is sometimes used to contrast YHWH's great, vast, and enduring *ḥsd* with the fleeting, perishable *ḥsd* of humanity. YHWH must supply *ḥsd* and related [ENTITIES] to sustain relationship with YHWH's people.

51. E.g., the Baals (Hos 2:19–20 [2:21–22 MT], with the contrast in vv. 16–17 [18–19 MT]).
52. E.g., the wicked one is tormented, but *ḥsd* surrounds the one who trusts in YHWH (Ps 32:10).

4.1.7. **Ḥsd** ***and Closely Related Hebrew Nouns***

For this study of *ḥesed* and the New Testament, it is important to distinguish *ḥsd* from nouns with which it may be confused. Studying the semantic relations between "elements" of the lexical field of *ḥsd*,[53] Clark concludes that human *ḥsd* is closely related to *ḥnn*, *rḥmym*, and *ʾmwnh*, but not *ʾhb*. According to Clark, *ḥsd* includes "grace," "mercy," "compassion," "faithfulness," "reliability," and "confidence," but it is more than each of these. It also includes, but has broader connotations than, "love."[54] The phrase "overlaps with" seems more accurate than "includes" in this context, but even overlaps in meaning can be confusing.

Shared LXX translations add to the confusion. I limit my discussion of this issue to the most frequent translation of *ḥsd*: *eleos*. Among other words in the MT (see table A2.1), *eleos* also renders *ḥn* ("grace/favor") in Gen 19:19 and Num 11:15 LXX,[55] and *rḥmym* ("mercy/compassion") in Deut 13:18; Isa 47:6; 54:7; 63:7; Jer 49:12; and Dan 9:9, 18 LXX. On the other hand, the usual LXX rendering for *ḥn* is *charis* (cf. *ḥsd* in Esth 2:9).

In addition, *ʾhbh* ("love") is often confused with *ḥsd* because some scholars think that *agapē* (which is used in the LXX to render *ʾhbh*) is the New Testament equivalent to *ḥsd*.[56] Therefore, this section highlights contrasts between *ḥsd* and *ḥn*, between *ḥsd* and *rḥmym*, and between *ḥsd* and *ʾhbh*.

4.1.7.1. Ḥsd *and* Ḥn

Instead of being "done" (*ʿśh*; [AGENT'S_ACTIVITY]) by a situationally more powerful party ([AGENT]) with a situationally less powerful party ([PATIENT]; cf. ARTICLE_OF_TRANSACTION_*ḤSD*), *ḥn* is "found" (*mṣʾ*) by a [SEEKING_PARTY] in the eyes of a [PERCEIVING_PARTY]. The [SEEKING_PARTY] makes a request of the [PERCEIVING_PARTY], and the [PERCEIVING_PARTY] may grant the request. But, unlike with *ḥsd*, there is no expectation of reciprocity,[57] nor any relational "tie or claim."[58]

Ḥn is usually the Direct Object of *mṣʾ* in the Protasis of a Conditional Sentence (i.e., "If I have found favor [*ḥn*] in your eyes . . ."; e.g., Gen 18:3). The only Hebrew Bible instance where *ḥn* has a suffix is in Gen 39:21 (i.e., "his favor [*ḥn*]"). *Ḥn* has no prototypical partner noun and it does not occur in the plural.

53. Clark, *Word Hesed*, 35.
54. Ibid., 267–68.
55. *Eleos* also renders *tḥnh* (Josh 11:20; Jer 43:7; 44:20; 45:26; 49:2 LXX), *ḥnynh* (Jer 16:13), and *tḥnwn* (Dan 9:3).
56. See §6.1.1.
57. Joosten, "חסד, 'Benevolence', and ἔλεος, 'Pity'," 99: "'Pity' will always . . . be unilateral."
58. Lofthouse, "*Ḥen* and *Ḥesed*," 33; also noted by Sakenfeld in *Meaning of Hesed*, 4.

4.1.7.2. Ḥsd *and* Rḥmym

Rḥmym is often paired with *ḥsd* and behaves much like *ḥsd* (e.g., Zech 7:9). It is featured in the same subcategories as *ḥsd*, except that it is a [GIFT], not an [ARTICLE_OF_TRANSACTION]. That is, the *rḥmym* are prototypically "given/granted" (*ntn*) to a new [POSSESSOR] (e.g., Jer 42:12), not "done" (*ʿśh*) with a [PATIENT] ([AGENT'S_ACTIVITIES]).

Like [CHARACTERISTIC] *ḥsd*, *rḥmym* can have a [POSSESSOR] (e.g., 1 Kgs 3:26) and may be described as "great" or "abundant" (e.g., Isa 54:7). But *rḥmym* are gut-level emotions/yearnings directed toward an object (cf. Gen 43:14; 1 Kgs 3:26), rather than a disposition to act in accordance with covenant commitments. A plea for *rḥmym* often follows some wrongdoing by the potential [POSSESSOR], so they are undeserved (cf. Dan 9:18) and may be accompanied by an appeasement offering (e.g., Gen 43:14). There is particular emphasis on gathering God's people from the nations among the [MANIFESTATIONS] of *rḥmym* (e.g., Isa 54:7–8; Ps 106:46–47).

In addition, *ḥsd*'s characteristic loyalty, greater emphasis on [DURATION], and appearance in confidence motifs with *bṭḥ* ("trust"; e.g., Ps 52:10 MT) distinguish it from *rḥmym*.[59]

4.1.7.3. Ḥsd *and* ʾHbh

The noun *ʾhbh* behaves more like instances of CHARACTERISTIC_*ḤSD* or ENTITY_*ḤSD* than it does like the other subcategories of *ḤSD*. Like *ḥsd*, *ʾhbh* sometimes has a [POSSESSOR] (e.g., "love of YHWH"), and thus sometimes occurs in construct form (e.g., Hos 3:1), perhaps preceded by the prefix *b* (e.g., Zeph 3:17). Instead of a [PATIENT], however, it often has an [OBJECT] (e.g., Rachel [Gen 29:20]; Virgin Israel [Jer 31:3–4]; *ḥsd* [Mic 6:8]). Rarely is *ʾhbh* the Direct Object of an action, and there are few descriptions of its [MANIFESTATIONS], but it can provide a basis or strong motivation for various (sometimes intense) [RESPONSES] (e.g., Gen 29:20; Song 2:5; 5:8). It is hoped, rather than expected, that love will be returned. While *ʾhbh* is a powerful emotion that usually has positive connotations (e.g., Song 8:6), if the nature or [OBJECT] of love is inappropriate, the connotations are negative (e.g., 2 Sam 13:15). Unlike *ḥsd*, *ʾhbh* does not occur in the plural form and is rarely paired with any closely related nouns, but it is [CONTRASTED] with *śnʾh* ("hatred"; e.g., Prov 10:12).

59. Glueck, *Das Wort ḥesed*, 66; Glueck, *Ḥesed in the Bible*, 84, 102. See also Stoebe, "Gottes hingebende Güte und Treue," 132.

Norman Snaith's distinction between God's "Election-Love" (*ʾhbh*; "the cause of the covenant") and "Covenant-Love" (*ḥsd*; "the means of its continuance") is generally helpful,[60] although not every experience of *ḥsd* is dependent on the prior existence of a covenant (cf. the initiating aid in Judg 1:24).

4.1.8. General Themes

The following themes emerge across the subcategories of ḤSD:

4.1.8.1. Translations and Word Combinations

Eleos is the most frequent LXX rendering of *ḥsd*. Other renderings sometimes reflect the [MANIFESTATIONS] of *ḥsd* in their particular contexts, the books in which they are found, or the word combinations to which they belong. *Ḥsd* is most frequently paired with *ʾmt*.

4.1.8.2. Transactions

Ḥsd often occurs in Verbal Clauses, and the most common [AGENT'S_ACTIVITY] is "doing" (*ʿśh*) *ḥsd*. It is prototypically associated with transactions between two parties, and so a common grammatical construction is *ʿśh ḥsd ʿm* ("do *ḥsd* with").

4.1.8.3. YHWH and Ḥsd

YHWH/God is the most frequent and reliable [POSSESSOR] and [AGENT] of *ḥsd*. YHWH's *ḥsd* is abundant, great, vast, superior, faithful, and enduring ([QUANTITY]/[QUALITY]; [DURATION]). It is described using the constructions *rb ḥsd* and *ky lʿwlm ḥsdw*. Requests are often made on the basis of YHWH's *ḥsd*, so it is also connected to prepositions and pronominal suffixes (e.g., *kḥsdk*). Demonstration of *ḥsd* is commonly [JUSTIFIED] by relationship with or the reputation of YHWH/God. YHWH, who delights in *ḥsd*, is also one of the most frequent [PERCEIVERS] of *ḥsd* (or the lack thereof), but YHWH is rarely described as a [PATIENT] of *ḥsd*.

4.1.8.4. Humans and Ḥsd

In contrast to that of YHWH/God, human *ḥsd* is fleeting. Certain people or types of people are usually involved (or not involved) in *ḥsd* events, and the

60. Snaith, *Distinctive Ideas*, 95. Cf. Exod 20:5–6; Mal 1:2–3 (verb *ʾhb*); 2 Chr 2:11 (2:10 MT); 9:8.

demonstration of *ḥsd* is commonly [JUSTIFIED] by mutuality/reciprocity, recipients' good/faithful conduct, or the principle of reaping what one has sown. Kings, leaders, and their associates feature among the human [AGENTS], [PATIENTS], and [PERCEIVERS] of *ḥsd.* Thus, *ḥsd* is sometimes [LOCATED] in particular houses/households. The people of Israel are also [PATIENTS] and [PERCEIVERS], especially patriarchs, groups of faithful people, and psalmists. Human [RESPONSES] to *ḥsd* are vocal/musical, written, cognitive, emotional, or behavioral. Particular groups are appointed to give thanks to YHWH for his enduring *ḥsd.*

4.1.8.5. Covenant Relationship

Ḥsd is often associated with the relationship between YHWH/God and YHWH/God's people / covenant partners and is situated in [LOCATIONS]/[CONTEXTS] connected to YHWH and YHWH's people. YHWH keeps the covenant and *ḥsd,* and *ḥsd* is contrasted with covenant transgressions.

4.1.8.6. Need, Distress, and Change

There is a wide range of [MANIFESTATIONS] of *ḥsd,* usually matched to the presenting needs and [CONTEXTS] of the [PATIENTS]. [MANIFESTATIONS] highlighted in particular subcategories include answered prayer and remembrance, protection, deliverance, salvation, redemption and preservation of lives, sustaining a dynasty and cultic reforms, compassion, comfort, and support. In particular, demonstrations of *ḥsd* are often associated with immediate needs, change/transitions/milestones, or ongoing continuity. Thus, *ḥsd* is commonly situated in [CONTEXTS] of dislocation/distress (including potential death). Sometimes, *ḥsd* is communicated "in the morning," perhaps after the distress of the night ([TIME]/[DURATION]).

4.1.8.7. Contrasting Outcomes

Positive outcomes from *ḥsd* events include granted requests and fulfilled promises, subsequent requests, and YHWH's intervention. There can be negative or unexpected outcomes, especially when *ḥsd* is not done, reciprocated, or appreciated.

4.1.9. Developments

Of the four main subcategories of *ḤSD*, ARTICLE_OF_TRANSACTION_*ḤSD* is the most clearly defined and prototypical subcategory from which the others extend. CHARACTERISTIC_*ḤSD* emphasizes the [QUALITY], [QUANTITY], and [DURATION] of YHWH's *ḥsd*, along with human [RESPONSES] (esp. appeals for YHWH to act in accordance with YHWH's *ḥsd* disposition). SPECIFIC_DEMONSTRATION_OF_*ḤSD* includes metonymic extensions of *ḤSD*, where the term profiles a specific demonstration of *ḥsd*, rather than a general state or ongoing commitment. ENTITY_*ḤSD* includes more schematic occurrences of *ḥsd*. The most common elements to be figuratively extended or compared are [AGENT] (personification), [QUANTITY]/[QUALITY], [DURATION], and [OUTCOME]. Other developments in the category *ḤSD* relate to the [MANIFESTATIONS], [POSSESSORS], [PATIENTS], and grammatical constructions of *ḥsd*, as outlined below.

4.1.9.1. Manifestations

The personification of *ḥsd* emphasizes its [MANIFESTATIONS], because *ḥsd* is commissioned to carry out particular tasks on behalf of YHWH. Some LXX translations of *ḥsd* also emphasize its [MANIFESTATIONS] (specialization). With respect to the dating of texts, it is difficult to say whether the regular use of *eleos* as a translation for *ḥesed* reflects an increased use of *ḥesed* to convey God's willingness to forgive relationship breaches in exilic and postexilic writings, as Sakenfeld suggests, but the problematic status of the covenant during the exile is certainly an issue in some verses containing *ḥsd* (e.g., Jer 16:5; Ps 89:49 [89:50 MT]).[61]

One particular [MANIFESTATION] of *ḥsdym* associated with Nehemiah (Neh 13:14), and possibly Hezekiah (2 Chr 32:32) and Josiah (2 Chr 35:26), is cultic reform. The only other plural uses of *ḥsd* with human [POSSESSORS] are the "of David" constructions, one of which is in the context of Solomon's temple-dedication prayer (2 Chr 6:42). Thus, Sakenfeld's phrase "ritual- and temple-related content" seems fitting to describe a special focus in four of these plural uses. The constancy of YHWH's *ḥsd* is emphasized throughout the Hebrew Bible, but the forms of its "expression" do not necessarily remain constant.[62]

4.1.9.2. Possessors and Patients

In Isa 40:6, the *ḥsd* of "all flesh" is compared to a flower of the field. This figurative use of *ḥsd* illustrates an occasional expansion in the possessors of *ḥsd* to include all humanity.[63] Then again, some uses of *ḥsd* suggest a "narrowing" to focus on only faithful followers of YHWH (e.g., Ps 103:11, 17).

61. Sakenfeld, *Meaning of Hesed*, 119, 129.

62. Ibid., 153, 213.

63. Glueck, *Das Wort ḥesed*, 21; Glueck, *Ḥesed in the Bible*, 56.

4.1.9.3. Grammatical Constructions

First Chronicles 16:41 records David's decision to appoint certain people to give thanks to YHWH ("for his *ḥsd* is forever") as part of regular worship. Thus, *ḥsd* becomes embedded in the repeated liturgical formula *ky lʿwlm ḥsdw*. In contrast, the expression *tśʾ ḥsd* in Esth 2:9, 17 is unique. According to Sakenfeld, in this instance, the actor is not addressing an essential need or taking responsibility for the recipient, as the term *ḥesed* would traditionally imply.[64] However, the extent to which Sakenfeld's interpretation here is accurate depends on how Esther actually "lifted up" *ḥsd* "before" King Ahasuerus and his official.[65]

The trends indicated by these category developments and extensions raise issues for the New Testament to address, such as how God's loyalty to the covenant will continue to be made manifest after the exile, and whom the faithful people of *ḥsd* will eventually include.

4.1.10. Distinguishing Features

Analysis of Hebrew Bible occurrences of *ḥsd* (and their LXX translations) indicates that potential New Testament instances of the category *ḤSD* are likely to reflect the following features. Instances will be attributes/entities/experiences within interpersonal relationships. The relationships will probably be based on covenants involving responsibilities for each party. Actions or requests of the parties will be motivated by loyalty to kinship/covenant ties, mutuality and reciprocity, or the recognition of need and power imbalance.

A transaction between two parties where the situationally more powerful party meets the present need of the situationally less powerful party (ARTICLE_OF_TRANSACTION_*ḤSD*) is most typical. In some cases, an appeal could be made to someone with a reputation for meeting such needs (CHARACTERISTIC_*ḤSD*), and the appropriate response would be thanksgiving or praise. There may also be specifically identifiable demonstrations of loyal help/devotion that can be remembered, considered, and even recorded (SPECIFIC_DEMONSTRATIONS_OF_*ḤSD*). However, schematic instances of the category (ENTITY_*ḤSD*) may be communicated only as perceptions of the presence/absence of the entity. Some instances of the category may be associated with figurative language, especially personification or agricultural/natural imagery.

Instances of *ḤSD* will not be found by a [SEEKING_PARTY] in the eyes of a [PERCEIVING_PARTY], but "done" by a situationally more powerful party ([AGENT]) with a situationally less powerful party ([PATIENT]). Instances of

64. Sakenfeld, *Meaning of Hesed*, 159, 161.
65. See Nelson, "What About the Women of *Ḥesed*?," 161–63.

ḤSD are more likely to be [ARTICLES_OF_TRANSACTION] than [GIFTS]. They will involve more disposition to act in accordance with covenant commitments ([CHARACTERISTIC]) than gut-level emotion or yearning, and they are more likely to be directed toward a [PATIENT] who benefits from the experience than a human or nonhuman [OBJECT]. They will always have positive connotations.

The remainder of this study utilizes this Hebrew Bible and LXX data in two main ways: First, the most common LXX translations, prototypical scripts, and distinguishing features of *ḥsd* are helpful for identifying New Testament instances of the category ḤSD. Second, New Testament instances of ḤSD are analyzed according to the same criteria as Hebrew Bible instances, so that the two sets of data can be compared and New Testament emphases identified.

4.2. *Ḥsd* in Other Literature of the Second Temple Period

4.2.1. Ḥsd *in the Dead Sea Scrolls*

The influence of the Hebrew Bible (*BHS*) and the LXX on New Testament engagement with the concept corresponding to *ḥesed* is more obvious than that of the nonbiblical texts from Qumran (DSS texts hereafter). Therefore, I will limit my discussion about *ḥsd* in that literature to key similarities and differences in comparison to the Hebrew Bible data.

There is a higher incidence of plural forms among the 141** occurrences of *ḥsd* in the DSS texts[66] than there is in the Hebrew Bible (*BHS*) occurrences. The plural construct form is especially frequent.[67] The subcategory ENTITY_ḤSD also features proportionally more often in these texts (e.g., 1QS V, 4) than in the Hebrew Bible.

The relationship between *ḥsd* and covenant observed in the Hebrew Bible remains important in the DSS texts. The covenant is called a "Covenant of *Ḥsd*" (*bryt ḥsd*; 1QS I, 8),[68] and covenant people are called "Sons of *Ḥsd*" (*bny ḥsd*; 1QH^a XV, 23). *Ḥsd* is received by those who love God and keep God's commandments (CD XIX, 1–2; 1QH^a VIII, 34–35; 4Q393 3, 2). However, according to The Rule of the Community (1QS), covenanters commit to the covenant community where that rule is established and to the statutes of God (1QS I, 7–8, 16).

66. *DSSC* 1:270–71, and Stegemann, Schuller, and Newsom, *Qumran Cave 1.III*, 347. See the list of occurrences in table A3.1. I do not deal here with the biblical texts found at Qumran.

67. 1QS I, 22; II, 4; X, 4, 16; XI, 12, 13; 1QM XII, 3; XIV, 9; XVIII, 11; 1QHa V, 22; VIII, 30, 30; IX, 34; X, 25; XII, 38; XIV, 12; XV, 30, 38; XVII, 7, 10, 14; XIX, 8, 21, 31, 33, 34; XXIII, 25; XXV, 11; XXVI, 32; 4Q176 8–11, 10; 4Q185 1–2ii1; 1–2ii13; 4Q215a 1ii4; 4Q258 IX, 1; 4Q286 1ii8; 4Q372 1, 19, 25; 4Q381 33+35, 5, 6; 46a+b, 2; 4Q400 1i18; 1i20; 4Q403 1i23; 4Q423 3a, 2; 4Q437 2i5; 4Q509 3, 5; 4Q511 26, 2; 36, 2; 11Q5 XIX, 9, 13; XXII, 5; 11Q6 4–5, 10.

68. In addition, *bryty wḥsdy* occurs in 4Q463 1, 3, and *hbryt whḥsd* occurs in CD XIX, 1; 4Q393 3, 2.

Ḥsd is also associated with some combinations of words in the DSS texts that differ from those featured in the Hebrew Bible. In 1QS IV, 5, it is the "sons of *ʾmt* ['faithfulness']" who receive an abundance of *ḥsdym*. However, *ḥsd wʾmt* occurs only twice** in the DSS texts (1QHᵃ VIII, 34; 11Q5 XXVI, 10). Similarly, *ʿśh* ("to do/make") takes *ḥsd* or *rwb ḥsd* as its object only three times (CD XX, 21; 1QHᵃ VIII, 26–27; 4Q385a 7, 2). These totals are considerably less than in *BHS*.[69] On the other hand, paired or parallel uses of *ḥsd* and *rḥmym* are still prominent in the DSS texts.[70] Among the verbs that take *ḥsd* as their object (though infrequently) in the DSS texts, *ʾhb*, *gml*, *ḥrt*, *ydʿ*, *smk*, *šlm*, and *šʿn* do not take *ḥsd* as their object in *BHS*. And *ḥsd* is associated with *ʾhbh* more frequently in the DSS texts than in *BHS*. When people are the agents of *ḥsd*, it is coupled with *ʾhbh* (i.e., *ʾhbt ḥsd*).[71]

There is a higher proportion of attributive formulations that include *ḥsd* (especially *ʾhbt ḥsd*) in the DSS texts than in *BHS*,[72] and *ḥsd* has become more dependent on other substantives. However, the presence of characteristic grammatical constructions containing *ḥsd* (e.g., *brwb ḥsdw* in 1QS IV, 4) and quotations of Hebrew Bible texts (e.g., Deut 7:9; CD XIX, 1–2) indicates that its "original meaning" is still important.[73]

In summary, when compared with the Hebrew Bible (*BHS*), the nonbiblical Dead Sea Scrolls contain proportionally more plural and attributive uses of *ḥsd*, and there are some different combinations of words involving *ḥsd*. Covenant fidelity remains an important aspect of the corresponding concept, but a particular community of God's people is emphasized.

4.2.2. **Ḥsd** ***in Sirach***

The Wisdom of Ben Sira (Sirach) also provides a helpful comparison for the present study because it is extant in both Hebrew and Greek. However, the diversity of Greek equivalents for *ḥsd* supports Benjamin Wright's general conclusion

69. E.g., there are fifteen** MT occurrences of *ḥsd wʾmt* and another seven close variants of the phrase.

70. In addition to the constructions in 1QS I, 22; II, 1 (cf. 4Q403 1i23; 4Q405 3ii15), I observe in the DSS texts five parallel uses of *ḥsd* and *rḥmym* (1QS XI, 13; 1QHa XV, 30; XIX, 21; 4Q372 1, 19; 4Q418 81+81a, 8) and six additional instances where these words are paired together (1QHa IX, 33–34; XII, 38; XVIII, 16; 4Q286 1ii7–8; 11Q5 XIX, 8 // 11Q6 4–5, 9).

71. CD XIII, 18; 1QS II, 24; V, 4, 25; VIII, 2.

72. McCune, "Contribution of the Dead Sea Scrolls," 14–18, and Zimmerli, *Studien zur alttestamentlichen Theologie*, 277–78. The phrase *ʾhbt ḥsd* occurs in CD XIII, 18; 1QS II, 24; V, 4, 25; VIII, 2; X, 26; 4Q258 II, 4; 4Q299 54, 3; 4Q502 14, 5. This phrase is partially reconstructed in 4Q418 169+170, 3; 4Q437 4, 4; 4Q438 4ii4 (so Strugnell and Harrington, "Instruction," 391, and Weinfeld and Seely, "Barkhi Nafshi," 320, 330). Nouns also follow *ḥsd* in formulations such as *ḥsdy ʿwlm*.

73. Contra Stoebe, "חֶסֶד *ḥesed*," 2:463.

that "the grandson was not concerned to give a formal representation of Ben Sira's Hebrew."[74]

There are twenty-eight** occurrences of *ḥsd* in Hebrew Sirach,[75] twenty-two of those in chapters 44–51, including fourteen in repetitions of the refrain "For his [YHWH's] *ḥsd* is forever" after each description of YHWH in Sir 51:12a–n (material found only in the Hebrew texts). The expectation for *ḥsd* to endure is also evident prior to 51:12.[76]

The heritage of *ḥsd* among Israel's ancestors is especially evident in a hymn (chs. 44–49) honoring the "men of *ḥsd*" (*andras endoxous* [44:1]; *andres eleous* [44:10]), all of whom are Hebrew Bible figures. However, not all of these men are named as agents or patients of *ḥsd* in the Hebrew Bible. In contrast, no women are named in this hymn, even though there are women of *ḥsd* in the Hebrew Bible.[77]

4.2.3. Significance for This Study

In light of this data, we should not be surprised to observe some diversity in the word combinations containing New Testament equivalents for *ḥsd*. We shall see in the New Testament whether the expectation for God's *ḥsd* to endure is fulfilled and the nature/range of participation in the covenant community is reexamined.

74. Wright, *No Small Difference*, 116. Comparing Hebrew and Greek Sirach, *ḥsd* matches *eleos* five times and *charis* twice, and *gmylwt/gymylwt ḥsd* matches *eucharistia* once. Otherwise, Greek equivalents occur once or there is no obvious match between the Hebrew and the Greek.

75. *Book of Ben Sira*, https://www.bensira.org. See table A3.2. Singular *ḥsd* is more frequent than the plural.

76. Human: 7:33; 41:11; divine: 40:17; 47:22; 51:8.

77. See Nelson, "What About the Women of *Ḥesed*?," 152–67.

CHAPTER 5

Ḥsyd in the Hebrew Bible and Other Literature of the Second Temple Period

Findings from my category analysis of the thirty-two* Hebrew Bible (*BHS*) occurrences of the adjective *ḥsyd*[1] indicate that there are two subcategories of ḤSYD: ONE_DEVOTED_TO_COVENANT_RELATIONSHIP and ONE_DEVOTED. I summarize and interpret my findings about the Hebrew Bible (*BHS*) instances in each subcategory (and their LXX renderings) (§5.1) and then do the same for instances in other literature of the Second Temple period (§5.2).[2] I highlight trends and developments in the category ḤSYD, noting how this information, together with the information in chapter 4, forms a basis for the New Testament investigation presented in chapters 11–12.

5.1. *Ḥsyd* in the Hebrew Bible

There has been some disagreement about whether a *ḥsyd* practices[3] or receives[4] *ḥsd*, but the key elements in *ḥsyd* clauses are not [AGENT] and [PATIENT]. They are [DEVOTED_PARTY] (usually human) and [POSSESSIVE_PARTY] (usually God). The description "party" is more consistent with Rudolf Kittel's idea that the *ḥsydym* are called "the people" not because of their goodness but because of their relationship to YHWH,[5] although YHWH is also described as *ḥsyd*.

Identifying and labeling the subcategories of ḤSYD has been challenging. PERSON_OF_ḤSD would be a satisfying equivalent for *ḥsyd* because it does not emphasize either the demonstration or receipt of *ḥsd*. But neither does it

1. This figure includes twenty-five** occurrences in Psalms. The occurrences of *ḥsyd* in 4Q88 II, 19 (Ps 107:15; treated as *ḥsd*) and 11Q5 XVII, 3 (Ps 145:13) (so *DSSC* 3:260) are not included in this analysis. Table A1.2 presents all *BHS* instances of the categories ḤSD and ḤSYD.

2. Table A1.1 presents definitions of the clause elements included in the analyses on which the data in this chapter is based.

3. So, e.g., Glueck, *Das Wort ḥesed*, 34; Glueck, *Ḥesed in the Bible*, 69.

4. So, e.g., Sakenfeld, *Meaning of Hesed*, 242, except in the two instances where *ḥāsîd* is used of God (Jer 3:12; Ps 145:17).

5. Kittel, *Die Psalmen*, 184; Glueck, *Ḥesed in the Bible*, 69.

adequately describe the divine *ḥsyd*, nor account for subtle differences in the way that particular occurrences of *ḥsyd* may be translated into English (e.g., *ḥsydk* in Ps 16:10 vs. *ḥsyd lw* in Ps 4:3 [4:4 MT]). Sakenfeld identifies three groupings of people labeled by the plural uses of *ḥāsîd*: all Israel, "the faithful and/or the upright," and a priestly class.[6] From specific examples, Glueck observes that the "*ḥasid*" is portrayed "als Gegenteil vom Sünder" ("as the opposite of the sinner"), "gleich dem Redlichen und Gerechten" ("identical with the honest and the just"), and "gleich dem Getreuen" ("identical with the faithful").[7] However, *ḥsyd* is not always presented in parallel or contrast with those terms, nor is the referent of *ḥsyd* always obvious. Instead, I distinguish different uses of the term within its grammatical and semantic contexts. I label the two subcategories ONE_DEVOTED_TO_COVENANT_RELATIONSHIP and ONE_DEVOTED, and I label *ḥsyd* the [DEVOTED_PARTY], although I do not intend to emphasize either the activity or the receptivity of the *ḥsyd* by these choices.

The instances of each subcategory of *ḤSYD* were analyzed with regard to Obligatory and Optional Clause Elements. In my summary of analysis results for ONE_DEVOTED_TO_COVENANT_RELATIONSHIP, I include a script and a prototypical exemplar. This subcategory has only one Obligatory Element ([DEVOTED_PARTY]), but a [POSSESSIVE_PARTY], to whom the [DEVOTED_PARTY] belongs/relates, is usually also involved. ONE_DEVOTED is a more generalized development of ONE_DEVOTED_TO_COVENANT_RELATIONSHIP, but the subcategory boundaries should not be considered rigid.

5.1.1. ONE_DEVOTED_TO_COVENANT_RELATIONSHIP_(WITH)

The central/prototypical subcategory of *ḤSYD* is ONE_DEVOTED_TO_COVENANT_RELATIONSHIP. This label is inspired by Ps 50:5, where YHWH's *ḥsydym* are placed in parallel with those who made a covenant with YHWH by sacrifice. That occurrence of *ḥsyd* also illustrates the need for the optional "with" at the end of the label (i.e., "those devoted to covenant relationship with me" or "my devoted ones").

5.1.1.1. Findings from the Analysis

Most instances of *ḤSYD* in this subcategory occur in Psalms and are rendered by *hosios* in the LXX. The presence of *l'* before associated verbs produces or

6. Sakenfeld, *Meaning of Hesed*, 243–44.

7. Glueck, *Das Wort ḥesed*, 31–34; Glueck, *Ḥesed in the Bible*, 66–69. The English phrases are headings, recorded in all uppercase letters.

should produce a positive experience (e.g., not being "forsaken" [*ʿzb*]). Apart from cases where an entire pericope is largely duplicated (2 Sam 22:26 // Ps 18:25 [18:26 MT]), the only repeated clause involving *ḥsyd* is *ky ḥsyd ʾny* ("For I am *ḥsyd*"; Jer 3:12; Ps 86:2), although *ḥsyd* does occur more often in the plural than in the singular, and it is usually in construct form with a pronominal suffix.[8] Within this subcategory, the only referent of these pronominal suffixes is YHWH. *Kl ḥsydyw* ("all his *ḥsydym*") also occurs more than once (e.g., Ps 148:14), indicating that individual *ḥsydym* belong to the collective group of those devoted to covenant relationship with YHWH. Words used in construct form before *ḥsydym* denote the [POSSESSIONS] of the *ḥsydym* (e.g., *rgly ḥsydw* ["the feet of his *ḥsyd*"]; 1 Sam 2:9).

There is no particular clause role to which *ḥsyd* is most suited,[9] and no word/s that are repeatedly paired with *ḥsyd*, but there are certain groups or types of people whose descriptors occur in parallel with *ḥsyd*.[10] The only Obligatory Element is [DEVOTED_PARTY], but the referent of [DEVOTED_PARTY] is not usually specified explicitly. The only specified [DEVOTED_PARTIES] are YHWH and YHWH/God's people (including psalmists and those groups mentioned in parallel).

Regarding Optional Elements, psalmists and other writers/speakers document perceptions of *ḥsydym*. Where possession is indicated, the *ḥsydym* belong/relate to YHWH ([POSSESSIVE_PARTY]). Therefore, in this subcategory, either YHWH Godself is *ḥsyd* (e.g., Jer 3:12) or the relationship is between the *ḥsyd/ḥsydym* and YHWH. Various [POSSESSIONS_OF_THE_DEVOTED_PARTY] are also considered worthy of attention.[11]

The majority of [RESPONSES_OF_THE_DEVOTED_PARTY] are forms of vocal thanksgiving, praise, and blessing toward YHWH (e.g., Ps 30:4 [30:5 MT]) or positive attitudes (e.g., gladness; 2 Chr 6:41). All of YHWH's [RESPONSES] toward the *ḥsydym* are positive (e.g., protection, deliverance; Ps 97:10). [REASONS] for these positive [RESPONSES] often concern YHWH Godself. For example, YHWH will not forsake YHWH's *ḥsydym*, because YHWH loves justice (Ps 37:28). In addition, the *ḥsydym* are [CONTRASTED] with those opposed to YHWH's ways (e.g., the wicked; 1 Sam 2:9).

8. *Ḥsydy* (Ps 50:5); *ḥsydyk* (e.g., Ps 52:9 [52:11 MT]); *ḥsydyw* (e.g., Ps 97:10).

9. Verbal Clauses are more common than other clause types. *Ḥsyd* can fulfill the roles of Subject, Direct Object, Indirect Object, and Complement, or occur within a Modifier.

10. E.g., "servants" (Ps 79:2), "priests" (Ps 132:9), those who are devout, pure, or faithful (2 Sam 22:26–27; Pss 18:25–26 [18:26–27 MT]; 31:23 [31:24 MT]).

11. Feet (1 Sam 2:9); face (Jer 3:12); flesh (Ps 79:2); *npš* (Pss 86:2; pl. 97:10); death (Ps 116:15); way (Prov 2:8).

5.1.1.2. Script

The *ḥsyd*, who belongs to YHWH and is devoted to covenant relationship with YHWH, praises YHWH for YHWH's characteristics and deeds.

5.1.1.3. Prototypical Exemplar: Psalm 30:4–5 (30:5–6 MT)

YHWH's *ḥsydym* are instructed to sing praises to YHWH and give thanks to his holy name, for they spend a short time in YHWH's anger, but a lifetime in YHWH's pleasure.

5.1.2. ONE_DEVOTED_(TO)

For five occurrences of *ḥsyd*, it is not clear that the *ḥsyd* is associated specifically with the relationship between YHWH and YHWH's people, the *ḥsyd* is absent, and/or the sense of *ḥsyd* is general and abbreviated. For example, in Ps 132:16, the *ḥsydym* belong to Zion, the place of God's habitation (v. 13; cf. 2 Sam 6),[12] and the [CONTEXT] of *ḥsyd* in Ps 12:1 (12:2 MT) relates to humanity in general. These five occurrences make up the subcategory ONE_DEVOTED.

5.1.2.1. Findings from the Analysis

Four of the five occurrences of *ḥsyd* in this subcategory are found in Psalms and rendered by *hosios* in the LXX. Four occurrences are singular, including those in a collective/representative sense (e.g., Ps 12:1 [12:2 MT]). The words paired or contrasted with *ḥsyd* indicate that *ḥsyd* is also a faithful, upright person (e.g., Mic 7:2). The only Obligatory Element in this subcategory is [DEVOTED_PARTY], but the identity of these *ḥsydym* is not made explicit. Regarding Optional Elements, the only named [POSSESSIVE_PARTY] is Zion (Ps 132:13, 16). YHWH is an ["OBJECT"_OF_DEVOTION] (Ps 4:3 [4:4 MT]).[13] YHWH, psalmists, and the prophet Micah communicate perceptions of *ḥsydym* (or the lack thereof). Negated statements concern [LOCATIONS]/[CONTEXTS] (e.g., Mic 7:2) and [DURATION] (e.g., Ps 12:1 [12:2 MT]). The only recorded [RESPONSE_OF_A_DEVOTED_PARTY] is rejoicing (Ps 132:16). Other [RESPONSES] relate to the positive attention and intervention of YHWH (e.g., Ps 4:3 [4:4 MT]) or the absence of *ḥsydym* (e.g., Ps 43:1).

Thus, in this subcategory, the *ḥsyd* is devoted, but not necessarily to a particular covenant relationship with YHWH. A perceiver reports responses to the *ḥsyd*, responses by the *ḥsyd*, or absence of the *ḥsyd*.

12. Goldingay, *Psalms 90–150*, 555–57.
13. See table A1.2, n. 24.

5.1.2.2. Exemplar: Psalm 132:13–18

A psalmist declares that YHWH has chosen Zion as a habitation. YHWH says that he will "abundantly bless" (*brk ʾbrk*) the provisions of Zion and satisfy her poor. Her *ḥsydym* will "shout aloud for joy" (*rnn yrnnw*).

5.1.3. Ḥsyd *and a Closely Related Hebrew Adjective*

For this study of *ḥesed* and the New Testament, it is important to distinguish *ḥsyd* from any adjective with which it may be confused. *Hosios* and *hagios* are often thought to be synonymous because they share the English translation "holy / holy one."[14] But, in the LXX, *hosios* usually renders *ḥsyd* and *hagios* renders *qdwš/qdš*. Therefore, in this section, I consider the distinguishing features of the categories *ḤSYD* and *QDWŠ*.

The subcategories of *QDWŠ* are more distinct from each other than those of *ḤSYD*. The first relates to a general DESCRIPTOR for a variety of different entities, including a nation, a city, the temple, those left in Zion, and even YHWH (of hosts). Other subcategories include HEAVENLY_BEING (e.g., Job 15:15), CHARACTERISTIC/MEMBER_OF_YHWH'S_PEOPLE/CONGREGATION (e.g., Num 16:3), and YHWH'S_TITLE (i.e., "the Holy One of Israel"; e.g., Isa 1:4).

An explicit [REASON] is given for YHWH's people to be *qdšym* ([CHARACTERISTIC/MEMBERS_OF_YHWH'S_PEOPLE/CONGREGATION]): YHWH is incomparably *qdwš* ([DESCRIPTOR]; e.g., Lev 11:44, 45). *Qdšym* (including YHWH) may have [POSSESSORS] (cf. "all his holy ones" [Deut 33:3]; "your Holy One" [Isa 43:15]), although possession is more pronounced with *ḥsydym*, for whom covenant relationship with YHWH is the central focus.

YHWH is occasionally referred to as *ḥsyd*, but *qdwš yśrʾl* becomes a regular title for YHWH. There are various positive and negative [RESPONSES] *to* YHWH as "the Holy One of Israel," from praising (Ps 71:22) to defying (Jer 50:29), and various [RESPONSES] *of* YHWH in that role (e.g., choosing Israel [Isa 49:7]; glorifying Zion [Isa 60:9]).

5.1.4. General Themes and Developments

The majority of instances of *ḤSYD* are rendered by *hosios* in the LXX. Most instances occur in Psalms.

YHWH is either *ḥsyd* Godself or the main [POSSESSIVE_PARTY] of human *ḥsydym*. All of YHWH's [RESPONSES] toward the *ḥsydym* and their [POSSESSIONS]

14. E.g., Mounce, *Pastoral Epistles*, 108.

are positive. The reasons concern YHWH Godself. Apart from YHWH, the only [POSSESSIVE_PARTY] of *ḥsydym* is Zion.

The human *ḥsyd* is a faithful, upright person, usually in covenant relationship with YHWH, and sometimes with a special role. Thus, the *ḥsydym* are [CONTRASTED] with those opposed to YHWH's ways. *Ḥsyd* is also often found in the plural construct form (i.e., multiple *ḥsydym* belonging to YHWH). [RESPONSES_OF_THE_DEVOTED_PARTIES] include positive attitudes and various forms of vocal response toward YHWH. Two distinctive features of the smaller subcategory of *ḤSYD* are the shift from specific ("one devoted to covenant relationship") to general or abbreviated usage ("devoted") and the introduction of Zion as an additional [POSSESSIVE_PARTY] to *ḥsydym*.

5.1.5. Distinguishing Features

Analysis of Hebrew Bible occurrences of *ḥsyd* (and their LXX translations) indicates that potential New Testament instances of the category *ḤSYD* are likely to be rendered by *hosios* and to reflect the following features: Human devoted ones will probably be referred to as a group. Prototypically, they will be devoted to covenant relationship with YHWH and praise YHWH for YHWH's characteristics and deeds. Words evoking *ḥsyd* are unlikely to name particular qualities of objects/places or describe ways of life, and likely to refer to parties carrying out responsibilities in order to maintain relationships.

This Hebrew Bible and LXX data is utilized in two main ways in the remainder of this study. First, the most common LXX translation and the prototypical script of *ḥsyd* are helpful for identifying New Testament instances of the category *ḤSYD*. Second, the New Testament instances of *ḤSYD* are analyzed according to the same criteria as the Hebrew Bible instances, so that the two sets of data can be compared and the New Testament emphases identified.

5.2. *Ḥsyd* in Other Literature of the Second Temple Period

5.2.1. Ḥsyd *in the Dead Sea Scrolls*

There are eleven** occurrences of *ḥsyd* in the nonbiblical texts from Qumran (DSS texts hereafter).[15] In these texts, as in the Hebrew Bible (*BHS*), YHWH and Zion are [POSSESSIVE_PARTIES] of *ḥsydym*. The [POSSESSIVE_PARTIES] respond positively to their *ḥsydym*: YHWH's [RESPONSES] include giving Thumim and

15. *DSSC* 1:272. See table A3.1. I do not deal here with the biblical texts found at Qumran.

Urim (4Q175 14; cf. Deut 33:8), being gracious (*ḥnn*; 4Q380 2, 5), and crowning (*piel* of *ʿṭr*; 11Q5 XIX, 7). In addition, as an [OTHER_PARTY], the Lord will "attend to" (*piel* of *bqr*) or "honor" (*piel* of *kbd*) *ḥsydym* (4Q521 2ii+4, 5, 7). Zion's [RESPONSE] is to boast (*hithpael* of *pʾr*) in the deeds of its *ḥsydym* (11Q5 XXII, 6). Generations of *ḥsydym* will be Zion's splendor (11Q5 XXII, 3–4). The *ḥsydym* are set in parallel with the righteous ones (*ṣdyqym*; 4Q521 2ii+4, 5; 11Q5 XVIII, 10) and with Zion's prophets (11Q5 XXII, 5–6). In 11Q5 XVIII, 10, there is a new association between Wisdom and the assembly of *ḥsydym*.

A significant occurrence of *ḥsyd* for this study is in 4Q408 3+3a, 6: YHWH is blessed and called *ḥsyd* because of his judgments (cf. Rev 16:5).[16]

5.2.2. Ḥsyd *in Sirach and* Asidaioi *in 1–2 Maccabees*

There is only one occurrence of *ḥsyd* in Sirach (a plural in 51:12o; cf. Ps 148:14).[17] The clause speaks in praise of YHWH, who raised up "a horn for his people, praise for all his *ḥsydym*." "All his *ḥsydym*" is set in parallel to "his people." YHWH ([POSSESSIVE_PARTY]) raises up praise ([RESPONSE]) for the *ḥsydym*.

The *ḥsydym* probably also feature in 1–2 Maccabees, under the derived name *Asidaioi* (NRSV: "Hasideans").[18] In the postexilic period, this group of Jews supported commitment to the Torah.[19] According to Robert Siebeneck, the group was forming at the time "when Sirach wrote." Thus, during the Maccabean crisis, the "*ḥăsîdîm*" were probably inspired and encouraged by "Sirach's historical survey," which gave them "roots in the past." Like the prophets and judges of old, they would deliver YHWH's people from foreign domination and insist on YHWH's moral demands.[20]

Some joined the priest Mattathias and his sons and associates, in resisting the practices of Seleucid rulers/officials in Judah (1 Macc 1:41–50; 2:42; 7:13; 2 Macc 14:6).[21] But the nature of the "Hasidean" group, whether nationalist, a sect, or otherwise, is debated. For example, Paul Redditt thinks that limiting the concern of the Hasideans to "religious law and not Jewish nationalism" overlooks the nature of 1 Macc 7:12–17, the nature of the split, and their involvement in the Maccabean Revolt.[22] According to Philip Davies, however, if one leaves references to "*Ḥasidim*" in 1 Maccabees out of consideration, then

16. Reconstructed text in Steudel, "408. 4QApocryphon of Mosesc?," 305.
17. *Book of Ben Sira*, https://www.bensira.org. See table A3.2.
18. Cf. Redditt, "Hasideans," 3:66. See 1 Macc 7:13, 17 (quoting selected parts of Ps 78:2–3 LXX [79:2–3 MT]).
19. Redditt, "Hasideans," 3:66.
20. Siebeneck, "May Their Bones Return to Life!," 417–19.
21. Redditt, "Hasideans," 3:66, and Baer and Gordon, "חסד," 2:218. See also Stoebe, "חֶסֶד *ḥesed*," 2:463.
22. Redditt, "Hasideans," 3:66.

"II Macc's portrayal of the *Ḥasidim* can be interpreted exactly in accordance with the meaning of the term *ḥasid* in the O.T."[23]

There does appear to be some shift from the Hebrew Bible portrayal of *ḥsydym* to the Maccabees portrayal of *Asidaioi*. In some Hebrew Bible texts, the *ḥsydym* are presented as equivalent to the Israelites (e.g., Ps 148:14). Where a distinction is made between *ḥsydym* and others, its basis is often abstract and spiritual: the general state of being genuinely devoted to God as opposed to being *ḥsyd* by ancestral heritage only (e.g., Ps 97:10). The exception is the priestly group presented in parallel to the *ḥsydym* in Ps 132:16 and 2 Chr 6:41 (cf. Deut 33:8). Thus, Sakenfeld hypothesizes that "the more general application of *ḥāsîd* to all of God's [covenant] people" existed alongside a more occasional use "for special religious functionaries."[24] In Maccabees, however, the *Asidaioi* are not presented as equivalent to the Israelites. They are viewed as a recognizably distinct subgroup ("first among the Israelites" [1 Macc 7:13]; "those of the Jews called Hasideans" [2 Macc 14:6]). Perhaps then, for the Maccabean context, *ḥsyd* was used for special military or nationalistic functionaries.

Scholars are divided about which subsequent group (Pharisee, Sadducee, Essene) "descended from the Hasideans."[25] The word *Asidaioi* does not occur in the New Testament; however, if the *Asidaioi* had become involved with sectarian, military, or nationalistic concerns, then New Testament findings about those most closely aligned with the *ḥsydym* suggest a shift to other priorities (see ch. 11 and §14.3.4).

23. Davies, "*Ḥasidim*," 136–39.

24. Sakenfeld, *Meaning of Hesed*, 244–45. According to Eerdmans, "The Chasidim . . . held a position between the priests and the great prophets of the 8th Cent. B.C." They were pious laymen that knew the historical traditions and could play instruments / compose songs ("Chasidim," 254).

25. Redditt, "Hasideans," 3:66.

CHAPTER 6

Greek Words That Evoke *Ḥsd* or *Ḥsyd*

For this study, it is important to know not only the behavior patterns of *ḥsd* and *ḥsyd* but also the Greek words that are likely to evoke those terms. I do not propose a single New Testament "equivalent" for either term, as it is doubtful that New Testament writers would consistently choose one Greek word to evoke *ḥsd* and one Greek word to evoke *ḥsyd*. Nonetheless, in comparison to proposed alternatives and in light of the scriptural tradition, I consider *eleos* (§6.1) and *hosios* (§6.2) as the *most likely* words to evoke *ḥsd* and/or *ḥsyd* in the New Testament. Section 6.3 outlines my approach for chapters 7–12, which discuss occurrences of *eleos* and *hosios* in specific New Testament books.

6.1. *Eleos*

6.1.1. Charis, Agapē, *and* Eleos

Greek words already proposed as New Testament "equivalents" for *ḥsd* are also connected with related Hebrew nouns, as discussed in section 4.1.7. One such "equivalent" is *charis* ("grace").[1] In particular, a considered alternative for some scholars is that *plērēs charitos kai alētheias* ("full of grace and truth") in John 1:14 is a direct allusion to / rendering of *rb ḥsd w'mt* ("abounding in *ḥsd* and faithfulness"; LXX: *polyeleos kai alēthinos*), a phrase from Exod 34:6.[2] Conversely, a few authors deny any connection between *ḥsd w'mt* and *charitos kai alētheias*, partly because, in the LXX, *charis* usually renders *ḥn*, not *ḥsd*.[3] While I do not deny the possibility of a direct rendering of this Hebrew

1. Sakenfeld rejects "grace" as an older, unsuitable alternative (*Ruth*, 24).
2. E.g., Carson (*Gospel According to John*, 129) and Keener (*Gospel of John*, 1:416–17) highlight this.
3. Bultmann, *Das Evangelium des Johannes*, 50n, and de la Potterie, "Χάρις Paulinienne et Χάρις Johannique," 258–59. In the LXX, *charis* ("grace/favor") renders *ḥsd* only once (Esth 2:9) but *ḥn* sixty-two times. In addition, Esth 2:17 LXX has *kai heuren charin* in place of *wtś' ḥn wḥsd*

expression, the wider biblical evidence lends weight to the influence of LXX translations on New Testament vocabulary. For example, Jas 4:6 and 1 Pet 5:5 cite Prov 3:34 LXX, where *charis* renders *ḥn*.[4]

Another proposed New Testament "equivalent" for *ḥsd* is *agapē* ("love"). On the one hand, both terms refer to love that is kind, endures, and bears things for the sake of another (1 Cor 13:4, 7). On the other hand, in the LXX, *agapē* renders *ʾhbh* ("love"), not *ḥsd*. Moreover, *agapē* in the New Testament has links with citations of Lev 19:18, where *agapaō* (2sg. fut.) renders *ʾhb* (2 masc. sg. pf. consec.) (Rom 13:9–10; Gal 5:13–14).[5] This evidence does not support understanding New Testament occurrences of *agapē* as evoking *ḥsd*.

Setting aside *charis* and *agapē* then, I focus on *eleos*, the most frequent LXX rendering of *ḥsd*.[6] The great majority of occurrences of *eleos* in LXX texts with Hebrew *Vorlage* are translations of *ḥsd*.[7] There is also some resonance with Hebrew Bible passages that contain *ḥsd* among the occurrences of *eleos* in LXX texts without Hebrew *Vorlage*.[8] For example, Pss. Sol. 2:33 speaks of the *eleos* of the Lord being upon those who fear him, while Ps 102:17 LXX (103:17 MT) states that the *eleos* of the Lord (MT: *ḥsd yhwh*) is "from everlasting even to everlasting on those who fear him."[9] Likewise, *kata to plēthos tou eleous sou* ("according to the abundance of your *eleos*") features in Dan 3:42 LXX, while the same phrase renders *krb ḥsdk* in 2 Esd 23:22 LXX.[10] In addition, some other prototypical features of *ḥsd* (LXX: *eleos*) mentioned in chapter 4 are evident

("and she lifted up grace and *ḥsd*"). These figures** do not include occurrences in Greek Sirach, where *charis* matches *ḥsd* in 7:33 (MS A) and 40:17 (MSS B, M), but *ḥn* in 4:21 (MSS A, C); 7:19 (MS A); 26:15 (MS C); and 32:10 (MS B).

4. NA[28], 692, 706, 856.

5. Matt 5:43; 19:19; 22:39; Mark 12:31, 33; Luke 10:27; and Jas 2:8 also cite Lev 19:18. Matt 22:37; Mark 12:30, 33; and Luke 10:27 cite Deut 6:5 (where *agapaō* renders *ʾhb*). NA[28], 841, 843.

6. See table A1.3. Aside from *eleos* and *polyeleos*, *dikaiosynē* is the next most frequent term used to render *ḥsd* in the LXX (nine times), but it renders *ṣdqh* 131 times, *ṣdq* eighty-one times, and *ṣdyq* seven times. (These figures** do not include occurrences in Greek Sirach, where *dikaiosynē* matches *ṣdq* in 16:22 [MS A], and *ḥsd* in 44:10 [MSS B, M]). Furthermore, Rom 4:3, 22; Gal 3:6; and Jas 2:23 cite Gen 15:6; 2 Cor 9:9 cites Ps 112:9 (111:9 LXX); and Heb 1:9 cites Ps 45:7 (44:8 LXX), where *dikaiosynē* in each of these Old Testament texts renders *ṣdqh* or *ṣdq*. In addition, 1 Cor 1:30 includes *dikaiosynē*, and v. 31 cites Jer 9:23–24 (9:22–23 LXX), where *dikaiosynē* renders *ṣdqh*. NA[28], 488, 489, 520, 569, 582, 658, 689, 837, 852, 855, 862.

7. See table A2.1. Out of 334 occurrences of *eleos* in 322 LXX verses* (including eighty-three verses with no Hebrew *Vorlage*), 211** occurrences translate *ḥsd*.

8. Table A2.1 lists verses and parts of verses without Hebrew equivalents.

9. NETS.

10. Other examples include 1 Macc 4:24, where the army of Judas sang *hoti eis ton aiōna to eleos autou* ("for his *eleos* is for ever"; cf. Dan 3:89, 90). This is identical to the consistent LXX translation for *ky lʿwlm ḥsdw* (e.g., Ps 136 [135 LXX] refrain). *Eleos kai oiktirmous* occurs in 1 Macc 3:44 (cf. variants in Ps 102:4; Hos 2:21; and Zech 7:9 LXX, where the MT equivalent of *eleos* is *ḥsd*). *Poly eleos* (Tob 8:16; Odes 12:14) and *polyeleos* (3 Macc 6:9; Odes 12:7) resemble a typical LXX translation of *rb ḥsd* (e.g., Exod 34:6).

in the LXX material without Hebrew equivalents. For instance, *eleos* is often portrayed as characteristic of God (e.g., Pss. Sol. 4:25) and sometimes paired with *alētheia* ("faithfulness")[11] or *oiktirmos* ("compassion").[12]

On the other hand, in Isa 63:15, *eleos* within the phrase *to plēthos tou eleous sou* corresponds to the plural of *mʿh* ("entrails"), and in Sir 16:12, *poly eleos* translates *rb rḥmym* ("abundant compassion"). There are also some phrases and word pairs involving *eleos* that are more evident in LXX texts without Hebrew *Vorlage* than in LXX translations of verses containing *ḥsd* (e.g., *charis kai eleos* ["grace and *eleos*"]; Wis 3:9; 4:15).[13]

Therefore, *eleos* in the LXX often, but not always, conveys the sense of *ḥsd*. Given the influence of the LXX on the New Testament, *eleos* is therefore also arguably the *most likely* word to evoke *ḥsd* in the New Testament.

6.1.2. **Ḥsd** ***and*** **Eleos**

This raises the issue of convergence between the senses of *ḥsd* and *eleos*. Among the BDAG renderings of *eleos*, "kindness or concern expressed for someone in need" comes closest to the sense of *ḥsd*, and the "Moral and Ethical Qualities and Related Behavior" domain, to which Johannes Louw and Eugene Nida assign *eleos*, resembles CHARACTERISTIC_*ḤSD*.[14] But Rudolf Bultmann's description of the Greek usage of *eleos* does not resonate strongly with the consistently positive character of *ḥsd*. In particular, Bultmann speaks of *eleos* not as "a moral relationship to others" but as a *pathos*, "the emotion roused by contact with an affliction which comes undeservedly on someone else." *Eleos* is an emotion that makes judges partial, one that Stoics regarded as "a sickness of the soul," and the opposite of *orgē*.[15]

In the works of Philo and Josephus,[16] *eleos* is often an emotion/response to which one may be moved, an attribute, or an entity that is sometimes shown/sought/granted. Many of the forty-six* occurrences of *eleos* in Philo's works have the sense of "mercy" as compared with "judgment" (e.g., *Quod Deus sit immutabilis* 74–76) or "pity" felt toward someone suffering injustice or misfortune (e.g., *De specialibus legibus* 1.308). Sometimes, *eleos* is combined with

11. E.g., Pss. Sol. 17:15; cf. *ʾmt* (e.g., Mic 7:20).

12. E.g., 1 Macc 3:44; cf. *rḥmym* (e.g., Hos 2:19 [2:21 MT]).

13. Other examples include *en hēmerais eleous* ("in the days of *eleos*"; Pss. Sol. 18:9; cf. 14:9; 18:5), *epiphanas to eleos autou* ("having revealed his *eleos*"; 3 Macc 6:39; cf. 2:19), and *mē apostēsēs to eleos sou* ("do not withdraw your *eleos*"; Pss. Sol. 16:6; Dan 3:35; cf. 2 Sam 7:15).

14. BDAG, s.v. "ἔλεος, ους, τό." According to L&N, *eleos* shares the subdomain "Mercy, Merciless" with *eleaō*, *eleeō*, and other cognate words (s.v. "ἐλεάω or ἐλεέω; ἔλεος, ους").

15. Bultmann, "ἔλεος, ἐλεέω," 2:477–78.

16. Greek texts of Philo from Borgen, Fuglseth, and Skarsten, *Works of Philo*, and those of Josephus from *Flavii Josephi opera*.

lambanō (along with *oiktos*) giving the idea of "taking pity upon" someone (e.g., *De specialibus legibus* 3.4). There are thirty-eight* occurrences of *eleos* in the works of Josephus. Among these, I note the connection between *eleos* and *pathos* (e.g., *Bellum judaicum* 1.195), and the association between *eleos* and vulnerable people (e.g., *A.J.* 14.480 [neg.]).

On the other hand, "taking pity / having mercy on" (e.g., Ps 51:3 MT [*ḥnn*]; 50:3 LXX [*eleeō*]) someone in need is a manifestation of *ḥsd* (LXX: *eleos*), rather than a sense. With *ḥsd*, there is more emphasis on relational commitment than on emotional response. Therefore, as Sakenfeld point outs, while *eleos* is probably the term that best fits what the Greek translators understood to be the meaning of *ḥesed*, that meaning may not always have been "the central content of *ḥesed*."[17] The lack of an evident pattern in the distribution of *dikaiosynē* ("righteousness") and *eleos* as translations for the pentateuchal occurrences of *ḥsd* may be an indication that the translators were struggling to render the Hebrew term adequately.[18]

I give further consideration to the relationship between the senses of *ḥsd* and *eleos*, and the effects of their frequent association, as I consider each of the twenty-seven* New Testament occurrences of *eleos* and evaluate their potential for denoting instances of the category ḤSD.[19]

6.2. *Hosios*

Considering *hosios* as distinct from *hagios*—the Greek term with which it commonly shares the English translation "holy / holy one"—may enrich our understanding of New Testament texts that include *hosios*. In addition, identifying the particular senses of *hosios* in the LXX, as distinct from its general Greek use, helps with discerning which occurrences of *hosios* are likely to evoke *ḥsyd*.

6.2.1. Distinguishing **Hosios** *from* **Hagios**

Hagios and *hosios* are often thought to be synonymous,[20] but this is somewhat misleading. In the LXX texts with Hebrew *Vorlage*, *hagios* usually renders *qdwš/qdš*, but never *ḥsyd*, and *hosios* usually renders *ḥsyd*, but never *qdwš/qdš*.

17. Sakenfeld, *Meaning of Hesed*, 15.

18. This is inspired by Sakenfeld's insights about the use of *dikaiosynē* in Genesis and Exodus (*Meaning of Hesed*, 15). Contra Joosten, "חסד, 'Benevolence', and ἔλεος, 'Pity'," 101.

19. By limiting my discussion to the Greek word that has the most supporting intertextual evidence, I do not imply that entities or situations denoted by New Testament uses of other Greek words should necessarily be excluded from the category ḤSD.

20. E.g., Mounce, *Pastoral Epistles*, 108.

Hagios occurs much more frequently in the LXX than *hosios*. Of the 792* LXX occurrences of *hagios*, 123** are in Leviticus, in contexts mostly to do with holy days, the tabernacle, offerings, attire, and priests/people imitating the Lord. Holy things are kept from the unclean (12:2–5) and from becoming profane or defiled (19:8; 20:3). The Lord's name (e.g., 1 Chr 29:16), the covenant (e.g., Dan 11:30), the temple (e.g., Hab 2:20), the city of Jerusalem/Zion (e.g., 2 Esd 21:1 LXX), and the "holy ones" are among the additional items described as *hagios* elsewhere.

On the other hand, most of the seventy-seven* LXX occurrences of *hosios* are used to describe the Lord's people and their attributes or the Lord / God.[21] In these occurrences, there is more emphasis on the Lord's people belonging to or trusting the Lord, and on uprightness or covenant loyalty/faithfulness, particularly in distressing circumstances. It is not surprising, then, that *hosios* is the most frequent rendering of *ḥsyd* in the LXX,[22] that the majority of occurrences of *hosios* in LXX passages with Hebrew *Vorlage* translate *ḥsyd*,[23] and that *hosios* is also used to translate *ḥsd* in one LXX text (Isa 55:3). In addition, from the LXX occurrences of *hosios* that have no Hebrew equivalent,[24] the relationship between *hosios* and *eleos* (cf. *ḥsyd* and *ḥsd*) is most apparent in Pss. Sol. 2:36 and 13:12. Psalms of Solomon 2:36 speaks of the Lord doing to his *hosioi* according to his *eleos*, and 13:12 says, "But upon the *hosioi* [is] the *eleos* of the Lord." However, *hosios* is sometimes used to translate other Hebrew words (e.g., *yšr* in Deut 32:4). Thus, *hosios* in the LXX often, but not always, renders *ḥsyd*. This also makes *hosios* a likely choice to evoke *ḥsyd* in the New Testament.

It is reasonable to conclude then that, while there is some overlap in the meanings of *hagios* and *hosios*, the LXX translators carefully distinguish renderings of the two Hebrew terms, and where New Testament authors select words to evoke those Hebrew terms, they are likely to have made similarly careful distinctions.

21. The exceptions are 2 Macc 12:45; Prov 2:11 (thought or insight); Prov 22:11; Dan 3:87 LXX (heart/s); Wis 6:10; Isa 55:3 (things); Amos 5:10 (word).

22. See table A1.4.

23. See table A2.3.

24. There are thirty-seven** such occurrences (see table A2.3). Some prototypical features of *ḥsyd* are also evident among these occurrences: God is the most frequent possessor of *hosios* (e.g., Pss. Sol. 8:23), God treats the *hosioi* specially (e.g., Pss. Sol. 2:36) and/or deals with that which is troubling them (e.g., Pss. Sol. 12:4), praise is among the responses of *hosioi* (e.g., Dan 3:87; Pss. Sol. 8:34), and the *hosios* / the righteous is contrasted with the sinners (e.g., Pss. Sol. 12:6; 14:6–10). However, Wisdom is personified as the rescuer, renewer, and rewarder of *psychas hosias* ("*hosios* souls") and *laon hosion/hosiois* ("*hosios* people") (Wis 7:27; 10:15, 17).

6.2.2. Ḥsyd *and* Hosios

Setting aside temporarily the one LXX occurrence of *hosios* that renders *ḥsd,* I address the issue of convergence between the senses of *ḥsyd* and *hosios.*

In general Greek use, *hosios* may describe actions, persons, or things. It refers to that which is considered "right and good" before humanity and before the gods. The sense may depend on whether *hosios* is associated with *dikaios* (righteous, lawful, dutiful) or *hieros* (holy, of the temple, sacred). The challenge in making a judgment comes when "what is felt to be truly moral" conflicts with a human commandment.[25]

Among the sixty-five* occurrences of *hosios* in Philo's works and thirty-five* in Josephus's works, *hosios* is often used to make an evaluative judgment about whether a thing/action/word/choice does or does not seem right/moral in a particular situation (e.g., Josephus, *A.J.* 8.8; Philo, *De vita Mosis* 1.254).[26] *Hosios* can also describe a personal characteristic (along with "devout" or "just"; e.g., Josephus, *A.J.* 8.295), a doctrine/commandment (e.g., Philo, *De aeternitate mundi* 76), a manner/way of doing things (esp. in the adverbial form; e.g., Josephus, *A.J.* 6.87), or even God (e.g., Philo, *De sobrietate* 10). Comparative and superlative forms are used to indicate the quality/quantity of *hosios* (e.g., Philo, *In Flaccum* 134).

There is some overlap between the semantic range of *hosios* and that of *ḥsyd,*[27] but in Hebrew Bible usage, *ḥsyd* describes only people or God. Being *ḥsyd* also involves right and moral conduct before God and humanity, but that conduct is the expected outworking of belonging to YHWH's covenant people, so it could more accurately be termed "faithful" or "devoted" conduct. Thus, when *hosios* is used to translate *ḥsyd,* there is specialization in its semantic range.

I give further consideration to the relationship between the senses of *ḥsd, ḥsyd,* and *hosios,* as I consider the eight New Testament occurrences of *hosios* and evaluate their potential for denoting instances of the categories *ḤSD* and *ḤSYD*.[28] New Testament engagement with *hosios* seems to be influenced by both general usage and more specialized application of the word. For example,

25. Hauck, "ὅσιος, ὁσίως," 5:489–90, 492 (including the quoted phrases), and LSJ, sv. "ὅσιος, α, ον." *Dikaios* and *hieros* sometimes accompany *hosios* in the works of Philo (e.g., *De fuga et inventione* 63; *De confusione linguarum* 27) and Josephus (e.g., *A.J.* 15.138; *Bellum judaicum* 2.1 [*hieron*]).

26. *Anosios* is also used this way.

27. Among the BDAG renderings of *hosios,* "devout" and "pious" come closest to the meaning of *ḥsyd* (s.v. "ὅσιος, ία, ον").

28. By limiting my discussion to the Greek word that has the most supporting intertextual evidence, I do not imply that entities or situations denoted by New Testament uses of other Greek words should necessarily be excluded from the categories *ḤSD* or *ḤSYD*.

in 1 Tim 2:8, hands are described as *hosios*, and in Rev 15–16, the connections between *hosios* and *dikaios*, as well as those between *hosios* and judgment, are reflected in the faithful and righteous judgments of the *hosios*. On the other hand, in Acts 2:27 and 13:34, 35, *hosios* is located in quotations from Ps 16:10 (15:10 LXX) and Isa 55:3, where it originally rendered *ḥsyd* and *ḥsd*, respectively.[29]

6.3. New Testament Occurrences of *Eleos* and *Hosios*

In the following chapters, I deal with the New Testament occurrences of *eleos* and then the New Testament occurrences of *hosios*. Key occurrences of *eleos*, considered in chapters 7–10, are sequenced according to the probability that they denote instances of the category *ḤSD*. I deal with Matthew's Gospel first (ch. 7), because two Matthean occurrences of *eleos* are in quotations from Hos 6:6, where *eleos* renders *ḥsd*. Chapter 8 addresses the Pauline letters, focusing particularly on Rom 15:9, where *eleos* occurs just prior to two scriptural quotations that, in their original Hebrew contexts, are followed by verses containing *ḥsd*. Chapter 9 deals with *eleos* in Luke's Gospel, where there are several probable allusions to *ḥsd* with indirect links to YHWH's attribute formula (Exod 34:6). Lastly, chapter 10 considers other uses of *eleos* in the New Testament, the most significant of which is in 1 Pet 1:3.

Of the New Testament occurrences of *hosios*, those most likely to denote instances of the categories *ḤSD* and *ḤSYD* are associated with the occurrences in Acts, so I deal with them first, in chapter 11. Chapter 12 deals with the other five occurrences of *hosios*, focusing on the two in Revelation because they are accompanied by allusions to Hebrew Bible texts containing *ḥsd* or *ḥsyd*.

29. Psalm 16:10 is the only verse containing *ḥsyd* in the Hebrew Bible (15:10 LXX: *hosios*) that is quoted in the New Testament (Acts 2:27; 13:35). Isaiah 55:3 (quoted in Acts 13:34) is the only verse where *hosios* (LXX) translates *ḥsd* (MT). Thus, *ta hosia* in Acts 13:34 is a unique instance of *hosios*, assigned to L&N's "communication" domain ("promise" subdomain) (s.v. "ὅσιος, α, ον," "τὰ ὅσια").

CHAPTER 7

Eleos in Matthew's Gospel: A Weighty Matter of the Law

In the middle of a series of woe statements (Matt 23:13–36), Jesus calls the scribes and Pharisees "hypocrites" because they tithe mint, dill, and cumin but neglect weightier things of the law: "justice [*krisis*], mercy [*eleos*], and faithfulness [*pistis*]" (v. 23). This is the only use of *eleos* in Matthew's Gospel apart from two quotations of an excerpt from Hos 6:6a, which includes *ḥsd* in the MT. Thus, intertextual and intratextual evidence indicates that, in the context of this woe statement, the Greek word translated "mercy" (*eleos*) evokes *ḥsd*.[1] *Eleos* (cf. *ḥsd*) is a "weighty" priority for genuine law observance.

This chapter addresses the intertextual connections between *eleos* in Matthew's Gospel and *ḥsd* in the Hebrew Bible (§7.1), Matthew's engagement with the category ḤSD (§7.2), and the exegetical value of recognizing that engagement (§7.3).

7.1. Intertextual Connections Between *Eleos* in Matthew's Gospel and *Ḥsd* in the Hebrew Bible

Two of the three verses in Matthew's Gospel that contain *eleos* (9:13; 12:7)[2] include identical quotations from Hos 6:6a: "I desire *eleos* and not sacrifice." In Hosea MT, this clause reads, *ky ḥsd ḥpṣty wlʾ zbḥ* ("For I delight in *ḥsd* and not sacrifice"). Therefore, *eleos* in the quoted text renders *ḥsd*. In this section, I consider (1) the sense of *ḥsd* (LXX: *eleos*) in the context of Hos 6:6a, (2) Matthew's

1. Cf. Davies and Allison, *Commentary on Matthew XIX–XXVIII*, 294. It is not necessarily manifested as "mercy to those who do wrong." This phrase is quoted from Wilkins's list of the "more important matters" of the law based on Jesus's woe statement recorded above (*Matthew*, 753).

2. On the other hand, *eleeō* occurs in Matt 5:7 (pass.); 9:27; 15:22; 17:15; 18:33, 33; 20:30, 31. Except for 5:7, which also includes *eleēmōn*, each of these occurrences could be translated with a variation on the phrase "have mercy on [me]!" (cf. *ḥnn* in the Hebrew Bible; e.g., Pss 51:3 MT [50:3 LXX]; 123:3 [122:3 LXX]).

use of an excerpt from that text, and (3) the third occurrence of *eleos* in this Gospel (23:23), as a corollary to my argument about *eleos* in 9:13 and 12:7.

7.1.1. Hosea 6:6

Ḥsd occurs six times in Hosea, each time addressing a void in the land of Israel.[3] The people and priests of the northern kingdom were unfaithful to their God (1:2; 4:9; 5:1; 6:9),[4] and the basic aspects of covenant relationship and lifestyle—"faithfulness" (*ʾmt*), *ḥsd*, and "the knowledge of God" (*dʿt ʾlhym*)—were not evident in the land (4:1–2).[5] In the context of Hosea's prophecy, *ḥsd* has the figurative sense of devotion that marriage partners are meant to share with one another (cf. the betrothal gifts offered by YHWH; Hos 2:19–20 [2:21–22 MT]),[6] but which was lacking from one side of this partnership.

Hosea 6 begins with a call to return to YHWH and to press on to know him (vv. 1–3). Then YHWH expresses his own disappointment and anguish at the fleeting displays of *ḥsd* by Ephraim/Judah (v. 4). The judgment for their unfaithfulness (v. 5) will be according to the terms of the covenant that the people have broken.[7] In verse 6, YHWH continues to explain his disappointment:

Hos 6:6 MT:

כי חסד חפצתי ולא זבח	For I delight in *ḥsd* and not sacrifice,
ודעת אלהים מעלות	and the knowledge of God,
	rather than[8] burnt offerings.

Hos 6:6 LXX:

διότι ἔλεος θέλω καὶ οὐ θυσίαν	For I desire *eleos* and not sacrifice,
καὶ ἐπίγνωσιν θεοῦ ἢ	and the knowledge of God,
ὁλοκαυτώματα.	rather than burnt offerings.

In verses 7–10, YHWH describes the shameful transgressions (bloodshed, murder, prostitution) that have caused him such concern.

The phrase *wlʾ zbḥ* (LXX: *kai ou thysian*) in Hos 6:6 is problematic. Does Hosea reject the sacrificial system itself, and more generally, do the

3. Hosea 2:19 (2:21 MT); 4:1; 6:4, 6; 10:12; 12:6 (12:7 MT).

4. Dearman, *Book of Hosea*, 155.

5. Hosea 4:1–3 includes three parts of a covenant lawsuit: the statement introducing the case (v. 1), the indictment (vv. 1–2), and the sentence (v. 3) (cf. Deut 32:4–6, 15–18, 19–29, respectively). Ibid., 146–47 (cf. Mic 6:3–8; Hubbard, *Hosea*, 96), and Wright, "Lawsuit of God," 52.

6. Abel, "Marriage Metaphor," 23, and Kidner, *Message of Hosea*, 36.

7. Stuart, *Hosea—Jonah*, 109–11, and Sweeney, *Micah, Nahum, Habakkuk*, 43.

8. Andersen and Freedman, *Hosea*, 430.

eighth-century prophets believe that the cult is no longer essential or helpful for Israel's relationship with YHWH?[9] Or is sacrifice merely relegated to "second place,"[10] while the prophetic critique focuses on ritual without obedience,[11] or as a way of persuading one's deity to act?[12]

J. J. M. Roberts draws attention to the intertextual relationship between this text and 1 Sam 15:22,[13] where the issue is the priority of obedience over sacrifice.[14] Roberts also provides another example of *ʾl* and *mn* set in parallelism. The issue in Prov 8:10 is not the rejection of riches but rather the choice of "instruction and knowledge" over "silver and fine gold."[15] While silver and gold do not provide a straightforward parallel to the sacrificial system, the interpretive point is fair. Like the "better" choice of Wisdom's instruction (Prov 8:10–11), the people of Israel here needed to make *ḥsd* and the knowledge of God their priorities. In light of these interpretive parallels, then, Hosea's point would be that, by neglecting the fundamental priorities of the law, God's people had misunderstood the true nature of worship and covenant relationship.

7.1.2. Matthew 9:13 and 12:7

An excerpt from Hos 6:6 is cited in Matt 9:13 and 12:7. These quotations agree almost exactly with the LXX,[16] which, in turn, is a close rendering of the Hebrew:

Hos 6:6a MT:	
כי חסד חפצתי ולא זבח	For I delight in *ḥsd* and not sacrifice.
Hos 6:6a LXX:	
διότι ἔλεος θέλω καὶ οὐ θυσίαν	For I desire *eleos* and not sacrifice.
Matt 9:13; 12:7 quotations:	
ἔλεος θέλω καὶ οὐ θυσίαν	I desire *eleos* and not sacrifice.

9. Ibid.
10. Ibid.
11. Sakenfeld, *Meaning of Hesed*, 172–73. Cf. 1 Sam 15:22–23; Isa 1:10–20; Jer 7:21ff.; Amos 5:21–24; Mic 6:6–8 (all references per Sakenfeld).
12. Dearman, *Book of Hosea*, 197.
13. Roberts, "Hosea and the Sacrificial Cultus," 26.
14. See Firth, *1 and 2 Samuel*, 175.
15. Roberts, "Hosea and the Sacrificial Cultus," 16–17.
16. I.e., the text represented in the Rahlfs edition and recorded here. The opening *dioti* (Hos 6:6a LXX) is deleted in the Matthean quotations to suit the new contexts. I set aside the alternative notions, first, that the LXX^{B} *hē* be taken as the preferred original, *kai ou* in LXX^{AQOr} is "influenced by the NT," and Matthew "independently renders the Hebrew" (explored by Gundry, *Use of the Old Testament*, 111), and, second, that this may indicate a deliberate undermining of the sacrificial system (Meier, *Matthew*, 94).

For *eleos* still to carry the connotations of *ḥsd* for Matthew,[17] however, the New Testament author must have been familiar with those connotations.

While acknowledging some debate regarding the authorship of this Gospel,[18] I proceed with the understanding that it was written by a Jew who was familiar with the Scriptures in both Hebrew and Greek, probably the apostle Matthew.[19] There is no evidence from early centuries that the Gospel was ever attributed to any other author.[20] Furthermore, quotations in the material unique to this Synoptic are distinctive from other scriptural quotations, possibly representing Matthew's own translation of the Hebrew text.[21] It is likely, therefore, that the author of this Gospel (hereafter referred to as Matthew) was at least aware of the concept corresponding to *ḥesed* and its connection with Hos 6:6. Moreover, his quotations from Hos 6:6 are unique among the Synoptics,[22] suggesting that he was deliberately drawing attention to that concept. The relevance of Hosea's point about *ḥsd* for the contexts into which Jesus came and Matthew wrote is the topic for sections 7.2 and 7.3.

7.1.3. Corollary: Matthew 23:23

Matthew 23:23 contains the only other occurrence of *eleos* in this Gospel. The central woe of seven such statements included in Jesus's speech about the scribes and Pharisees reads:

Matt 23:23–24:

Οὐαὶ ὑμῖν, γραμματεῖς καὶ Φαρισαῖοι ὑποκριταί, ὅτι ἀποδεκατοῦτε τὸ ἡδύοσμον καὶ τὸ ἄνηθον καὶ τὸ κύμινον καὶ ἀφήκατε τὰ βαρύτερα τοῦ νόμου, τὴν κρίσιν καὶ τὸ ἔλεος καὶ τὴν πίστιν· ταῦτα [δὲ][23] ἔδει	Woe to you, scribes and Pharisees, hypocrites, for you tithe mint and dill and cumin and have neglected the weighty things of the law, justice and *eleos* and faithfulness; these things it was necessary to do

17. Davies and Allison present this possibility (*Commentary on Matthew VIII–XVIII*, 105).

18. E.g., Nolland considers it "most unlikely" that the apostle Matthew composed the canonical Gospel (*Gospel of Matthew*, 3–4), but Hagner prefers to take the testimony of Papias seriously (*Matthew 1–13*, xlvi).

19. After thorough consideration of the evidence, Davies and Allison conclude, "Since Matthew knew Hebrew, he was almost certainly a Jew" (*Introduction and Commentary on Matthew I–VII*, 33). Matthew would have been exposed to the Hebrew Scriptures through school and synagogue attendance. Blomberg, "Matthew," 1.

20. France, *Gospel of Matthew*, 15, and Nolland, *Gospel of Matthew*, 3.

21. Gundry, *Matthew*, 4; Hagner, *Matthew 1–13*, lvi; Pao, "Old Testament in the Gospels," 634. Morris points out the "play on the words 'Jesus' and 'Savior' in 1:21, which is natural in Hebrew" (*Gospel According to Matthew*, 17).

22. Hill, "On the Use and Meaning," 107.

23. Omitted in א D Γ Θ; included in B C K L W Δ. NA[28], 77.

ποιῆσαι κἀκεῖνα μὴ ἀφιέναι. ὁδηγοὶ τυφλοί, οἱ διϋλίζοντες τὸν κώνωπα, τὴν δὲ κάμηλον καταπίνοντες.	while not neglecting those things. Blind guides, (those) who strain out the gnat but swallow the camel!

I treat this occurrence of *eleos* as a corollary to the argument outlined above. In addition, the grouping of entities in verse 23 supports the connection between *eleos* here and *ḥsd*. The group of herbs and the group of characteristics are both recorded in noun triplets linked together by *kai*. The terms in the latter triplet—*krisis* ("justice"), *eleos*, and *pistis* ("faithfulness")—have been listed among the Lord's characteristics in the LXX. For example, *krima* (MT: *mšpṭ* ["justice"]; cf. *krisis*), *eleos* (MT: *ḥsd*), and *pistis* (MT: *ʾmwnh* ["faithfulness"]) are three of the Lord's betrothal gifts in Hos 2:21–22 LXX. *Krima* (MT: *mšpṭ*) and *eleos* (MT: *ḥsd*) also occur in the Mic 6:8 LXX trio of things required by the Lord.[24] These intertextual and intratextual connections indicate that *eleos* in Matt 23:23 denotes the third instance of the category ḤSD in Matthew's Gospel.

Therefore, in terms of Hays's tests for echoes, the key issue concerning *eleos* in Matthew's Gospel is **volume**: that is, the prominence of Hos 6:6. In the following sections, I demonstrate how the third instance of the category ḤSD in this Gospel also brings **thematic coherence** to Matthew's argument.

7.2. The Category ḤSD in Matthew's Gospel

Given that an excerpt from Hos 6:6 is cited in Matt 9:13 and 12:7, I compare the elements of the category ḤSD present in Hos 6:6 with those in the literary contexts of the Matthean citations and the related woe statement (Matt 23:23).[25]

7.2.1. ḤSD *in Hosea 6:6*

In Hos 6:6 MT, YHWH speaks to Ephraim and Judah (communication; location; relational context), whose *ḥsd* has previously been compared to a morning cloud and the dew that goes away quickly (v. 4). Yet YHWH ([PERCEIVER]) delights in ([PERCEIVER'S_RESPONSE]) *ḥsd* ([ENTITY]), not *zbḥ* ("sacrifice"; [CONTRAST]). *Ḥsd* is set in parallel with "knowledge of God." A judgment precedes that statement, and some crimes against the covenant follow it (vv. 5,

24. Hare, *Matthew*, 269.

25. Here and elsewhere, I distinguish elements found within the sentence that contains *ḥsd*, *ḥsyd*, *eleos*, or *hosios* ([SMALL_CAPITALS]) from those found elsewhere (plain text). The form of communication and the relational context are also signaled in plain text, but they are not elements.

7–10), so the desired manifestation of *ḥsd* is probably the opposite of those crimes (i.e., covenant obedience). *Ḥsd* is the Direct Object of a Transitive Verb (1sg. pf. of *ḥpṣ*: "I delight/ed in"), within a Causal Verbal Clause ("for . . .").

The same category elements are present in Hos 6:6 LXX: "The Lord our God" ([PERCEIVER]; v. 1) desires ([PERCEIVER'S_RESPONSE]) *eleos* ([ENTITY]), not *thysia* ("sacrifice"; [CONTRAST]). The same clues concerning the desired manifestation of *eleos* are also present. *Eleos* is the Direct Object of a Transitive Verb (1sg. pres. of *thelō*: "I desire"), within a Causal Verbal Clause. Matthew's removal of *dioti* also removes the causal aspect of the quoted clause.

7.2.2. ḤSD *in Matthew 9:13*

In the context of Matt 9:9–13, the words from Hos 6:6 are communicated in Jesus's speech (vv. 12–13) while he is reclining at a table in the house of Matthew, a tax collector (location; time; vv. 9–10).[26] Jesus responds indirectly to a question that the Pharisees posed (nonperceivers' response) to his disciples: "On what basis does your teacher eat with tax collectors and sinners?" (communication; v. 11).[27] Jesus perceives that the Pharisees (nonperceivers) lack understanding about *eleos* and sends them away to learn more ([OUTCOME])[28] about the statement,[29] "I ([PRIMARY_PERCEIVER]; YHWH) desire ([PRIMARY_PERCEIVER'S_RESPONSE]) *eleos* ([ENTITY]) and not sacrifice ([CONTRAST])" (v. 13). The Pharisees do not perceive that Jesus acts as an agent of *eleos* by sharing table fellowship with sinners, but Jesus indicates that it was for the purpose of calling sinners that he came (manifestation; v. 13; cf. v. 9).[30] He reinforces this with an analogy: "Those who are healthy have no need of a physician but those who are poorly/sick" (contrast). By implication, Jesus is the physician and sinners are the sick who recognize their need of a physician (patients; justification; v. 12). Metaphorically, then, *ELEOS*_IS_MEDICAL_AID, where PHYSICAL_IS_SPIRITUAL (context).

26. Jesus was probably "the guest of honor" at a special meal in the tax collector's house, rather than the host (cf. the Luke parallel). France, *Gospel of Matthew*, 352–53, and Hagner, *Matthew 1–13*, 238 (including the quoted phrase).

27. The Pharisees believed that purity before God involved keeping separate from sinners and avoiding contact with the "morally suspect." Nolland, *Gospel of Matthew*, 386.

28. Secondary perceiver's response; recommended [RESPONSE] for potential possessors/agents.

29. The rabbinic idiom ("Go and learn!") urges the Pharisees to "discern the *sense* of," or make valid inferences from, the scriptural text. Hill, "On the Use and Meaning," 111; emphasis original.

30. Suggestions for that to which Jesus calls sinners include "repentance" (cf. Luke 5:32), the kingdom of God (cf. Matt 21:31), and discipleship. Davies and Allison, *Commentary on Matthew VIII–XVIII*, 105; Hagner, *Matthew 1–13*, 240; Morris, *Gospel According to Matthew*, 222.

7.2.3. ḤSD *in Matthew 12:7*

In the context of Matt 12:1–8, the words from Hos 6:6 are communicated in Jesus's direct response (Matt 12:3–8) to the Pharisees' exclamation: "Look, your disciples are doing what is not permitted (to do) on the Sabbath!" (time; v. 2).[31] At the time, Jesus and his disciples were going through the grainfields (location) and they began to pluck heads of grain to eat (v. 1). Jesus's justifications for allowing this conduct include two analogies where key figures also do what is unlawful on the Sabbath (time; vv. 3–5)[32] and a principle from Hos 6:6: "I ([PRIMARY_PERCEIVER]; YHWH) desire ([PRIMARY_PERCEIVER'S_RESPONSE]) *eleos* ([ENTITY]) and not sacrifice ([CONTRAST])" (Matt 12:7). It seems from the way that Jesus introduces the quotation ("If you had known what is [*ti estin*]"; neg. [SECONDARY_PERCEIVERS'_RESPONSE]), that he (perceiver) thinks the Pharisees (neg. [SECONDARY_PERCEIVERS]) lack understanding about *eleos* and its priority on the Sabbath (time).

The Pharisees (nonperceivers) do not understand (contrast) that Jesus, the Lord of the Sabbath (v. 8), behaves on that day as an agent of *eleos* should, allowing his disciples (patients; relational context) to pluck grain and, later, healing a man with a shrivelled hand (vv. 9–13; manifestations).[33] The Pharisees' exclamation to Jesus about his disciples' behavior condemns the innocent ([OUTCOME]; v. 7). The Pharisees also challenge Jesus about healing on the Sabbath and plot how they might kill Jesus (nonperceivers' responses/outcome; vv. 10, 14).

7.2.4. ḤSD *in Matthew 23:23*

Jesus's speech in Matt 23 addresses his disciples and the crowds, but it concerns the scribes and Pharisees (communication). Jesus's (perceiver) series of woe statements follows an initial explanation about why his audience should follow what the scribes and Pharisees say but not what they do (recommended response; vv. 2–12). The fourth woe statement says, "Woe to you ([PERCEIVER'S_RESPONSE]/[OUTCOME]), scribes and Pharisees—hypocrites (neg. [AGENTS]), for you tithe mint, dill, and cumin ([CONTRAST]), and have neglected (actual [ACTIVITY/RESPONSE]) the weighty things of the law, justice, *eleos* ([ENTITY]),[34] and faithfulness; these things it was necessary to do (neg. [AGENT'S_ACTIVITY/

31. Cf. Exod 20:10; Deut 5:14. Hagner, *Matthew 1–13*, 328.

32. France explains that later Jewish exegesis assumes the incident in 1 Sam 21 occurred on the Sabbath (*Gospel According to Matthew*, 202).

33. Edin points out that Jesus demonstrates "mercy" by healing this man. She connects "Mercy in Matthew's Gospel" with *ḥesed*, but does not distinguish the sense of *eleos* from that of *eleeō* ("Learning What Righteousness Means," title, 357–58).

34. I treat this occurrence of *eleos* as an [ENTITY] because of its schematic nature, even though there is a definite article before it.

RESPONSE]) while not neglecting those things. Blind guides, who strain out the gnat but swallow the camel (hyperbolic figurative contrast)!" The implied comparison is *ELEOS*-NEGLECT_IS_LIKE_A_CAMEL, where SIZE/WEIGHT_IS_IMPORTANCE. *Eleos* is one of the Direct Objects of a Transitive Verb (2pl. aor. of *aphiēmi*: "you have neglected"), in a Contrastive-Causal Verbal Clause.

7.2.5. General Observations

Ḥsd and *eleos* are [ENTITIES] in Hos 6:6 and Matthew's Gospel. In Matthew's citations of Hos 6:6 MT, the perfect verb form ("delight/ed") is rendered in present tense ("desire"), and the clause type changes from Causal to Verbal. Shifting to a Transitive Verb with negative connotations in Matt 23:23 ("neglect"), the Subject also changes from the Lord (1sg.) to the scribes and Pharisees (2pl.).

7.2.5.1. Critique of Misplaced Priorities and Hypocrisy

Within Jesus's speeches, the quotation from Hosea suggests a comparison between participants in the scenes described by Matthew and those addressed in the prophetic oracle. YHWH initiates the interaction with Ephraim and Judah concerning their lack of covenant obedience (neg. manifestation), while Jesus responds directly or indirectly to the Pharisees' critique on two occasions (communication). In each case, the speaker (YHWH or Jesus) [PERCEIVES] and strongly critiques a misplaced priority and a corresponding neglect of *ḥsd* or *eleos* ([ENTITIES]).[35] Those who appeared to be keeping the covenant meticulously and should have been agents of *ḥsd/eleos* were not.[36] Thus, Jesus calls his antagonists hypocrites. On the other hand (contrast), the Pharisees do not perceive that Jesus (implied agent) understands and does *eleos* (calling sinners, feeding the hungry, healing the sick; manifestations). Jesus instructs the Pharisees to gain greater understanding of the saying from Hos 6:6a and recommends that his disciples do as the Pharisees say, but not as they do. The Pharisees condemn the innocent and plot to kill Jesus (responses; [OUTCOMES]).

7.2.5.2. Redefining the People of Eleos

Matthew introduces new and unexpected locations and patients for *eleos*. One of the conversations takes place in the house of a tax collector, after Jesus calls him from his tax booth! Jesus's disciples and sinners who recognize their need for a savior are among the people of *eleos* (cf. *ḥsd*).

35. Cf. France, *Gospel According to Matthew*, 203–4.
36. *Eleos* is "the real intent of the Law." Hicks, "Sabbath Controversy in Matthew," 88.

7.2.5.3. Interpreting the Law with Authority

Jesus, the Lord of the Sabbath, indicates that it is lawful to do *eleos* on the Sabbath (time). *Ḥsd/eleos*, which the Lord delights in / desires ([RESPONSE]), is [CONTRASTED] with sacrifice. Demonstrating *eleos* is [CONTRASTED] with observing legal minutiae. Jesus compares the difference in importance between these two extremes to the difference in weight between a camel and a gnat. This final analogy governs the sense of the [ENTITY] *eleos* (cf. *ḥsd*) in Matthew's Gospel: It is a weighty matter of the law (Hays: **thematic coherence**).

7.3. Exegetical Value of Recognizing Engagement with the Category *ḤSD* in Matthew's Gospel

Matthew's versions of the tax collector's call and the Sabbath grain-picking episode include an excerpt from Hos 6:6 not found in the parallel narratives in Mark or Luke. This suggests that Matthew includes the prophetic statement to make special points in his argument.[37] This study is concerned with not only the contribution of Hos 6:6a to Matthew's argument, but more specifically the exegetical value of recognizing that the occurrences of *eleos* in Matthew's quotations of that text, and in Matt 23:23, denote instances of the category *ḤSD*. Four themes connected with *ḤSD* are particularly relevant to Matthew's argument: meeting needs, law observance, genuine righteousness, and belonging to God's covenant people.

7.3.1. ḤSD *and Meeting Needs*

Ḥsd is done when a situationally powerful party freely offers help to another party in need.[38] In Ps 107:4–32, each manifestation of YHWH's *ḥsd* (labeled as *ḥsd* in vv. 8, 15, 21, 31) matches a particular need: satisfying the thirsty and filling the hungry (vv. 4–9), bringing out those who sit in darkness and gloom and breaking prisoners' bonds (vv. 10–16), healing and saving the foolish (vv. 17–22), and calming a storm (vv. 23–32). There is some similarity between these manifestations of YHWH's *ḥsd* and the deeds of those who inherit the kingdom prepared for them when the Son of Man comes in his glory in Matt 25:31–40:[39] allowing the hungry to eat and the thirsty to drink, receiving the stranger as a

37. Hagner, *Matthew 1–13*, 237, 239.

38. Sakenfeld, *Faithfulness in Action*, 131, and *Meaning of Hesed*, 24.

39. Luz relates "mercy" in Matt 23:23 to "works of charity" in 25:35–39, 42–44 (*Matthew 21–28*, 124).

guest, clothing the naked, caring for the sick, and going to the prisoners.[40] These deeds also resemble the experiences that the religious leaders of Jesus's day neglected. They challenged Jesus for healing and allowing the hungry to pick grain on the Sabbath (12:1–14),[41] and unlike the tax collector, presumably they did not "receive" Jesus and his disciples (9:9–13).[42] In response, Jesus told the Pharisees to learn the meaning of the prophetic principle "I desire *eleos* and not sacrifice." In this respect, Matthew's list of kingdom deeds (25:35–39) might be considered manifestations of *eleos* (cf. *ḥsd*). As the religious leaders of Jesus's day had not done these things for one of the least of Jesus's brothers (cf. his disciples; 10:42; 23:23–24; 25:45), they had not done *eleos* for Jesus.

According to Matthew's account, Jesus understands the needs associated with doing *eleos* (cf. *ḥsd*) as both physical and spiritual. Jesus applies a proverbial metaphor to his own ministry among tax collectors and sinners (Matt 9:12, 13b):[43] "Those who are healthy have no need of a physician but those who are poorly/sick. . . . For I did not come to call righteous ones but sinners."[44] Thus, Jesus compares (1) those who are healthy to the righteous, as neither has any particular need to be addressed, (2) those who are sick to sinners,[45] as both have obvious needs, and (3) himself to the physician, as he has come to call those who (recognize they) have need.[46] Jesus's instruction to go and learn the meaning of the principle about *eleos* is inserted between the metaphor and its application. Although the Pharisees do not recognize it, Jesus does *eleos* (cf. *ḥsd*) to the "sick" in this scene. He is the only one who can meet the dire spiritual need of sinners. On the other hand, those who reject his "help" are ultimately left with the greater need.[47]

7.3.2. ḤSD *and the Law*

The category *ḤSD* is also associated with observing the law. Sakenfeld even describes *ḥesed* in some "religious" contexts as "a one-word summary of the

40. Cf. the items added to those who seek first God's kingdom and righteousness (Matt 6:31–33).

41. The Pharisees' question implies that Jesus is either oblivious to the situation or has allowed his disciples to do this activity. But Jesus's reply suggests that allowing them to satisfy their hunger demonstrates *eleos* and/or that the Pharisees have neglected to demonstrate *eleos*.

42. Receiving Jesus also means receiving the one who sent Jesus and a righteous person's reward (see §7.3.3). Those who give one of Jesus's disciples a cup of water will also be rewarded (Matt 10:40–42).

43. Cf. Hagner, *Matthew 1–13*, 239–40; Morris, *Gospel According to Matthew*, 221; Nolland, *Gospel of Matthew*, 386–87.

44. C K L Γ^{c} Θ add *eis metanoian* ("to repentance"), probably as an interpretation. NA^{28}, 24. Cf. Justin, *1 Apologia* 15.8 (PG 6:349), and Ottenheijm, "Shared Meal," 19–20.

45. Cf. Exod 15:26; Sir 21:3; 38:15. Ottenheijm, "Shared Meal," 12, 14.

46. Hosea indicates that YHWH alone, and not foreign powers, can offer spiritual healing to YHWH's people (e.g., 5:13; 6:1; 7:1).

47. Cf. Hagner, *Matthew 1–13*, 240.

decalogue," both God-oriented and community-oriented.[48] In Exod 20:4–6, YHWH, the jealous God who forbids the making and worship of idols, speaks of doing *ḥsd* to those who keep the commandments. However, in Hosea, the divine "husband" is in anguish when his covenant devotion is not reciprocated. The priests and people of Ephraim/Judah are not living in accordance with the covenant (6:7–7:2). They have neglected the priorities of the law, including *ḥsd*, and misunderstood the true nature of worship (4:1; 6:4–6).

Similar issues are also associated with *eleos* (cf. *ḥsd*) in Matthew's Gospel. Writing in a Jewish way for an audience probably made up largely of Jewish Christians (e.g., Matt 5:17–19, 47; 23:23),[49] Matthew explains the new kingdom movement in terms of its Jewish roots (e.g., Jesus fulfilling the Law and the Prophets).[50] It seems appropriate, therefore, for Matthew also to connect aspects of Jesus's ministry with a concept associated with the Decalogue (i.e., that corresponding to *ḥesed*). He contrasts Jesus, the true interpreter and exemplary doer of the law,[51] who discerns and (by implication) does such weighty matters as *eleos* (cf. *ḥsd*), with those not living in accordance with the covenant, whose actions are inconsistent with their words.[52] The current religious leaders prioritize external ritualism and legal minutiae over doing *eleos* (23:1–36).

The relationship between *eleos* and the law is particularly evident in the Matt 12:1–8 narrative, where the Pharisees challenge Jesus because his disciples pluck and eat grain on the Sabbath. Matthew's portrayal of Jesus using the principle from Hos 6:6 (Matt 12:7) shows Jesus's authoritative interpretation of this scriptural tradition.[53] He demonstrates what a higher standard of "loyalty to the sabbath" means within the new kingdom context.[54] As the Son of Man is lord of the Sabbath (12:8) and the Lord desires *eleos* above sacrifice on the Sabbath,[55] the disciples should not have been condemned for plucking grain on that day.[56] Jesus's words imply that the disciples plucking and/or eating grain on the Sabbath, or permitting them to do so, is consistent with covenant relationship and/

48. Sakenfeld, *Meaning of Hesed*, 181.

49. Hagner, *Matthew 1–13*, lxiv–lxv, and Nolland, *Gospel of Matthew*, 18.

50. Cf. France, *Gospel According to Matthew*, 17–18.

51. Hagner, *Matthew 1–13*, lxii, 240, 330.

52. Keener, *Commentary on the Gospel of Matthew*, 549–52.

53. The quotation is introduced as an interpretive principle. Hicks, "Sabbath Controversy in Matthew," 88. Cf. Hagner, *Matthew 1–13*, 240.

54. Hagner, *Matthew 1–13*, 330–31, and Nolland, *Gospel of Matthew*, 485. Cf. Matt 5:19–20, 21–22, 27–28, 31–32, 38–39, 43–44.

55. Jesus's claim that he was "lord of the sabbath" would have put him on the level of God (cf., e.g., Exod 31:13). France, *Gospel of Matthew*, 463.

56. As Nolland claims, Matthew writes "to [have people] engage with Jesus" (*Gospel of Matthew*, 38).

or obedience (cf. the sense of *ḥsd* [LXX: *eleos*] in Hosea), even though the activity profanes the Sabbath and is considered unlawful (cf. 12:4–5).

If, as I argue above, the merciful acts listed in Matt 25:35–39 (e.g., feeding the hungry, caring for the sick) are potential manifestations of *eleos*, it follows that Jesus's exegesis of the Sabbath rest commandment permits those acts on the Sabbath (cf. 12:12).[57] If one neglects to do *eleos* in these ways, one does not fulfill the Law and the Prophets, nor inherit the kingdom (7:12; 23:23; 25:34, 46). In this sense, *eleos* does seem to involve pitying others in their affliction, as in Greek usage or the LXX rendering of *ḥnn* (e.g., Ps 123:3 [122:3 LXX]), but only as a manifestation of *eleos*, not as the essence of *eleos* itself. In this context, *eleos* evokes the broader notion of "fidelity to the law."[58]

With these insights in mind, I now read Jesus's two analogies (Matt 12:3–5) taken from the Law and the Prophets[59] in light of the Hos 6:6 principle. Jesus, the one in whom the weary find rest (Matt 11:28–30),[60] and whose presence is greater than the temple (12:6),[61] reads the Law and the Prophets as not only permitting, but prioritizing the doing of *eleos* (12:7), even on the Sabbath.[62] Therefore, like David and those with him,[63] Jesus's disciples were hungry and they ate (12:1, 3–4).[64] But, more than the priests who were considered innocent when they performed covenant rituals in the temple on the Sabbath,[65] Jesus

57. Hagner, *Matthew 1–13*, 331. As Church points out, Jesus's use of an example from the Pharisees' own practice (Matt 12:11) indicates their instinctive understanding that the Torah should be interpreted according to *eleos* ("Jesus and His People," 91).

58. Hagner speaks of "Jesus' fidelity to the law" (*Matthew 1–13*, lxiv).

59. France, *Gospel of Matthew*, 458, and Hagner, *Matthew 1–13*, 329–30.

60. Davies and Allison, *Commentary on Matthew VIII–XVIII*, 305; Hagner, *Matthew 1–13*, 331; Wilkins, *Matthew*, 442. "Rest" (*mnwḥh*) is a manifestation of *ḥsd* in Ruth 1:8–9 (cf. Exod 33:14).

61. Jesus says, "But I say to you," as in the Sermon on the Mount. Nolland, *Gospel of Matthew*, 485. "Greater" translates *meizon* from the majority of MSS (see NA[28] and Morris, *Gospel According to Matthew*, 303n15). In light of other uses of the neuter comparative *meizon* (Matt 13:32; 23:19), the "greater thing" could be either "the dawning of the messianic age," which has brought the kingdom of heaven near (Matt 4:16–17; cf. Dan 4:10–12, 21; 7:14; Hagner, *Matthew 1–13*, lxiv), or the presence of God, embodied in the Messiah (France, *Gospel According to Matthew*, 203), to whom the temple, its sacrifices, and other legal observances point.

62. Morris, *Gospel According to Matthew*, 299–300, 304.

63. David entered the house of God and ate "the bread of the presence" (cf. 1 Sam 21:1–6 [21:2–7 MT]). Mark 2:26 indicates that David also gave some to his companions. But only priests on duty were ordinarily permitted to eat those loaves (Lev 24:9). Davies and Allison, *Commentary on Matthew VIII–XVIII*, 308–10, and Hagner, *Matthew 1–13*, 329.

64. See Nolland, *Gospel of Matthew*, 483, for a summary of opinions concerning how David's behavior generalizes to that of Jesus and his disciples. My focus here is the reference to hunger (*peinaō*) in both descriptions (vv. 1, 3).

65. Scholars propose various options for what made the priests' activity permissible (see, e.g., France, *Gospel of Matthew*, 460, and Hagner, *Matthew 1–13*, 329). But the Matthean text records only the time and location of their "apparently unlawful behaviour." Nolland, *Gospel of Matthew*, 484. Priests made burnt offerings (Num 28:9–10) (e.g., Morris, *Gospel According to*

and his disciples should be considered innocent (12:7). For something more important than external practices like sacrifice is taking place here. It is *eleos* (cf. *ḥsd*), an experience at the heart of covenant relationship.

7.3.3. ḤSD *and Being Righteous*

While "righteousness" (MT: *ṣdq/ṣdqh*; LXX: *dikaiosynē*) is more closely allied with "justice" (MT: *mšpṭ*; LXX: *krima*) than with *ḥsd* (e.g., Ps 89:15 MT [88:15 LXX]), it does have some relationship with *ḥsd* in the Hebrew Bible.[66] For Hosea, *ḥsd* (LXX: *zōē*) is the harvest of *ṣdqh* (LXX: *dikaiosynē*; Hos 10:12). Similar imagery occurs in Prov 11:17–18: "A person of *ḥsd* does [so to] his *npš*, but a cruel one ruins his flesh. The wicked do false [MT: *šqr*; LXX: *adikos*] labor,[67] but one who sows righteousness [MT: *ṣdqh*; LXX: *dikaios*] [reaps] a true reward [MT: *śkr*; LXX: *misthos*]." Matthew's use of the highlighted Greek vocabulary appears to be consistent with the scriptural tradition. For example, according to Matt 10:41, "The one who receives a righteous person [*dikaios*] in the name of a righteous person, will receive the reward [*misthos*] of a righteous person."[68]

Righteousness is an important theme in Matthew's Gospel.[69] Jesus's disciples are to seek first God's kingdom and his righteousness, and as they do, the Father will meet their physical needs (6:31–33). Moreover, the king (Jesus) will allow the righteous (who feed the hungry, care for the sick, and so on) to enter eternal life and inherit the kingdom (25:34–46). However, from Matthew's perspective, Jesus and the other religious leaders do not share a common understanding of what being righteous involves. Of the three Matthean pericopes that feature *eleos*, this issue is especially evident in 9:9–13 and 23:1–36.

Jesus's instruction to go and learn what "I desire *eleos* and not sacrifice" means comes immediately before his comment: "For I did not come to call the righteous, but sinners" (9:13). The Pharisees, who think they are righteous, neither recognize their need of salvation nor address the need of sinners.[70]

Matthew, 302) and laid out the loaves of bread before YHWH ("a covenant forever"; Lev 24:8–9) on the Sabbath.

66. *Ḥsd* is translated by *dikaiosynē/dikaios* ten times in the LXX (see table A1.3).

67. Cf. *adikeō* in Gen 21:23 LXX.

68. See also Matt 5:10–12; 6:1; 20:8, 13; 25:46.

69. Hagner, *Matthew 1–13*, lxi. Within this Gospel, *dikaios* ("righteous") occurs seventeen times, *dikaiosynē* ("righteousness") seven times, and *dikaioō* ("declare righteous") twice.** At least four key themes emerge from these occurrences: (1) *dikaiosynē* is a way of life (e.g., 3:15; 5:6, 10; 6:33; 21:32); (2) the apparent righteousness of the scribes and Pharisees must be exceeded (5:20) to receive a reward in heaven (6:1; 23:28, 29; cf. 10:41); (3) conversely, those who are genuinely "righteous" (*dikaios*; 1:19; 27:19) are not always perceived to be so; (4) the righteous are distinguished from the evil/neglectful and judged accordingly (12:37; 13:43, 49; 25:37, 46).

70. However, Przybylski is careful to distinguish between salvation and righteousness in Matthew's Gospel (*Righteousness in Matthew*, 116).

But Jesus has already warned his disciples that, if their righteousness does not exceed that of the scribes and Pharisees, they will not enter the kingdom of heaven (5:20).[71] In contrast, Jesus demonstrates that he is truly righteous by meeting the spiritual need of sinners (doing *eleos*). Indeed, according to Mary Hinkle Edin, the conflicts recorded in Matt 9:9–13 and 12:1–8 are an indication that, in this Gospel, "to be righteous is to show mercy." Furthermore, for readers of this Gospel to learn what "I desire *eleos* and not sacrifice" means, they must recognize "the steadfast love of the God of Israel as it is embodied and enacted by Jesus."[72] Just as YHWH showed more commitment to the desert-wandering Israelites than they deserved by renewing the covenant (cf. *ḥsd* in Exod 34:6, 7),[73] Jesus shows more commitment toward sinful Jews than they deserve by sharing table fellowship with them.[74] Despite this apparently scandalous behavior, when Jesus is later on trial before Pilate, Pilate's wife declares that Jesus is in fact righteous (27:19).

In the speech recorded in Matt 23, Jesus indicates that the teaching of the scribes and Pharisees should be followed because they sit on Moses's seat, but not their practice because that is inconsistent with their words (vv. 2–3).[75] Jesus teaches his disciples to humble themselves instead of doing things for people to see, as these religious leaders do (vv. 5–12). The speech also contains seven woe oracles, the fifth and sixth considering inner and outer righteousness from different angles (vv. 25–28).[76]

The fourth and central woe (23:23–24) provides a practical illustration of the contrast between inner and outer righteousness depicted in the woes that follow. The scribes and Pharisees tithe mint, dill, and cumin but omit the weightier things of the law: justice, *eleos* (cf. *ḥsd*), and faithfulness.[77] Jesus does not deny the value of tithing herbs, but he relates its level of importance in comparison with demonstrating justice, *eleos*, and faithfulness to the minute size of a gnat in comparison with a camel (23:24).[78] R. T. France suggests that Hos 6:6 could "sum up the contrast" in Matt 23: the hypocritical religion of the Pharisees and

71. Edin, "Learning What Righteousness Means," 355–56.

72. Ibid., 356, 362.

73. Cf. Lane, "Echo of Mercy," 82.

74. Hagner points out that, by doing so, Jesus was communicating his acceptance of and oneness with these people (cf. 8:11) (*Matthew 1–13*, 238).

75. Edin, "Learning What Righteousness Means," 359, and Keener, *Commentary on the Gospel of Matthew*, 549–52.

76. Hagner, *Matthew 14–28*, 671–72.

77. *Pistis* is usually translated "faith" elsewhere in this Gospel (e.g., NRSV; ESV; Nolland, *Gospel of Matthew*, 937–38).

78. The "camel" (Aramaic: *gml'*) and "gnat" (Aramaic: *qlm'*) were unclean creatures, the biggest and smallest in Palestine. France, *Gospel of Matthew*, 874, and Nolland, *Gospel of Matthew*, 938.

scribes, which focuses on externals (pretentious righteousness), is compared to "sacrifice" without *eleos* (cf. *ḥsd*), but Jesus doing the will of God (genuine righteousness) is compared to the *eleos* (cf. *ḥsd*) that God desires.[79] Thus, the truly righteous person (in this case, Jesus, who fufills all righteousness; cf. 3:15) is known by his/her *eleos* (cf. *ḥsd*).

In light of the relationship between righteousness and *eleos* (cf. *ḥsd*) evident in Matthew's Gospel, I now return to a manifestation of *ḥsd* in Ps 107:8–9 MT: "Let them give thanks to YHWH [for] his *ḥsd* [LXX: *eleos*]. . . . For he satisfies [*hiphil* of *śbʿ*; LXX: *chortazō*] the thirsty *npš* [*npš šqqh*; LXX: *psychēn kenēn*; cf. *dipsaō* in v. 5] and fills the hungry *npš* [*npš rʿbh*; LXX: *psychēn peinōsan*] with what is good." The vocabulary in Matt 5:6 brings to mind those psalm verses: "Blessed are those who hunger [*peinaō*] and thirst [*dipsaō*] for righteousness, for they will be satisfied [*chortazō*]" (cf. priorities for the *psychē* in 6:25; Hays: **volume**). *Eleos* (cf. *ḥsd*) is indeed a practice and a reward of the righteous.

7.3.4. ḤSD *and Belonging*

In Matthew's Gospel, as in the Hebrew Bible,[80] the category *ḤSD* is associated with belonging to God's covenant people. In the account following Matthew's call, the Pharisees' question about Jesus eating with sinners may reveal their concern to enforce boundaries for table fellowship—in this case, who should be excluded.[81] But the connection with *ḥsd*,[82] created by including a principle from Hosea, suggests a deeper issue: who could or could not be considered "acceptable" for covenant relationships.[83] Like Hosea calling God's people back to their God and to *ḥsd*, Jesus reminds his audience what it means to belong to the people of *eleos*. The religious leaders maintain separatist boundaries, observe ceremony and its restrictions, and appear to keep the covenant meticulously. But Jesus restores people to true covenant relationship through forgiveness of sins (cf. Matt 9:1–13).[84] He exposes misplaced priorities, eats with sinners, and offers a tax collector the call to discipleship![85] Thus, the conflict, which would eventually result in Jesus's crucifixion, escalates.[86]

79. France, *Gospel of Matthew*, 873.
80. E.g., Exod 20:6; 34:6–7; Deut 7:12; Isa 55:3; Ps 25:10.
81. Jews and Gentiles sat at different tables. Hagner, *Matthew 1–13*, 238.
82. Evoked by *eleos* in Matt 9:13.
83. See Hagner, *Matthew 1–13*, 238, and Keener, *Commentary on the Gospel of Matthew*, 296.
84. Davies and Allison, *Commentary on Matthew VIII–XVIII*, 100.
85. Hagner, *Matthew 1–13*, 236, 240, and Morris, *Gospel According to Matthew*, 219.
86. Cf. Turner, *Matthew*, 33.

7.4. Conclusions

Intertextual and intratextual evidence indicates that all three occurrences of *eleos* in Matthew's Gospel denote instances of the category *ḤSD*. For Matthew, *eleos* does not primarily communicate "mercy to those who do wrong."[87] It evokes the concept corresponding to *ḥesed*, especially as portrayed by the prophet Hosea (i.e., devotion within covenant relationship, obedience to the commandments). Recognizing Matthew's engagement with this concept, I should read the passages concerned from within a "*ḥesed* framework."

From a Jewish background and speaking to a Jewish audience, Matthew uses the scriptural tradition to establish the validity of the new kingdom movement and Jesus's ministry. In Matthew's Gospel, Jesus (perceiver) uses an excerpt from Hosea to highlight the misplaced priorities and corresponding neglect of *eleos* (cf. *ḥsd* hereafter) in the outwardly meticulous behavior of the Pharisees. By demonstrating *eleos* in unexpected locations to unexpected patients, Jesus redefines what it means to be the people of *eleos*. As lord of the Sabbath, Jesus also indicates that it is lawful to do *eleos* on the Sabbath (time), for the Lord ([PRIMARY_PERCEIVER]) desires ([RESPONSE]) *eleos* more than sacrifice or the tithing of herbs ([CONTRASTS]). In contrast, the Pharisees do not perceive that Jesus (implied agent) understands and does *eleos*, so they condemn the innocent and plot to kill Jesus ([OUTCOMES]).

By evoking *ḥsd*, Matthew's use of *eleos* highlights issues of covenant relationship (e.g., who can belong to God's special people) as a motivation for meeting personal needs, both physical and spiritual, in ways that extrabiblical Greek usage of *eleos* could not. For Hosea, sacrifice without *ḥsd* is a poor substitute for true worship and covenant relationship. For Matthew, the pretentious righteousness of outwardly meticulous legal observance is a poor substitute for true *eleos* (covenantal devotion). But Jesus, the authoritative interpreter of the law, understands the "weighty" priority of doing *eleos*.

87. Implied by Wilkins, *Matthew*, 753.

CHAPTER 8

Eleos in Paul's Letters: The Reason for Gentiles Glorifying God

Eleos in Paul's letters is often viewed as a response to sinfulness.[1] However, in the pericope to which the Rom 15:9 occurrence of *eleos* belongs, there is no explicit reference to sinfulness and Paul's engagement with *eleos* is not ultimately about God having mercy on sinners. Rather, intertextual connections and prototypical language patterns indicate that this occurrence of *eleos* denotes an instance of the category ḤSD that emphasizes covenant relationship and Gentile response.

This chapter considers nine occurrences of *eleos* located in the New Testament letters attributed to Paul as potentially denoting instances of the category ḤSD (§8.1). While I do not seek to challenge traditional views on Pauline authorship of Ephesians and the Pastoral Epistles,[2] I deal with Eph 2:4; 1 Tim 1:2; 2 Tim 1:2, 16, 18; and Titus 3:5 separately from Rom 9:23; 11:31; 15:9; and Gal 6:16 in order to acknowledge the disputes about this matter.[3] The strongest intertextual connections between *eleos* in Paul's letters and Hebrew Bible texts containing *ḥsd* are evident in Rom 15:7–13. Therefore, my discussions about Paul's engagement with the category ḤSD (§8.2) and the exegetical value of recognizing his engagement (§8.3) are based principally on quotations/allusions/echoes within that pericope.

1. E.g., in his comment about Rom 15:8–9a, Byrne describes the benefit that came to the Gentiles in Christ as "an act of pure 'mercy'" to sinners (*Romans*, 429–30).

2. Cf., e.g., Arnold, "Letter to the Ephesians," 240–42; Barth, *Ephesians*, 41; Knight, *Pastoral Epistles*, 52.

3. See Best, *Critical and Exegetical Commentary*, 20, 25, 27, 34–36, regarding issues pertaining to the authorship of Ephesians, and Trebilco and Rae, *1 Timothy*, 2–3, regarding reasons why "the Pauline authorship of the Pastoral Epistles has been questioned." Cf. Marshall, *Critical and Exegetical Commentary on the Pastoral Epistles*, 57–92.

8.1. Intertextual Connections Between *Eleos* in Paul's Letters and *Ḥsd* in the Hebrew Bible

Born and raised in "a religiously observant Jewish family," educated under "a leading Jewish teacher," and a Pharisee with respect to the law (Acts 22:3; 23:6; 26:5; Phil 3:5), Paul would have been familiar with scriptural uses of both *ḥsd* and its usual LXX rendering, *eleos*.[4] Intertextual evidence indicates that, within the letters attributed to Paul, the occurrence of *eleos* in Rom 15:9 is the most likely to denote an instance of the category *ḤSD*, but I also consider the occurrences of *eleos* in Rom 9:23; 11:31; and Gal 6:16 as corollaries to the Rom 15:9 argument. I survey briefly the remaining occurrences of *eleos* in letters attributed to Paul.

The concept corresponding to *ḥesed* is also hinted at in 1 Cor 1:9, 31; 10:13; and 2 Cor 3:3; 10:17, where scriptural verses that include *ḥsd* in the Hebrew are quoted or alluded to, in part. For example, the original reason for the boasting recorded in the text partially quoted in 1 Cor 1:31 and 2 Cor 10:17 (i.e., Jer 9:23–24 [9:22–23 MT/LXX]) is comprehending and knowing YHWH, "who does *ḥsd* [LXX: *eleos*], justice, and righteousness in the land/earth."[5] As the words translating *ḥsd* are excluded from the Corinthian appropriations, however, I do not consider these texts further.

8.1.1. Romans 15:9

Romans 15:7–13 is a significant pericope within this letter because it acts as a conclusion for the previous exhortations (12:1–15:6) and summarizes themes from the entire letter.[6] After an exhortation for strong believers to bear with the failings of the weak and all of them to live in harmony with one another (15:1–6), the paragraph opens with *dio* ("therefore") and another exhortation to accept one another as Christ accepted them (v. 7). The reason follows (vv. 8–9a):

4. Bruce, "Paul in Acts and Letters," 681–82. Cf. Morris, *Epistle to the Romans*, 18, and Stenger, "Paul the Jew," 504–6. Porter indicates that Paul may have been able to copy Greek and possibly Hebrew Scriptures periodically ("Paul and His Bible," 122).

5. Cf. the theme of writing on the tablet of the heart in 2 Cor 3:2–3. In Prov 3:3, *ḥsd* and faithfulness are written on that tablet.

6. Wagner, "Christ, Servant of Jew and Gentile," 473. E.g., "God's faithfulness to his promises to Israel" and "the inclusion of Gentiles in the people of God" (vv. 8, 9a). Moo, *Letter to the Romans*, 889–90.

Rom 15:8–9a:

λέγω γὰρ Χριστὸν διάκονον γεγενῆσθαι περιτομῆς ὑπὲρ ἀληθείας θεοῦ, εἰς τὸ βεβαιῶσαι τὰς ἐπαγγελίας τῶν πατέρων, τὰ δὲ ἔθνη ὑπὲρ ἐλέους δοξάσαι τὸν θεόν, καθὼς γέγραπται·	For I declare that Christ has become a servant of [the] circumcision for the sake of the faithfulness of God, in order to confirm the promises of [made to][7] the patriarchs, but[8] the Gentiles are to glorify God for the sake of *eleos*, just as it is written:

The citation formula *kathōs gegraptai* ("just as it is written") introduces four quotations taken from the Law, the Prophets, and the Psalms,[9] each featuring the word *ethnos* ("nations/Gentiles"; vv. 9–12).[10] The Hebrew texts of two of those quotations are immediately followed by verses containing *ḥsd* (LXX: *eleos*): the quotations of Pss 18:50 MT (17:50 LXX) and 117:1 (116:1 LXX) recorded in Rom 15:9b, 11.

Romans 15:9b includes a quotation from Ps 17:50 LXX (with *kyrie* omitted):[11]

Ps 18:50 MT:	
על כן אודך בגוים יהוה ולשמך אזמרה	For this reason I will confess you among the nations, O YHWH, and let me sing to your name.
Ps 17:50 LXX:	
διὰ τοῦτο ἐξομολογήσομαί σοι ἐν ἔθνεσιν, κύριε, καὶ τῷ ὀνόματί σου ψαλῶ	Because of this I will confess you among [the] nations, O Lord, and I will sing praise to your name.
Rom 15:9:	
διὰ τοῦτο ἐξομολογήσομαί σοι ἐν ἔθνεσιν καὶ τῷ ὀνοματί σου ψαλῶ.	Because of this I will confess you among [the] nations/Gentiles, and I will sing praise to your name.

The following verse of that psalm records a reason for the praise:

7. Longenecker, *Epistle to the Romans*, 987.

8. After lengthy consideration of various alternatives for construing the Greek, Cranfield settles on "I declare that . . . but that the Gentiles are glorifying . . ." (i.e., *ta de ethnē* . . . is dependent on *legō* in v. 8) (*Commentary on Romans IX–XVI and Essays*, 742–43).

9. Moo, *Romans*, 478–79, and *Letter to the Romans*, 894–95 (using the label "writings"). For Paul, no illustrations from Jesus's life are necessary: "The Bible ends all argument." Morris, *Epistle to the Romans*, 499, 505.

10. Ps 18:50 MT (17:50 LXX) (// 2 Sam [2 Kgdms LXX] 22:50); Deut 32:43; Ps 117:1; Isa 11:10. NA^{28}, 845, 847, 851, 855, 858.

11. Cf. 2 Kgdms 22:50 LXX: *dia touto exomologēsomai soi, kyrie, en tois ethnesin kai en tō onomati sou psalō*.

Ps 18:51 MT:[12]

מגדל ישועות מלכו ועשה חסד למשיחו לדוד ולזרעו עד עולם	He makes great the victories/tri- umphs ["salvations"] of his king and does *ḥsd* to his anointed one, to David and to his offspring forever.

Ps 17:51 LXX:

μεγαλύνων τὰς σωτηρίας τοῦ βασιλέως αὐτοῦ καὶ ποιῶν ἔλεος τῷ χριστῷ αὐτοῦ, τῷ Δαυιδ καὶ τῷ σπέρματι αὐτοῦ ἕως αἰῶνος.	He makes great the victories/tri- umphs ["salvations"] of his king and does *eleos* to his anointed one, to David and to his offspring forever.

Eleos in Ps 17:51 LXX renders *ḥsd*. Thus, the psalmist confesses YHWH among the nations and sings to YHWH's name because YHWH does *ḥsd* to his anointed one by making great his victories/triumphs (cf. 17:44–46 LXX [18:44–46 MT]).[13] In addition, Ps 18:25 (18:26 MT; 17:26 LXX) includes the words, "With *ḥsyd* you [i.e., YHWH] will prove yourself *ḥsyd* [*ttḥsd*]" (cf. 2 Sam [2 Kgdms LXX] 22:26). The victories/triumphs spoken about in verse 50 (51 MT/LXX) are set in parallel with YHWH doing *ḥsd* (LXX: *eleos*) to YHWH's anointed one David (his *ḥsyd*) and David's offspring forever.[14]

The third quotation in Paul's series (v. 11) comes from Ps 117:1 (116:1 LXX):[15]

Ps 117:1 MT:

הללו את יהוה כל גוים שבחוהו כל האמים	Praise YHWH, all you nations; extol him, all you peoples.

Ps 116:1 LXX:

Αἰνεῖτε τὸν κύριον, πάντα τὰ ἔθνη, ἐπαινέσατε αὐτόν, πάντες οἱ λαοί	Praise the Lord, all you nations; extol him, all you peoples.

Rom 15:11:

αἰνεῖτε, πάντα τὰ ἔθνη, τὸν κύριον καὶ ἐπαινεσάτωσαν[16] αὐτὸν πάντες οἱ λαοί.	Praise, all you Gentiles, the Lord,[17] and let all the peoples extol him.[18]

12. Second Samuel 22:51 MT has *mgdyl* in place of *mgdl*.

13. God has given David "victory over Gentile nations." Moo, *Letter to the Romans*, 895.

14. *Yšʿ* (noun), *yšʿ* (verb), and *yšwʿh* occur a total of five times in Ps 18:26–51 // 2 Sam 22:26–51 MT.

15. NA^{28}, 855.

16. *Epainesatōsan* (3pl.) in P^{46} ℵ A B C D Ψ; *epainesate* (2pl.) in F G L P, as in Ps 116:1 LXX. NA^{28}, 512.

17. This unique word order matches Rom 15:10, which begins with the "Gentiles" rejoicing (emphasis) and ends with "his [the Lord's] people."

18. Paul inserts *kai* before the aorist imperative.

Once again, the verse that follows the verse Paul quotes is significant. That is, Ps 117:2 is the key to understanding the relationship between the quoted verse (Ps 117:1 in Rom 15:11) and *eleos* in Rom 15:9. Psalm 117:2 (116:2 LXX) reads,

Ps 117:2 MT:

כי גבר עלינו חסדו ואמת יהוה לעולם הללו יה	For his *ḥsd* was superior[19] [strengthened] / prevailed toward us, and the faithfulness of YHWH is forever. Praise YHWH!

Ps 116:2 LXX:

ὅτι ἐκραταιώθη τὸ ἔλεος αὐτοῦ ἐφ' ἡμᾶς, καὶ ἡ ἀλήθεια τοῦ κυρίου μένει εἰς τὸν αἰῶνα.	For his *eleos* was strengthened / prevailed toward us, and the faithfulness of the Lord remains forever.

This verse reveals the basis for all the peoples/nations praising YHWH (v. 1): the strength and endurance of YHWH's *ḥsd* and *ʾmt*. The parallelism typical of *ḥsd* (LXX: *eleos*) and *ʾmt* (LXX: *alētheia*) is reflected in Rom 15:8–9.[20] Christ became a servant to the circumcised "to show" God's *alētheia* (cf. *ʾmt*), and the Gentiles are praising God "for" *eleos* (cf. *ḥsd*).[21] Douglas Moo confirms this connection, noting that, in Rom 15:8–9 as in Ps 117 (116 LXX), God's *eleos* and *alētheia* are cited as reasons for Gentiles to praise God / the Lord.[22] If, then, *alētheia* (15:8) and *eleos* (15:9) evoke *ʾmt* and *ḥsd,* respectively, why does the Greek word order not also follow the predominant pattern for this word pair—*ḥsd* followed by *ʾmt?*

Reading Rom 15 in light of an almost unique reversal of these terms in Mic 7:20a would suggest that the Romans order is deliberate.[23]

Mic 7:20a MT:

תתן אמת ליעקב חסד לאברהם	You give faithfulness to Jacob, *ḥsd* to Abraham.

19. *HALOT*, s.v. "גבר."

20. Michel notes the correspondence between "ἀλήθεια und ἔλεος" and *ḥsd wʾmt* (*Der Brief an die Römer*, 322n3).

21. The quoted words are ESV renderings.

22. Moo, *Romans*, 481.

23. The reversed order also occurs in Hos 4:1 (*ʾmt*) and Ps 89:25 (*ʾmwnh*) MT, but Mic 7:20 is more relevant to the Romans context (see NA^{28}, 868).

Mic 7:20a LXX:

δώσεις ἀλήθειαν τῷ Ιακωβ,	You give faithfulness to Jacob,
ἔλεον τῷ Αβρααμ	*eleos* to Abraham.

Just as "*ʾmt* to Jacob" and "*ḥsd* to Abraham" are parallel in Mic 7:20, so also "circumcision for the sake of *alētheia*" and "the Gentiles . . . for the sake of *eleos*" could be interpreted as parallel in Rom 15:8–9.[24] The circumcision (Rom 15:8) presumably relates to the line of "Jacob," while the gospel's impact on the nations/Gentiles (15:9) was foreshadowed by the promises to "Abraham" (Gen 12:1–3; 17:5; cf. Rom 4:16).[25]

Therefore, two quotations and one allusion in Rom 15:7–13 indicate that *eleos* in verse 9 denotes an instance of the category *ḤSD*. Christ became a servant of the circumcision for the sake of God's *alētheia* (cf. *ʾmt*), but the Gentiles are to glorify God for the sake of *eleos* (cf. *ḥsd*), in this case referring to God's covenant loyalty to Abraham. Jews and Gentiles are to accept one another as Christ has accepted them and glorify God together in one voice (15:6–7).

Regarding Hays's tests for echoes (allusions here), there are multiple allusions to the category *ḤSD* in one section of text (Rom 15:7–13; **recurrence**) and the assertion in verses 8–9 introduces in a satisfying way the appropriations of scriptural texts that follow (**satisfaction**). The value of these allusions for Paul's argument (**thematic coherence**) is the topic for section 8.3.

8.1.2. Corollaries: Romans 9:23; 11:31; and Galatians 6:16

8.1.2.1. Romans 9:23 and 11:31

Positioned within the chapters "increasingly seen as the heart of Romans"[26] are two further occurrences of *eleos* (9:23; 11:31). Given that the occurrence of *eleos* in Rom 15:9 almost certainly evokes *ḥsd* and that 15:7–13 sums up themes in this letter, one might expect that the occurrences of *eleos* in chapters 9–11 also evoke *ḥsd*. But scholars rarely distinguish the senses of the noun *eleos* and the verbs *eleaō* and *eleeō* (which are usually associated with different Hebrew roots in the LXX),[27] perhaps owing to the clustering of these terms.[28]

24. The clauses that Wright labels "parallel" differ from these ("Letter to the Romans," 747).

25. Moo, *Letter to the Romans*, 894.

26. Brands, "Vessels of Mercy," 23.

27. *Ḥsd*, and *ḥnn* or *rḥm*. Tables A2.1 and A2.2 list the Hebrew words rendered by *eleos* and *eleeō*, respectively. In Ps 36:26 and Prov 14:31, *eleaō* renders *ḥnn*; in Ps 114:5 and Isa 49:10, it renders *rḥm*; and in Prov 21:26, it renders *ntn* (LXX references).

28. In Romans, *eleos* occurs in 9:23; 11:31; 15:9; *eleeō* in 9:15, 15, 18; 11:30, 31, 32; and *eleaō* in 9:16; 12:8. Thus, for example, Moo writes in his comment on Rom 9:23, "Some receive mercy (v. 18), those 'vessels' of mercy whom God chooses (vv. 15–16)" (*Letter to the Romans*, 628).

In Rom 9:19–24, Paul employs the metaphor of God as a potter and humans as vessels of various types to compare the notion of humanity resisting the will of God to that which is molded saying to its molder, "Why have you made me like this?"[29] A potter has the right to make, out of one lump of clay, one "vessel" (*skeuos*) for honorable use and another for dishonorable use (vv. 19–21). Verses 22–23 read,

Rom 9:22–23:

εἰ δὲ θέλων ὁ θεὸς ἐνδείξασθαι τὴν ὀργὴν καὶ γνωρίσαι τὸ δυνατὸν αὐτοῦ ἤνεγκεν ἐν πολλῇ μακροθυμίᾳ σκεύη ὀργῆς κατηρτισμένα εἰς ἀπώλειαν, καὶ ἵνα γνωρίσῃ τὸν πλοῦτον τῆς δόξης αὐτοῦ ἐπὶ σκεύη ἐλέους ἃ προητοίμασεν εἰς δόξαν;	But [what] if God, wanting to demonstrate wrath [*orgē*] and to make known his power, has endured in much patience vessels [pl. of *skeuos*] of wrath [*orgē*] prepared for destruction,[30] (and) in order to make known the riches of his glory for vessels [pl. of *skeuos*] of *eleos*, which he prepared beforehand for glory?[31]

Paul provides scriptural backing for his rhetorical question from Hos 2:23 (2:25 MT/LXX) and 1:10 (2:1 MT/LXX) and concluding statements for this section of the letter from Isa 10:22–23 and 1:9 (Rom 9:25–29).[32] Those verses indicate that, in keeping with YHWH's compassion/love, those who were not YHWH's people would be called YHWH's people, and a remnant (of Jacob; cf. Isa 10:21) would "return" ("be saved"; cf. Rom 9:27).

The references to Moses and Pharaoh in Rom 9:15, 17 are clues that 9:14–18 should be read with Exodus as a backdrop. Paul quotes from Exod 9:16 and from 33:19, where *eleeō* translates *ḥnn* ("to favor"). But *eleos* occurs only three times in Exodus LXX (20:6; 34:6 [*polyeleos*], 7), each time translating *ḥsd*.[33] Moreover, the situation that began with a declaration of *orgē* ("anger/wrath") in 32:10 ended up with a declaration of *polyeleos* ("abundant *ḥsd*") and *eleos* in 34:6–7. This observation supports the connection between Rom 9:22 and Exod

29. Byrne, *Romans*, 297–98, and Moo, *Romans*, 311–12.

30. Hoover translates *katērtismena* in the middle voice: "having made themselves fit" ("Wealth of God's Glory," 54).

31. In vv. 22–23, the beginning "if" is not followed up by an apodosis. Morris, *Epistle to the Romans*, 366–67. See Moo, *Romans*, 312, regarding decisions made in the NIV translation.

32. NA^{28}, 857–58, 867, and Longenecker, *Epistle to the Romans*, 821–23.

33. Similarly, in Hosea, *eleos* always translates *ḥsd*, and in Isaiah, it translates various words including *ḥsd*, but not *ḥnn*. In Exodus, those who refuse to cooperate (4:14), oppose YHWH (15:7), or worship other "gods" (32:7–12), experience YHWH's *orgē* ("wrath"). Those who love YHWH and keep his commandments experience YHWH's *eleos* (20:6; 34:7).

34:6 noted by James Dunn: "God endures the 'vessels of wrath' ἐν πολλῇ μακροθυμίᾳ,[34] possibly a rejoinder to the μακρόθυμος καὶ πολυέλεος of Exod 34:6."[35]

In addition, there could be several allusions involved in the pottery metaphor, including Isa 29:16; 45:9; and Wis 15:7 (cf. Rom 9:20–21).[36] But the most relevant allusions for this study are Jer 18:1–11 and Pss. Sol. 17:23.[37] Jeremiah 18 begins with YHWH speaking to the prophet concerning the potter's house.[38] A vessel[39] of clay was spoiled in the potter's hand, "and he reworked it into another vessel, as seemed good to him" (v. 4 NRSV). Paul also speaks of two types of vessels in Rom 9:22–24: vessels of *orgē* prepared for destruction and vessels of *eleos* prepared in advance for glory (cf. 15:7).

In the wider Jeremiah context, the presence and absence of divine or human *eleos* (when translating *ḥsd*) in Judah/Israel leads to positive and negative responses/outcomes, respectively.[40] The Lord's *orgē* is often directed toward Judah/Israel or Jerusalem, but in a message of assurance, the Lord speaks of gathering his people from the places where he scattered them in his *orgē* (MT: *ʾp*; 39:37 LXX [32:37 MT]). These people resemble the remnant mentioned in Mic 7:18 LXX. God does not hold to his *orgē* (MT: *ʾp*) as a testimony, for God desires *eleos* (MT: *ḥsd*).[41]

Reading Rom 9:22–24 in light of these intertextual connections, it seems fitting that vessels of *orgē* are endured patiently. As Dunn indicates, the echo of Jer 18:1–11 would invite the Roman readers to recognize "that the pot made for a disreputable use could be remade into a work to be treasured."[42] In other words, God's patience may provide the opportunity for vessels characterized by *orgē* (cf. *ʾp*) to be re-"molded" according to *eleos* (cf. *ḥsd*).[43] This is helpful, for vessels of *eleos*, those Jews and Gentiles whom God has called,[44] have the riches of God's glory made known to them (Rom 9:23–24).

34. NRSV: "with much patience."

35. Dunn, *Romans 9–16*, 559. Dunn notes "the repetition and development of Exod 33:19 in 34:6" (552).

36. NA[28], 858–59, 874. Cranfield, *Commentary on Romans IX–XVI and Essays*, 491–92.

37. I consider the allusion to Pss. Sol. 17:23 in the discussion about Rom 11:31 that follows.

38. Jeremiah 18:6 is linked with Rom 9:21 in particular. NA[28], 862.

39. *Kly*; LXX: *angeion*; usually translated *skeuos*.

40. In Jeremiah LXX, the use of *eleos* is varied: it translates *ḥsd* four times (2:2; 9:23; 39:18 [32:18 MT]; 40:11 [33:11 MT]), *tḥnh* ("plea") four times (43:7 [36:7 MT]; 44:20 [37:20 MT]; 45:26 [38:26 MT]; 49:2 [42:2 MT]), *ḥnynh* once (16:13), and *rḥmym* once (49:12 [42:12 MT]). Among other Hebrew terms, *orgē* translates *ḥrwn* four times and *ʾp* four times in this book.

41. The concluding section of Micah begins with this text (7:18) and ends with the text to which Rom 15:8–9 alludes (7:20).

42. Dunn, *Romans 9–16*, 565. Cf. Cranfield, *Commentary on Romans IX–XVI and Essays*, 495.

43. Cf. Cranfield, *Commentary on Romans IX–XVI and Essays*, 497.

44. Cf. Jacob (Rom 9:10–13).

Paul returns to the topic of a remnant in Rom 11 (cf. 9:27). The elect remnant has obtained what Israel sought, but the rest of Israel experiences a hardening until the fullness of the Gentiles has come in (11:5–7, 25). Figuratively, these Gentiles are wild branches grafted into the cultivated olive tree of Israel (11:11–24).[45] In light of this, Paul addresses the Gentiles:

Rom 11:30–32:

ὥσπερ γὰρ ὑμεῖς ποτε ἠπειθήσατε τῷ θεῷ, νῦν δὲ ἠλεήθητε τῇ τούτων ἀπειθείᾳ, οὕτως καὶ οὗτοι νῦν ἠπείθησαν τῷ ὑμετέρῳ ἐλέει, ἵνα καὶ αὐτοὶ [νῦν] ἐλεηθῶσιν. συνέκλεισεν γὰρ ὁ θεὸς τοὺς πάντας εἰς ἀπείθειαν, ἵνα τοὺς πάντας ἐλεήσῃ.	For just as you were once disobedient to God, but now you have been shown mercy for the disobedience of these ones, so also these ones have now been disobedient for your *eleos*, in order that they also (now)[46] might be shown mercy. For God consigned all to disobedience, in order that he might show mercy to all.

Verses 30 and 31 present the parallel treatment of Jews and Gentiles. Two occurrences of the verb *eleeō* ("show mercy") are matched, two occurrences of the verb *apeitheō* ("be disobedient") are matched, and "your *eleos* [noun]" corresponds to "the disobedience [*apeitheia*; noun] of these ones." Keeping the sense of the noun consistent with the verb would preserve the pattern here.[47] But many commentators also link *eleos* in 11:31 with *eleos* in 9:23 and 15:9.[48]

Dunn associates God's "unrepentance" over the calling of Israel (Rom 11:29) with the expanded attribute formula in Joel 2:13 and Jonah 4:2 (where *polyeleos* translates *rb ḥsd*, *eleēmōn* translates *ḥnwn*, and *eleeō* does not occur).[49] Dunn also suggests that Paul had "the language of Pss 31:8 [LXX 30:9] and 78 [LXX 77]:50, 62" in mind when he spoke of being "consigned" (*synkleiō*; Rom 11:32; ESV).[50] In Ps 30:10 LXX, the psalmist asks the Lord to "have mercy upon" (*eleeō*; MT: *ḥnn*) him. But there are also three occurrences of *eleos* within that psalm (vv. 8, 17, 22), each one rendering *ḥsd* in a setting relevant to Paul's thought. In particular, verses 8–9a read, "I will exult and rejoice in your *eleos*

45. Dunn, *Romans 9–16*, 675.

46. See Kaden, "Methodological Dilemma," 167–82, for a detailed appraisal of the textual variant associated with the second *nun* in this sentence. It is included in ℵ B D*.c, but omitted from P46 A D1 F G L Ψ. NA28, 505.

47. Moo, *Letter to the Romans*, 747–48. Murray notes the three terms for mercy, the three references to disobedience, and an implied lesson (*Epistle to the Romans*, 2:102).

48. E.g., Jewett, *Romans*, 710.

49. The expanded formula includes YHWH's "repenting." Dunn, *Romans 9–16*, 688.

50. Actually, Dunn translates *synkleiō* with "confine or imprison" instead (ibid).

(MT: *ḥsd*), that . . . you did not consign [aor. of *synkleiō*] me into the hands of [the] enemy." In addition, YHWH's *ḥsydym* are connected with those who wait for / hope in YHWH in the concluding cola of Ps 31:24–25 MT.[51]

"Hope" (*elpis/elpizō*) and *eleos* are also themes in Pss. Sol. 17.[52] In this case, a psalmist prays that the Lord, the hope of Israel, will hasten his *eleos* upon Israel (v. 45; cf. Rom 15:9, 12–13). In addition, Pss. Sol. 17 includes *kerameus* ("potter") and *skeuos* ("vessel"; v. 23;[53] cf. Rom 9:21–23),[54] *doxazō* ("glorify") and *doxa* ("glory"; vv. 5, 6, 30–31; cf. Rom 9:23; 15:6–9), ten** occurrences of *ethnos* ("nation/Gentile"; cf. Rom 9:24; 15:9–12), and one of only four LXX occurrences of *apeitheia* ("disobedience"; v. 20; cf. Rom 11:32). Considering that Pss. Sol. 17 shares this vocabulary with the Romans passages where *eleos* occurs, it is also noteworthy that, in Pss. Sol. 17, *eleos* and *eleeō* behave much like *ḥsd* and *ḥnn*, respectively (vv. 3, 9, 15, 34, 45).[55] In particular, 17:15 records the lack of "one who does *eleos* [cf. *ḥsd*] and *alētheia* [cf. *ʾmt*] in Jerusalem," and 17:34 refers to the Lord "having mercy upon" (*eleeō*) "nations/Gentiles" (*ethnos*).

If, then, *eleos* in Rom 11:31 also evokes *ḥsd*, Paul could be saying, "So these ones also have now been disobedient for your *ḥsd* (*eleos*), in order that they also might be shown mercy [aor. pass. subjunctive of *eleeō*; cf. *ḥnn*]."[56] *Eleos* (cf. *ḥsd*) has come to the Gentiles in order that the Jews "might be shown mercy" (*eleeō*; cf. *ḥnn*).

On the basis that *eleos* in Rom 15:9 almost certainly denotes an instance of the category *ḤSD*, I have considered Rom 9:23 and 11:31 as corollaries. Acknowledging that the boundaries between *eleos*, *eleeō*, and *eleaō* in Romans are fuzzy, I nevertheless offer a combined reading of these three texts containing *eleos*: God called a remnant of Jews and Gentiles to be vessels of *eleos* (cf. *ḥsd*) and prepared them for glory. The disobedience of Israel was for the *eleos* (cf. *ḥsd*) of the Gentiles, and so that Israel might also be shown mercy (*eleeō*; cf. *ḥnn*) and be saved. As a result of Christ becoming a servant of the circumcision, promises made to the patriarchs are confirmed and the Gentiles glorify God for the sake of *eleos* (cf. *ḥsd*).

51. In Ps 30 LXX, this is the last of five uses of *elpizō* ("hope for").

52. See vv. 2, 3, 15, 33–34, 39, 45.

53. Paul contrasts vessels of wrath prepared for destruction with vessels of *eleos* prepared for glory. The psalmist asks God to raise up a king from the line of David (cf. Cranfield, *Introduction and Commentary on Romans I–VIII*, 58) who will destroy the arrogance of the sinner as a potter's vessel (vv. 21–23) and restore "those scattered throughout the Diaspora" (vv. 26–28). Dunn, *Romans 9–16*, 681.

54. This psalm also includes *dynatos* ("power"; vv. 34, 37), *orgē* ("anger"; v. 12), and *apōleia* ("destruction"; v. 22). Cf. Hays: **volume**.

55. This distinction is also established elsewhere in the LXX. See tables A2.1 and A2.2.

56. Cf. Ps 51:3 MT (50:3 LXX), where another psalmist appeals to God's *ḥsd* (*eleos*) when asking for mercy (*ḥnn*; LXX: *eleeō*).

8.1.2.2. Galatians 6:16

I propose a third corollary within Paul's letters: that *eleos* in Gal 6:16 also denotes an instance of the category *ḤSD*. Following declarations that he boasts only in the cross of Christ and that what counts is neither circumcision nor uncircumcision but a new creation,[57] Paul writes:

Gal 6:16: καὶ ὅσοι τῷ κανόνι τούτῳ στοιχήσουσιν, εἰρήνη ἐπ' αὐτοὺς καὶ ἔλεος καὶ ἐπὶ τὸν Ἰσραὴλ τοῦ θεοῦ.	And to as many as will follow this rule,[58] "peace" [*eirēnē*] upon them and *eleos* also/even upon the Israel of God.[59]

The order of *eirēnē* and *eleos* in Gal 6:16 is "somewhat strange."[60] Other New Testament benedictions use the reverse order (1 Tim 1:2; 2 Tim 1:2; 2 John 3). The only LXX precedent for this combination of terms within a benediction is Sir 50:22–24, where *eirēnē* matches *šlwm* (v. 23) and *eleos* matches *rṣwn* (v. 22) or *ḥsd* (v. 24).[61] But I see only the mention of Israel in verse 23 as a potential connection with Gal 6:16 in that context. In other LXX benedictions with Hebrew equivalents, *eirēnē* and *eleos* occur separately. The blessing "peace [*eirēnē*; MT: *šlwm*] upon Israel" concludes Pss 124 LXX (125 MT) and 127 LXX (128 MT).[62] The blessings in 2 Kgdms 2:6 and 15:20 combine *eleos* (MT: *ḥsd*) with *alētheia* (MT: *'mt*), not *eirēnē*, and in Ruth 1:8 and Ps 32:22 LXX (33:22 MT), *eleos* (MT: *ḥsd*) is the only component of the blessing.[63]

Nevertheless, there are other scriptural texts where *eirēnē* and *eleos* (or *šlwm* and *ḥsd*) occur together (e.g., Ps 84:11 LXX [85:11 MT]; Isa 54:10[64]).[65] In Jer 16:5 MT, YHWH speaks of having taken away his "peace" (*šlwm*), *ḥsd*, and "compassion" (*rḥmym*). The only attribute included in the LXX translation of that

57. The statement in v. 15 was probably a traditional maxim. Longenecker, *Galatians*, 296–97.

58. Longenecker thinks this rule refers to the statement made in v. 15 (ibid., 297).

59. Of the many interpretive issues relating to this verse, I focus on the identity of those upon whom the blessing of *eleos* is bestowed. See nn. 71 and 73 below. Another difficulty relates to the sense and function of the second and third occurrences of *kai*. See Eastman, "Israel and the Mercy of God," 371–72, for three possible interpretations of this verse.

60. This is Longenecker's description (*Galatians*, 297).

61. MS B.

62. Martyn, *Galatians*, 566.

63. In Ruth 2:20 and 3:10, *ḥsd* is not a component of the blessing, but the basis for the blessing. In Sir 51:29, *en tō eleei autou* matches בישיבתי in position (MS B), but it is not a direct translation of the Hebrew term.

64. Cf. Gal 4:27 (quoting Isa 54:1). Wright, *Paul and the Faithfulness of God*, 2:1150.

65. *Šlwm* is frequently included in blessings in the DSS, but the combination with *ḥsd* is rare. *Ḥsd* comes before *šlwm* in 1QS II, 4.

verse is *eirēnē*.[66] But in Jer 33 MT, each of these attributes is restored (vv. 6, 9, 11, 26 [*rḥm*]),[67] and *šlwm* and *ḥsd* are both translated (LXX: *eirēnē* and *eleos*, respectively). These texts relate to that which is removed from or restored to the covenant people of God—the offspring (collective sg.) of Abraham, Isaac, and Jacob (v. 26)—and their land/city. But Gal 3:14 and 3:16 state that believers (including Gentiles) are blessed "in Christ," because the promises were made to Abraham and his offspring (sg.), who is Christ.[68] The restoration of *eirēnē* (cf. *šlwm*) and *eleos* (cf. *ḥsd*) occur for the sake of Christ.

In Gal 6:16, Paul invokes the blessing of *eirēnē* and *eleos* upon "as many as will follow this rule" (i.e., the rule of new creation),[69] and upon "the Israel of God." My conclusions about *eleos* in Rom 9:23; 11:31; and 15:9, along with the broader Romans context, suggest that "as many as will follow this rule" and "the Israel of God" are set in parallel here,[70] as two descriptions of one group receiving both *eirēnē* and *eleos*,[71] and that *eleos* in Gal 6:16 evokes *ḥsd*. The vessels of *eleos* (cf. *ḥsd*) discussed in Rom 9:23–24 include both Jews and Gentiles whom God has called.[72] It is likely, therefore, that "the Israel of God" (Gal 6:16) does not include all ethnic Israel, but all those Jews and Gentiles whom God has "called" as vessels of *eleos* (cf. *ḥsd*), those who follow the rule of new creation.[73] In Rom 11:30–31, Paul speaks of the disobedience of Israel being for the *eleos* (cf. *ḥsd*) of the Gentiles, and so that the Jews might be shown mercy (cf. *ḥnn*) by God. Drawing Rom 11:7, 23–24 into the picture as well then, "the Israel of God" could include all the (believing) branches of the olive tree who partake of the blessings promised to Abraham[74] and trust in God's *eleos* (cf. *ḥsd*; Ps 52:10 MT [51:10 LXX]). Reading Gal 6:16 in light of connections with *ḥsd*, both Jews and Gentiles "in Christ" are among those upon whom *eirēnē* and *eleos* (cf. *ḥsd*) are bestowed, because Christ is the offspring of Abraham to

66. Jeremiah 16:5 LXX is shorter than 16:5 MT.

67. *Šlwm* is now revealed and *ḥsd* is now a reason for thanksgiving.

68. Martyn, *Galatians*, 338–40. Cf. Gen 12:7; 13:15–16; 17:7–9, 19; 22:17–18; 26:4; 28:4, 14; Jer 33:26.

69. Ibid., 566–67.

70. Cf. Martyn's translation of Gal 6:16 (ibid., 559).

71. The *kai* before *epi ton Israēl tou theou* makes it difficult to determine the particular recipients of *eirēnē* and/or *eleos*. See Fung, *Epistle to the Galatians*, 310–11; Longenecker, *Galatians*, 297–99; Martyn, *Galatians*, 567. Paul could be repeating himself (i.e., "all who follow this rule" is identical to "Israel of God") or "adding a new group" (McKnight, *Galatians*, 302–3). However, as Wright points out, leaving out the second *kai* would be a clearer way of indicating that each group received a different blessing (*Paul and the Faithfulness of God*, 2:1149).

72. Cf. children of the promise, the true offspring of Abraham (Rom 9:6–8; Gal 4:28).

73. There are various views on that to which "the Israel of God" refers (see McKnight, *Galatians*, 303–4). But, if Paul meant something other than the believing church ("the majority view"), he would have undermined points made in the rest of his letter. Wright, *Paul and the Faithfulness of God*, 2:1151.

74. See Rom 4:9–17; 11:17–18. Das, "'Praise the Lord, All You Gentiles,'" 93.

whom the promises were made (Gal 3:16). Christ became a servant of the circumcision (Rom 15:8; cf. Gal 6:15), and the Gentiles now glorify God for *eleos* (cf. *ḥsd*; Rom 15:9).

8.1.3. Ephesians 2:4; First Timothy 1:2; Second Timothy 1:2, 16, 18; and Titus 3:5

Of the remaining occurrences of *eleos* in letters attributed to Paul, the one most likely to denote an instance of the category ḤSD is in Titus 3:5, but other occurrences also display particular prototypical features of that category. For example, in light of the covenantal issues in Eph 2 (vv. 11–12; cf. 19), the description of God as "rich in *eleos*" (*plousios ōn en eleei*; v. 4) could be another way of rendering *rb ḥsd* ("abounding in *ḥsd*"),[75] although the LXX renders this phrase by *polyeleos*[76] or *plēthos tou eleous*.[77] By including *eleos* (cf. *ḥsd*) within blessings for individuals/households (1 Tim 1:2; 2 Tim 1:2, 16, 18), the author reinforces his pastoral emphasis on not forsaking the faith or the faithful ones.[78] The blessing associated with Onesiphorus also resembles the *ḥsd* tradition. If you cannot repay *ḥsd* yourself, you commit the person who has shown you *ḥsd* (and their household) to YHWH's *ḥsd* (cf. 2 Sam 15:20; Ruth 1:8).[79] Likewise, Paul invites the Lord to grant *eleos* to Onesiphorus and his household because Onesiphorus showed loyalty to Paul (2 Tim 1:16–18).[80]

In Titus 3, Paul explains that God "saved" (*sōzō*) believers who were once "foolish, disobedient, deceived, and enslaved"[81] not because of their righteous works "but according to his *eleos*, . . . through the washing of regeneration" (vv. 3–5). The outworking of God's *eleos* in regeneration is also signaled in Corpus hermeticum (13.3, 8, 10).[82] However, the grammatical construction *kata*

75. Cf. Barth, *Ephesians*, 218, and Lincoln, *Ephesians*, 100, who link this text with Exod 34:6.

76. Exod 34:6; Num 14:18; 2 Esd 19:17; Pss 85:5, 15; 102:8; Joel 2:13; Jonah 4:2 (LXX references).

77. Or by similar phrases. See 2 Esd 23:22; Pss 5:8; 68:14; 105:7, 45; Lam 3:32 (LXX references).

78. E.g., 2 Tim 1:13–15; 4:9–10.

79. Sakenfeld explains that the invocation of God's *ḥsd* in these two verses "may be understood as a formal way of ending the voluntary relationship within which the parties have accepted responsibility for one another" (*Meaning of Hesed*, 109).

80. In the Hebrew Bible, *ḥsd* is "given/granted" only occasionally (Mic 7:20). "Find" (*mṣ*ʾ) is usually associated with *ḥn* (i.e., "find favor"), rather than *ḥsd*, but *ḥn* is almost always translated by the accusative form of *charis* in the LXX, not *eleos*. "Find" in 2 Tim 1:18 may be a play on the same verb from 1:17. Johnson, *First and Second Letters to Timothy*, 361, and Knight, *Pastoral Epistles*, 386.

81. Paul joins himself with all believers here. Mounce, *Pastoral Epistles*, 446.

82. Bultmann, "ἔλεος, ἐλεέω," 2:478.

to autou eleos[83] and the specific manifestation of God's *eleos* (i.e., salvation)[84] hint that *ḥsd* is evoked here.

In conclusion, while the boundaries between *eleos* and related verbs are fuzzy, intertextual connections to *ḥsd* influence the sense of *eleos* in some texts from letters attributed to Paul. As the most relevant intertextual evidence in these letters relates to the occurrences of *eleos* in Rom 15:9 and corollary texts, those occurrences form the basis of the discussion in the remaining sections of this chapter.

8.2. The Category *ḤSD* in Romans and Galatians

Having established the intertextual connections between *eleos* in Rom 15:9 and *ḥsd* in Pss 18:50 (18:51 MT); 117:2; and Mic 7:20, I now compare the elements of the category *ḤSD* associated with those Hebrew Bible texts and Rom 15:9, together with the corollary texts.

8.2.1. ḤSD *in Psalm 18:51 MT (17:51 LXX)*

Psalm 18 (cf. 2 Sam 22) is a song attributed to David, YHWH's servant (perceiver), and addressed to YHWH (communication), on the day when YHWH delivered David from the hands of Saul and all his enemies (context). In Ps 18:51 MT, *ḥsd* (LXX: *eleos*) is the Direct Object of the Participle of *ʿśh* (LXX: *poieō*) within a Verbal Clause; that is, YHWH ([AGENT]) does (pres. [AGENT'S_ACTIVITY]) *ḥsd* ([ARTICLE_OF_TRANSACTION]). The [PATIENTS] of YHWH's *ḥsd* are YHWH's anointed one, David (cf. the *ḥsyd* in v. 26 MT), and his offspring forever ([DURATION]). Therefore, the relationship exists between YHWH and YHWH's anointed one / his descendants.

According to the superscription, the king is also the psalmist. He is righteous and blameless before YHWH (justification; vv. 21–25 MT). Given that "does *ḥsd* to his anointed" is parallel to "makes the victories of his king great" (*mgdl yšwʿwt mlkw*), the probable [MANIFESTATION] of *ḥsd* is "victories"

83. See §§10.1.2 and 10.3.1, regarding 1 Pet 1:3, for further discussion about the connections between *kata to autou eleos*, *kḥsd*, and regeneration. *Kata to eleos autou* in Isa 63:7 is associated with *rḥmym*, but *kata to eleos* in Pss 24:7; 108:26; 118:88, 124, 149 LXX is associated with *ḥsd*. Quinn notes the use of *eleos* as "the bridge" to pass faith about YHWH's *ḥesed* "into Hellenistic Jewish congregations." YHWH's *ḥesed/eleos* is the reason/motive for initiating both the original covenant and the new covenant (*Letter to Titus*, 217).

84. E.g., "Save [*hiphil* imperative of *yšʿ*; LXX: *sōzō*] me, according to your *ḥsd* [LXX: *eleos*]!" (Ps 109:26b [108:26b LXX]).

("salvations"; pl. of *yšwʿh*). Those victories are the result of "deliverance" (*plṭ*; *nṣl*) from enemies and violent people (v. 49 MT). In response, the psalmist gives thanks and praise among the nations (location; v. 50 MT). In contrast, the psalmist's enemies who cry for help are not saved (v. 42 MT).

8.2.2. ḤSD *in Psalm 117:2 (116:2 LXX)*

In Ps 117:1–2, the psalmist (perceiver) calls all nations to praise YHWH and all peoples to extol[85] him (communication; universal [PERCEIVERS'/PATIENTS'_RESPONSES]), because YHWH's ([POSSESSOR]) *ḥsd* (LXX: *eleos*; [CHARACTERISTIC]) was strengthened/superior ([QUALITY]) toward "us" ([PATIENTS]; i.e., Israel),[86] and YHWH's *ʾmt* (LXX: *alētheia*) is forever. Thus, the relationship is between YHWH and Israel. "His *ḥsd*" (LXX: *to eleos autou*) is the Subject of an Intransitive Verb (pf. of *gbr*: "was strengthened/superior"; LXX: aor. pass. of *krataioō*) in a Causal Verbal Clause.

8.2.3. ḤSD *in Micah 7:20*

In Micah's oracle (communication) about the incomparable nature of God, who does not retain anger forever but delights in *ḥsd* (contrast; Mic 7:18), the prophet (perceiver) writes, "You ([AGENT]; i.e., God) will give (impf. [AGENT'S_ACTIVITY]) faithfulness to Jacob, *ḥsd* ([ARTICLE_OF_TRANSACTION]) to Abraham ([PATIENT]), which you swore (pf. [AGENT'S_ACTIVITY]) to our ancestors ([PATIENTS]) from days of old ([TIME]/[DURATION])" (v. 20). Therefore, the relationship is between God and Abraham / Abraham's descendants. God will "cast" (*šlk*) all their sins into the sea (parallel statement in v. 19; possible manifestation).[87] By ellipsis, *ḥsd* (LXX: *eleos*) is the second Direct Object (the first being *ʾmt*; LXX: *alētheia*) of a Transitive Verb (2sg. impf. of *ntn*: "you will give"; LXX: 2sg. fut. of *didōmi*) in a Verbal Clause.

8.2.4. ḤSD *in Romans 15:9*

Paul ([PERCEIVER]) writes to all those in Rome who are beloved of God and called to be saints (communication; Rom 1:7). In the context of Rom 15:9, *eleos*

85. NRSV.

86. The referent of "toward us" could be everybody, or, as my decision here reflects, Israel (i.e., all nations and peoples praise YHWH for blessing Israel, and there is no direct benefit for the other nations). Schaefer, *Psalms*, 287–88, and Allen, *Psalms 101–50*, 159.

87. However, if this *ḥsd* is linked with YHWH swearing to Abram *byn btryʾ* ("between the pieces"; Cathcart and Gordon, *Targum of the Minor Prophets*, 128n52; cf. Gen 15: *byn hgzrym*), the manifestation would relate to the multitude of Abraham's descendants and the land given to them.

(cf. *ḥsd*) is an [ENTITY]. It occurs within the Adverbial Prepositional Phrase *hyper eleous* ("for the sake of *eleos*"), which modifies the aorist infinitive of *doxazō* ("to glorify") in a Contrastive-Purpose Verbal Clause. That is, while Christ became a servant of circumcision for the sake of the *alētheia* (cf. *ʾmt*) of God ([CONTRAST]), the Gentiles ([PERCEIVERS]) glorify God ([PERCEIVERS'_RESPONSE]) for the sake of *eleos* (cf. *ḥsd*). These experiences are seen as the fulfillment of what is written in Ps 18:49 (18:50 MT; 17:50 LXX); Deut 32:43; Ps 117:1 (116:1 LXX); and Isa 11:1, 10, concerning the Gentiles and God's people ([JUSTIFICATION]).

8.2.5. ḤSD *in Romans 9:23; 11:31; and Galatians 6:16*

Romans 9–11 is the section of Paul's (perceiver) letter to the Roman saints devoted to the topic of Israel's relationship to the gospel (communication). In 9:19–23, Paul speaks metaphorically about vessels of *eleos* (part of an Adjectival Prepositional Phrase in a Purpose Verbal Clause).[88] Building on the metaphor CREATOR_IS_A_POTTER ([AGENT]), it follows that *ELEOS*_IS_ONE_TYPE_OF_POTTER'S_VESSEL. In 11:31, *eleos* occurs in the Adverbial Prepositional Phrase *tō humeterō eleei* ("for your *eleos*"), which modifies the third-person plural aorist of *apeitheō* ("they have been disobedient") in a Comparative Verbal Clause. Galatians 6:11–18 is written in Paul the apostle's (perceiver) own hand, the final section of his letter to the churches of Galatia (communication). In Gal 6:16, *eleos* is a Subject of the Nominal Clause (Blessing) *eirēnē epʾ autous kai eleos* ("peace [be] upon them and *eleos*").

In Rom 9:23 and 11:31, the [POSSESSORS] of [CHARACTERISTIC] *eleos* are (metaphorically speaking) "vessels"[89] (9:23–24) and Gentiles (11:13). God is an [AGENT] of *eleos* in that he formed the vessels (9:21–23). In Gal 6:15–16, the [ENTITY] *eleos* is part of a blessing invoked by Paul upon the Israel of God, as many as will follow the rule of new creation ([SECONDARY_PATIENTS]). This implies that God is also the agent of *eleos* (although this is not stated explicitly), and God's relationship is with believers who follow the rule of new creation (3:9; 6:16)—that is, children of the promise made to Abraham and his offspring (i.e., Christ; primary patient; 3:8, 14, 16; 4:28; cf. Gen 12:3; 26:24, 29).

[MANIFESTATIONS] of *eleos* include the opportunity to become God's people (Rom 9:25–26) and "compassion/mercy" (*eleeō*; Rom 11:30–32). [JUSTIFICATIONS] include the will and calling of God (Rom 9:21–24; cf. 11:28–29) and the cross of Christ (Gal 6:14). [CONTEXTS] include the calling of God and the rule of new creation, as contrasted with the rule pertaining to circumcision/

88. "Vessels of *eleos*" are also that which "he prepared beforehand" (3sg. aor. of *proetoimazō*).
89. I.e., those whom God has called, from the Jews and the Gentiles.

uncircumcision (Gal 6:15). The [OUTCOME] for [POSSESSORS] of *eleos* is glory (Rom 9:23). There is an inheritance for the "offspring" of Abraham (Gal 3:16, 18).

[POSSESSORS] respond by presenting their bodies as a living sacrifice, thinking reasonably, loving without hypocrisy, and not answering back to God (Rom 9:20; 12:1, 3, 9). The [AGENT'S_ACTIVITIES/RESPONSES] are preparing vessels for glory and making known the riches of his glory. Vessels of *eleos* are [CONTRASTED] with vessels of *orgē*, which are endured with patience and prepared for destruction (Rom 9:22–23). God has consigned all to disobedience, in order that he might show mercy to all, but the Gentiles are [CONTRASTED] with Israel, who have been disobedient for the *eleos* of the Gentiles (Rom 11:11, 31–32). The perceiver responds by praying to God that Israel might be saved, making his "own people" (NRSV) jealous, glorifying God, and boasting in the cross of Christ (Rom 10:1; 11:14, 33–36; Gal 6:13–14).

8.2.6. General Observations

Comparing elements of the category ḤSD in Romans and Galatians with those in Paul's scriptural sources, I observe the following. In the Hebrew Bible texts, *ḥsd* (LXX: *eleos*) is an [ARTICLE_OF_TRANSACTION] (Direct Object) or a [CHARACTERISTIC] (Subject). In Rom 9:23 and 11:31, *eleos* is a [CHARACTERISTIC] (included in Modifiers), but in Rom 15:9 (cf. Mic 7:18) and Gal 6:16, it is an [ENTITY] (Subject or included in Modifier).

8.2.6.1. YHWH/God

In the texts to which Paul refers, YHWH/God is the only [POSSESSOR] and/or [AGENT] of *ḥsd*. Furthermore, YHWH/God's *ḥsd* is strengthened/superior and endures throughout the history of YHWH/God's people ([QUALITY]; [DURATION]). Therefore, it is not surprising that God's *eleos* (cf. *ḥsd*) also appears in these New Testament contexts. For Paul, the [CONTEXTS]/[JUSTIFICATIONS] for *eleos* include the will and calling of God. God prepares vessels for glory, makes known the riches of his glory, and consigns all to disobedience that he might also have compassion/mercy on them all ([AGENT'S_ACTIVITIES]/[RESPONSES]). Consequently, [PERCEIVERS] praise/glorify YHWH/God ([RESPONSE]).

8.2.6.2. Christ, the Cross, and New Creation

Various elements of the category ḤSD reflect developments resulting from the work of Christ. In Ps 18, the psalmist is righteous/blameless (justification), there are great acts of salvation/victories ([MANIFESTATION] of *ḥsd*),[90] and the psalmist is delivered from the hand of enemies (context for *ḥsd*). Thus, a text from that psalm about praising God is cited and interpreted in light of Christ's victory. According to Paul, new [JUSTIFICATIONS] for *eleos* include the fulfillment of Scripture and the cross of Christ (in which Paul boasts; response). Believers are now blessed "in Christ" (primary patient). [MANIFESTATIONS] of *eleos* include receiving mercy and becoming God's people, now through the activity of Christ. A [CONTEXT] for *eleos* is the rule of new creation.

8.2.6.3. Jews, Gentiles, and Contrasts

As with Micah, who contrasts God's *ḥsd* with God's anger/wrath, Paul [CONTRASTS] vessels of *eleos* (those called from among the Jews and the Gentiles; [POSSESSORS]) with vessels of wrath. Paul also appropriates a psalm where the psalmist (the implied [PATIENT] of *ḥsd*) is contrasted with his enemies. But the key [CONTRAST] for Paul is between the present season for some of Israel and the present season for the Gentiles: what is needed for the natural olive branches and what is appropriate for the grafted branches (Rom 11:17–24, 31); the rule of circumcision/uncircumcision and that of new creation; Christ's response to the circumcision (becoming a servant) for the sake of God's *alētheia* and the Gentiles' [RESPONSE] to God (glorification) for the sake of *eleos*. Ultimately, Paul is concerned that the Jews and Gentiles might glorify God together in one voice.

Other elements also reflect this goal: [PATIENTS] of *ḥsd* in the source texts are those in covenant relationship with YHWH/God (Abraham, David, Israel, and their descendants), but [PATIENTS] of *eleos* (cf. *ḥsd*) in Paul's letters include the "Israel of God." In the source texts, *ḥsd* is perceived by a psalmist or prophet, but *eleos* in Paul's letters is perceived also by the apostle Paul and the Gentiles. Paul prays for the salvation of Israel.

8.3. Exegetical Value of Recognizing Engagement with the Category *ḤSD* in Romans and Galatians

The intertextual connections and category analysis recorded above indicate that, when Paul uses *eleos*, he is not necessarily concerned with God's mercy toward Gentile sinners. Sometimes, he is concerned with the Gentiles as perceivers of *eleos* (cf. *ḥsd*). To Paul's arguments in Romans and Galatians, the category ḤSD brings association with certain covenant relationships and certain promises that included the nations/Gentiles.

90. By allusion to Mic 7:18–20, forgiveness is also available (casting sins into the sea).

8.3.1. ḤSD *and Covenant Relationships*

The category *ḤSD* is associated with covenant relationships. Three such relationships are evident in texts that Paul quotes or alludes to in Rom 15:7–13. Psalm 18 mentions the line of David,[91] Ps 117 mentions YHWH's *ḥsd* toward Israel ("us"), and Mic 7 concludes with the parallel statements "*ʾmt* to Jacob" and "*ḥsd* to Abraham."

For Paul, covenant promises to David's line are fulfilled in Jesus, David's anointed descendant. The excerpt from Ps 18 (17 LXX) quoted in Rom 15:9b indicates that the psalmist will praise God among the nations/Gentiles. Dunn understands the words of this passage as "the words of the devout Jew (David) foreshadowing the situation of the diaspora Jew, and now particularly of the Jewish Christian."[92] However, the ones who benefit from YHWH's *ḥsd* (LXX: *eleos*) in Ps 18:51 MT (17:51 LXX) are YHWH's anointed one, King David, and his descendants. If, as the superscription implies, the psalmist is also David, then the one who praises the Lord in Rom 15 is not a representative "Jewish Christian," but one specific Jew, a descendant of David. Indeed, when reflecting on the significance of David's victory for the Rom 15 context, Moo suggests that Paul may include the quotation "as a claim of the risen Christ."[93] This "messianic" interpretation of Ps 17:50 LXX is consistent with the omission of *kyrie* in the quotation[94] and Paul's attribution of the words of another psalm "of David" to Christ (Ps 68:10 LXX in Rom 15:3).[95] In Ps 68 LXX, the appeal for salvation/deliverance is also on the basis of the Lord's *eleos* (MT: *ḥsd*; vv. 2, 14–15). But, for Paul, *eleos* (MT: *ḥsd*) is demonstrated by the great "salvation/victory" (*sōtēria*; Ps 18:50 [18:51 MT; 17:51 LXX]) for King David's descendant, Christ Jesus (Rom 15:8–9; cf. 10:9–13; 11:11).

Regarding the Lord's *eleos* (MT: *ḥsd*) toward Israel, Paul refers to another psalm (Rom 15:11).[96] Psalm 116 LXX is concerned with the response of all peoples and nations to the Lord's *eleos* (MT: *ḥsd*) toward Israel and the Lord's abiding *alētheia* (MT: *ʾmt*). Reading Rom 15:8–9 in light of the parallelism between *eleos* and *alētheia* in that psalm, it appears that Christ becoming a servant to the circumcised is an expression of God's abiding *alētheia*, and the Gentiles are praising the Lord for his *eleos* toward his covenant people. Indeed,

91. Cf. the allusion to Pss. Sol. 17 in Rom 9:22–23 (see §8.1.2.1).

92. Dunn, *Romans 9–16*, 849.

93. Moo, *Letter to the Romans*, 895. For New Testament writers, Jesus's deliverance "from death itself" holds the deeper significance of "the deliverance of God's *anointed* from the 'cords of death' ([MT Ps 18] vv 5–6)" (emphasis original). Craigie and Tate, *Psalms 1–50*, 177.

94. The *kyrios* speaks. So Hays, *Conversion of the Imagination*, 103.

95. Hays, *Echoes of Scripture in the Letters*, 72.

96. Ps 117 (116 LXX). NA[28], 855.

Paul consistently emphasizes God's faithfulness to the covenant with / promises to Israel.[97]

On the other hand, this combination of terms occurs also in Mic 7:20, in the same order as in Rom 15:8–9 (first, *alētheia* [cf. *'mt*]; second, *eleos* [cf. *ḥsd*]). Building on the idea that, in Christ, "God has been faithful . . . to the promises he made to Abraham" (Rom 4; 9; 11),[98] the distinction between *alētheia* and *eleos* in Rom 15:8–9 may also be explained in terms of the associations between the Gentiles and the Lord's promises to Abraham (Gen 18:18), between the Jews and the Lord's promises to Jacob (as well as Abraham). This interpretation would bring a fitting culmination to an overarching theme of Romans, introduced in 1:16–17, that the gospel is the power of God for salvation to everyone who believes—first the Jew and also the Greek.[99]

Thus, in Rom 15:9, as in each scriptural quotation/allusion discussed here, *eleos* evokes YHWH/God's *ḥsd*, expressed within covenant relationships. According to Paul, the events he describes occur or have occurred on the basis of those covenants.

8.3.2. ḤSD *and the Gentiles*

Each quotation in Rom 15:9–12 includes the plural of *ethnos* (MT: *gwym*; "nations"/"Gentiles"). First, a psalmist (cf. Christ) praises YHWH/God among the nations/Gentiles (Ps 18:50 MT [17:50 LXX]; Rom 15:9). Psalm 18:51 MT (17:51 LXX) indicates that this is because YHWH does *ḥsd* (LXX: *eleos*) to his anointed one (his "Christ"). Next, the nations/Gentiles rejoice with YHWH/God's people (Deut 32:43 LXX; Rom 15:10).[100] Deuteronomy 32:43 indicates that this is connected with avenging the blood of his servant(s)/son(s). Then, all the peoples and nations/Gentiles praise YHWH / the Lord (Ps 117:1 [116:1 LXX]; Rom 15:11). Psalm 117:2 (116:2 LXX) states that this is because of his superior/strengthened *ḥsd* (LXX: *eleos*) and abiding *'mt* (LXX: *alētheia*). Finally, the nations/Gentiles will hope in "the root of Jesse" ("a messianic designation";[101] Isa 11:10 LXX;[102] Rom 15:12).[103]

97. Wright, "Letter to the Romans," 402.

98. Wright, *Climax of the Covenant*, 234. In the Romans story, Abraham serves as the "archetype" for both Gentile and Jewish believers. Hays, *Echoes of Scripture in the Letters*, 56.

99. The 15:7–13 pericope also integrates the section of counsel into that overarching theme. Dunn, *Romans 1–8*, lxiii.

100. *Meta* ("with") is added in the Greek. Cf. Morris, *Epistle to the Romans*, 505, and Dunn, *Romans 9–16*, 849.

101. Moo, *Letter to the Romans*, 896. Both Judaism and the early church recognize Isa 11:10 as messianic. Kruse, *Paul's Letter to the Romans*, 534. Cf. Matt 12:21; Rev 5:5. NA[28], 858.

102. Jewish and Gentile Christians alike hope in Jesus. Fitzmyer, *Romans*, 708.

103. Recalling the introductory statement about the resurrected descendant of David and the Gentiles among whom Paul is an apostle (Rom 1:3–5), the Isaiah text about the "root of Jesse" seems a fitting conclusion to Paul's whole argument. Wright, "Letter to the Romans," 748.

The two Psalms quotations in the Rom 15 series point to evidence that the relationship between *eleos* (MT: *ḥsd*) and *ethnos* (MT: *gwym*), emphasized in verse 9, already existed in the scriptural tradition.[104] Thus, while *ḥsd* is usually associated with God's covenant people, God's choice of Israel as his people "always had this wider call in view."[105] None of these Scriptures explicitly claims that the Gentiles become members of the covenant people, but God has called Gentiles to be among the vessels of *eleos* (cf. *ḥsd*; Rom 9:23–24), Gentiles have become possessors of *eleos* (Rom 11:31), and the "Israel of God," on whom Paul invokes a blessing of *eleos*, is composed of "as many as will follow" the rule of new creation (Gal 6:16). Therefore, Leslie Allen's claim seems appropriate: "Israel's would-be hired choristers were destined eventually to become their partners in faith in the international religion of the NT."[106]

8.4. Conclusions

In the New Testament letters attributed to Paul, at least some events involving *eleos* are primarily concerned not with mercy shown to sinners but rather with the concept corresponding to *ḥesed.* In Rom 15:7–13, Paul utilizes the terms *eleos* and *alētheia* in parallelism (cf. *ḥsd wʾmt*), claiming that the Gentiles glorify God for *eleos* (Rom 15:9). In support of this claim, he alludes indirectly to *eleos* (MT: *ḥsd*) in Pss 17:50–51; 116:1–2; and Mic 7:20 (LXX references). Corollaries indicate that God has called both Jews and Gentiles to be vessels of *eleos*, that Gentiles can possess *eleos*, and that a blessing of *eleos* is bestowed upon the "Israel of God" (Rom 9:23–24; 11:31; Gal 6:16).

Recognizing the category *ḤSD* in Romans and Galatians, I read the passages concerned in light of associated themes, including covenant relationships and the response of Gentiles. First, the fact that *eleos* (evoking *ḥsd*) still features in these New Testament texts is evidence of God's abiding commitment to his covenant promises (duration). God's promises to Abraham, Israel, and David are fulfilled in Christ. For Paul, God is the primary and praiseworthy [AGENT] of *eleos*, and [POSSESSORS] of *eleos* include those whom God has called to receive mercy and become his people ([MANIFESTATIONS]). Fulfillment of the Scriptures, God's will and calling, and the cross of Christ [JUSTIFY] engagement with *eleos*.

104. Cf., e.g., Josh 2:12–14; Ruth 1:8.
105. Dunn, *Romans 9–16*, 569.
106. Allen, *Psalms 101–50*, 159.

Second, Paul employs quotations from the scriptural tradition to support his argument that salvation has come first to the Jew and also to the Greek. The original literary contexts of two quotations already include the intention for the nations/Gentiles to praise God for *eleos* (MT: *ḥsd*), along with Israel. Paul's main concern in relation to *eleos* is the [CONTRAST] between the current circumstances of the Jews (circumcision) and those of the Gentiles. Both Jews and Gentiles can follow the rule of new creation ([CONTEXT]) and [POSSESS] *eleos*. Gentiles glorify God ([PERCEIVERS]; [RESPONSE]) for *eleos*. But this is the season of *eleos* for the wild branches grafted into the olive tree. A season of fullness will come for the natural branches, and then Jews and Gentiles in "the Israel of God" will glorify God together for *eleos*. In the meantime, Paul prays for the salvation of Israel (response).

CHAPTER 9

Eleos in Luke's Gospel: A Basis for Remembered Promises and Neighborly Actions

The title "Good Samaritan" is used to describe one who does acts of compassion for those left wounded on the road of life. But intertextual and intratextual evidence in Luke's Gospel indicates that the activity of the Samaritan in Jesus's parable is more than an expression of compassion. It is also a demonstration of *ḥsd*.[1]

Within Luke's Gospel, *ḥsd* is evoked by the term *eleos*,[2] which occurs five times in the first infancy narrative (1:50, 54, 58, 72, 78), highlighting remembered promises, and once in the narrative frame of the "Good Samaritan" parable (10:37), indicating the basis for a neighborly action. I consider the intertextual connections between those occurrences of *eleos* and *ḥsd* in the Hebrew Bible (§9.1), Luke's engagement with the category ḤSD in this Gospel (§9.2), and the exegetical value of recognizing that engagement (§9.3).

9.1. Intertextual Connections Between *Eleos* in Luke's Gospel and *Ḥsd* in the Hebrew Bible

Luke is usually believed to be of non-Jewish descent,[3] writing for a predominantly Gentile Christian audience,[4] and the influence of the LXX in Luke's writing seems great.[5] However, it is at least possible that Luke also consulted

1. Bailey, *Through Peasant Eyes*, 50.

2. *Eleos* does not occur in Acts, where *hosios* evokes *ḥsd* and *ḥsyd* instead.

3. Nolland, *Luke 1–9:20*, xxxv. Cf. Bock, "Gospel of Luke," 496; Morris, *Luke*, 23. Contra Edwards, *Gospel According to Luke*, 8–10. Note *euangelion kata loukan* ("Gospel According to Luke") at the end of the Third Gospel in P75 and the probable implication in Col 4:10–14 that Luke is not "of the circumcision." Fitzmyer, *Gospel According to Luke (I–IX)*, 35, 41–53. The Muratorian Canon attributes the Third Gospel to Luke, a physician and companion of Paul. Nolland, *Luke 1–9:20*, xxxv.

4. Luke's Gospel and Acts are both dedicated to someone with a Greek name and show how "the salvation promised to Israel" also relates to Gentiles. Fitzmyer, *Gospel According to Luke (I–IX)*, 57–58. On the other hand, Nolland sees "a very significant Jewish setting" for Luke's writings (*Luke 1–9:20*, xxxvii).

5. Fitzmyer, *Gospel According to Luke (I–IX)*, 125.

Hebrew sources[6] and/or was exposed to the Hebrew language while traveling with Paul or through educational opportunities.[7] If so, the covenantal associations of the concept corresponding to *ḥesed* would make it a relevant choice for Luke to communicate foundational issues like the messianic identity of Jesus and/or the place of Gentiles within a movement that originated amongst Jews.[8]

The infancy narratives in Luke 1–2 have a marked Hebraic flavor that may indicate Luke's imitation of biblical language or someone's translation from a Hebrew source.[9] In any case, there are strong intertextual connections with *ḥsd* in the background of the occurrences of *eleos* in Luke 1:46–80. The usual English translation "mercy" does not do justice to the links with the Abrahamic and Davidic covenants evident in that narrative.

The five occurrences of *eleos* in Luke 1:46–80 form a pattern: two occurrences in the Magnificat, (mirrored by) two in the Benedictus, and one in between those hymns, as follows:

1:50: καὶ τὸ ἔλεος αὐτοῦ εἰς γενεὰς καὶ γενεὰς τοῖς φοβουμένοις αὐτόν
And his *eleos* is to generations and generations (i.e., many generations) for those who fear him.

1:54: ἀντελάβετο Ἰσραὴλ παιδὸς αὐτοῦ, μνησθῆναι ἐλέους
He came to the aid of Israel his servant, in remembrance[10] of *eleos*.

1:58: καὶ ἤκουσαν οἱ περίοικοι καὶ οἱ συγγενεῖς αὐτῆς ὅτι ἐμεγάλυνεν κύριος τὸ ἔλεος αὐτοῦ μετ' αὐτῆς
And her neighbors and relatives heard that the Lord had abundantly/lavishly[11] demonstrated his *eleos* with her.

1:72: ποιῆσαι ἔλεος μετὰ τῶν πατέρων ἡμῶν καὶ μνησθῆναι διαθήκης ἁγίας αὐτοῦ
To do *eleos* with our fathers and to remember his holy covenant

1:78a: διὰ σπλάγχνα ἐλέους θεοῦ ἡμῶν
Because of the heart/affections of *eleos* of our God

6. It is possible that the "conceptual form" of some arguments included in Luke-Acts had a Hebrew source (Bock, *Proclamation from Prophecy and Pattern*, 271). See also Buth, "Aramaic Language," 89, on possible Hebrew sources. Contra Fitzmyer, who writes, "There is no evidence that Luke knew any Hebrew" (*Gospel According to Luke [I–IX]*, 118).

7. Irenaeus of Lyons describes Luke as "inseparable from Paul" in *Adversus haereses* 3.14.1 (PG 7:913; trans. *ANF* 1:437). According to Bovon, the author's language indicates that "Jewish methods of exegesis" were part of his education (*Luke 1*, 8). Similarly, Luke makes positive and accurate reports on "Jewish [worship,] practices and parties." Edwards, *Gospel According to Luke*, 10; cf. Hengel, "Zur urchristlichen Geschichtsschreibung," 51.

8. Bock, "Gospel of Luke," 498; Edwards, *Gospel According to Luke*, 10.

9. Johnson, *Gospel of Luke*, 7, and Morris, *Luke*, 29.

10. NRSV; ESV.

11. Cf. "lavished." Culy, Parsons, and Stigall, *Luke*, 47.

Hays's **volume** test is significant in this context, because Luke gives a certain precursor text prominence. Nathan Lane claims that each of the Luke 1 references to *eleos* is "directly or indirectly related to the credo of Exod. 34.6–7."[12] I deal with each of these occurrences of *eleos* in turn, starting from the upper section of the pattern (1:50, 54), moving to the lower section (1:72, 78), and finishing in the center (1:58). The intertextual connections between these occurrences and *ḥsd* in the Hebrew Bible support Lane's claim to a point, and they provide evidence that each occurrence of *eleos* here denotes an instance of the category ḤSD. I discuss the only other occurrence of *eleos* in this Gospel (10:37) as a corollary to that argument.

9.1.1. The Magnificat

The Magnificat (Luke 1:46–55)[13] magnifies God for the great things God has done for his servants, Mary and Israel. Luke 1:50 reveals one reason to magnify the Lord: "And his *eleos* is to many generations [*eis geneas kai geneas*] for those who fear him."[14]

Others have observed the connection between Luke 1:50 and Ps 103:17a (102:17a LXX).[15] This allusion links *eleos* in Luke 1:50 with *ḥsd*:

Ps 103:17a MT:	
וחסד יהוה מעולם ועד עולם על יראיו	But the *ḥsd* of YHWH is from everlasting (and) to everlasting upon those who fear him.
Ps 102:17a LXX:	
τὸ δὲ ἔλεος τοῦ κυρίου ἀπὸ τοῦ αἰῶνος καὶ ἕως τοῦ αἰῶνος ἐπὶ τοὺς φοβουμένους αὐτόν	But the *eleos* of the Lord is from everlasting (and) to everlasting upon those who fear him.

In Ps 103:15–17 MT, the psalmist contrasts YHWH's everlasting *ḥsd* (LXX: *eleos*) with the fleeting lifespan of a human. Elsewhere, the psalmist urges his *npš* to bless YHWH because, among other reasons, it is crowned with *ḥsd* (LXX: *eleos*) and *rḥmym* ("compassion"; v. 4), he interprets an abbreviated version of YHWH's

12. Lane, "Echo of Mercy," 80–81. In Exod 34 LXX, *polyeleos* renders *rb ḥsd* (v. 6) and *eleos* renders *ḥsd* (v. 7). Substantial repetitions of the "credo" (YHWH's self-description, also called the "attribute formula") occur in Num 14:18; Joel 2:13; Jonah 4:2; Pss 86:15; 103:8; 145:8; and Neh 9:17.

13. Also Odes 9:46–55.

14. "To many generations" (a Hebraism): so Marshall, *Gospel of Luke*, 83.

15. NA[28], 854 (**history of interpretation**). E.g., Ringgren, "Luke's Use of the Old Testament," 230. Nolland observes the similarity of thought with Ps 102:17 LXX and views God's "mercy" as "active faithfulness to his covenant commitment to Israel" (*Luke 1–9:20*, 71).

attribute formula (vv. 8–10; an indirect link to Exod 34:6–7; cf. Lane's claim cited above)[16] that includes *rb ḥsd* (LXX: *polyeleos*),[17] and he declares, "For as high as the heavens are above the earth, so great is his *ḥsd* [LXX: *eleos*] toward those who fear him [*ʿl yrʾyw*; LXX: *epi tous phoboumenous auton*]" (v. 11). That which the psalmist says about those who fear YHWH could also be said of "those who fear" (*tois phoboumenois*) the Lord, according to the Magnificat.

In addition, the phrase *eis geneas kai geneas* is loosely connected to *ḥsd*. *Eleos* (cf. *ḥsd*) is sometimes set in parallel/comparison with things that exist (or do not exist) for many generations, including the Lord's *alētheia* ("faithfulness/truth"; Pss 88:2; 99:5 LXX; MT: *ʾmwnh*).[18] These parallel/comparative statements also resemble YHWH's promise to keep the covenant and the *ḥsd* (LXX: *eleos*) to the "thousands" (*chilias geneas* in Deut 7:9 LXX) of those who love YHWH and keep his commandments.[19]

These intertextual connections indicate that *eleos* in Luke 1:50 evokes *ḥsd*. Indeed, Howard Marshall sees a nuance different from "compassion and mercy to the unfortunate" conveyed by *eleos* in this verse, because of its function in the LXX to render *ḥsd*. He associates it with mutual relationship and God's covenant (cf. Exod 20:6).[20]

The Magnificat concludes with the words "He has come to the aid of Israel, his servant,[21] to remember *eleos* [*mnēsthēnai eleous*], just as he said to our ancestors, to Abraham and to his seed/offspring forever" (vv. 54–55). *Zkr* ("to remember"; LXX: *mimnēskomai*) has various connections with *ḥsd* (LXX: *eleos*) in the Hebrew Bible (e.g., Ps 25:7 [24:7 LXX]; 2 Chr 6:42). But, in terms of the most likely Scriptures alluded to in verses 54–55, scholars focus on Ps 98:3 (concerning remembrance of *ḥsd* [LXX: *eleos*] to Israel) and 2 Sam 22:51 / Mic 7:20 (concerning *ḥsd* [LXX: *eleos*] to ancestors):[22]

Ps 98:3 MT:

זכר חסדו ואמונתו לבית ישראל	He has remembered his *ḥsd* and his faithfulness to the house of Israel;
ראו כל אפסי ארץ את ישועת אלהינו	all the ends of the earth have seen the salvation of our God.

16. See §9.1.

17. YHWH will not keep his anger forever, nor will YHWH deal with his people according to their sins.

18. Cf. the Abrahamic covenant confirmed to Israel (1 Chr 16:15–18). See also Pss 76:9; 84:6b, 8 LXX.

19. Cf. Lane, "Echo of Mercy," 79.

20. Marshall, *Gospel of Luke*, 83.

21. This form of "servant" (*pais*) is used in the servant passages (Isa 42:1; 52:13; Fitzmyer, *Gospel According to Luke [I–IX]*, 368) and used of David in Luke 1:69.

22. See, e.g., NA[28], 181 (**history of interpretation**).

Ps 97:3 LXX:

ἐμνήσθη τοῦ ἐλέους αὐτοῦ τῷ Ιακωβ καὶ τῆς ἀληθείας αὐτοῦ τῷ οἴκῳ Ισραηλ,	He remembered his *eleos* to Jacob and his faithfulness to the house of Israel;
εἴδοσαν πάντα τὰ πέρατα τῆς γῆς τὸ σωτήριον τοῦ θεοῦ ἡμῶν.	all the ends of the earth saw the salvation of our God.[23]

2 Sam 22:51 MT:

מגדיל[24] ישועות מלכו	He magnifies the salvation(s)/ victories of his king
ועשה חסד למשיחו	and does *ḥsd* for his anointed one,
לדוד ולזרעו עד עולם	for David and for his seed forever.

2 Kgdms 22:51 LXX:

μεγαλύνων σωτηρίας βασιλέως αὐτοῦ	He magnifies the salvation(s) of his king
καὶ ποιῶν ἔλεος τῷ χριστῷ αὐτοῦ,	and does *eleos* for his anointed one,
τῷ Δαυιδ καὶ τῷ σπέρματι αὐτοῦ ἕως αἰῶνος.	for David and for his seed forever.

Mic 7:20a MT:

תתן אמת ליעקב	You will give faithfulness to Jacob,
חסד לאברהם	*ḥsd* to Abraham.

Mic 7:20a LXX:

δώσεις ἀλήθειαν τῷ Ιακωβ,	You will give faithfulness to Jacob,
ἔλεον τῷ Αβρααμ	*eleos* to Abraham.

The equivalence between *eleos* and *ḥsd* in each of these texts confirms that *eleos* in Luke 1:54 also denotes an instance of the category *ḤSD*. Micah 7:20 is particularly relevant, because the patient of *ḥsd* in that context is Abraham (cf. Luke 1:55).[25] In addition, the Mic 7:18–20 hymn shares vocabulary with Exod 34:6–7 (e.g., three Hebrew words for wrongdoing),[26] suggesting that Micah had the Exod 34 tradition in mind.[27] This is an indirect connection between *eleos* in Luke 1:54 and the Exod 34 formula (cf. Lane's claim).

23. Psalm 97:3 LXX inserts a reference to Jacob, but does not mention Abraham. This psalm also mentions the "arm" (*brachiōn*) of the Lord (cf. Luke 1:51).

24. *Qere*: *mgdwl* (*BHS*, 551).

25. In 2 Sam 22:51, the patient of *ḥsd* is David. Cf. Ringgren, "Luke's Use of the Old Testament," 231.

26. *ʿwn, pšʿ, ḥṭʾt.* Waltke, "Micah," 762–63.

27. Andersen and Freedman, *Micah*, 598.

9.1.2. The Benedictus

In the Benedictus (Luke 1:68–79), two of the purposes stated by Zechariah for the Lord raising up a "horn of salvation" from the house of David are "to do *eleos* with our ancestors" and "to remember his holy covenant, [the] oath that he swore to Abraham, our ancestor" (vv. 72–73). Zechariah also declares that his child will go before the Lord to prepare his ways and to give his people the knowledge of salvation through the forgiveness of sins, "because of the heart/affections [*splanchna*] of *eleos* of our God,[28] by which the sunrise from on high will visit[29] us" (vv. 76–79). Thus, it is because of the *eleos* of God that the Messiah will visit (cf. Isa 60:1; Mal 4:2) and bring salvation to his people.[30]

The connection between *eleos* in Luke 1:72 and *ḥsd* is obvious to scholars. For example, Joseph Fitzmyer associates "mercy" in this context with "Yahweh's covenantal attribute, *ḥesed*,"[31] and Marshall sees "*ʿāśāḇ ḥeseḏ ʿim*" reflected in *poiēsai eleos meta*.[32] In addition, various echoes or allusions are identified in connection with the phrases "our ancestors" and "to remember his holy covenant," including Pss 105:8 (104:8 LXX); 106:45 (105:45 LXX); and Mic 7:20.[33] Psalm 106:45 (105:45 LXX)[34] and Mic 7:20[35] are particularly relevant to this discussion, because both include *ḥsd* (LXX: *eleos*) in contexts where other items resonate with Luke 1:68–74: a requested/anticipated salvation (Ps 106:47 [105:47 LXX]; Mic 7:7; cf. Luke 1:69, 71); a "remembered" covenant (Ps 106:45 [105:45 LXX]; cf. Luke 1:72); that which was sworn to ancestors, especially Abraham (Mic 7:20; cf. Luke 1:73); and the downfall of enemies (Mic 7:10 NRSV; cf. Luke 1:74). In addition to the intertextual connections between Mic 7:18–20 and Exod 34:6–7 discussed in relation to the Magnificat, Ps 106:45 MT includes the same description of YHWH's *ḥsd* as found in Exod 34:6 (*rb ḥsd*).[36] This group of connections indicates that Luke 1:72

28. *Splanchnon* is always plural in the New Testament. According to BDAG, it refers to "the inward parts of a body" but can be rendered by "heart" (i.e., "the seat of the emotions"; s.v. "σπλάγχνον, ου, τό").

29. א * B L W Θ: *episkeptomai* ("will visit"); א² A C D K Γ Δ Ξ Ψ: *epeskepsato* ("has visited"). NA[28], 183. According to Marshall, "Most scholars regard the aorist as being due to assimilation to v. 68 . . . and accept the better attested future, which fits in with the tense in v. 76" (*Gospel of Luke*, 94).

30. Green, *Gospel of Luke*, 119.

31. Fitzmyer, *Gospel According to Luke (I–IX)*, 384. Cf. *ḥsd* texts listed in Bovon, *Luke 1*, 74n62.

32. Marshall, *Gospel of Luke*, 92.

33. E.g., Fitzmyer, *Gospel According to Luke (I–IX)*, 384, and Marshall, *Gospel of Luke*, 92.

34. "He remembered (to them) his covenant and became remorseful [*HALOT*, s.v. "נחם"] according to the abundance of his *ḥsd*."

35. Discussed in §9.1.1.

36. "Abundance of [noun] / abounding in [adjective] *ḥsd*."

contains another instance of the category *ḤSD* and another indirect link with the Exod 34 attribute formula.

There is less agreement about the sense of *eleos* in Luke 1:78, for *splanchna eleous* has no LXX precedent.[37] But the covenant-devotional sense of *ḥsd* is still relevant here (i.e., "the devoted heart/affections of our God"),[38] especially considering verses like Isa 42:6–7, where the one given as a covenant to the people and a "light" to the nations brings forth "those who sit in darkness" (cf. Luke 1:79; Mic 7:8), and Ps 107:10–16 (106:10–16 LXX),[39] where YHWH does the same as a manifestation of YHWH's *ḥsd* (LXX: *eleos*).[40] In fact, Joel Green compares Zechariah's Song, which "revolves around 'tender mercy,'" to Ps 130:7–8, which "roots redemption and freedom from iniquities in the Lord's 'steadfast love'" (i.e., *ḥsd*).[41] These intertextual connections, along with the mirror effect of the two hymns in Luke's infancy narrative, suggest that *eleos* in Luke 1:78 denotes another instance of the category *ḤSD*. Links to YHWH's attribute formula are weaker in this instance, but still conceivable.[42]

9.1.3. Luke 1:58

Like the Benedictus, the central occurrence of *eleos* in Luke's infancy narrative is associated with the birth of John the Baptist. When the Lord had taken away the stigma of Elizabeth's barrenness (cf. 1:25) and she had given birth to a son (1:57),[43] her neighbors and relatives heard "that the Lord abundantly/lavishly demonstrated his *eleos* [*emegalynen kyrios to eleos autou*] with her" (1:58).

There is some similarity between Luke 1:58 and Gen 19:19,[44] although in that case, *ḥsd* is translated by *dikaiosynē*, not *eleos*:

Gen 19:19 MT:

ותגדל חסדך	And you have greatly demonstrated your *ḥsd*,
אשר עשית עמדי	(which you have made/done) with me.

37. Nolland, *Luke 1–9:20*, 89. However, the whole passage also appears in Odes 9:68–79.

38. Contra Marshall, who thinks the phraseology in 1:78 reflects "*raḥᵉmayim*" (*Gospel of Luke*, 94).

39. Cf. Bovon, *Luke 1*, 76, and NA[28], 854.

40. See also "light/shine" in Pss 31:16; 118:27–29.

41. Green, *Gospel of Luke*, 118.

42. E.g., connections between Ps 130 and Exod 34:6–9 (Goldingay, *Psalms 90–150*, 526–27, and Hossfeld and Zenger, *Psalms 3*, 438) and themes shared with the exodus tradition (e.g., redemption [LXX: *lytroō*] in Mic 6:4 and forgiveness [LXX: *aphaireō*] in Exod 34:9) (cf. *lytrōsis* and *aphesis* in Luke 1:68, 77).

43. Fitzmyer, *Gospel According to Luke (I–IX)*, 373.

44. Nolland, *Luke 1–9:20*, 78, and NA[28], 837 (**history of interpretation**).

Gen 19:19 LXX:	
καὶ ἐμεγάλυνας τὴν δικαιοσύνην σου,	And you have greatly demonstrated your righteousness / righteous responsibility,
ὃ ποιεῖς ἐπ' ἐμέ	(which you undertake / carry out) toward me.

I also detect another indirect allusion to the Exodus attribute formula with the occurrence of *eleos* in Luke 1:58. An abbreviated version of that formula occurs in Num 14:18, but in 14:19, a request is made in accordance with YHWH's "great *ḥsd*" (LXX: *mega eleos*).

Therefore, the intertextual evidence indicates that all five occurrences of *eleos* in Luke 1 denote instances of the category *ḤSD*, and Lane's claim is correct to the extent that an indirect (rather than direct) relationship between Exod 34:6–7 and this group of occurrences is likely.[45]

9.1.4. Corollary: The Devoted Samaritan Parable

The only occurrence of *eleos* in Luke's Gospel located outside of chapter 1 occurs in the narrative frame of Jesus's parable about three men, each of whom saw another man left half-dead on the road from Jerusalem to Jericho. Of the three, only the Samaritan helped the wounded man. Concluding the parable, Jesus asks his conversation partner, "Which of these three seems (to you) to become[46] a neighbor of the one who fell among the robbers?" The expert in the law answers:

Luke 10:37:	
ὁ ποιήσας τὸ ἔλεος μετ' αὐτοῦ.	Lit.: "The one who did the *eleos* with him."

Given that intertextual links to *ḥsd* have already been established for the other occurrences of *eleos* in Luke's Gospel, I treat this sixth occurrence as a corollary to the previous arguments. But there is an additional clue that this occurrence denotes an instance of the category *ḤSD*. The clause *ho poiēsas to eleos met' autou* is not usually translated literally in English (as above) because that seems awkward. But similar constructions are used in the LXX to translate variations on the Hebrew phrase *ʿśh ḥsd ʿm* (lit. "do *ḥsd* with").[47] Thus, I con-

45. Cf. Lane, "Echo of Mercy," 80–81.

46. ESV. *Ginomai* ("to become") replaces *eimi* ("to be") in the lawyer's question (10:29).

47. Discussed in ch. 3; cf. Luke 1:72 above. *Eleos* is associated with *plēsion* in Sir 18:13; 29:1, but neither text is in the Hebrew manuscripts. *Eleos* in the characteristic LXX phrase *poiēseis eleos*

sider Luke's use of this clause as an echo of both the concept corresponding to *ḥesed* and that grammatical construction, rather than an allusion to a specific Hebrew Bible text.

In summary, the Hebraic flavor of the Lucan infancy narratives, the intertextual connections presented in section 9.1, and the relevance of *ḥesed* to issues faced by the early Christian movement all support the conclusion that the six occurrences of *eleos* in Luke's Gospel denote instances of the category *ḤSD*.

9.2. The Category *ḤSD* in Luke's Gospel

In Luke's Gospel, engagement with the category *ḤSD* is signaled by allusions and echoes involving *eleos* (cf. *ḥsd*), rather than quotations. Therefore, there is more evidence of themes and grammatical constructions / word patterns connected with *ḥsd* than exactly replicated clauses. Given the series of indirect allusions to Exod 34:6–7 in the Luke 1 infancy narrative, I compare elements of the category *ḤSD* in that Hebrew Bible text with those in the Lucan texts containing *eleos* (grouped as in §9.1).

9.2.1. ḤSD *in Exodus 34:6–7*

Ḥsd occurs twice in Exod 34:6–7, the record of YHWH's proclamation after descending in a cloud to stand with Moses (communication) on Mount Sinai (location). The first occurrence of *ḥsd* is in the list of [CHARACTERISTICS] pertaining to YHWH ([POSSESSOR]/[PERCEIVER]), an Incomplete Clause that includes the Construct/Adjectival Phrase *rb ḥsd wʾmt* ("abounding in *ḥsd* and faithfulness"; LXX: *polyeleos kai alēthinos*). Even though YHWH's people have broken the covenant (context; cf. Exod 32; 34:1), YHWH's *ḥsd* abounds ([QUANTITY]). The second occurrence is the Direct Object of *nṣr* (ptc.) in a Relative Verbal (Participle) Clause in which YHWH ([AGENT]/[PERCEIVER]) is described as "keeping" (pres. [AGENT'S_ACTIVITY]) *ḥsd* ([ARTICLE_OF_TRANSACTION]) to the thousands ([PATIENTS]; [DURATION]). In Exod 20:6, the "thousands" relate to those who love God and keep his commandments (justification). The [MANIFESTATIONS] of *ḥsd* are probably linked with the description "forgiving [ptc. of *nśʾ*] iniquity [*ʿwn*], transgression [*pšʿ*], and sin [*ḥṭʾh*]." This forgiveness is [CONTRASTED] with visiting iniquity on descendants (34:7). Moses responds to the proclamation by bowing his head, worshipping YHWH

meta (or similar) renders *ḥsd*, not *ḥnn* or *rḥmym*. Philo and Josephus do not use *ho poiēsas to eleos* (or similar). Fitzmyer recognizes a "Septuagintism" here (*Gospel According to Luke [X–XXIV]*, 888), and Dickey, a "Hebraism" ("Development of the Hebrew Idea," 105).

(v. 8), and then making three subsequent requests of YHWH: ongoing presence (*hlk*) with his people, pardoning (*slḥ*) iniquity and sin, and taking (*nḥl*) Israel for his inheritance (outcomes; v. 9).

9.2.2. ḤSD *in the Magnificat*

When Elizabeth recognizes Mary's blessed state (context; Luke 1:42–45), Mary responds with the Magnificat (vv. 46–55; communication). In this song, *to eleos autou* ("his *eleos*"; [CHARACTERISTIC]) is the Subject of a Nominal Clause (v. 50), and *eleos* ([ENTITY]) is the Direct Object of *mimnēskomai* (aor. inf.: "to remember"; v. 54) in a Purpose Verbal Clause. That is, the Lord is the [POSSESSOR] and [AGENT] of *eleos* (vv. 50, 54), and the Lord's help is in remembrance of *eleos* spoken to ancestors, Abraham and his offspring ([RESPONSE]; [REASON]; vv. 54–55). [PATIENTS] of *eleos* are the Lord's servant Israel (v. 54), and more particularly, those who fear the Lord (v. 50; [JUSTIFICATIONS]) from generation to generation (i.e., "to many generations"; [DURATION]). The specified [MANIFESTATION] of the Lord's *eleos* to Israel is "assistance" (*antilambanō*; v. 54). Other manifestations may include the great things that the Lord has done for Mary (v. 49) and the reversals for particular groups among God's people (vv. 51–53).[48] The Lord responds differently to those who are proud, rulers, and rich from those who are lowly and hungry (contrast). Mary and "all generations" of those who know of Mary's situation perceive the Lord's *eleos*. Mary's soul magnifies the Lord, her spirit rejoices in God her Savior (response; vv. 46–48). She gives birth to a son, Christ the Lord (outcome; 2:7, 11), and "all generations" will call her blessed ([RESPONSE]; v. 48).

9.2.3. ḤSD *in the Benedictus*

After Elizabeth gave birth and the child was named/circumcised, Zechariah prophesied about the salvation of the Lord's people (context; Luke 1:57–79). In his prophecy (vv. 68–79; communication), *eleos* is a reason for the events taking place. Thus, *eleos* ([ARTICLE_OF_TRANSACTION]) is the Direct Object of *poieō* (aor. inf.: "to do"; [AGENT'S_ACTIVITY]) in a Purpose Verbal Clause (v. 72), and *dia splanchna eleous theou hēmōn* ("because of the heart/affections of *eleos* of our God"; [CHARACTERISTIC]) is a Prepositional Phrase within a Causal Verbal Clause (v. 78), probably modifying *didōmi* (aor. inf.: "to give"; v. 77) in the previous clause.

48. Scattering the proud, bringing down the rulers, exalting the lowly, filling the hungry, and sending the rich away empty. Cf. 1 Sam 2:1–10. Hays, *Echoes of Scripture in the Gospels*, 197–98.

The Lord God of Israel ("our God") is the [POSSESSOR] and [AGENT] of *eleos* (vv. 72, 78). It is set in parallel with the Lord's holy covenant ([JUSTIFICATION]; v. 72). The [PATIENTS] are "us" (presumably the Lord's people, Israel)[49] and "our ancestors" (vv. 72, 78). The Lord's people are [CONTRASTED] with their enemies (vv. 71, 74). [MANIFESTATIONS] of *eleos* may include redemption (v. 68), raising up a horn of salvation in the house of David (v. 69), salvation/deliverance from enemies (vv. 71, 74), forgiveness of sins (v. 77), and the visitation from on high ([LOCATION]) of a messianic figure described as the "(sun)rise" (vv. 68, 78).[50] Zechariah (perceiver) [RESPONDS] by blessing the Lord God of Israel (vv. 67–68). [OUTCOMES] include deliverance (v. 74), light, and guidance (v. 79). The Lord's people serve the Lord in uprightness and righteousness all their days (vv. 74–75).

9.2.4. ḤSD *in Luke 1:58*

Mary's relative Elizabeth is an elderly, righteous (justification), and previously barren woman (Luke 1:6–7, 36). Elizabeth's own experience of *eleos* is narrated (communication) in between the Magnificat and the Benedictus. When the time is fulfilled for Elizabeth to give birth, she bears a son (manifestation; v. 57), and her neighbors and relatives ([PERCEIVERS]) hear that the Lord ([POSSESSOR]/[AGENT]) has made great ([AGENT'S_ACTIVITY]; [QUANTITY]) his *eleos* ([ARTICLE_OF_TRANSACTION]/[CHARACTERISTIC]) with Elizabeth ([PATIENT]; v. 58). Thus, *to eleos autou* ("his *eleos*") is the Direct Object of *megalynō* (3sg. aor.: "he made great / lavishly demonstrated"; [AGENT'S_ACTIVITY]) in an Object Verbal Clause. The neighbors and relatives rejoice with Elizabeth ([RESPONSE]; v. 58). On the eighth day, the child is circumcised and named (vv. 59–63). He grows and becomes strong in spirit (v. 80). He will be called the prophet of the Most High (v. 76; outcomes).

9.2.5. ḤSD *in the Devoted Samaritan Parable*

In reply to the question of an expert in the law—"Who is my neighbor?"—Jesus tells a parable (Luke 10:29–35). Jesus concludes with a different question, concerning three characters in the parable (communication): "Which of these three seems (to you) to become a neighbor?" (v. 36). *Eleos* occurs within the lawyer's ([PERCEIVER]) response to that question: the character in the parable who became a neighbor to the wounded man ([PATIENT]) was the one ([AGENT]) who did ([AGENT'S_ACTIVITY]) the *eleos* ([SPECIFIC_DEMONSTRATION]/

49. Cf. Nolland, *Luke 1–9:20*, 90.

50. I.e., "the coming of the Messiah." Green, *Gospel of Luke*, 119. Marshall explains that *anatolē* could refer to "the Shoot of Jesse (Is. 11:1ff.) and the star from Jacob (Nu. 24:17)," both descriptions associated with the Davidic messiah (*Gospel of Luke*, 95).

[ARTICLE_OF_TRANSACTION]) with him (v. 37). Thus, *to eleos* ("the *eleos*") is the Direct Object of *poieō* (aor. ptc.: "one who did") in an Object Participial Phrase (i.e., what is said).

The conversation in the parable frame points to information about the elements of the category ḤSD deduced from the parable itself. The [PATIENT] of *eleos* is a man who fell among robbers and was stripped, beaten, and left half-dead on the road from Jerusalem to Jericho (location/context; v. 30).[51] The [AGENT] is neither a priest[52] nor a Levite (contrast), but a Samaritan man (vv. 31–35). As the Samaritan was traveling on that route (time), he saw the wounded man and "had compassion" (*splanchnizomai*; manifestation; v. 33), binding up the wounds, taking him to an inn, and paying for his care there (vv. 34–35).[53]

On the other hand, the outcomes associated with each layer of interaction are deduced only from the parable frame.[54] According to the law (vv. 26–27), the wounded man would be expected to love as himself the Samaritan who became his neighbor (v. 37). The so-called "expert in the law" is to become a neighbor by doing *eleos* with those in need ("do likewise"; v. 37) and to love his own neighbors as himself (v. 27).[55] Those who love God and love as themselves people who do *eleos* with them inherit eternal life (vv. 25–28). In light of other New Testament teaching, it could also be said that the lawyer's eternal life depended on him admitting that he was in need of salvation[56] and loving Jesus, who eventually even laid down his life for his people.

9.2.6. General Observations

All ḤSD subcategories are evident in Luke's Gospel, and *eleos* is usually the Direct Object of a verb or part of a Complement/Modifying Phrase.

51. This man is presumed to be Judean. So Johnson, *Gospel of Luke*, 173. Contra Green, who emphasizes the anonymity of the man in need throughout the story (*Gospel of Luke*, 429n114).

52. Bailey explains that, without "distinctive dress" or speech, the priest cannot identify the wounded man. If the wounded man is dead, the priest will be defiled through contact with him and thus not be able to deal with tithes (*Through Peasant Eyes*, 44).

53. Cf. the sense of "secular" *ḥesed* as described by Sakenfeld (*Meaning of Hesed*, 234): a situationally powerful party (though a Samaritan) performs this act of *eleos* for a situationally weak party (a wounded man); the Samaritan provides for an essential need (recovery) and delivers from "dire straits" (being left half-dead on the road); he is "the sole source of assistance available" to the wounded man at the time of this encounter and is free to withhold assistance (a prerogative exercised by both priest and Levite).

54. Reported interaction (Jesus and a lawyer; v. 25), potential interaction (this lawyer, God, and the lawyer's neighbor; vv. 27–28), and hypothetical interaction (characters in Jesus's parable).

55. It is difficult to discern from the text whether the lawyer is actually a dynamic character (as Lane argues ["Echo of Mercy," 74, 82]). Luke does not record the outcome of the dialogue.

56. Cf. the relationship between *ḥsd* and *yšʿ* ("to save") or *yšwʿh/tšwʿh* ("salvation") in Pss 13:6; 18:51; 57:4; 85:8; 86:15–16; 98:3; 108:5–7; 109:26; 119:41 (MT references).

9.2.6.1. *The Lord God and the Lord God's Choices*

Luke emphasizes the abundant, enduring nature of the Lord's *eleos* (cf. *ḥsd*), mostly within hymn-like texts (communication). The events surrounding the Messiah's appearance have occurred because the Lord keeps *eleos* through the generations ([DURATION]; cf. *ḥsd* in Exod 34:7). The Lord God of Israel is the only [POSSESSOR] and one of only two [AGENTS] of *eleos* in this Gospel. The Lord not only "does" *eleos*, but makes it great ([AGENT'S_ACTIVITY]; [QUANTITY]).

The Lord acts in remembrance of *eleos*. The Lord makes it manifest to the people of Israel, the Lord's servant, and in particular, those who fear the Lord or are righteous ([PATIENTS]; [JUSTIFICATIONS]). They experience *eleos* for the sake of covenant promises made to their ancestors, especially Abraham. But the patients/perceivers of *eleos* also include some unexpected choices: a virgin girl who becomes the mother of the Son of the Most High and an elderly barren woman who becomes the mother of a prophet of the Most High. The lowly are favored and lifted up, and the hungry are filled with good things (manifestations). In contrast, the Lord scatters the proud, brings down the powerful, and sends the rich away empty. Where Moses responded to YHWH's proclamation involving *ḥsd* by bowing his head and worshipping, [RESPONSES] to the Lord's *eleos* include rejoicing and blessing.

9.2.6.2. *Messianic Visitation*

In the context of the Exodus covenant renewal, [MANIFESTATIONS] of *ḥsd* were likely to include forgiveness of iniquity, transgression, and sin.[57] [MANIFESTATIONS] of the Lord's *eleos* in Luke 1 all relate to the visitation of a messianic figure who fulfills covenantal promises, including those in Exod 34:6–7 ([JUSTIFICATION]/[REASON]). The [MANIFESTATIONS] may include forgiveness of sins, great things (e.g., miraculous conceptions), reversed circumstances, assistance, salvation/deliverance from enemies, and redemption. The Lord's visitation leads to more positive ways of life: those who sit in darkness receive light and guidance into the way of peace, and the Lord's people serve the Lord in holiness and righteousness all their days ([OUTCOMES]).[58]

57. Prophetic echoes of the Exodus covenant and attribute formula indicate that the covenant is eventually renewed with a faithful remnant of God's people (cf. Jer 31:31–34; Mic 7:18–20).

58. In addition, those who love God and love their neighbors as themselves inherit eternal life.

9.2.6.3. A Priest, a Levite, and a Samaritan

Aside from the Lord God of Israel, the only other [AGENT] of *eleos* in Luke's Gospel is a Samaritan man. A legal expert ([PERCEIVER]) recognizes the hypothetical demonstration of *eleos* in Jesus's parable: a Samaritan meets the urgent need of a wounded man ([PATIENT]) left for dead on the road from Jericho to Jerusalem (location). In contrast, a priest and a Levite exercise their prerogative not to become involved. By his acts of compassion (manifestation), the Samaritan becomes a neighbor to the wounded man. The law commands love for such a neighbor.[59]

9.3. Exegetical Value of Recognizing Engagement with the Category *ḤSD* in Luke's Gospel

The preceding analysis indicates that the category *ḤSD* is relevant to at least three key issues in Luke's Gospel: remembered promises, reciprocal relationships, and the nature of the covenant people.

9.3.1. ḤSD *and Remembered Promises*

In the Hebrew Bible, YHWH "keeps" (*šmr*) the covenant and *ḥsd* "for those who love him and keep [*šmr*] his commandments."[60] YHWH "keeps" *ḥsd* in the sense that he fulfills his obligations and is true to his word. YHWH also keeps his *ḥsd* to the house of David (2 Sam 7:15; 1 Kgs 3:6; 2 Chr 1:8; 6:14–17), even though the outworking of associated promises is not obvious for a season (Ps 89:49 [89:50 MT]). In addition, the verb "remember" (*zkr*; i.e., implement one's commitment[61]) is associated with *ḥsd* (e.g., Ps 106:7, 45; 2 Chr 6:41–42). Of particular relevance to this study, Ps 98:3 reads, "He has remembered [3 masc. sg. pf. of *zkr*; Ps 97:3 LXX: *mimnēskomai*] his *ḥsd* and his faithfulness to the house of Israel. All the ends of the earth have seen the salvation [*yšwʿh*; LXX: *sōtērion*] of our God" (see §9.1.1).

It is fitting, then, that the category *ḤSD* is present in Luke's Gospel, where fulfillment of scriptural promises is a key theme.[62] In particular, in Luke 1, demonstrations of God's *eleos* (cf. *ḥsd*), including the coming of the Messiah,

59. Luke's interest in reciprocity is well served by the concept corresponding to *ḥesed*. See below, and the discussion on household reciprocity in Elliott, "Temple Versus Household," 236–38.

60. Deut 7:9; Neh 1:5; Dan 9:4.

61. Cf. Tate, *Psalms 51–100*, 524.

62. Marshall, *Gospel of Luke*, 35.

are connected to God's covenant with the ancestors of Israel (Luke 1:54–55, 72). In fact, 1:72a reads literally, "to do *eleos* with our fathers," indicating that the patient of this *eleos* is still Israel's ancestors.

Luke strongly communicates that the demonstrations of *eleos* recorded in this infancy narrative are continuous with the tradition of *ḥsd* (LXX: *eleos*) extended to Israel throughout the generations (1:50). In Luke 1, *eleos* and the covenant are both associated with the verb *mimnēskomai* ("remember"; vv. 54, 72). The remembered *eleos* and covenant result in the Lord assisting Israel (v. 54) and raising up "a horn of salvation [*sōtēria*]" in the house of David (v. 69; cf. vv. 71, 77).[63] The Lord does indeed keep his promises to the house of Israel (esp. as spoken to Abraham; vv. 55, 73; cf. Ps 98:3 [97:3 LXX]) and the house of David. Thus, in this context, the sense of *eleos* is closer to "covenant devotion" than it is to "mercy."

9.3.2. ḤSD *and Reciprocal Relationships*

There are several examples in the Hebrew Bible where people expect reciprocal *ḥsd*. For instance, Abimelech says to Abraham, (lit.) "according to the *ḥsd* that I have done with you, you will do with me" (Gen 21:23). This example includes an adaption of the common grammatical construction associated with ARTICLE_OF_TRANSACTION_*ḤSD* ("do *ḥsd* with") that, in itself, reflects this expectation. Even the Sinai/Horeb covenant stipulates mutual obligations: YHWH "keeps" (*šmr*) the covenant and *ḥsd* "for those who love him and keep [*šmr*] his commandments" (Deut 7:9).

There are indications in the Luke 10 parable and its frame that the relationship initiated by the Samaritan's act of *eleos* also involves mutuality and reciprocity.[64] First, *eleos* (v. 37) occurs in a phrase that resonates with the grammatical construction involving *ḥsd* mentioned above ("did *ḥsd* with"). Instead of the awkward literal translation, NRSV and ESV render *ho poiēsas to eleos met' autou* as "the one who showed him mercy." But a translation such as "dealt faithfully with" (cf. 2 Sam 10:2 NRSV) would communicate the relationality, reciprocity, and ongoing commitment involved in a *ḥsd/eleos* transaction better than "showed mercy."[65]

63. YHWH's *ḥsd* is sometimes manifested in acts of salvation (e.g., Ps 109:26 MT; cf. §§4.1.1–4.1.2). In Luke's Gospel, "salvation" is from enemies (1:69, 71), but it also involves forgiveness of sins and restored relationships (1:77; 19:9), dire needs of all humanity.

64. There is no indication of any preexisting relationship between the Samaritan and the man he helps. Nolland, *Luke 9:21–18:34*, 596.

65. Concerning *eleos* in Luke 1, Bibb highlights a "subtlety of faithfulness arising from a mutual relationship" associated with *eleos* by LXX use ("Characterization of God," 280). Evans refers to the lawyer's reply as a "thoroughly Semitic expression" and human "*mercy* (*eleos*)" as "acts of succour to be expected of those who have claims on one another" (*Saint Luke*, 471).

Second, the law promotes love among neighbors, and Jesus's parable illustrates that neighbors are those who do *eleos* with one another. The pericopes about "love" in Luke's Gospel form a pattern: chapters 3 and 20 speak of "beloved" (*agapētos*) sons,[66] chapters 6 and 16 highlight the contrast between "loving" (*agapaō*) and "hating" (*miseō*),[67] and chapters 7 and 11 contrast the genuine "love" (*agapaō*) of a Gentile and a sinner with the superficial "love" (*agapaō*) of the Pharisees.[68] The center of this "love" pattern falls in chapter 10, where Luke records the words that form "the heart of Jewish religion":[69] "You shall love [*agapaō*] the Lord your God, . . . and your neighbor as yourself" (v. 27; cf. Deut 6:5; Lev 19:18).

Jesus's parable clarifying the nature of a neighbor (Luke 10:30–35) provides another example of the contrast between those who are genuine and those who are superficial in their love (cf. chs. 7 and 11). When a priest and a Levite saw a man who had been left half-dead on the road, they passed by on the other side. But when a Samaritan saw the wounded man, he went and assisted him. In reply to Jesus's question, "Which of these three seems (to you) to become a neighbor of the one who fell to the robbers?" (10:36),[70] the lawyer says, "The one who did the *eleos* with him" (v. 37).[71] By hypothetical implication then, the wounded man would be expected to love as himself the one who became a neighbor to him—that is, the Samaritan who did *eleos* with him. This does not actually involve reciprocal *eleos*, but it does build a bond of love between neighbors on a foundation of *eleos*. Furthermore, those who love the Lord (v. 27) also engage with one who does *eleos* (cf. *ḥsd*) with them, for the Lord has promised to do *eleos* (cf. *ḥsd*) to the thousandth generation of those who love him and keep his commandments (Exod 20:6; Deut 7:9).

66. Jesus at his baptism and the son of the vineyard owner in the parable about wicked tenant-farmers are both referred to as "beloved" sons (3:22; 20:13).

67. In Luke 6:27, 32, and 35, Jesus sets a higher standard with respect to love. Jesus's disciples should love not only those who love them, but also their enemies. They should do good to those who hate them. In return, God will reward them. The love–hate (*agapaō–miseō*) dualism is also included in 16:13, this time in relation to choosing a master to serve. Cf. the dualism in Exod 20:5–6, where YHWH rewards those who "love" (*'hb/agapaō*) YHWH by doing *ḥsd/eleos* with them.

68. In Luke 7, those who love might previously have been considered "enemies" of God / God's people (vv. 5, 42, 47). In Luke 11, Jesus condemns the Pharisees for loving public recognition and honor (v. 43), instead of loving God (v. 42). In 11:42, Luke uses "the love [*agapē*] of God" where Matthew (23:23) has *eleos* ("mercy") and *pistis* ("faithfulness").

69. Omitting the verb, Luke adds part of Lev 19:18 to the first commandment. Marshall, *Gospel of Luke*, 443–44.

70. Crossan reflects on an inconsistency in the Luke 10 meanings of *plēsion* ("neighbour"): "he to whom love must be offered" (10:27, 29) and "he who offers mercy to another's need" (10:36) ("Parable and Example," 68).

71. Nolland concludes, "It is from the perspective of the ditch where one lies helpless and battered . . . that one should reflect upon the question 'who is my neighbor?'" (*Luke 9:21–18:34*, 592).

The sense of *eleos* in Luke 10:37 includes "mercy," to the extent that acts of compassion (cf. *splanchnizomai* in v. 33) are the manifestation of *eleos* here. However, the ideas communicated by "devotion," "responsibility," "solidarity," and "mutual aid" are closer to the sense of *ḥsd* evoked by *eleos* in this context. A neighbor is one who does *eleos* (cf. *ḥsd*) by taking responsibility for meeting another's need. But the one who does *eleos* with the wounded man in Jesus's parable is a Samaritan!

9.3.3. ḤSD *and the Covenant People*

In the Hebrew Bible, YHWH's *ḥsd* is primarily associated with members of YHWH's covenant community (cf. Deut 7:12), even to the extent that they are called *ḥsydym* (Ps 50:5 MT). In Luke's Gospel, *eleos* is also associated with God's covenant community, although Luke appears to be signaling a redefinition of that community by the selection of participants in events involving *eleos*. Individuals who share in God's *eleos* (cf. *ḥsd*), such as a priest and a Levite, do not demonstrate *eleos*.[72] Instead, Jesus's audience would be shocked to realize that the only agent of *eleos* in Jesus's parable is a Samaritan! But Luke's first audience would be even more bewildered to realize that the only other agent of *eleos* in this Gospel is God.[73] Considering this, Green's description of the Samaritan as participating in "the compassion and covenant faithfulness of God, who sees and responds with salvific care,"[74] seems startlingly accurate.

For Luke, membership in the covenant community (cf. the *ḥsydym*) is more about one's *practice* of *eleos* than one's ethnicity, "inherited status," or role.[75] Just as the Lord acts in accordance with his word concerning *eleos* (Luke 1),[76] so too the importance of action leading to eternal life is emphasized by the fourfold repetition of *poieō* ("do") in the "Good Samaritan" pericope:[77] "what must I do?" (10:25), "do this" (10:28), "the one who did the *eleos*" (10:37a), and "do likewise" (10:37b).[78] But the only human who "does" *eleos* in Luke's Gos-

72. Levi is compared to *ḥsyd* (Deut 33:8), and YHWH's priests are compared with *ḥsydym* (Ps 132:9; 2 Chr 6:41).

73. There are also four uses of *eleeō* ("have mercy") in Luke's Gospel: pleas for mercy to "Father Abraham" (16:24), "Jesus, Master" (17:13), and "Jesus, Son of David" (18:38, 39). But, in the LXX, *eleeō* is most frequently associated with *ḥnn*.

74. Green, *Gospel of Luke*, 431. Note the cognates of *splanchnon* in 1:78 and *splanchnizomai* in 10:33 (cf. 7:13; 15:20).

75. Cf. ibid., 23. As Nolland puts it, from the point of view of a desperate victim, "the practice of mercy . . . makes a passerby [even a Samaritan] into a neighbor" (*Luke 9:21–18:34*, 596, 598).

76. Green identifies words in Luke 1:54–55 that point back to God's nature and history with Israel (e.g., "servant," "Abraham") (*Gospel of Luke*, 105).

77. Bailey points out that both "rounds" of questions and answers in this pericope conclude "with a command to *do* something" (*Through Peasant Eyes*, 34, 55; emphasis original).

78. Cf. Green, *Gospel of Luke*, 425.

pel is someone whom an Israelite would probably have considered an outsider,[79] ineligible for covenant relationship—a Samaritan!

When the expert in the law asked Jesus, "Who is my neighbor?" (Luke 10:29), his motive was probably to find out where the limits of neighborliness lay—in particular, who could be excluded from the definition.[80] According to Lev 19:34, the resident alien (*gēr*) was included among those whom Israelites should love as themselves, but in Jewish usage, that did not include Samaritans or foreigners.[81] Nevertheless, the neighbor in Jesus's parable was a Samaritan who did *eleos*. In light of the command to "love your neighbor," then, Jesus implied that the wounded man in his parable must love someone who would have been considered his enemy (10:27; cf. 6:27, 35).[82] Kim Huat Tan explains how "Jesus' exposition of the Shema" in this context, which names "the Samaritan as the faithful son of the covenant," would be perceived as "a redefinition of the covenant community."[83]

The covenant associations of *ḥsd*, especially the covenant renewal connected with Exod 34:6–7, make its frequent LXX equivalent, *eleos*, an obvious choice for highlighting issues such as covenant community redefinition in Luke's Gospel. Of course, the Samaritan agent of *eleos* is not the only one who belongs in that redefined community. The selection of patients/perceivers and manifestations of *eleos* (including great things for a virgin girl, an elderly barren woman bearing a child, and reversals for the lowly and hungry) is consistent with Luke's emphasis on accepting outcasts and those otherwise rejected on the basis of human standards.[84] Luke's readers are left to ponder whether the legal expert who asked Jesus to define "neighbor" now also comprehends and accepts this shift.

9.4. Conclusions

An accumulation of intertextual evidence indicates that each of the six occurrences of *eleos* in Luke's Gospel denotes an instance of the category *ḤSD*.

79. Cf. Bailey, *Through Peasant Eyes*, 50.

80. Jewish ideas seem to limit the meaning of "neighbor" to the nation Israel, rather than all humankind. Geldenhuys, *Commentary on the Gospel of Luke*, 311, and Morris, *Luke*, 205–6.

81. Marshall also notes the Pharisaic tendency to exclude "ordinary people" and the Qumran community's exclusion of "the sons of darkness" (e.g., 1QS I, 10) (*Gospel of Luke*, 444).

82. Note Jesus's reasons to rebuke two disciples in Luke 9:52–55. Bock writes, "The idea of a good Samaritan was an oxymoron to a Jew" (*Luke*, 301). In terms of the social hierarchy (see Gourgues, "The Priest, the Levite, and the Samaritan," 713), Luke's audience would have expected "an Israelite layman" to come after the priest and Levite, and certainly not a Samaritan! Morris, *Luke*, 207.

83. Tan, "Community, Kingdom and Cross," 138.

84. Evans, *Saint Luke*, 95, 99, and Johnson, *Gospel of Luke*, 21–22, 24. Bovon explains that Luke's outlook on women, children, the neglected, poverty, and weakness would have been "startlingly novel" for his time (*Luke 1*, 10).

Despite the traditional emphasis on the Gentile authorship and readership of this Gospel, it is conceivable that the author understood and chose to evoke a Hebrew concept. Luke's emphasis on acceptance of outcasts may also indicate a need to address the place of Gentiles within a movement that originated amongst Jews.

The occurrences of *eleos* in the Luke 1 infancy narrative allude indirectly to the themes of Exod 34:6–7, especially *ḥsd.* Luke emphasizes the abundant, enduring, and covenantal nature of the Lord's *eleos*, now made [MANIFEST] by the coming of the Messiah. The construction involving *eleos* in the narrative frame of the "Good Samaritan" parable echoes a common grammatical construction involving *ḥsd.* Indeed, the compassionate activity of the Samaritan in that parable is a demonstration of *eleos* (cf. *ḥsd*). Luke contrasts those expected to practice/receive *eleos* (cf. *ḥsd*) with those who actually do.

Recognizing the category *ḤSD* in Luke's Gospel, I pay attention to the Lord's remembered promises, the importance of reciprocal relationships, and the redefined nature of the covenant people. In remembrance of his *eleos*, the Lord has sent the Messiah, keeping covenant promises made to Abraham and David ([JUSTIFICATION]/[REASON]; [MANIFESTATION]). Demonstrations of *eleos* recorded in the Luke 1 infancy narrative are continuous with the tradition of *ḥsd* extended to Israel throughout the generations ([DURATION]). The reciprocal nature of *ḥsd* is reflected in a grammatical construction involving *eleos* and implied by the "love your neighbor as yourself" command in the "Good Samaritan" parable frame. Unexpected human personnel involved in *eleos* experiences suggest a redefinition of covenant community. Thus, in Luke's Gospel, *eleos* means more than "mercy." It evokes notions associated with *ḥsd.*

CHAPTER 10

Eleos in Other New Testament Books: Characteristic of God, Reason for Hope

In addition to occurrences of *eleos* in Matthew's Gospel, Luke's Gospel, and the letters attributed to Paul, *eleos* occurs eight more times in the New Testament: Heb 4:16; Jas 2:13, 13; 3:17; 1 Pet 1:3; 2 John 3; and Jude 2, 21. In this chapter, I consider experiences/entities described by each of these remaining occurrences to see whether they resemble *ḥsd* experiences/entities.

There are few clues in the Hebrews, James, 2 John, and Jude contexts to determine whether the sense of *eleos* there is influenced by the extrabiblical Greek notion of pity stirred by affliction or the LXX use of the term to translate *ḥsd*. Consequently, I comment briefly on those occurrences, before focusing on 1 Pet 1:3–2:10, which has the strongest intertextual connections to *ḥsd* (§10.1). I consider engagement with the category ḤSD (§10.2) and the exegetical value of recognizing that engagement (§10.3), only in relation to 1 Peter. In that context, *eleos* is characteristic of God and a reason why Christians have living hope.

10.1. Intertextual Connections Between *Eleos* in Hebrews, James, First Peter, Second John, and Jude and *Ḥsd* in the Hebrew Bible

10.1.1. Hebrews 4:16; James 2:13, 13; 3:17; Second John 3; and Jude 2, 21

The association between *eleos* and "well-timed help [*boētheia*]" in Heb 4:16 resembles the script for ARTICLE_OF_TRANSACTION_ḤSD in which one party helps another party in his/her time of need. However, links between *eleos* and *boētheia* in the LXX are not strong.[1] Similarly, there seems to be only a loose connection between the combination of *eleos* and *alētheia* in 2 John 3 and the common word pair *ḥsd* and *ʾmt* (cf., e.g., Josh 2:14 LXX: *eleos kai alētheian*).

Eleos, *eirēnē* ("peace"; cf. Gal 6:16; §8.1), and *agapē* ("love") occur together in the Jude 2 benediction. *Eleos* and *agapē* occur again in Jude 21, where the

1. See Pss 61:8, 13; 88:20, 25; 107:5, 13 LXX.

author speaks of "waiting [*prosdechomai*] for the *eleos* of our Lord Jesus Christ [leading] to eternal life." In Ps 33:18–19 (32:18–19 LXX), the psalmist indicates that the eye of YHWH is on those who "wait/hope" (MT: *yḥl*) for YHWH's *ḥsd* (LXX: *eleos*) to deliver their *npš* from death and keep them alive in famine, although the LXX translation of *yḥl* in verse 18 is *elpizō*, not *prosdechomai*.[2]

Among this set of texts, however, the occurrences of *eleos* in James have the most resonance with the category *ḤSD*. The combination of *poieō* and *eleos* in Jas 2:13 resembles the expression "do *ḥsd*." It is difficult, however, to determine whether the judgment being *aneleos* ("without *eleos*") for one who does not "do *eleos*" (cf., e.g., Judg 8:35) also evokes *ḥsd*. The phrase *katakauchatai eleos kriseōs* ("*eleos* boasts/triumphs over judgment") in the same verse shares key words with Jer 9:22–23 LXX, where the grounds for "boasting" (*kauchaomai*) include knowing the Lord, who "does [*poieō*] *eleos* [MT: *ʿśh ḥsd*] and justice/judgment and righteousness on the earth."[3] *Mestē eleous* ("full of *eleos*") in Jas 3:17 may also reflect either *rb ḥsd* ("abounding in *ḥsd*") or *gdl ḥsd* ("great in *ḥsd*"), although *mestos* is not used in LXX translations of those constructions.

10.1.2. First Peter 1:3

10.1.2.1. Eleos *and* Eleeō *in First Peter 1:3–2:10*

The only occurrence of *eleos* in 1 Peter is located in the opening verse of a unit about the identity of God's people (1:3–2:10).[4] Scholars draw attention to the inclusio between *eleos* in 1:3 and two occurrences of *eleeō* in 2:10.[5] However, intertextual connections suggest that those related words evoke different Hebrew terms (*ḥsd* and *rḥm*, respectively).

Eleos occurs within the sentence that stretches from 1:3 to 1:9. The first three of those verses read:

1 Pet 1:3–5:

Εὐλογητὸς ὁ θεὸς καὶ πατὴρ τοῦ κυρίου ἡμῶν Ἰησοῦ Χριστοῦ ὁ κατὰ τὸ πολὺ αὐτοῦ ἔλεος	Blessed is the God and Father of our Lord Jesus Christ, who, according to his great *eleos*, has

2. Cf. *anamenō* in Sir 2:7.

3. In addition, Jas 3:14–15 includes the instruction not to "boast" (*katakauchaomai*) in earthly wisdom (cf. Jer 9:22–23 LXX) and v. 18 concerns the harvest of righteousness (cf. Prov 11:17–18).

4. Michaels, *1 Peter*, xxxvii.

5. E.g., Elliott, *I Peter*, 331.

ἀναγεννήσας ἡμᾶς εἰς ἐλπίδα ζῶσαν δι' ἀναστάσεως Ἰησοῦ Χριστοῦ ἐκ νεκρῶν, εἰς κληρονομίαν ἄφθαρτον καὶ ἀμίαντον καὶ ἀμάραντον τετηρημένην ἐν οὐρανοῖς εἰς ὑμᾶς τοὺς ἐν δυνάμει θεοῦ φρουρουμένους διὰ πίστεως εἰς σωτηρίαν ἑτοίμην ἀποκαλυφθῆναι ἐν καιρῷ ἐσχάτῳ	rebegotten us into a living hope through the resurrection of Jesus Christ from the dead, into an imperishable and undefiled and unfading inheritance, being kept in heaven for you, (the ones) [who are] being guarded by the power of God, through faith, into a salvation prepared to be revealed in [the] last time.[6]

It is "according to his great *eleos*" (*kata to poly autou eleos*) that God has rebegotten the elect into (1) a living hope, (2) an imperishable, undefiled, and unfading inheritance being kept in heaven for them, and (3) a salvation ready to be revealed in the last time.

A phrase identical to *kata to poly autou eleos* except for the inversion of the last two words occurs in Greek Sir 16:12, matching *krb rḥmyw* in Hebrew MS A. Thus, it is possible that *eleos* in 1 Pet 1:3 alludes to *rḥmym* ("compassion"), just as *eleeō* in 1 Pet 2:10 alludes to *rḥm* from Hos 1:6; 2:25 MT.[7] However, unlike that of 1 Pet 1:3–2:10, the context of Sir 16:12 emphasizes punishment of sin. Alternatively, *polyeleos* in LXX translations of YHWH's attribute formula renders *rb ḥsd* (e.g., Exod 34:6).[8] Furthermore, *krb ḥsdw* occurs in Ps 106:45[9] and Lam 3:32 MT, both times rendered *kata to plēthos tou eleous autou* in the LXX, a phrase slightly different from but related to that in 1 Pet 1:3. In each case, it is according to YHWH's abundant *ḥsd* that YHWH relents and gives his people to compassion / has compassion (*nḥm/rḥmym*; *rḥm*). The LXX translations of those texts do not include *eleeō*.[10] However, in Deut 30:1–5 LXX, which speaks of the gathering of those who are scattered as an outworking of the Lord's mercy/compassion, *eleeō* translates *rḥm*.[11]

Finally, in Isa 54:7–8, *ḥsd*, *rḥm* (LXX: *eleos* and *eleeō*, respectively), and the notion of gathering occur together. YHWH says to the barren one (vv. 1, 6), "For a short while I abandoned you, but with great compassion [*rḥmym*; LXX: *eleos*], I will gather [*qbṣ*; LXX: *eleeō*] you. In overflowing wrath I hid

6. The sense of salvation in 1 Peter is "a goal toward which the Christian progresses (2:2)." Davids, *First Epistle of Peter*, 20. Cf. Michaels, *1 Peter*, lxxi.

7. NA[28], 866–67, 872.

8. Also in Num 14:18; Joel 2:13; Jonah 4:2; Pss 86:15 (85:15 LXX); 103:8 (102:8 LXX); Neh 9:17 (2 Esd 19:17 LXX). Cf. Ps 86:5 (85:5 LXX).

9. Cf. vv. 46–47: "He gave them to compassion [*rḥmym*] . . . gather us from among the nations."

10. In Ps 105:45–46 LXX, *metamelomai* translates *nḥm* and *oiktirmos* translates *rḥmym*. In Lam 3:32 LXX, *oiktirō* translates *rḥm*.

11. Table A2.2 lists references for all LXX texts where *eleeō* renders *rḥm*.

my face from you for a while, but with everlasting *ḥsd* [LXX: *eleos*], I have compassion on [*rḥm*; LXX: *eleeō*] you" (vv. 7–8 MT).[12] This LXX translator kept the second phrase in each verse the same and varied the first. If, then, 1 Pet 1:3 and 2:10 are read in light of Isa 54:8, it could be said that God "had compassion on" (*eleeō*; cf. *rḥm*) the elect exiles (2:10), in accordance with God's great (abundant) *eleos* (cf. *ḥsd*; 1:3). The expectation is, therefore, that these exiles will eventually be gathered from all the peoples where they have been scattered (cf. Deut 30:1–5 [*qbṣ* in vv. 3, 4]; Isa 54:6–8).[13] But an inheritance kept in heaven (1 Pet 1:4) is the ultimate goal for this gathering of God's people.

Thus, intertextual and intratextual connections suggest that Peter utilizes the relevant inner-Greek resonances in a way similar to the LXX, *eleos* in 1 Pet 1:3 denotes an instance of the category *ḤSD*,[14] and the occurrences of *eleeō* in 1 Pet 2:10 denote instances of the category *RḤM*.

10.1.2.2. First Peter and Isaiah

The opening sentence of 1 Pet 1:3–2:10 can also be better interpreted in light of themes from elsewhere in that unit and from one of Peter's favorite sources, Isaiah. Nestle-Aland[28] lists fourteen verses quoted from Isaiah in 1 Peter,[15] along with additional allusions (Hays: **recurrence**).[16] From those verses and their literary contexts, three key themes provide encouragement for the "elect exiles" whom Peter addresses.

First, there are reassuring and affirming descriptions of believers / God's chosen people in a time to come. An *eklektos* ("chosen"), *entimos* ("precious") *lithos* ("stone") that the Lord is laying in Zion becomes *proskomma* ("a cause for stumbling") for those who do not trust but keeps from shame those who do (Isa 8:14;[17] 28:16[18] LXX; cf. 1 Pet 2:4, 6–8). Likewise, in a new act of deliver-

12. This is not the only time that *eleos* in the LXX renders *rḥmym* (v. 7), but it is not according to YHWH's *rḥmym* that YHWH has compassion (*rḥm*). YHWH has compassion (*rḥm*) according to YHWH's *ḥsd* (LXX: *eleos*; v. 8).

13. Cf. Isa 14:1, which reports that YHWH will "have compassion" (*rḥm*; LXX: *eleeō*) on Jacob. He will place them upon their land and the alien will join himself to them.

14. See also connections made with "mercy" in Hosea (Elliott, *I Peter*, 331), Ps 65:20 LXX (Michaels, *1 Peter*, 18), and regeneration resulting from God's "mercy or covenant-faithfulness" in Exod 20:6; 34:7 (Davids, *First Epistle of Peter*, 51). In each of the associated LXX texts, *eleos* renders *ḥsd*.

15. Isa 8:12–13 in 1 Pet 3:14–15; Isa 8:14 in 1 Pet 2:8; Isa 10:3 in 1 Pet 2:12; Isa 11:2 in 1 Pet 4:14; Isa 28:16 in 1 Pet 2:6; Isa 40:6, 8 in 1 Pet 1:24–25; Isa 43:21 in 1 Pet 2:9; Isa 53:4, 5, 12 in 1 Pet 2:24; Isa 53:6 in 1 Pet 2:25; Isa 53:9 in 1 Pet 2:22. NA[28], 857–60.

16. Isa 28:16 in 1 Pet 2:4; Isa 42:12 and 43:20 in 1 Pet 2:9. NA[28], 858–59.

17. In addition, in Isa 8:12–13 (cf. 1 Pet 3:14–15), readers are urged to fear not what "this people" fears (Aram or Assyria) but the Lord, who is holy. Watts, *Isaiah 1–33*, 120.

18. Following the woe oracle concerning Ephraim, the focus in Isa 28:1–29 shifts to the rulers in Jerusalem (v. 14), who boast that they have made a covenant with death and a lie their shelter. But

ance, the Lord will provide for those he calls *to genos mou to eklekton* ("my elect/chosen race") and *laon mou, hon periepoiēsamēn* ("my people, whom I obtained for my own possession"; Isa 43:20–21 LXX; cf. 1 Pet 2:9).[19]

More specifically, there is the prediction of good things for a remnant of people who remain faithful through a time of exile. The spirit of YHWH/God will rest on a shoot from the stump/root of Jesse (Isa 11:1–2; cf. those who are insulted; 1 Pet 4:14),[20] the nations will inquire of the root of Jesse on "that day" (MT), and the dispersed ones will be gathered (Isa 11:10–12 NRSV). Unlike the proud "crown/garland" (LXX: *stephanos*) of the drunkards of Ephraim and the fading/withering flower of its glorious beauty (LXX: hired ones, fallen flower, glory; Isa 28:1–4), YHWH / the Lord will be "the crown/garland of glory" (LXX: hope; *ho stephanos tēs elpidos*) and "the woven-wreath of beauty" (LXX: glory; *ho plakeis tēs doxēs*) (cf. the elders' reward in 1 Pet 5:4) for the remnant of YHWH / the Lord's people (Isa 28:5).[21]

There is also the example of one who has suffered righteously for the sake of others but then obtained glory (1 Pet 1:11; cf. 2:21). Peter expounds quotations from and allusions to the Isa 53 Servant Song (53:4–6, 9b, 12b; cf. 52:13) in 1 Pet 2:22–25[22] to describe Christ, his suffering, and his response.

In addition, 1 Pet 1:3–2:10 includes a quotation of the only text where *doxa* (LXX) renders *ḥsd* (MT) (Isa 40:6 quoted in 1 Pet 1:24). Themes from Hebrew Bible, LXX, and New Testament contexts of that text are relevant to 1 Pet 1:3–9. Peter cites Isa 40:6, 8 (40:6–8 LXX; 1 Pet 1:24–25)[23] as scriptural endorsement for his claim about an imperishable seed and his exhortation to love one another constantly (1:22–23):[24]

---

the Lord's response to the boast refers to a precious/honored cornerstone in Zion (v. 16). Oswalt, *Isaiah*, 317, 319.

19. Childs, *Isaiah*, 336–37, and Michaels, *1 Peter*, 107–9. There are also shared themes of "priesthood" (1 Pet 2:5, 9; cf. Exod 19:6 LXX [Davids, *First Epistle of Peter*, 90–92, and Elliott, *I Peter*, 437–38]; Isa 61:6), coming out of darkness / moving into light (1 Pet 2:9; cf. Isa 2:5; 9:1 LXX; 42:16; 49:9; 58:8, 10; 60:1), and on the other hand, a day of visitation (1 Pet 2:12; cf. Isa 10:3).

20. Elliott, *I Peter*, 782.

21. Cf. Davids, *First Epistle of Peter*, 182, and Elliott, *I Peter*, 834–35. Those who shepherd God's flock will receive a "crown/garland" (LXX: *stephanos*; a victor's wreath made of flowers) when the chief shepherd appears (1 Pet 5:4). Michaels, *1 Peter*, 287–88. Cf. Isa 61:3: the anointed one gives to those who mourn in Zion "a garland [NRSV; MT: *p'r*; LXX: *doxa*] instead of ashes."

22. NA[28], 860. Goldingay and Payne, *Isaiah 40–55*, 2:285.

23. Allusions to Isa 40:6–7 in Jas 1:10–11 "stress the transitoriness of the wealthy" (Davids, *First Epistle of Peter*, 79), but *doxa* (MT: *ḥsd*) is not mentioned there. In Ps 103:15–18 MT, the days of humanity are compared to the blossoming of a flower, which is no more when the wind passes over it. But YHWH's *ḥsd* is from everlasting to everlasting upon those who fear YHWH and keep YHWH's covenant.

24. "Constantly": BDAG, s.v. "ἐκτενῶς." The introductory *dioti* ("for") is probably in place of "for it is written." The early Christian movement could not survive in its hostile environment,

Isa 40:6b–8 MT:

כל הבשר חציר	All (the) flesh is grass,
וכל חסדו כציץ השדה	and all its *ḥsd* is as a flower of the field.
יבש חציר נבל ציץ	Grass dries and a flower fades/withers,
כי רוח יהוה נשבה בו	for the breath of YHWH blows on it;
אכן חציר העם	surely the people are grass.
יבש חציר נבל ציץ	Grass dries and a flower fades/withers,
ודבר אלהינו יקום לעולם	but the word of our God will stand forever.

Isa 40:6b–8 LXX:

Πᾶσα σὰρξ χόρτος,	All flesh is grass,
καὶ πᾶσα δόξα ἀνθρώπου ὡς ἄνθος χόρτου,	and all the *doxa* of humanity is as a flower of grass,
ἐξηράνθη ὁ χόρτος, καὶ τὸ ἄνθος ἐξέπεσεν,	the grass dries, and the flower falls,
τὸ δὲ ῥῆμα τοῦ θεοῦ ἡμῶν μένει εἰς τὸν αἰῶνα.	but the word of our God abides forever.

1 Pet 1:24–25a:

πᾶσα σὰρξ ὡς χόρτος	All flesh is as grass[25]
καὶ πᾶσα δόξα αὐτῆς ὡς ἄνθος χόρτου·	and all its *doxa* is as a flower of grass;
ἐξηράνθη ὁ χόρτος καὶ τὸ ἄνθος ἐξέπεσεν·	the grass dries and the flower falls;
τὸ δὲ ῥῆμα κυρίου μένει εἰς τὸν αἰῶνα.	but the word of the Lord abides forever.

Like the grass that dries up and the flower that fades/withers (LXX: "falls"), all flesh and all the *ḥsd* of all flesh (LXX: the *doxa* of humanity) do not endure for long in their original glorious form. They are evidently of "perishable" (*phthartos*) seed. But those in Peter's audience have been "begotten anew" (*anagennaō*) of "imperishable" (*aphthartos*) seed, through the living and

without the kind of devotion to one's group included in the ancient understanding of love. Elliott, *1 Peter*, 386–90.

25. Peter includes *hōs* before *chortos*, making the initial metaphor into a simile. Michaels, *1 Peter*, 77.

abiding "word" (*logos*) of God (1:23–24).[26] In contrast to the *doxa* of humanity, the "word" (*rhēma*) of God will stand/abide forever (1:25).[27]

Only Isa 40:7 MT indicates that YHWH's breath (*rwḥ*) is the cause of the drying and fading/withering in this analogy.[28] YHWH, the Creator of the heavenly host, also blows upon the princes and rulers of the earth. They dry up and are carried off, but YHWH strengthens the weary and powerless who wait for him (40:22–31; cf. 41:16). This suggests that the imagery in 40:6–8 is concerned with the impermanence of political leaders and their perceived power.[29] On the other hand, the "elect exiles" in Peter's audience might be included among the powerless who are strengthened.

Isaiah 40:9–10 records the commissioning of herald/s of good news (LXX: repeated use of *ho euangelizomenos*) to Jerusalem and the cities of Judah. YHWH comes with strength and a reward. Interpreting verse 8 in light of this news, as well as the intertextual link between the "judgment" in verses 6b–8a and the promised transformation of a proud crown/garland's "fading/withering" flower ("in that day") in 28:3–6, one might assume that the word (LXX: *rhēma*) of God that abides forever is one of salvation after judgment: "Isaiah's proclamation of the coming new age."[30]

Peter gives clues that the words proclaimed in Isaiah are "fulfilled in the gospel proclaimed . . . in Asia Minor."[31] Whether this is Peter's deliberate choice or based on different manuscripts, the use of "the word of the Lord" (1 Pet 1:25a) instead of "the word of our God" (Isa 40:8) allows for application to God or Jesus Christ.[32] Peter's commentary (1 Pet 1:25b) indicates that "this word [*rhēma*]" is "the good news" (*to euangelisthen*) preached to the elect

26. The only LXX occurrences of *phthartos* or *aphthartos* are in 2 Macc 7:16; Wis 9:15; 12:1; 14:8; 18:4; and Isa 54:17. In Isa 54:17 LXX, *pan skeuos phtharton* ("every perishable/corruptible vessel/thing") roughly corresponds to the Hebrew *kl kly ywṣr* ("Every vessel/weapon that is formed").

27. Jobes suggests that Peter distinguished "the external preaching of God's word" (*rhēma*; 1:25) from "the internal effect of regeneration" in believers of the word (*logos*; 1:23) ("Got Milk?," 3).

28. YHWH used the image of the hot, dry, and persistent "sirocco or khamsin" wind to warn the people of Judah about a "threatened Babylonian devastation" (e.g., Jer 4:11–12), but the prophet now laments because the threat was carried out. Goldingay, *Message of Isaiah 40–55*, 25.

29. Cf. Blenkinsopp, *Isaiah 40–55*, 193, and Watts, *Isaiah 34–66*, 624.

30. Childs, *Isaiah*, 300. *To sōtērion tou theou* ("the salvation of God") is inserted in parallel with *doxa* in Isa 40:5 LXX (cf. 12:2; 60–62). Brockington highlights the connection between "this concern for salvation" and the use of *doxa* or *doxazō* ("Greek Translator of Isaiah," 32). The offer of "comfort, 'good news,' and the prospect of salvation" to people exiled and oppressed in Babylon (Deutero-Isaiah) is particularly relevant to the situation addressed in 1 Peter. Elliott, *I Peter*, 390.

31. Schreiner, *1, 2 Peter, Jude*, 97.

32. Michaels, *1 Peter*, 78–79.

exiles (cf. v. 12),[33] and he emphasizes the Greek pronoun forms for "you."[34] As Ramsey Michaels explains, concluding the section with *eis hymas*, the same phrase used in 1 Pet 1:4, emphasizes that "everything that God planned from the beginning, everything that he accomplished through the death and resurrection of Jesus Christ, everything still waiting to be revealed, is for the sake of the Christians in Asia Minor who read Peter's words."[35]

Having identified relevant themes from Isaiah and elsewhere in 1 Pet 1:3–2:10, I now highlight the same themes in 1 Pet 1:3–9: Peter blesses the God and Father of the Lord Jesus Christ, who, according to his great (abundant) *eleos*, has caused the "elect" (*eklektos*; 1:1; cf. Isa 28:16; 43:20 LXX) exiles to be "rebegotten" (*anagennaō*; 1:3; cf. v. 23) into a living "hope" (*elpis*; 1:3; cf. v. 21; Isa 28:4 LXX), an "imperishable" (*aphthartos*; 1:4; cf. v. 23), undefiled, and "unfading" (*amarantos*; 1:4; cf. v. 24 [*xērainō/ekpiptō*]; Isa 40:7 LXX) inheritance, and a "salvation" (*sōtēria*) yet to be revealed (1:5, 9; cf. 2:2; Isa 40:5 LXX [*sōtērios*]). The tested genuineness of their faith is more "precious" (*polytimos*; 1:7; cf. *entimos* in Isa 43:4 LXX) than gold that "perishes" (*apollymi*; 1:7; cf. *phthartos* in vv. 18, 23),[36] and it results in praise, glory (*doxa*/*doxazō*; 1:7–8; cf. v. 24; Isa 40:5–6; 43:4; 52:13 LXX), and "honor" (*timē*; cf. 2:7; Isa 11:1–2, 10 LXX; not shame [Isa 28:16 LXX]). This sentence is evidently meant to be interpreted in light of connections within the letter and with Isaiah.

10.1.2.3. First Peter 1:3–2:10 and Ḥsd

Finally, I consider whether the concept corresponding to *ḥesed* could have been within Peter's frame of reference when he included *ho kata to poly autou eleos* in 1 Pet 1:3 and/or the quotation from Isa 40:6–8 in 1 Pet 1:24–25. For the apostle Peter, this matter is complex.[37] He was an uneducated Galilean (Matt

33. Ibid., 79. Peter's interpretation resembles the "this is that" style of *pesher* interpretation. Longenecker, *Biblical Exegesis in the Apostolic Period*, 84, and Schutter, *Hermeneutic and Composition*, 126–27. The things proclaimed to Peter's audience (1:12) are discussed in connection with inquiries about the sufferings of Christ and the glories that follow (cf. vv. 10–11). This suggests that the good news to them is associated with the expectation that demonstrating solidarity with Christ in his suffering will also result in vindication and glories (cf. vv. 6–9). Elliott, *I Peter*, 448.

34. After the initial "your souls" (v. 22a), there is no other occurrence of *su* ("you") in 1:22–25 until the last word of the chapter. Having built a sense of anticipation, Peter declares that "this word" is the gospel that was preached "to you" (*eis hymas*; v. 25b). Michaels, *1 Peter*, 79–80.

35. Ibid., 79.

36. Cf. Isa 52:3.

37. I adopt here the traditional view on authorship. See Michaels, *1 Peter*, lxvi–lxvii. Contra, Elliott, *I Peter*, 124–25, and Senior, "1 Peter," 4–6, who conclude that 1 Peter is probably a pseudonymous letter. Davids concludes, on the basis of 5:12, that this letter was written in the style of Silvanus but attributed to Peter (*First Epistle of Peter*, 6–7).

4:18; Acts 4:13), the language in 1 Peter is strongly influenced by the LXX,[38] and some scholars find no evidence that the author "was translating from a Hebrew original."[39] Then again, the Hebrew *Vorlage* may have been accessible to him,[40] he was probably exposed to the Hebrew language during worship times and interactions as a disciple of Jesus,[41] and the concept corresponding to *ḥesed* was prominent in the Jewish heritage.

Given Peter's dependence on Isaiah LXX, with its fluid translation of terms, both *eleos* and *doxa* could denote instances of the category ḤSD in 1 Pet 1:1–2:10.[42] Indeed, Peter may have quoted the only LXX verse where *doxa* renders *ḥsd* to remind his audience of the sad outcomes for those in the past whose mutuality, solidarity, and loyalty (cf. 1:22) have been fleeting in the face of trials and temptations (Isa 40:6 LXX; cf. 28:1–4). On the other hand, the liberal use of *doxa* and *doxazō* in Isaiah LXX[43] and elsewhere in this letter[44] may indicate that the sense of *doxa* in 1 Peter merely reflects the theme of glory in Isaiah LXX. As the connection between *doxa* in 1 Pet 1:24 and *ḥsd* is unique and uncharacteristic, I analyze *eleos* in verse 3 as denoting an instance of the category ḤSD (§10.2) and refer to *doxa* in verse 24 as an interpretive comparison, but do not generalize to Peter's other uses of *doxa*.

38. Achtemeier, *1 Peter*, 6–7.

39. So Bigg, *Critical and Exegetical Commentary*, 3. Achtemeier does not think that the Semiticisms indicate "a direct dependence . . . on Hebrew thought-forms" (*1 Peter*, 4).

40. Greenspoon, "Old Testament Versions, Ancient," 754. *Hoti agapē kalyptei plēthos hamartiōn* ("for love covers a multitude of sins"; 1 Pet 4:8) is closer to the MT *wʿl kl pšʿym tksh ʾhbh* ("and love covers over all transgressions") than is the equivalent clause in Prov 10:12b LXX, although the Hebrew form may have existed as "a detached maxim." Elliott, *I Peter*, 13, 751.

41. In the synagogue, each passage of Scripture was meant to be read in Hebrew and then interpreted orally. Chilton, "Targums," 800. Abegg refers to evidence supporting the likelihood that Jesus "spoke Hebrew in his interactions with the scribes, Pharisees and Sadducees" ("Hebrew Language," 462).

42. In Isaiah LXX, *eleos* occurs twelve times, translating *ḥsd* four times (16:5; 54:8, 10; 63:7) and *rḥmym* ("compassion") three times (47:6; 54:7; 63:7). *Eleos* also renders *yšʿ*, *ṣdqh*, *rṣwn*, *mʿh*, and a pronominal suffix, once each. *Doxa* occurs sixty-eight** times, translating *kbwd/kbd* ("glory") thirty-one** times (often describing the presence or splendor of God, or the honor of people), and *tpʾrt/tpʾrh* ("splendor") eleven** times. *Doxa* also renders *hdr* four times (2:10, 19, 21; 53:2), *gʾwn/gʾwt* three times (14:11; 24:14; 26:10), the verb *pʾr* twice (60:21; 61:3), the noun *pʾr* twice (3:20; 61:3), *ʿz* twice (12:2; 45:24), and several other Hebrew words (including *ḥsd*) once each. It is equivalent to a phrase in 11:3 and has no/uncertain matches in 22:22 and 30:18.

43. In Isaiah LXX, *doxa* is even used in place of Hebrew words that are translated by different terms elsewhere (e.g., *pʾr* [NRSV: "garland"] in 61:3).

44. *Doxa*: 1 Pet 1:7, 11, 21; 4:11, 13, 14; 5:1, 4, 10. *Doxazō*: 1 Pet 1:8; 2:12; 4:11, 16. Elliott draws attention to the high proportion of "references to glory and glorification" in 1 Peter (*I Peter*, 470). In this letter, *doxa* is used to refer to a gift, time/period, attribute, spirit, symbol, or experience of glory/honor (e.g., 1:21; 5:4), sometimes revealed/bestowed (e.g., 5:1) after a period of trial/suffering (e.g., 1:11; 5:10) and at the revelation of Jesus Christ (e.g., 1:7). Cf. Michaels, *1 Peter*, 31, 69–70.

10.2. The Category ḤSD in First Peter 1:3–2:10

Engagement with the category ḤSD in 1 Pet 1:3–2:10 is primarily by way of an echo of *krb ḥsdw* in 1:3. Therefore, rather than comparing my analysis of elements of the category ḤSD associated with 1 Pet 1:3 with one specific Hebrew Bible text, I consider how this echo resembles and develops the tradition associated with YHWH's abundant *ḥsd*. I make particular reference to the attribute formula (first recorded in Exod 34:6) and the Hebrew Bible texts that include *krb ḥsdw* (Ps 106:45; Lam 3:32).

10.2.1. ḤSD *in First Peter 1:3*

Peter (perceiver) opens the first main section (1 Pet 1:3–2:10) of his letter to the elect exiles (communication) by blessing ([PERCEIVER'S_RESPONSE]) the God and Father of "our" Lord Jesus Christ ([POSSESSOR]), the one who rebegot (*anagennaō*; [MANIFESTATION]) "us" (presumably Peter and the elect exiles of Asia Minor) according to his abundant ([QUANTITY]) *eleos* (cf. *ḥsd*; [CHARACTERISTIC]; 1:3). Thus, *eleos* is part of an Adverbial Prepositional Phrase in a Relative Verbal Clause, modifying the verb *anagennaō*. The relationship is between God and God's "elect people" (*genos eklekton*; cf. 2:9). The new birth is into a living hope, an imperishable, undefiled, and unfading inheritance, and a salvation prepared to be revealed in the last time ([OUTCOMES]). The "newly begotten ones" (*artigennētos*) should "grow up" into this salvation (outcome; 2:2).[45] The recommended [RESPONSE] is rejoicing (1:6).[46] The imperishable inheritance is contrasted with perishable things (gold, silver, seed, the glory of all flesh; 1:18, 23–24).

10.2.2. General Observations

YHWH, the God and Father of "our" Lord Jesus Christ, is blessed ([PERCEIVER'S_RESPONSE]), for he alone is the [POSSESSOR] of abundant ([QUANTITY]) *ḥsd* or *eleos* ([CHARACTERISTIC]). The Construct/Adjectival description (*rb ḥsd*) in the attribute formula becomes a Construct/Adverbial Phrase[47] when the [CHARACTERISTIC] becomes the basis for YHWH's expected or realized intervention and for new transformations that should lead to rejoicing ([RESPONSE]).

45. Note the familiar connection between salvation (1:5, 9, 10) and glory (1:7, 11, 21, 24) in 1 Pet 1:3–2:10 (cf. Isaiah).

46. See also 1:22: "Love one another constantly."

47. *Krb ḥsdw / kata to plēthos tou eleous autou; kata to poly autou eleos.*

10.2.2.1. Renewal Leading to Hope and Salvation

YHWH / the Lord's abundant *ḥsd* is or will be [MANIFESTED] in forgiveness (in the context of the covenant renewal; Exod 34:1, 6–7), relenting (concerning his people who are held captive; Ps 106:45), and compassion (toward those who are rejected and grieved; Lam 3:31–32). Subsequent requests include YHWH's ongoing presence (Exod 34:9), salvation, gathering from the nations (Ps 106:47), and judging a cause (Lam 3:58–59; outcomes). Through the resurrection of Jesus Christ, God's abundant *eleos* is [MANIFESTED] by begetting anew God's elect exiles into a living hope, an imperishable, undefiled, and unfading inheritance, and a salvation prepared to be revealed in the last time ([OUTCOMES]; 1 Pet 1:3–5). The newly begotten ones are to long for pure spiritual milk, so that they may grow up into salvation (outcome; 1 Pet 2:1–2). Clearly, YHWH provides opportunities for renewed relationship (cf. Lam 3:31; 1 Pet 2:25).

10.2.2.2. The Perishable and the Imperishable

Peter contrasts the abundant *eleos* of the God who begets anew of imperishable seed and into an imperishable inheritance ([OUTCOME]) with all the *doxa* of all flesh, which perishes ([DURATION]; [QUALITY]) like a flower of the grass that falls (cf. gold, silver, seed; 1 Pet 1:18, 23–24; [OUTCOME]).

10.3. Exegetical Value of Recognizing Engagement with the Category ḤSD in First Peter 1:3–2:10

Three factors associated with *ḥsd* contribute to the interpretation of 1 Pet 1:3–2:10: (1) God's motivation for helpful action, (2) God's relationship with God's chosen people, and (3) the expectation of enduring commitment/solidarity.

10.3.1. **ḤSD** *and God's Motivation*

In the Hebrew Bible, YHWH's characteristic *ḥsd* is a basis for YHWH's helpful action toward his people (e.g., redemption; Exod 15:13).[48] Therefore, when Israelites need help, they appeal to YHWH's disposition to act "according to *ḥsd*" (e.g., Neh 13:22).[49] In particular, the abundance of YHWH's *ḥsd* (LXX: *eleos*)

48. Cf. *bḥsd* (Pss 21:8; 52:10 MT); *brb ḥsdk* (Pss 5:8; 69:14 MT); *bḥsdk* (Exod 15:13; Pss 13:6; 31:8, 17; 143:12 MT).

49. Cf. *krb ḥsdw* ("according to the abundance of his *ḥsd*"; Ps 106:45; Lam 3:32 MT); *kḥsdk / kgdl ḥsdk* ("according to your [great] *ḥsd*"; Num 14:19; Pss 25:7; 51:3; 109:26; 119:88, 124, 149, 159

is the basis for YHWH showing compassion (*krb ḥsdw*; Ps 106:45–47; Lam 3:32). YHWH's compassion was withheld (neg. *rḥm*; LXX: *oiktirō*) because of the people's disobedience (Isa 27:11). But it will eventually be restored (*rḥm*; LXX: *eleeō*; *hileōs*), and they will be gathered, on account of YHWH's everlasting *ḥsd* (LXX: *eleos*), which is more immovable than the mountains (Isa 54:7–10).[50] It is fitting, therefore, that God's *eleos* (cf. *ḥsd*) is also the basis/motivation for the compassion now shown (*eleeō*) to the elect exiles of Asia Minor (1 Pet 1:3; 2:10; Hays: **satisfying** use of related terms).

Nevertheless, there is a more explicit manifestation of the abundant *eleos* of God described in 1 Pet 1:3–2:10: regeneration (1:3–9; cf. v. 23).[51] First Peter 1:3 and Titus 3:5 present biblical examples of God's *eleos* demonstrated through "regeneration" (*anagennaō*; *palingenesia*).[52] The choice of terms in these examples implies that the work of regeneration is consistent with the tradition of God's covenant loyalty throughout salvation history.[53]

As for loyalty to a particular covenant, the presence of *poly . . . eleos* in 1 Pet 1:3 suggests association with the Sinai covenant, as "abundant" *ḥsd* (LXX: *polyeleos*) is included in YHWH's attribute formula (cf., e.g., Exod 34:6; Num 14:18; Ps 103:8). But terms in 1 Pet 1:1–2:10 also resemble language and imagery connected with the Isaianic servant-messiah figure, suggesting that this loyalty pertains to promises concerning Israel and an anointed leader called for Israel's sake (cf. Isa 45:1, 4). *Genos eklekton* ("chosen race/people") in 1 Pet 2:9 alludes to *to genos mou to eklekton* ("my chosen race/people") in Isa 43:20. Earlier in Isa 43, the Lord refers to the Lord's people as *ho pais*, *hon exelexamēn* ("the servant whom I chose"; v. 10). The servant is both Jacob/Israel, the offspring of Abraham (Isa 41:8–9; 44:1, 21; 45:4; 49:3), and one who carries out the Lord's initiative regarding *diathēkēn genous* ("a covenant [to] a race/people"; Isa 42:6;

[MT references]). There is also an appeal based on a demonstration of human *ḥsd* in Gen 21:23 (*kḥsd*).

50. Isaiah 54:10 indicates that, while the mountains may withdraw and the hills sway, YHWH's *ḥsd* (LXX: *eleos*) will not withdraw from the barren one, and his covenant of peace will not sway. Isaiah 55 opens with a call to respond to the restorative work of YHWH (Goldingay, *Message of Isaiah 40–55*, 23) and the promise of an everlasting covenant (cf. the faithful *ḥsdym* [LXX: *hosia*] of David; v. 3). The speaker calls for the wicked/unrighteous one to return to YHWH, who will "have compassion" (*rḥm*; LXX: *eleeō*) on him (v. 7). But this chapter and the whole of Deutero-Isaiah close with a description of the mountains and hills "bursting forth," as they have been commanded to do when YHWH has compassion (55:12; cf. 49:13).

51. See Bultmann, "ἔλεος, ἐλεέω," 2:477–78.

52. Titus 3:5 reads, "According to his own *eleos* through the washing of *palingenesia* and renewing of the Holy Spirit. . . ." Cf. Michaels, *1 Peter*, 18.

53. E.g., *ho kata to poly autou eleos . . . eis sōtērian* (1 Pet 1:3–5); *kata to autou eleos esōsen hēmas* (Titus 3:5); cf. *sōson me kata to eleos sou* (Ps 108:26 LXX).

49:6 [LXX only]).[54] In addition, Peter refers to a chosen cornerstone laid in Zion (1 Pet 2:4, 6; cf. Isa 28:16), which the Targum of Isaiah interprets as a future king.[55] Indeed, the prophet had already predicted that one in the tent of David would sit in "faithfulness" (*ʾmt*) on a throne established in *ḥsd* (LXX: *eleos*; Isa 16:5; cf. 9:6–7).[56] Thus, God regenerating (*anagennaō*) believers, according to / motivated by his abundant *eleos*, and through the resurrection of Jesus the Messiah, is probably also an outworking of the everlasting covenant of peace, which brings together promises made to the Israelites who "come" and the faithful *ḥsdym* of David (Isa 54:10; 55:3).

10.3.2. ḤSD *and God's People*

In 1 Pet 1:3, 23, and only here within the New Testament, *anagennaō* is used to describe God the Father's action as he "begot anew" (manifestation) the elect exiles, according to God's abundant *eleos*. Unlike the *doxa* of all flesh (evidently of perishable seed), which is compared to a flower that perishes, God has begotten these believers anew from imperishable seed (vv. 23–24). *Anagennaō* never occurs in the LXX, as rebegetting is a uniquely New Testament experience, but *gennaō* ("beget") is common. Although *gennaō* is not associated with LXX manifestations of *eleos* (MT: *ḥsd*), an intriguing use of the term occurs in the Song of Moses in Deut 32: "You were unmindful of the Rock [LXX: *theos*] [who] begot [LXX: *gennaō*] you;[57] you forgot the God who brought you forth" (v. 18 MT).[58] God begot Israel as a race/people, and God begot anew these elect exiles as a race/people (1 Pet 1:3, 23; 2:9).[59] This also fits with the language appropriated from Hos 2:25 LXX (cf. 1:6, 9; 2:1) to communicate the reconstitution of a "people" (*laos*; 1 Pet 2:10).[60] Yet Gentile Christians probably comprise the majority of those to whom Peter writes.[61]

54. Isaiah 42:6–7 also mentions a light of/to the nations (cf. 49:6) that will bring out from prison those who sit in darkness, and 1 Pet 2:9 features one who calls the *genos eklekton* out of darkness and into light.

55. Excerpt from Targum Jonathan Isa 28:16: *mmny bṣywn mlk mlk tqyp gybr wʾymtn* ("I am about to appoint in Zion a king, a strong king, powerful and terrible"; trans. Childs, *Isaiah*, 208).

56. Targum Jonathan Isa 16:5 has *bkyn mšyḥʾ dyśrʾl* ("*the* throne *of the Messiah of Israel*"; trans. Chilton, *Isaiah Targum*, 35; emphasis original).

57. *Gennaō* often refers to the father's role in a child's birth. Cf. Grudem, *First Epistle of Peter*, 55. "Unmindful": NRSV.

58. Note the male and female imagery here.

59. Trebilco notes that Jews in Asia Minor also thought that they belonged to "a 'people' or a 'race'" ("Jewish Communities," 564).

60. Peter applies words that describe the reconstitution of Israel as God's people (Hos 2:23 [2:25 MT/LXX]) to the Christian community (1 Pet 2:10). Achtemeier, *1 Peter*, 70.

61. Elliott, *I Peter*, 89, 96, and Michaels, *1 Peter*, xlvi. Cf. Achtemeier, *1 Peter*, 51; Davids, *First Epistle of Peter*, 8; Donelson, *I and II Peter and Jude*, 9.

Using language previously associated with God's covenant people (e.g., "elect" [1:1],[62] "You shall be holy" [1:16],[63] "aliens and sojourners/exiles" [2:11],[64] and "Babylon" [5:13]),[65] Peter addresses Christians, including those from a Gentile background, "as if they were Israel."[66] With respect to the title "elect," John Elliott explains that, through Israel's history, appeal to divine election "is frequently directed to a minority people or a remnant experiencing spatial dislocation and social alienation."[67] In the case of those whom Peter addresses, the "elect exiles" (*eklektos*; 1:1) have become God's "elect" people (*eklektos*; 2:9) by following the "elect" stone (*eklektos*; 2:6). In other words, a spatially dislocated and socially alienated group of Christians from the dispersion in Asia Minor (cf. Deut 30:1–5) is privileged to be among the remnant of God's special and honored people[68] who, through the redeeming work of Jesus Christ, will inherit that which was promised "to their ancestors in faith."[69]

It is also appropriate, therefore, that the elect exiles have been regenerated according to God's abundant *eleos* (cf. *ḥsd*), another term associated with keeping promises to God's covenant people, Israel. Indeed, Marshall highlights the possible ambiguity of the Greek word translated "mercy" (i.e., *eleos*). It is normally used for undeserved compassion, but in 1 Pet 1:3, it refers more to "God's acting in accordance with his character and his [covenant] promises." As in 2:10, Peter probably refers to the admission of Gentiles into "the covenant made centuries earlier with Israel and now renewed in Jesus."[70] Gentile believers have now "received compassion/mercy" (*eleeō*; 2:10; cf. *rḥm*) along with Jewish believers, because of God's abundant *eleos* (cf. *ḥsd*). They are among the reconstituted people of God, the people of *ḥsd*.

10.3.3. **ḤSD** *and Enduring Commitment*

Peter also explains what it means to be the reconstituted people of God in times of trial.[71] In a society where attaining *doxa* is a primary ethical objective,[72]

62. Cf., e.g., Isa 43:20–21.

63. "You shall be holy for I am holy" (Lev 11:44, 45; 19:2; cf. 20:7, 26 [variations]). Achtemeier, *1 Peter*, 70.

64. Cf. Gen 23:4; Ps 38:13 LXX. Schreiner, *1, 2 Peter, Jude*, 40.

65. Michaels, *1 Peter*, xlv. Peter applies to Christian experience the powerful metaphors of the Babylonian exile and resulting diaspora. They express the longing for "final peace" and the need to keep distant from the surrounding culture. Senior, "1 Peter," 9–10. Schreiner thinks that "Babylon" in 5:13 refers to Rome (*1, 2 Peter, Jude*, 37).

66. McKnight, *1 Peter*, 24. Cf. Achtemeier, *1 Peter*, 69–72, and Marshall, *1 Peter*, 26.

67. Elliott, *I Peter*, 445.

68. Ibid., 442, 446–49.

69. Senior, "1 Peter," 14.

70. Marshall, *1 Peter*, 34n.

71. See Schreiner, *1, 2 Peter, Jude*, 47.

72. Martin, *Metaphor and Composition*, 110; referring to Cicero, *De officiis* 2.9–11 (Miller, LCL).

the opposite is the current reality for the Christians,[73] who suffer harassment (taunts/insults; *sneidizō* in 1 Pet 4:14; cf. *sneidismos* in Lam 3:30, 61 LXX) and hostility, and are now considered "strangers" within their local communities.[74] Therefore, Peter presents an eschatological resolution:[75] After a short time of grief/suffering, Christ's *doxa* will be revealed, and they will obtain salvation (1 Pet 1:5–9; 4:13–14; 5:1, 4–6, 10).[76]

When compared to *doxa* in Christ (1 Pet 1:7; 5:10), the portrayal of the perishing *doxa* of all flesh (1:24) is not inspiring. Scholars provide a range of suggestions for what the simile adapted from Isa 40:6–8 and cited in 1 Pet 1:24–25 means for Christians in Asia Minor at the time of Peter's writing.[77] But the intertextual connection with Isa 40:22–26 suggests that the key issue is the perceived power of political leaders, which is impermanent and incomparable to that of the Holy One who created the heavenly host (cf. Isa 54:17 LXX).[78] This implies "good news" for the harassed members of Peter's audience.[79]

In contrast to the perishable outcomes typical of human *doxa*,[80] those rebegotten of imperishable seed through God's word and according to God's abundant *eleos* (1 Pet 1:3, 23; cf. *ḥsd*) are called to God's eternal *doxa* (5:10). Instead of yielding to the attractive but fragile "splendor of pagan society,"[81] the "elect exiles" of Pontus, Galatia, Cappadocia, Asia, and Bithynia could follow the example of the faithful remnant to whom YHWH of hosts promised a glorious crown/garland "in that day" (Isa 28:5; cf. 1 Pet 5:4).

In the meantime, Peter encourages the elect exiles to "love one another constantly" (1 Pet 1:22; cf. 4:8),[82] to live faithfully in their commitment to Jesus Christ (1:13–21; 2:4–5), and to "endure/wait/hope" (*hypomenō*; 2:20). Like the

73. Martin, *Metaphor and Composition*, 111.

74. Elliott, *I Peter*, 97–103. The values of Christians were misunderstood and resented, but their suffering was probably "local and sporadic harassment," rather than "official state persecution." Senior, "1 Peter," 7. The tension/conflict may have been with "society at large" (Elliott, *I Peter*, 103) or with local Jewish communities that presented alternative interpretations of the tradition (Trebilco, "Jewish Communities," 569).

75. Martin, *Metaphor and Composition*, 112.

76. Cf. Isa 40:5 LXX; 54:4; Lam 3:26, 31–33.

77. E.g., the strong nations of the world—the persecutors of Peter's day, "who seemed invincible but whose glory was short-lived" (Schreiner, *1, 2 Peter, Jude*, 96), or "the [transitory] glitter, pomp, and power of the Roman culture" (Achtemeier, *1 Peter*, 142).

78. Goldingay, *Message of Isaiah 40–55*, 58–59.

79. Elliott, *I Peter*, 97–103.

80. The fleeting, futile nature of human *doxa* is also raised in Ps 49:16–17 (48:17–18 LXX); Hos 9:11; Isa 10:12; 14:11; 16:14; 17:4; 21:16; 28:1, 4; Jer 2:11; 48:18 (31:18 LXX); Dan 4:29–32.

81. Michaels, *1 Peter*, 78. Cf. the fading/falling flower associated with glory for the drunkards / hired workers of Ephraim (Isa 28:1–4).

82. Bonds between God's reborn "children" (1:14) resemble those of "family and kinship loyalties." Elliott, *I Peter*, 107, 114.

implied author of Lam 3,[83] who thinks his "hope" (MT: *twḥlt*; LXX: *elpis*; v. 18) from YHWH is gone but then recalls his reason to "endure/wait/hope" (MT: *yḥl*; LXX: *hypomenō*)—YHWH's endless *ḥsd* and compassions (vv. 21–22, cf. 25–26)—these believers have reason for "hope" (*elpis*; 1 Pet 3:15; cf. Isa 28:5 LXX),[84] because of God's *polyeleos* (cf. *rb ḥsd*). The strength of their own mutuality/solidarity with God's people and devotion to God may waver, but they have been rebegotten into a living "hope" (*elpis*) through the resurrection of Jesus Christ from the dead (1 Pet 1:3, 21), according to God's abundant *eleos* (cf. *ḥsd*), which evidently endures.

10.4. Conclusions

Of the occurrences of *eleos* in Hebrews, James, 1 Peter, 2 John, and Jude, those in James and 1 Peter behave most like they denote instances of the category *ḤSD*. James includes the phrases "one who has done no *eleos*" (2:13; cf. "do *ḥsd*"), "*eleos* boasts/triumphs over judgment" (2:13; cf. Jer 9:22–23 LXX), and "full of *eleos*" (3:17; cf. *rb ḥsd* or *gdl ḥsd*).

In 1 Peter, *eleos* (1:3) is usually translated "mercy" and *eleeō* (2:10) is usually translated "have mercy," but intertextual connections suggest that these terms evoke *ḥsd* and its [MANIFESTATION] *rḥm*, respectively (cf. Isa 54:7–8). Consistent with the scriptural tradition, God's abundant *eleos* (cf. *ḥsd*) is both characteristic of God and reason for hope. In 1:3–9, Peter (perceiver) blesses ([PERCEIVER'S_RESPONSE]) the God and Father of the Lord Jesus Christ ([POSSESSOR]), who rebegot ([MANIFESTATION]) the "elect exiles" (cf. 2:9) into a living hope, an imperishable inheritance, and salvation ([OUTCOMES]), through the resurrection of Jesus Christ and according to his abundant ([QUANTITY]) *eleos* ([CHARACTERISTIC]). In contrast to perishable *doxa*, those rebegotten of the imperishable seed through God's word "grow up" into salvation (outcomes; 1:23–24; 2:2).

The following issues associated with the category *ḤSD* serve Peter's purpose and enhance my reading of 1 Pet 1:3–2:10: In the scriptural tradition, God has relationship with God's chosen people, and they appeal to God on the basis of God's *ḥsd* (cf. *eleos*; motivation) when help is required. There is also an expectation of enduring commitment/solidarity amongst God's people. Likewise, it is according to God's enduring *eleos* (cf. *ḥsd*) that there is now a

83. Bier observes the dialogical engagement of multiple voices in this book. She notes that the *gbr* speaks throughout ch. 3, but there is an "extreme" change in tone at 3:21 (*"Perhaps There is Hope,"* 1, 105, 114).

84. And they should always be ready to give account for their hope (1 Pet 3:15).

regenerated people of God that includes Jews and Gentiles. Despite the social tensions and harassment suffered by these Christians, they can show devotion to God and solidarity with the Christian community, knowing they will eventually attain eternal *doxa*.

CHAPTER 11

Hosios in Acts: A Gift and Promises Concerning David and His Descendant

"Holy" is a common English translation for both *hosios* and *hagios* in Acts, and elsewhere in the New Testament.[1] But the lack of distinction between these two words is unhelpful, especially when *hagios* occurs 233* times in the New Testament, sometimes within quotations of or allusions to scriptural verses where *hagios* translates *qdš* (e.g., Exod 3:5 quoted in Acts 7:33), while *hosios* occurs only eight times, including three occurrences in quotations of scriptural verses where *hosios* translates either *ḥsd* or *ḥsyd* (Acts 2:27; 13:34, 35). Louw and Nida hint at a distinction between the two Greek terms by translating *hagios* in Mark 6:20 "holy" and *hosios* in Acts 2:27 "devoted one," but they group both texts together as examples within the subdomain "Dedicate, Consecrate" (domain: "Religious Activities").[2] Intertextual and categorization evidence (§§11.1–11.2) indicates that more significance should be given to the distinction.

Unlike the fifty-three occurrences of *hagios* in Acts, the three occurrences of *hosios* in the same book all denote instances of the categories ḤSD and ḤSYD. I consider the exegetical value of recognizing engagement with those categories in Acts (§11.3), noting particular connections with the Davidic covenant.

11.1. Intertextual Connections Between *Hosios* in Acts and *Ḥsd* or *Ḥsyd* in the Hebrew Bible

Assuming common authorship for Luke-Acts (Luke 1:3; Acts 1:1),[3] and having considered issues pertaining to authorship in section 9.1, I merely reiterate here

1. E.g., NRSV; ESV.
2. L&N, s.v. "ἅγιος, α, ον; ὅσιος, α, ον."
3. Fitzmyer claims that common authorship is "widely admitted today" (*Acts of the Apostles*, 49). Barrett asserts that *logos* in Acts 1:1 "refers to the gospel of Luke" (*Preliminary Introduction and Commentary*, 64). Contra Pervo, who does not consider the "unities of Luke and Acts" as "presuppositions to be exploited" (*Acts*, 19).

that ancient tradition attributes the Third Gospel to Luke, and parts of the material in that Gospel that are not shared with Mark or Matthew have a distinctly Hebrew flavor. Scholars often acknowledge Luke's facility in imitating a biblical style and the significant influence of the LXX on his writing,[4] but some of Luke's points could equally be based on the Hebrew text.[5]

A relevant illustration occurs in Acts 13:33–35. Two of the scriptural verses cited in this section of Paul's speech that share the word *hosios* are interpreted according to the *gezerâ šawâ* technique involved (cf. Hays, **thematic coherence**).[6] However, comparing the MT and LXX texts of the quoted verses highlights another level of connection: Luke has combined a LXX verse where *hosios* renders *ḥsyd* (Ps 16:10 [15:10 LXX]) with the *only* LXX verse where *hosios* renders *ḥsd* (Isa 55:3).[7] I explore the significance of the connection between *ḥsd* and *ḥsyd* in the background of those quoted texts, especially in relation to Luke's argument in Acts.

In addition to the occurrences of *hosios* in the quotations in Acts 13:34, 35, *hosios* occurs only once more in Acts (2:27; another quotation of Ps 16:10 [15:10 LXX]). I consider *hosios* in Ps 15:10 LXX and its appropriations in Acts 2:27 and 13:35, followed by *hosios* in Isa 55:3 LXX and its appropriation in Acts 13:34.

11.1.1. Psalm 16:10 (15:10 LXX) and Acts 2:27; 13:35

Psalm 16 (15 LXX) must have held particular interest for Luke, because he included excerpts from this psalm with accompanying "commentary" in two speeches within Acts:[8] "Peter's message on the day of Pentecost and Paul's address at Antioch of Pisidia."[9]

Almost all of Ps 15:8–11 LXX is quoted in the former speech (Acts 2:25–28), but only Ps 15:10b LXX is quoted in the latter (Acts 13:35). Psalm 16:10 (15:10 LXX) and its two New Testament quotations read:

4. Fitzmyer, *Acts of the Apostles*, 116, and Pervo, *Acts*, 7–8.

5. Marshall, "Acts," 516.

6. *Gezerâ šawâ* is a rabbinical technique of arguing from analogy. Pervo, *Acts*, 339; Shade and Nicholls, *Acts*, 207–8; Strack and Stemberger, *Introduction to the Talmud and Midrash*, 21. The rare use of *hosios* in the New Testament heightens the significance of its recurrence in this context. So Keener, *Acts*, 2:2072. These verses are also linked by introductory comments, the repetition of *didōmi*, and association with David. Chance, *Acts*, 219.

7. Neut. acc. pl. of *hosios* translates masc. pl. const. of *ḥsd*.

8. Cf. Trull, "Peter's Interpretation," 432.

9. Kaiser, "Promise to David," 219.

Ps 16:10 MT:

כי לא תעזב נפשי לשאול לא תתן חסידך לראות שחת	For you will not abandon my *npš* to Sheol, you will not give your *ḥsyd* to see the pit.

Ps 15:10 LXX; Acts 2:27 quotation:

ὅτι οὐκ ἐγκαταλείψεις τὴν ψυχήν μου εἰς ᾅδην οὐδὲ δώσεις τὸν ὅσιόν σου ἰδεῖν διαφθοράν.	For you will not abandon my soul to Hades, nor will you give your *hosios* to see corruption.

Acts 13:35b quotation:

οὐ δώσεις τὸν ὅσιόν σου ἰδεῖν διαφθοράν.	You will not give your *hosios* to see corruption.

The quotations of Ps 15:10b LXX in Acts 2:27b and 13:35b are exact, except that *oude* has been changed to *ou* to suit the context in 13:35.[10] The links between *ḥsyd* in Ps 16:10b MT and *hosios* in the Acts quotations indicate that these occurrences of *hosios* denote instances of the category *ḤSYD*.

Hosios (MT: *ḥsyd*) occurs in the final subsection (vv. 10–11) of Ps 15 LXX (16 MT),[11] a psalm attributed to David. After petitioning the Lord to keep/protect him (v. 1), contrasting himself with those whose weaknesses were multiplied (NRSV: "who . . . multiply their sorrows"; vv. 2–4), and expressing confidence in the Lord's goodness toward him (vv. 6–9), the psalmist states that the Lord will not abandon the psalmist's soul to Hades/Sheol, nor give the Lord's *hosios* (MT: *ḥsyd*) to see "corruption" (*diaphthora*; MT: *šḥt* ["the pit"]; v. 10). Instead, the Lord will cause the psalmist to know the ways of life,[12] fullness of joy with/in the Lord's presence, and pleasures at the Lord's right hand (v. 11; the opposite of v. 10).[13]

In the context of Peter's message, the quotation of Ps 15:8–11 LXX, introduced by the first of two explanatory uses of *gar* ("for"; Acts 2:25, 34), provides scriptural "proof" for the claim that God loosed Jesus from the pains of death because he could not be held back by it (Acts 2:24; cf. 2 Kgdms 22:6 LXX).[14]

10. Barrett, *Preliminary Introduction and Commentary*, 648.

11. That subsection begins with the third use of *ky*.

12. In the MT, "way" (*'rḥ*) is singular.

13. Mays describes the understanding of "death" in the psalms as "the polar opposite of life" (*Psalms*, 87).

14. Weiser notes how important it was for the early church that the experiences of Jesus be harmonized with the Old Testament (*Die Apostelgeschichte*, 1:93, and Fitzmyer, *Acts of the Apostles*, 256–57 [translation]). Bruce lists four "elements" of early apostolic preaching also present in Peter's proclamation, including "citation of Old Testament scriptures" fulfilled in Jesus's "ministry, death, and triumph" (*Book of Acts*, 63).

Peter interprets key points from the psalm in Acts 2:29–36: The patriarch David died, was buried, and did not ascend into the heavens. But David was a prophet who knew that God had sworn to set one of his descendants on the throne. Thus, David spoke about the resurrection of the Christ when he said that his flesh did not see corruption,[15] for God raised up Jesus, he is exalted at God's right hand, and God has made him both Lord and Christ.

In the context of Paul's address, the content of Ps 15:10 LXX is part of what God promised to the ancestors of the people of Israel and has now fulfilled, and proof that God raised Jesus (Acts 13:32–34). Paul's interpretation of this text continues in Acts 13:36–37: The words of Ps 15:10b LXX (16:10b MT) could not refer to David himself, because he "fell asleep" (*koimaō*) and saw corruption, but when God "raised up" (*egeirō*) Jesus from the dead and he did not see corruption,[16] the promise was fulfilled.[17]

Two contentious issues concerning the interpretation of Ps 16:10 (15:10 LXX) and its appropriations in Acts are particularly relevant when identifying elements of the category *ḤSYD*. First, there is the question of whether the psalmist expected to be kept from untimely death,[18] hoped to be preserved after death, or spoke of the messiah being resurrected from death[19] when he said, "You will not give your *ḥsyd* [LXX: *hosios*] to see *šḥt* [LXX: *diaphthora*]." If YHWH does not give his *ḥsyd* to see *šḥt* (the "pit"), then *ḥsyd* does not go to the place of the dead, but continues on the path of life (vv. 10–11 MT). If the Lord does not give his *hosios* to see *diaphthora* ("corruption"), then the *hosios* may expect to be raised to life, after death but before decay sets in (vv. 10–11 LXX; Acts 2; 13). However, if *šḥt* can be legitimately translated by "corruption," as some argue,[20] there is no difference between the original Hebrew meaning and the LXX / New Testament interpretation. John Goldingay challenges that translation: "LXX and Jerome translate *šaḥat* with words such as 'corruption,' as if it

15. Psalm 16:10b (15:10b LXX) does not mention flesh, but rather YHWH's *ḥsyd/hosios*.

16. The metaphor comparing sleep with death (cf. 1 Kgs 2:10) is also emphasized by the repeated use of *egeirō* (vv. 30, 37). Fitzmyer, *Acts of the Apostles*, 517–18, and Johnson, *Acts of the Apostles*, 235.

17. Cf. Zechariah's prophecy, which alluded to the description of YHWH in 2 Sam 22:3 // Ps 18:2: "The Lord God of Israel . . . has raised up [aor. of *egeirō*] a horn of salvation for us in the house of David his servant" (Luke 1:68–69).

18. Craigie and Tate speak of seeking "deliverance from an untimely death" (*Psalms 1–50*, 158).

19. Trull includes these options in his discussion about the meaning of Ps 16:10 ("Exegesis of Psalm 16:10," 320–21).

20. Trull argues that *šaḥat* can be rendered "corruption" in Ps 16, following Gesenius, who acknowledges two possible stems for *šaḥat* (*šûaḥ* and *šāḥat*; see *GKC* §95k) ("Exegesis of Psalm 16:10," 315–20; "Peter's Interpretation," 435). Murphy notes instances in the writings of Qumran where *šḥt* has the sense of "moral corruption" (e.g., CD XV, 7–8; cf. Gen 6:12) ("*Šaḥat* in the Qumran Literature," 61–62).

came from *šāḥat*, which would be plausible if there were not the ordinary noun *šaḥat*, meaning 'pit,' from *šûaḥ*."[21]

Šḥt is used in parallel or grouped with *š'wl* ("Sheol"), a name for the underworld (Ps 16:10; Job 17:13–14).[22] Other Hebrew Bible occurrences of *šḥt* also indicate that it refers to a dark,[23] confining[24] object or location, below ground level,[25] not a state.[26] This information suggests that, in Ps 16, the psalmist expected YHWH to stop him from going to the place of the dead (*šḥt*; v. 10) and to spare his life (v. 11).[27] On the other hand, the New Testament nuances of *diaphthora* include both the location and the state of the dead. Aside from the quotations from Ps 15:10 LXX in Acts 2:27 and 13:35, the noun *diaphthora* occurs within the New Testament only in Acts 2:31 and 13:34, 36–37. In 2:31, it probably denotes a *state* of decay ("nor did his flesh see [*eidon*] *diaphthora*"; cf. 13:36–37).[28] But the combination of *hypostrephō* and *diaphthora* in 13:34 suggests a specific *location* is in mind.[29] Thus, the LXX translator may have had the place of the dead in mind, but Luke's use of *diaphthora* highlights the ambiguity.

The other debated issue is the referent of *hosios*. Peter and Paul indicate that the psalmist (David) was speaking about Jesus when he said, "You will not give your *hosios* to see corruption" (Acts 2:22, 25, 27; 13:33–35). But it is debatable whether the psalmist referred to his descendant or not when he said, "You will not give your *ḥsyd* to see the pit" (Ps 16:10 MT). In the psalm, "your *ḥsyd*" is set in parallel with "my *npš*."[30] If this is synonymous parallelism, then verse 10b is the only place in this psalm that the author refers to himself in any way other than the first-person singular pronoun. Other occurrences of *ḥsyd* (esp. Ps 86:2 [85:2 LXX], which is attributed to David) suggest that it is proper when addressing YHWH to refer to oneself or one's group using relational descriptions (e.g., "your servant," "your *ḥsydym*").[31] In addition, David is associated with

21. Considering "dissolution of the body" after burial, Goldingay suggests that "the connotations of *šāḥat* [might] carry over to *šaḥat* when used in connection with death" (*Psalms 1–41*, 233).

22. According to Ps 103:4 MT, YHWH redeems the life of the psalmist's *npš* from *šḥt*, and crowns it with *ḥsd* and compassion. In Ps 86:13 MT, deliverance from *š'wl* is a manifestation of *ḥsd*.

23. E.g., Job 33:28, 30.

24. E.g., Ezek 19:4, 8; Jonah 2:6 (2:7 MT).

25. E.g., Ezek 28:8; Jonah 2:6 (2:7 MT); Ps 7:15 (7:16 MT).

26. Contra Trull, "Exegesis of Psalm 16:10," 315–20.

27. Knowing the "path of life" (MT) seems closer to an issue of wisdom than to a description of resurrection. However, in CD XIX, 1–2, "living" (*ḥyh*) for a thousand generations is presumed to be an outcome of YHWH "keeping" (*šmr*) his covenant and *ḥsd* to those who love him and "keep" (*šmr*) his commandments, perhaps indicating a growing expectation of resurrection.

28. *Diaphthora*: "**the condition or state of rotting or decaying, *destruction, corruption*** of the body" (BDAG, s.v. "διαφθορά, ᾶς, ἡ"; emphasis original).

29. Elsewhere in Luke-Acts, *hypostrephō* is associated with returning to or from people or places (e.g., Acts 1:12).

30. LXX: "your *hosios*" and "my soul [*psychē*]."

31. Cf. Deist, *Material Culture*, 272 (addressing a king); Tanner, "Psalm 86," 661.

ḥsd more than any other individual in the Hebrew Bible apart from YHWH.[32] While this evidence does not preclude the possibility of the psalmist referring to someone else as *ḥsyd*, it seems more likely that he is referring to himself, perhaps as a representative of all YHWH's *ḥsydym*. Furthermore, since both Peter and Paul explain why David could not have spoken of himself in that verse (Acts 2:29–36; 13:36–37), it seems reasonable to infer that the traditional interpretation gave at least some grounds to think otherwise. Therefore, resurrection from death was probably not the expectation of the psalmist. That was a distinctive experience of the Messiah (cf. Acts 2:30–31).

How then does one account for the discrepancy between the psalmist's expression of confidence that YHWH would spare his life and the New Testament interpretation that the psalmist (King David) was speaking about his descendant Jesus, whom God resurrected? As David's descendants failed to live up to ideals for the royal dynasty, "a latent messianic sense" surfaced in psalms like this.[33] Thus, the difference between the original sense and the latter interpretation of Ps 16 could have been the result of rabbinic hermeneutical processes (i.e., midrash or pesher), or reading "through the lens of the New Testament" to gain the fuller sense of the words (cf. Isa 7:14).[34]

11.1.2. Isaiah 55:3 and Acts 13:34

The second quotation in the series of three within Paul's speech at Pisidian Antioch (Acts 13:16–41) comes from Isa 55:3. Isaiah 55:3b and the excerpt quoted in Acts 13:34 read as follows:

Isa 55:3b MT:

ואכרתה לכם ברית עולם חסדי דוד הנאמנים	And let me make for you [masc. pl.] an everlasting covenant, the faithful *ḥsdym* of David.

32. David is a possessor, agent, patient, and perceiver of *ḥsd* in the Hebrew Bible. Except in lists like Sir 44–50, individual persons are rarely named as agents or patients of *ḥsd* in Sirach or the nonbiblical DSS texts. However, 4Q398 14–17 II, 1 includes the exhortation "Remember David, who was a man of *ḥsdym*."

33. Cf. Trull, "Views on Peter's Use," 206, and Waltke, "Canonical Approach," 7.

34. Trull, "Views on Peter's Use," 200, 204. Cf. Craigie and Tate, *Psalms 1–50*, 158–59, and Juel, "Social Dimensions of Exegesis," 547–50. Contra Trull, who elsewhere concludes that "διαφθοράν is a correct rendering," because "corruption is the proper sense of שַׁחַת" ("Peter's Interpretation," 435). Of the seven modern views about Peter's use of Ps 16:8–11 in Acts 2:25–32 analyzed by Trull, my explanation combines aspects of the "canonical approach" (the psalm's meaning developed through canonical stages), "typology" ("the hope of the psalmist" was ultimately fulfilled in Jesus's resurrection), and "*sensus plenior*" (the fuller sense of the psalm is read "through the lens of the New Testament") views but does not assume that the psalmist was originally speaking about a personal Messiah or resurrection ("Views on Peter's Use," 198–214).

Isa 55:3b LXX:	
καὶ διαθήσομαι ὑμῖν διαθήκην αἰώνιον,	And I will make for you an everlasting covenant,
τὰ ὅσια Δαυιδ τὰ πιστά.	the faithful *hosia* of David.
Acts 13:34 quotation:	
δώσω ὑμῖν τὰ ὅσια Δαυὶδ τὰ πιστά.	I will give you the faithful *hosia* of David.

This promise about the faithful *ḥsdym* of David comes from the concluding chapter of Deutero-Isaiah, where Israel is called to receive the restoration now offered.[35] In the surrounding verses, there is an invitation to "come" and "hear," in order that their *npš* might live and be richly satisfied (Isa 55:1–3a),[36] information about a leader that YHWH has established, a plea to seek YHWH, and the outcomes of doing so (vv. 4–13).

The excerpt from Isa 55:3 is included in Paul's speech as evidence that God resurrecting Jesus fulfilled for the people of Israel what was promised to their ancestors (Acts 13:32–34). Paul declares, "That he [God] raised [aor. of *anistēmi*] him [Jesus] up from [the] dead no longer about to return to corruption, he declared thus, 'I will give to you the faithful *hosia* of David'" (Acts 13:34).[37] Thus, the content of Isa 55:3b is interpreted as God's words, and Jesus's resurrection is seen as the faithful *hosia/ḥsdym* of David made manifest in the experience of the descendants of those to whom that promise was made. Citing Ps 15:10 LXX (16:10 MT) after Isa 55:3,[38] Paul connects Jesus, who would not return to corruption, with both promises: a *hosios* (MT: *ḥsyd*) would not see corruption and God would give to his people the faithful *hosia* (MT: *ḥsdym*) of David.[39]

There are at least two debatable issues concerning the interpretation of *ta hosia Dauid ta pista / ḥsdy dwd hnʾmnym* in these texts. The first relates to whether *ta hosia Dauid / ḥsdy dwd* is a subjective or objective genitive construction. Understanding *ḥsdy dwd* in Isa 55:3 MT as simply "*ḥsdym* of David" reflects the ambiguity.[40] The New Testament appropriation of the Greek translation does not remove the ambiguity. It could still be on account of *hosia* by David, God's *hosia* for David, or their mutual responsibilities (cf. Acts 13:22–23)

35. Oswalt, *Book of Isaiah*, 433–34.

36. Isaiah 55:3a LXX: "Offer your ears and follow my ways, hear me, and your soul will live among [the] good."

37. The uses of *didōmi* ("give") in Acts 13:34 and the following verse may be related. Marshall, *Acts of the Apostles*, 227, and Bruce, *Acts of the Apostles*, 310.

38. See §11.3.2, regarding the quotation from Ps 2:7 in this triad.

39. See Keener regarding the exegetical link connecting "the promise in Isaiah explicitly to the resurrection hope" (*Acts*, 2:2072).

40. See §4.1.3.4. In my analyses, David is the [POSSESSOR] of *ḥsdym / ta hosia*.

that God gives *ta hosia Dauid ta pista* to the descendants of the patriarchs. Nevertheless, the subject of most verbs in Acts 13:17–23, 30–35, including the first-person singular future of *didōmi* ("I will give") in verse 34 indicating that God made the "promise" (*epangelia*; v. 32) to give the *hosia*, leaves little doubt that God is the proactive party as *ta hosia Dauid ta pista* are given to this new generation.[41]

The second issue concerns how / to whom ([MANIFESTATION]; [POSSESSORS]) the *ḥsdy dwd / hosia Dauid* are passed on.[42] In Isa 55 MT, the covenant and *ḥsdym* are, in some sense, *for* the people ("you" pl.) called to "come" and "hear" (v. 3).[43] The same community is probably addressed in verse 5 ("you" sg.),[44] this time as a collective people.[45] Thus, the covenant and *ḥsdym* are for a community to whom nations run.[46] Luke's substitution of *dōsō hymin* in Acts 13:34 for the whole first clause of Isa 55:3b LXX, *kai diathēsomai hymin diathēkēn aiōnion*,[47] suggests that the promise about the everlasting covenant (cf. 2 Sam 23:5) was transumed information, brought to mind by *hymin* and *ta hosia Dauid ta pista*.[48] Acts 13:32–34, 38–39 indicates that God's promise of a gift/s to which those words allude is fulfilled for the present generation of people who respond to God's invitation.

In what sense, then, are these communities party to the faithful *ḥsdym/hosia* of David? Some scholars think that, according to Isa 55:3b–5 MT, the Davidic covenant was democratized.[49] Sakenfeld sees this as a transfer of role, from the Davidic ruler with respect to the Israelite people, to "Israel as a whole" with respect to the nations.[50] But democratization theory has also been challenged. For example, according to Walter Kaiser, if the promises to David are transferred to Israel, they will no longer be "*hanneʾemānîm*, 'certain', or 'unfailing.' "

41. Aside from the people asking for a king (v. 21), God performs all the actions in Acts 13:17–23.

42. Isaiah 55:3 involves ellipsis. Sakenfeld, *Meaning of Hesed*, 202–3. Isaiah 54:10 also links *ḥsd* with a covenant of peace. Brueggemann, *Isaiah 40–66*, 159.

43. Baltzer, *Deutero-Isaiah*, 470.

44. "See, you [masc. sg.] will call nations that you [masc. sg.] do not know."

45. So Goldingay and Payne, *Isaiah 40–55*, 2:374.

46. Cf. peoples making a pilgrimage to Zion (Isa 2:1–3). Baltzer, *Deutero-Isaiah*, 473.

47. Some combination of *diatithēmi* and *diathēkē* is the usual way of referring to the making of a covenant or treaty in the LXX. These words usually translate *krt* and *bryt* (e.g., Gen 21:32).

48. Luke uses *diathēkē* ("covenant") in connection with the Abrahamic covenant and the blood of the new covenant (Luke 1:72; 22:20; Acts 3:25; 7:8). He associates *diatithēmi* ("ordain/arrange") with the assigning of a kingdom to those who have remained with Jesus in his trials and the Abrahamic covenant (Luke 22:29; Acts 3:25). I find no occurrences of these words explicitly connected with the Davidic covenant, but a possible link is in Luke 1:68–75, where raising a horn of salvation in the house of David is portrayed as an outworking of God's holy covenant, sworn to Abraham.

49. E.g., von Rad thinks "the Messianic hope had no place" in the prophetic ideas of Deutero-Isaiah, and the realization of the promises made to David is for all Israel (*Theology of Israel's Prophetic Traditions*, 240). See also Goldingay and Payne, *Isaiah 40–55*, 2:372.

50. Sakenfeld, *Meaning of Hesed*, 203–4.

Instead, they were "*shared* with Israel" when the Davidic covenant was established (2 Sam 7).[51] Similarly, Joseph Blenkinsopp questions the use of "this analogy" (presumably that in Isa 55:1–5) without the author being persuaded that YHWH's "commitment to David and the dynasty" was permanent. The language here does not concern the restoration of that dynasty; it promises hearers experience of the same *ḥsdym* "that God performed in former times on behalf of David (as Ps 89:50)."[52] Kaiser and Blenkinsopp both make valid points. The acts of *ḥsd* are not limited to David's succession. They include support in battle (implied in Ps 89:43 NRSV [89:44 MT]), planting Israel in its own dwelling place, deliverance and rest from enemies, reputation, and exaltation (2 Sam 7:9–12; Ps 89:22, 24 [89:23, 25 MT]).

Luke's choice of vocabulary in Acts 13:23, 33–37 gives clues about how he understands the sharing of *ta hosia Dauid ta pista*. Luke contrasts Jesus (David's offspring [*sperma*]; v. 23) with David, who "fell asleep" (*koimaō*; v. 36), and links the promise recorded in 13:34 with God "raising" (*anistēmi*) Jesus from the dead (vv. 33, 34; cf. *egeirō* in vv. 22, 30, 37). These descriptions bring to mind 2 Kgdms 7:12 LXX: "If your days are fulfilled and you fall asleep [2sg. fut. pass. of *koimaō*] with your ancestors, . . . I will raise up [1sg. fut. of *anistēmi*] your offspring [*sperma*] after you."[53] Thus, the content of the Acts 13:34 promise is likely to include the resurrection and reign of David's offspring (cf. 2 Sam 7:12),[54] along with that which God is providing for those who "come" and "hear" (Isa 55:1–3a): an everlasting covenant (Isa 55:3b; 2 Sam 23:5; transumed content of Acts 13:34) involving renewed/eternal life (Isa 55:3a; cf. Acts 13:46) and "forgiveness" (*aphiēmi* [Isa 55:7]; *aphesis* [Acts 13:38]).

11.2. The Categories ḤSD and ḤSYD in Acts

Quotations that include *hosios* signal engagement with the categories ḤSD and ḤSYD in Acts. I compare the elements involved in two instances of the category ḤSYD in Acts with those in Ps 16:10 (15:10 LXX), and the elements involved in one instance of the category ḤSD within Acts with those in Isa 55:3.

51. Kaiser, "Unfailing Kindnesses," 96–97; emphasis original.

52. Blenkinsopp, *Isaiah 40–55*, 370. Note the plural form of *ḥsd* in both Ps 89:50 MT and Isa 55:3. Motyer, *Prophecy of Isaiah*, 453–54.

53. Jesus was "raised up" in both resurrection and reign. Fitzmyer, *Acts of the Apostles*, 513, 516.

54. See Marshall's preferred interpretations of the point of the quotation from Isa 55:3 in Acts 13:34 (*Acts of the Apostles*, 227–28). (Note, however, that, in Isa 55, "you" is plural in verse 3 and singular in verse 5.) Cf. Johnson's conclusion regarding Acts 13:35 that, according to Luke's reading, the oracle promised David that his seed would not see corruption (*Acts of the Apostles*, 235).

11.2.1. ḤSYD *in Psalm 16:10 (15:10 LXX) and Acts 2:27; 13:35*

In Ps 16:10 MT, *ḥsydk* is the Direct Object of a negated Transitive Verb (2 masc. sg. impf. of *ntn*: "you will give") in a Verbal Clause (following a Causal Verbal Clause). In Ps 15:10 LXX and Acts 2:27; 13:35, *ton hosion sou* is the Direct Object of a negated Transitive Verb (2sg. fut. of *didōmi*: "you will give") in a Verbal Clause, a close rendering of *lʾ ttn ḥsydk*. In Acts 2:27, the clause follows a Causal Verbal Clause; in Acts 13:35, it is the Object of *legō* (i.e., speech content).

The hopeful psalmist of Ps 16 (i.e., David, according to the superscription; [PERCEIVER]) asks for protection and refuge (v. 1), keeps YHWH before him (justification), and declares confidence in YHWH (communication; vv. 5–8), but the sorrow of others multiplies (contrast; v. 4). The psalmist's heart was glad, his tongue (MT: "glory") rejoiced, and his flesh will abide in security ([RESPONSES_OF_PERCEIVER/DEVOTED_PARTY]; v. 9), for YHWH ([POSSESSIVE_PARTY]) will not give/permit[55] (predicted neg. [ACTIVITY/RESPONSE_OF_POSSESSIVE_PARTY]) YHWH's *ḥsyd* ([DEVOTED_PARTY]) to see the pit (neg. [LOCATION]; v. 10). Neither will YHWH abandon the psalmist's *npš* to Sheol. In contrast, YHWH will cause the psalmist to know the path of life (impf. response of possessive party; v. 11).

According to Luke's account of Peter's Pentecost speech (communication) in Jerusalem in Acts 2:14–36, Peter (perceiver) considers the content of Ps 15:8–11 LXX to be the word of a prophet, spoken in foresight. The quotation is introduced with the words "For David ([PERCEIVER]) says with respect to him ([DEVOTED_PARTY])." The referent of "him" is "this [man]," Jesus of Nazareth, a descendant of the patriarch David, whom members of the house of Israel crucified (Acts 2:22–23, 29–32, 36). The relationship between the Lord / God and Jesus is, in this case, based on the Davidic covenant (justification; vv. 27, 29–31). David himself could not have been the [DEVOTED_PARTY], because he died, he was buried, his tomb is still present, and he did not ascend into the heavens (vv. 29, 34). In contrast, having loosed the pains of death (context; v. 24), God raised up "this Jesus" and made him Lord and Christ (responses of possessive party; vv. 30–36). Christ was not abandoned to Hades, and his flesh did not see corruption (v. 31). Thus, David said, "I saw the Lord always before me. . . . For you (the Lord; [POSSESSIVE_PARTY]) will not abandon my soul to Hades, nor give/permit[56] (neg. [ACTIVITY/RESPONSE_OF_POSSESSIVE_PARTY]) your *hosios* ([DEVOTED_PARTY]) to see corruption (neg. [CONTEXT])," with respect to "this [man]," Jesus (vv. 23, 25, 27). The Lord made known to Jesus

55. Barrett, *Preliminary Introduction and Commentary*, 127.
56. BDAG, s.v. "δίδωμι."

the paths of life (aor. response of possessive party; v. 28). By implication, Jesus's heart was glad, his tongue rejoiced greatly, and his flesh will abide in hope ([RESPONSES_OF_DEVOTED_PARTY]; v. 26).[57] Peter informs his audience that David spoke about the resurrection and exaltation of the Christ, Jesus (vv. 31–35). Those who hear this news are cut to the heart and ask what they should do in response (v. 37). Those who receive Peter's word are baptized (outcome; v. 41).

According to Luke's account of Paul's Sabbath-day speech (communication) in the synagogue at Pisidian Antioch in Acts 13:16–41, Paul (perceiver) considers the content of Ps 15:10b LXX (i.e., the words quoted in Acts 13:35; communication) as containing a promise made to the ancestors of those present, and fulfilled to their "children" by God raising Jesus from death and ensuring that he would not return to corruption (activities/responses of possessive party; contexts/locations; Acts 13:32–34): "You ([POSSESSIVE_PARTY]) will not give/permit (neg. [ACTIVITY/RESPONSE_OF_POSSESSIVE_PARTY]) your *hosios* ([DEVOTED_PARTY]) to see corruption (neg. [CONTEXT])." The original perceiver of the *hosios* is the psalmist David. When David had served the purpose of God in his generation, he fell asleep, was gathered to his fathers, and saw corruption (v. 36). In contrast, God raised Jesus from death and burial in a tomb, and Jesus did not see corruption (contexts/locations; vv. 29–30, 34, 37). Thus, the relationship is between the [POSSESSIVE_PARTY], God, and the [DEVOTED_PARTY] (*hosios*), Jesus, a descendant of David, the son of Jesse, presumably on the basis of the Davidic Covenant (vv. 22–23, 32–35). Paul refers to the [DEVOTED_PARTY] as "he whom God raised" (v. 37), and there is no evidence of a [DEVOTED_PARTY'S_RESPONSE] in Paul's retelling of the events. However, the appropriate responses of Paul's audience are knowing and believing, not scoffing (vv. 38–41).[58] Through this man, their sins can be "forgiven" (*aphesis*; cf. Isa 55:7 *aphiēmi*) and they can be "justified" (*dikaioō*) from that from which they could not be justified under the law of Moses (reason; contrasting outcomes; vv. 38–39).[59] Many Jews follow Paul and Barnabas (v. 43), but

57. My interpretation. Contra Barrett, who indicates that the two clauses in verse 26 do not have any bearing on the argument (*Preliminary Introduction and Commentary*, 145).

58. Habakkuk 1:5 LXX (which differs from MT) is cited in Acts 13:41. Fitzmyer, *Acts of the Apostles*, 519. See 1QpHab II, 1–2 (which relates to the LXX content better than to the MT) and the comment by Horgan (*Pesharim*, 23–24).

59. The decision to believe (or not) is also highlighted by repetition (vv. 39, 41, 48). Bruce notes the introduction of justification along with the forgiveness of sins already proclaimed (2:38; 3:19 [similar]; 5:31; 10:43) (*Book of Acts*, 262). Forgiveness (MT: *slḥ*; LXX: *aphaireō/aphiēmi*) is a manifestation of YHWH's *ḥsd* in Exod 34:6–9 and Num 14:18–19. In Isa 55:7, YHWH offers forgiveness (MT: *slḥ*; LXX: *aphiēmi*) to those who return to him. The connection between *ḥsd* and justification (LXX: *dikaioō* ["to justify"]) is not obvious (there is some association in Ps 51:1–4 [51:3–6 MT; 50:3–6 LXX]), but there is a stronger link with righteousness (LXX: *dikaiosynē*; see §7.3.3).

others contradict what Paul says, stirring up persecution and having Paul and Barnabas driven from the district (vv. 45, 50). Paul and Barnabas turn to the Gentiles, many of whom believe (contrasting outcomes; vv. 46, 48).

11.2.2. ḤSD *in Isaiah 55:3 and Acts 13:34*

In a prophetic oracle calling those who thirst and have no money to come (response; Isa 55:1, 3), YHWH (perceiver/[AGENT]) says (communication), "And let me make (impf. [AGENT'S_ACTIVITY]) for you ([SECONDARY_POSSESSORS]) an everlasting covenant, the faithful ([QUALITY]) *ḥsdym* ([SPECIFIC_DEMONSTRATIONS]) of David ([POSSESSOR]; [JUSTIFICATION])." Thus, by ellipsis, *ḥsdy dwd hnʾmnym* is the Direct Object of a Transitive Verb (1sg. impf. cohortative of *krt*: lit. "let me cut") in a Verbal Clause.[60] The relational context is the Davidic covenant, but the present interaction is between YHWH and those who come. Further invited responses include "inclining" (*hiphil* of *nṭh*) the ear, "listening" (*šmʿ*), "seeking" (*drš*), "calling upon" (*qrʾ*), and "returning" (*šwb*) to YHWH (vv. 3, 6–7). When these things take place (context; time), the outcomes include the nations running to Israel (v. 5) and YHWH "having mercy" (*rḥm*) / "forgiving" (*slḥ*) (v. 7). As the invited ones are led forth in peace, the mountains and hills will break into jubilation and clapping (v. 12; as commanded in 44:23; 49:13).[61]

In Luke's account of Paul's speech at Pisidian Antioch (Acts 13:16–41; communication), Paul (perceiver) announces good news: that which was promised to the ancestors of his audience, God has fulfilled to the present generation of Abraham's family ([SECONDARY_POSSESSORS]; time; justification) by raising Jesus (vv. 32–33). Paul's scriptural evidence for this claim is presented in a series of quotations. The second quotation is an excerpt from Isa 55:3b that reads, "I ([AGENT]) will give (fut. [AGENT'S_ACTIVITY]) you ([SECONDARY_POSSESSORS]) the faithful ([QUALITY]) *hosia* ([SPECIFIC_DEMONSTRATIONS]) of David ([POSSESSOR])" (v. 34). Thus, *ta hosia Dauid ta pista* is the Direct Object of a Transitive Verb (1sg. fut. of *didōmi*: "I will give") in an Object Verbal Clause (i.e., speech content). According to Luke, Paul introduces this quotation, saying, "But, that he raised him ([PATIENT]; i.e., Jesus) from the dead ([MANIFESTATION]), no longer to return to corruption ([LOCATION/CONTEXT]), he [i.e., God] has spoken in this way (communication)." Therefore, the key relationships are between God and Abraham (v. 26) and God and David (vv. 22–23).

60. The covenant that YHWH will "cut" (*krt*; v. 3) and the sign that will not be "cut off" (*krt*; v. 13b) are both "everlasting" (*ʿwlm*). Cf. Goldingay, *Message of Isaiah 40–55*, 558. In addition, *ḥsdy dwd hnʾmnym* is in apposition with *bryt ʿwlm* within Isa 55:3b.

61. In the LXX, the mountains and hills "leap out" in welcome, and the trees "rattle/clap" their branches.

David could not have been the [PATIENT] of the *hosia* in this context, because he saw corruption, but God kept Jesus from seeing corruption (vv. 34, 36–37). The audience responses and outcomes are the same as for the quotation of Ps 15:10 LXX in Acts 13:35 (above).

11.2.3. General Observations

Comparing Ps 16:10 and Isa 55:3 with their New Testament appropriations, I observe the following.

11.2.3.1. Agent's Activities and Syntactic Functions

The sole but significant change to elements of the quotation of Isa 55:3b in Acts 13:34 is the [AGENT'S_ACTIVITY], which is directly associated with the *hosia* of David in the abbreviated version and has shifted from "making" to "giving" (matching the verb in the following quotation). Unlike Isa 55:3, Luke's shortened quotation does not involve ellipsis or apposition. The syntactic functions of *ḥsydk* in Ps 16:10b MT and *ton hosion sou* in Ps 15:10 LXX and Acts 2:27; 13:35 are the same.

11.2.3.2. YHWH/God, the Proactive Agent and Possessive Party

YHWH/God is the [AGENT] of the faithful ([QUALITY]) *ḥsdym/hosia* of David (Isa 55; Acts 13) and the [POSSESSIVE_PARTY] of the *ḥsyd/hosios* (Ps 16; Acts 2; 13). God is the one who takes initiative and raises Jesus from the dead (Acts 2; 13). In Isa 55, YHWH "will make" the *ḥsdym* for YHWH's people; in Acts 13, God "will give" their descendants the *hosia* ([AGENT'S_ACTIVITIES]). In Ps 16 and Acts 2, YHWH / the Lord's [RESPONSES] toward YHWH / the Lord's *ḥsyd/hosios* are expressed both negatively (not giving/permitting him to see) and positively (causing him to know).

11.2.3.3. David and Jesus

A key relational bond in each context is the Davidic covenant. The [POSSESSOR] of the *ḥsdym* in Isa 55 and probably the [DEVOTED_PARTY] in Ps 16 is David (the patriarch who saw corruption), but the [DEVOTED_PARTY] and [PATIENT] of the *hosia* ([SPECIFIC_DEMONSTRATIONS]) in Acts 2 and 13 is David's descendant, Jesus (the Savior, whom the Lord / God did not give/permit to see corruption but raised; contrast). Where [DEVOTED_PARTIES'_RESPONSES] are recorded, they are reactive. Positive [RESPONSES] belong to the one who is both [PERCEIVER] and probable [DEVOTED_PARTY] in the psalm (the psalmist).

But according to Acts 2, the psalmist (David; [PERCEIVER]) attributes those [RESPONSES] to the [DEVOTED_PARTY], Jesus.

11.2.3.4. Death to Life

Together, Ps 16 and Acts 2 contrast preservation and resurrection, death and life. YHWH/God does not permit the [DEVOTED_PARTIES] to see the pit or corruption, both euphemisms for death ([LOCATION/CONTEXT]). But the Ps 16 *ḥsyd* is kept from death and the Acts 2 *hosios* is raised from death. Thus, YHWH will cause the psalmist to know the path of life and the Lord / God has made known to Jesus the paths of resurrected life (responses of possessive party). God raising Jesus from the dead is also the [MANIFESTATION] of the *hosia* in Acts 13.

11.2.3.5. A Gift to the Present Generation

As Isa 55:3b is appropriated in Acts 13:34, a new generation of God's people, referred to as "you," become the [SECONDARY_POSSESSORS] of the faithful ([QUALITY]) *ḥsdym/hosia* of David. The *hosia* are considered a gift to the generation of Abraham's family alive when God raised Jesus from the dead, even though the promise was made to their ancestors (time). Justification, not available through the law of Moses, is now made available by Jesus.

11.2.3.6. Invited and Realized Responses

In Isa 55 and Acts 2; 13, people are invited to respond to what is offered, but only the New Testament contexts indicate how particular groups do respond. Those who receive (response) Peter's word are baptized (outcome). The appropriate responses for Paul's audience are knowing and believing. Some Jews follow Paul and Barnabas and many Gentiles believe (cf. the nations in Isa 55:5), but some Jews stir up persecution against Paul and Barnabas and have them driven from the district (contrasting outcomes).

11.3. Exegetical Value of Recognizing Engagement with the Categories ḤSD and ḤSYD in Acts

Acts traces "a momentous transition in salvation history."[62] That statement signals both continuity and change. I consider the relationship between ḤSD, ḤSYD, and continuity and change.

62. Shade and Nicholls, *Acts*, 3 (quoted content is bold in the original).

II.3.1. ḤSD, ḤSYD, *and Continuity*

Luke interprets the events recorded in Acts as continuous with God's will and purpose in history (cf. Acts 2:23; 13:36).[63] For example, in Paul's Acts 13 speech, he recalls significant events from about 450 years of Israel's salvation history,[64] characterizing God as proactive and gracious toward God's people (vv. 19–21), before stating that, from the offspring of David, God brought to Israel the promised Savior, Jesus (v. 23). God "raised up" (*egeirō*) David (v. 22), and later "raised up" (*egeirō*) David's descendant, Jesus (vv. 30, 37; prefigurement).[65] Thus, Jesus's story is the "proper climax" of Israel's story.[66] The categories *ḤSD* and *ḤSYD* are appropriate for communicating the continuity of God's activity. In the Hebrew Bible, *ḥsd* and *ḥsyd* together denote a central concept, God is the primary possessor and agent of enduring *ḥsd* (e.g., Exod 34:6–7; Ps 136), and God does not forsake God's *ḥsydym* (e.g., Ps 37:28). God is also the possessive party for the *hosios* and agent of the *hosia* in Acts 2:27 and 13:34–35.

Furthermore, according to Luke's account, Peter and Paul appeal to members of God's chosen people in their speeches (e.g., "men of Israel," "sons of the family of Abraham"; Acts 2:22; 13:16, 26).[67] They argue in light of the assumed collective knowledge and values of their audiences (e.g., "the law of Moses"; 13:39)[68] and quote scriptural texts as "proof" of their claims (e.g., 2:24–25).[69] *Ḥsd* denotes one of those shared values (e.g., Jer 9:24 [9:23 MT]; Mic 6:8), and both speeches quote texts containing its most frequent LXX translation.

The issue of continuity is also evident in the "promise and fulfillment" motif (e.g., Acts 13:32–33; cf. Luke 1:54–55, 72).[70] For Luke, Christianity is the fulfillment of those "hopes of Judaism" expressed in Israel's Scriptures.[71] One such

63. By writing in the style of the LXX, Luke communicates continuity of theme with the Old Testament (Barrett, *Introduction and Commentary*, xlviii) and probably the understanding that he is "recording *sacred history*" (Marshall, *Acts of the Apostles*, 18; emphasis original). See also Fitzmyer, *Acts of the Apostles*, 60, 92.

64. Cf. Marshall, *Acts of the Apostles*, 23–24, and Pervo, *Acts*, 10.

65. "Luke sometimes finds in 'raising up' a double entendre for resurrection." Keener, *Acts*, 2:2062.

66. Ibid., 2:2069.

67. Cf. Stephen's speech in Acts 7. In Acts 13, Paul speaks as a member of the group (e.g., "for us," "brothers"; vv. 33, 38). Paul does not quote Scripture when evangelizing pagans (e.g., 17:22–31) in the same way that he does with Jews and Godfearers. Fitzmyer, *Acts of the Apostles*, 92.

68. Paul stood up to speak, following the reading of the Law and the Prophets (Acts 13:15). The condemnation of Jesus fulfills "the voices of the prophets, being read aloud during every Sabbath" (13:27). Suggested texts from which Paul's speech may have drawn content include Deut 1; 4:25–46; 1 Sam (1 Kgdms LXX) 13:14; 2 Sam (2 Kgdms LXX) 7:6–16. Bruce, *Book of Acts*, 254.

69. Cf. Acts 13:33–35, where Ps 2:7; Isa 55:3; and Ps 16:10 (15:10 LXX) are each introduced by a citation formula.

70. Fitzmyer, *Acts of the Apostles*, 92.

71. Chance, *Acts*, 18.

hope is the outworking of the Davidic covenant. YHWH's promises concerning David (2 Sam 7:15–16) were partially fulfilled in the experience of his son Solomon (1 Kgs 3:6;[72] cf. 2 Chr 1:8; 6:14–15), but later generations could not always perceive in their own experience evidence of the Lord's *ḥsdym* sworn to David (Ps 89:49 [89:50 MT]).[73] Nevertheless, the resurrection and exaltation of Jesus (Acts 2:27, 31; 13:30–37), David's descendant (Acts 13:23; cf. Luke 1:69), are evidence that God has not removed his *ḥsd* from the house of David, but has "proven himself *ḥsyd*" (*htḥsd*) with his *ḥsyd* (2 Sam 22:26; cf. Ps 16:10). The throne of David's descendant is established forever in *ḥsd* (2 Sam 7:16; Isa 16:5; Acts 2:34–36).[74]

Thus, while both Jesus and the things of God are holy (e.g., 1 Chr 23:13; Acts 4:27, 30), that is not the point of including scriptural quotations containing *hosios* in Acts 2 and 13. *Hosios* in these chapters is connected with YHWH's *ḥsyd* and specific demonstrations of *ḥsd* associated with David (cf. 2 Sam 7).

II.3.2. ḤSD, ḤSYD, *and Change*

Engagement with *ḤSD* and *ḤSYD* in Acts also highlights significant change. Peter and Paul appeal to Scripture as endorsement for new things taking place. A new manifestation of *ḥsd* introduces a new era in salvation history, involving new people.

If the *ḥsyd* of Ps 16 MT was kept from "untimely death," while the *hosios* of Acts 2 and 13 was "raised" from death, then the resurrection of Jesus is a distinctive New Testament manifestation of *ḥsd* (13:33–35).[75] Resurrection becomes the climax of the tradition associated with *ḥsd*, which involves "salvation" (*yšʿ*), "deliverance" (*nṣl*), and "revival" (*ḥyh*).[76] The resurrection offers new hope to all humans, who, despite perhaps seeking "deliverance from an untimely death" as the psalmist did, will still face "timely death" eventually.[77]

With this new manifestation of *ḥsd* comes the recognition that the *ḥsyd/hosios* spoken of in Ps 16:10b (15:10b LXX) is now present. Peter signals that the content of Ps 15:8–11 LXX should be interpreted messianically, by way of an

72. "You have kept for him [my father, David] this great *ḥsd*, and have given him a son to sit on his throne this day."

73. "Where is your initial *ḥsd*, Lord, which you swore to David in your faithfulness [*ʾmwnh*]?"

74. In both 2 Sam 7:12–16 and Acts 13:23, 32–34, "sonship" is obtained, and God raises up David's seed and makes a promise. Second Samuel 7 probably lies behind Paul's argument here. My exposition here is adapted from Kepple, "Hope of Israel," 236.

75. As Craigie and Tate put it, "In the experience of Jesus, death became a door" (*Psalms 1–50*, 158).

76. Descriptions of the trial, execution, and burial of Jesus build up to the announcement of the culminating initiative of God (Acts 13:30). Bruce, *Book of Acts*, 259.

77. Craigie and Tate, *Psalms 1–50*, 158–59.

introductory clause (Acts 2:25),[78] a reference to Ps 109:1 LXX (Acts 2:34–35),[79] and his claim that God has made the crucified Jesus both Lord and Christ (Acts 2:36; cf. v. 31).[80]

There are also indications in Paul's speech (Acts 13:16–41) that the *hosios* is a messianic figure. In Isaiah, YHWH describes the Persian king Cyrus as his *mšyḥ* ("anointed one"; 45:1), the one who will carry out his desire (44:28).[81] In 2 Sam 23:1, David is also referred to as *mšyḥ*. But in Acts 13:22–23, David is described as one who will do "all my desires,"[82] and Jesus is described as being "of this man's [i.e., David's] offspring," a Savior whom God brought to Israel. In addition, the quotations involving *hosios* recorded in Acts 13:34, 35 are meant to be interpreted in light of the preceding quotation from Ps 2:7: "You are my son, today I have begotten you" (Acts 13:33). Psalm 2, which was often understood messianically during the Second Temple period,[83] was probably composed for the coronation of a new king in David's dynasty,[84] a time when the king was said to be begotten by God (cf. 2 Sam 7:14). The appropriation of this excerpt in Paul's speech indicates that God has made the sonship of Jesus publicly known through the resurrection (Acts 13:34).[85] As promised in Ps 132:11–12 (131:11–12 LXX), God has indeed set on David's throne one from David's loins who keeps the covenant.[86] A new era has begun, because Jesus, the promised Messiah and *hosios* (cf. MT: *ḥsyd*), is no longer anticipated—he has come.

In this new era, the fulfillment of a promise about the faithful *hosia*/*ḥsdym* of David benefits a widening circle of people:[87] not only the descendants of those to whom the promise was made (cf. Isa 55:3), but all who know,[88] repent,

78. This indicates that Luke reads the psalm as David referring to Jesus of Nazareth.

79. Fitzmyer, *Acts of the Apostles*, 249, 260. Jesus interpreted this psalm messianically in Mark 12:35–37. Fernando, *Acts*, 103.

80. The midrash on Ps 16:10 (with comment on 16:9) refers to "the lord Messiah who will rise up out of me." Braude, *Midrash on Psalms*, 1:201. Cf. Bruce, *Book of Acts*, 65.

81. Fitzmyer, *Acts of the Apostles*, 512.

82. So Fitzmyer (ibid.).

83. 4Q174 discusses 2 Sam 7:10–14 and Ps 2:1–2 together. Keener, *Acts*, 2:2070. Psalms of Solomon 17:26 (cf. vv. 23–24) quotes Ps 2 "as a reference to Messiah." Shade and Nicholls, *Acts*, 207.

84. Fitzmyer, *Acts of the Apostles*, 516–17, and Jacobson, "Psalm 2," 65.

85. Bruce, *Book of Acts*, 259–60; Fitzmyer, *Acts of the Apostles*, 516–17; Keener, *Acts*, 2:2070–71.

86. Bruce, *Acts of the Apostles*, 126. The refrain in Ps 132:9, 16 MT indicates that the *ḥsydym* rejoice because YHWH has chosen Zion as his dwelling place (vv. 8, 13–14). The *mšyḥ* is favored in Zion for the sake of David (vv. 1, 10, 13, 17).

87. In Acts 1–14, Luke describes "a decisive step" that leads to the gospel, entrusted to a group of Jews, being communicated to those "of a different religious and racial background." Barrett, *Preliminary Introduction and Commentary*, 49.

88. I.e., know that, through Jesus, there is forgiveness of sins.

believe, are baptized,[89] and receive[90] (Acts 2:38; 13:38–39). While many Jews received the word (Acts 2:5, 41; 13:43), some rejected it, so Paul and Barnabas turned to the Gentiles, many of whom also believed (13:46–48; cf. 28:25–28).[91] They now belong to a renewed covenant people (cf. *ḥsydym*), the fulfillment of Israel's Scriptures and Israel's hopes.[92]

11.4. Conclusions

The occurrences of *hosios* in Acts denote two instances of the category ḤSYD and one instance of the category ḤSD. They are located in quotations of scriptural texts where *hosios* renders either *ḥsd* or *ḥsyd*. The two occurrences in Acts 13 are linked together using the *gezerâ šawâ* technique.

Luke reinterprets the *ḥsd/ḥsyd* tradition in light of Jesus's resurrection. Acts 2:25–28 cites Ps 15:8–11 LXX, and Acts 13:35 cites Ps 15:10b LXX. In Ps 16:10 MT, the psalmist (David) declares that YHWH will not give/permit YHWH's *ḥsyd* (LXX: *hosios*; [DEVOTED_PARTY]) to see the pit (LXX: "corruption"; neg. [LOCATION/CONTEXT]); that is, YHWH will not let him die. However, according to the speeches of Peter and Paul, David could not have been talking about himself, because David saw corruption. But Jesus's resurrection fulfills David's words. Contrasts in these instances of the category ḤSYD include Jesus and David, life and death, God's proactivity and Jesus's passive reactivity, and appropriate and inappropriate responses.

An excerpt from Isa 55:3b is quoted in Acts 13:34, introducing an instance of the category ḤSD. God's promise to give *ta hosia Dauid* is interpreted in light of Jesus's resurrection. Rereading Isa 55:3 through the lens of Acts 13, the content of the promises "shared" with the covenant people includes the "raising up" of David's offspring ([MANIFESTATION]; cf. 2 Sam 7) and associated good news for those who respond to YHWH's invitation to come. Promises connected with the Davidic covenant are interpreted messianically for a new generation of God's people. This is additional evidence for Luke's Gentile audience that they are becoming part of a movement that results from God's ongoing commitment to God's covenant people.

The categories ḤSD and ḤSYD are helpful for communicating themes of continuity and change associated with the resurrection of Jesus, God's *hosios*

89. I.e., baptized in Jesus's name.

90. I.e., receive the Holy Spirit.

91. Fernando, *Acts*, 31, and Fitzmyer, *Acts of the Apostles*, 519–22.

92. Chance describes "the Way" as "the fulfillment of Israel's own Scriptures and hopes" (*Acts*, 22).

(cf. *ḥsyd*). Evidently, *ḥsd* is still valued by God and God's covenant people, and the resurrection is viewed as the climactic demonstration of enduring *ḥsd* with respect to the house of David. But this new manifestation has also introduced a new era: the Messiah has now come and the covenant blessings and responsibilities are shared with believing Jews and Gentiles. The underlying issue in these experiences is not holiness, but devotion to covenant relationship.

CHAPTER 12

Hosios in Other New Testament Books: A Description of the One Who Makes Faithful and Righteous Judgments

In addition to the occurrences of *hosios* in Acts, *hosios* occurs five more times in the New Testament: 1 Tim 2:8; Titus 1:8; Heb 7:26; Rev 15:4; 16:5.[1] Once again, scholarship about these texts often blurs the distinction between *hagios* and *hosios*, because of the common translation "holy."[2] However, intertextual connections suggest that, at least in Revelation, a principal influence on the sense of *hosios* is its LXX association with *ḥsyd*, which has more to do with covenant devotion than holiness.

In this chapter, I explore intertextual connections between *ḥsd* and/or *ḥsyd* in the Hebrew Bible and the five remaining New Testament occurrences of *hosios* (§12.1), present an analysis of two instances of the category *ḤSYD* in Rev 15–16, where *hosios* is used to describe the One who makes faithful and righteous judgments (§12.2), and discuss the exegetical value of recognizing engagement with that category in Rev 15–16 (§12.3).

12.1. Intertextual Connections Between *Hosios* in First Timothy, Titus, Hebrews, and Revelation and *Ḥsyd* in the Hebrew Bible

Apart from the quotations from Ps 16 (15 LXX) and Isa 55 in Acts 2 and 13, intertextual connections between *hosios* in the New Testament and *ḥsyd* in the Hebrew Bible are established through allusions and echoes. I consider briefly the occurrences of *hosios* in 1 Tim 2:8; Titus 1:8; and Heb 7:26, before focusing on Rev 15:4 and 16:5, which contain the most likely instances of *ḤSYD* among these five texts.

1. Additionally, *anosios* occurs among the negative descriptions listed in 1 Tim 1:9 and 2 Tim 3:2.

2. E.g., Osborne thinks that *monos hosios* in Rev 15:4 indicates that God alone is holy, "set apart from this world, and stand[ing] above it" (*Revelation*, 567). L&N assigns this occurrence of *hosios* to the "Holy, Pure" subdomain within the "Moral and Ethical Qualities and Related Behavior" domain, together with *hagios* and *hosiōs* (s.v. "ἅγιος, α, ον; ὅσιος, α, ον; ὁσίως").

12.1.1. First Timothy 2:8; Titus 1:8; and Hebrews 7:26

The uses of *hosios* in 1 Tim 2:8; Titus 1:8; and Heb 7:26 probably reflect both Greek and Hebrew influences. *Hosious cheiras* ("holy hands"; 1 Tim 2:8) appears to reflect the general use of *hosios*, and the presence of *dikaios* and *hosios* in the list of characteristics of an overseer in Titus 1:7–9 is consistent with the frequent pairing of those terms in extrabiblical Greek literature.[3] But the sense of *hosios* in Titus 1:8 may also reflect LXX uses of *hosios* that render *ḥsyd*, such as those to which Philip Towner refers in his explanation of this verse (Deut 33:8; 2 Kgdms 22:26).[4] In that case, the overseers need to be "devoted to covenant relationship."

Craig Koester understands the sense of *hosios* in the list of characteristics of a permanent high priest in Heb 7:26–27 (cf. v. 24) as "holy,"[5] even though he illustrates his point about *hosios* in the Old Testament from Pss 29:5 and 30:24 LXX, where *hosios* translates *ḥsyd*.[6] If this use of *hosios* reflects the LXX sense of the term, the high priest would demonstrate "fidelity to the covenant" in his relationships to God and others.[7]

12.1.2. Revelation 15:4 and 16:5

In contrast to *hagios*, which occurs twenty-five** times in Revelation,[8] the only two occurrences of *hosios* in Revelation are located within a pair of related hymns (15:3–4; 16:5–7)[9] that occur in the account of the seven last plagues (15:1–16:21).[10] The Lord God the Almighty is described as *monos hosios* ("alone *hosios*") in 15:4 and *ho hosios* ("the *hosios* one") in 16:5. This limited but prominent usage of *hosios* (cf. Hays: **volume**) suggests that the term was purposefully

3. See §6.2.2. Hauck, "ὅσιος, ὁσίως," 5:490, 492.

4. Towner does not draw attention to *ḥsyd* in these verses (*Letters to Timothy and Titus*, 690; he writes "2 Kgs 22:26" for 2 Kgdms 22:26).

5. Koester, *Hebrews*, 366–67.

6. Ibid., 366.

7. Lane, *Hebrews 1–8*, 191.

8. The NRSV renders thirteen** of those occurrences using "saint/s," and four as describing the "holy city." In 6:10, the souls describe the Sovereign Lord as *ho hagios kai alēthinos* ("holy and faithful") and ask, "How long before you will judge and avenge our blood?" (ESV). Apparently, this cry is responded to in 16:5–7, where the Lord is described as *hosios* (see §12.1.2.2, n. 48).

9. Various terms in these two hymns mirror each other. In the first hymn, the Lord God the Almighty is incomparably *hosios* (15:4) and his ways are "righteous" (*dikaios*) and "faithful" (*alēthinos*; 15:3). The second hymn begins, "You are righteous [*dikaios*], who is and who was, *ho hosios*," and concludes describing the judgments of the Lord God the Almighty as "faithful" (*alēthinos*) and "righteous" (*dikaios*).

10. See the structure outlined by Michaels (*Revelation*, 31).

selected, arguably to evoke *ḥsyd*. Before drawing connections between these uses of *hosios* and Hebrew Bible texts containing *ḥsd/ḥsyd*, I consider the notion that the concept corresponding to *ḥesed* was known to the author of Revelation.

Three main possibilities have been proposed for the author of the Apocalypse: "John the apostle, another John (sometimes referred to as John the Elder), and someone else using 'John' as a pseudonym."[11] G. K. Beale rejects the last possibility, noting that an unknown author attempting to identify with "John the apostle" would probably use that fuller title.[12] That leaves John the apostle and John the Elder, who were both Jewish. The author exhibits an outstanding understanding of the Jewish scriptures.[13] The position of the majority of commentators is that this author was more influenced by the Hebrew text than the Greek translation,[14] although he probably depends on and modifies a combination of Semitic and Greek sources.[15] In either case, he would be familiar with *ḥsd* and *ḥsyd*.[16]

12.1.2.1. Revelation 15:4

Much of the imagery in Rev 15 may be understood in light of the exodus.[17] The chapter opens with the announcement of another sign in heaven (cf. 12:1–3): seven angels with seven plagues that resemble the plagues of Egypt (Exod 7–11; cf. Lev 26:21).[18] Verses 2–3 indicate that those who had conquered the beast, its image, and the number of its name are standing beside a sea of glass, singing the song of Moses and the song of the Lamb. The remainder of verse 3 and all of verse 4 record the song itself:[19]

11. Beale, *Book of Revelation*, 34.
12. Ibid.
13. Sweet, *Revelation*, 39–40. Cf. Aune, *Revelation 1–5*, cxxi.
14. Observed by Beale and McDonough ("Revelation," 1083). Charles claims that John thought in Hebrew and frequently reproduced Hebrew idioms. Charles provides examples of difficult phrases that "can be explained by retranslation into Hebrew" (*Critical and Exegetical Commentary*, 1:x, lxiv). Contra Swete, who concludes that there are other explanations for "the departures from the LXX" (*Apocalypse of St John*, clv).
15. Beale, *Book of Revelation*, 78.
16. Cf. Pattemore, *People of God*, 55, regarding the probable accessibility of Hebrew text / Greek translation for John's Jewish-Gentile Christian audience.
17. So, e.g., Keener, *Revelation*, 384–86.
18. Beale, *Book of Revelation*, 787, and Harrington, *Revelation*, 158.
19. Beale thinks the two titles describe a single song (*Book of Revelation*, 792). The title "Lamb" recalls the deliverance from plagues by the blood of a lamb (cf. Rev 12:11). Keener, *Revelation*, 384–85.

Rev 15:3–4:

μεγάλα καὶ θαυμαστὰ τὰ ἔργα σου,
κύριε ὁ θεὸς ὁ παντοκράτωρ
δίκαιαι καὶ ἀληθιναὶ αἱ ὁδοί σου,
ὁ βασιλεὺς τῶν ἐθνῶν·
τίς οὐ μὴ φοβηθῇ, κύριε,
καὶ δοξάσει τὸ ὄνομά σου;
ὅτι μόνος ὅσιος,
ὅτι πάντα τὰ ἔθνη ἥξουσιν
καὶ προσκυνήσουσιν ἐνώπιόν σου,
ὅτι τὰ δικαιώματά σου
ἐφανερώθησαν.

Great and wonderful are your works,
O Lord God, the Almighty;
righteous and faithful are your ways,
O King of the nations;
who will not fear, O Lord,
and glorify your name?
For you alone are *hosios*,
for all the nations will come
and worship before you,
for your righteous acts have been revealed.

The title "Song of Moses" suggests that either Exod 15 or Deut 32 is in mind.[20] However, the "sea" and "victory" motifs[21] and the reference to Moses as "the servant of God" in Rev 15:2–3 resonate more with Exod 14:31–15:18.[22] The Exodus song is about deliverance from Egypt, but Rev 15:3–4 speaks about "the much greater deliverance" achieved by the Lamb.[23] On the other hand, there is little similarity between the words following after the song title and those of either Exod 15 or Deut 32.[24] Aside from the phrase "just and faithful are your ways," which bears some resemblance to Deut 32:4, the song is a composite of allusions to various texts mainly from the Prophets and Psalms.[25] However, Beale claims that "the theme of the first exodus" (and its later developments) guides the selection of those texts.[26] From the acknowledged range of allusions in Rev 15:3–4,[27] I deal only with texts relevant to the issue of whether *hosios* in Rev 15:4 denotes an instance of the category *ḤSYD*.

20. Moyise, *Evoking Scripture*, 111. A third alternative, Ps 90, includes more lament about the consequences of sin than praise for what God has accomplished. Aune, *Revelation 6–16*, 872; Kraus, *Psalms 60–150*, 214–15; Tate, *Psalms 51–100*, 439.

21. Aune, *Revelation 6–16*, 872, and Mounce, *Book of Revelation*, 287. Beale refers to "the latter-day Red Sea setting" (*Book of Revelation*, 799).

22. Beale, *Book of Revelation*, 791–99, and Blount, *Revelation*, 286.

23. Beale, *Book of Revelation*, 792.

24. Moyise, *Evoking Scripture*, 112.

25. Beale, *Book of Revelation*, 794–98, and Moyise, *Evoking Scripture*, 112.

26. E.g., God's incomparability (Ps 86:9–10; Jer 10:7); cf. the "who is like" formula associated with the exodus redemption (Exod 15:11). Beale, *Book of Revelation*, 796–99.

27. Exod 15:1; Num 12:7; Deut 32:4; Josh 1:7; 14:7; Pss 86:9; 98:2; 111:2; 139:14; 145:17; Jer 10:7; 16:19; Mal 1:11. NA[28], 839, 842, 845, 853–55, 862, 869.

12.1.2.1.1. PSALM 86:8–10 (85:8–10 LXX)

There are several linguistic parallels between Rev 15:3–4 and Ps 86:8–10 (85:8–10 LXX),[28] including *megala/megas, ta erga sou, thaumasta/thaumasia, kyrie, theos/theois, kai doxasei/doxasousin to onoma sou, monos, panta ta ethnē, hēxousin kai proskynēsousin enōpion sou.*[29] The psalm and the Revelation hymn both take up phrases and themes from other scriptural texts.[30] In addition, *hosios* in Ps 85 LXX renders *ḥsyd*. In Ps 86 MT, the *ḥsyd* is the psalmist, who asks YHWH to protect and gladden his *npš* and to save him (vv. 2–4),[31] because "the Lord" (*ʾdny*) abounds in *ḥsd* (vv. 5, 15) and *ʾmt* (*alēthinos* [85:15 LXX]; cf. Rev 15:3), and he "alone" (*monos*; v. 10; cf. Rev 15:4) is God.[32] In light of the linguistic and thematic parallels,[33] the *hosios* in Rev 15:4 may also represent a *ḥsyd*, one devoted to covenant relationship.[34]

12.1.2.1.2. DEUTERONOMY 32:4 AND PSALM 145:17 (144:17 LXX)

Deuteronomy 32:4 and Ps 145:17 are further possible sources for *hosios* in Rev 15:4.[35] Deuteronomy 32:4 and Rev 15:4 have the stronger linguistic connection. Along with *hosios*, Deut 32:4 LXX includes all key terms in the clause "righteous and faithful are your ways" (*dikaios, alēthinos* [pl.], and *hodos* [pl.]). On the other hand, Ps 145:17 and Rev 15:3–4 have the closer thematic similarity in their literary contexts: both Ps 145 and the Revelation hymn praise the Lord and his deeds throughout.[36] In both Deut 32:4 and Ps 144:17 LXX, God / the Lord is the referent of *hosios*. But, in the former, *hosios* renders *yšr* ("upright"),[37] while in the latter, *hosios* renders *ḥsyd*. Thus, either sense (*yšr* or *ḥsyd*) is feasible for *hosios* in Rev 15:4.

28. Noted by Moyise in *Evoking Scripture*, 113. See also Aune, *Revelation 6–16*, 876; Beale, *Book of Revelation*, 797; Keener, *Revelation*, 385; Osborne, *Revelation*, 566.

29. Most of these parallel words/phrases were already identified by Moyise (*Evoking Scripture*, 114). There are also nine occurrences of *ky* (LXX: *hoti*) in Ps 86 (85 LXX) and three occurrences of *hoti* in Rev 15:4.

30. Ibid., 116; Schaefer, *Psalms*, 210; Goldingay, *Psalms 42–89*, 630.

31. Goldingay points out that "this suppliant prays as a member of the exodus people" (*Psalms 42–89*, 618); e.g., *slḥ* ("forgive/pardon") in Ps 86:5; cf. Exod 34:9 (622).

32. The beast and its image cannot be compared to "the true God"; they are merely "a parody." Beale, *Book of Revelation*, 797.

33. NA[28] (769, 853) indicates that Rev 15:4 quotes from Ps 86:9, but many scholars think there are only allusions and echoes in Revelation (e.g., Beale, *Book of Revelation*, 77).

34. Schaefer places vv. 5 and 15 of the psalm on opposite sides of a concentric pattern (*Psalms*, 211–12). In v. 13, YHWH's deliverance of the psalmist's *npš* from Sheol is set in parallel with the clause "For great is your *ḥsd* [*eleos*] toward me."

35. NA[28] (769, 770, 845, 855) indicates that Deut 32:4 is quoted in Rev 15:3 and alluded to in Rev 15:4, 5 and 16:5, while Ps 145:17 is quoted in Rev 15:3 and alluded to in Rev 16:5. See n. 33 above, regarding quotations/allusions in Revelation.

36. Moyise, *Evoking Scripture*, 115.

37. This is the only LXX text where that is the case.

While Deut 32:4 and Rev 15:3–4 share a few descriptive words, *hosios* is the only one used to describe the same entity (in this case, God / the Lord) in both texts.[38] There is a closer correspondence between the descriptions in Ps 145 and those in Rev 15:3–4. The psalmist refers to YHWH as his "God and King," and both titles are used of the Lord in Rev 15:3, this time within parallel phrases. Conversely, the expressions "your wondrous [MT: *pl'*; LXX: *thaumasios*] works" and "your greatness [MT: *gdwlh*; LXX: *megalōsynē*]," featured in separate statements in Ps 145:5–6 (144:5–6 LXX), are condensed within one colon in Rev 15:3 (*megala kai thaumasta ta erga sou*).[39] According to 11QPsalms[a], the *n* line "missing" in the MT text of this acrostic psalm is present in verse 13: "God is faithful in his words/affairs and *ḥsyd* in all his doings." Likewise, verse 17 (MT) states that YHWH is righteous (MT: *ṣdyq*; LXX: *dikaios*) in all his ways (cf. Rev 15:3) and *ḥsyd* (LXX: *hosios*)[40] in all his "doings."[41] Verse 19 indicates that YHWH will do "what is pleasing[42] to those who fear [*yr'*; LXX: *phobeō*] him" (cf. Rev 15:4), and he saves them.[43] Thus, evidently Ps 144 LXX provides the precedent for YHWH / the Lord as the referent of *hosios* (MT: *ḥsyd*) and confirms God's saving activity on behalf of those who fear him.

12.1.2.1.3. PSALM 98:2 MT

Psalm 98 is another "victory" (*yšʿ/yšwʿh*) song, praising YHWH for his "wonderful/miraculous deeds" (*pl'*; LXX: *thaumastos*; v. 1) and recalling exodus themes.[44] Verse 2 reads:

Ps 98:2 MT:

הודיע יהוה ישועתו לעיני הגוים גלה צדקתו	YHWH has made known his salvation/victory; before the eyes of the nations he has revealed his righteousness/vindication.

38. E.g., the Lord himself is *dikaios* in Deut 32:4 LXX, but the King's ways are *dikaios* in Rev 15:3.

39. The "works" in Rev 15:3 are probably plagues (cf. Deut 28:59–60 LXX: "great and amazing plagues"). Smalley, *Revelation to John*, 387.

40. Jeremiah 3:12 contains the only other MT reference to YHWH as *ḥsyd* (LXX: *eleēmōn*).

41. Cf. Ps 141:5 MT, where the same adjectives are used together. In addition, Ps 145:8 MT is an abbreviation of the attribute formula, in which YHWH is "great of *ḥsd*" (*gdl ḥsd*; LXX: *polyeleos*; cf. Num 14:19). YHWH's *ḥsydym* (LXX: *hosioi*) will speak of the glory of YHWH's kingdom (vv. 10–11). Thus, YHWH acts as *ḥsyd* with the *ḥsydym* (cf. Ps 18:26 MT).

42. *HALOT*, s.v. "רָזוֹן."

43. YHWH also "watches over all who love him, but all the wicked he will destroy" (v. 20).

44. Beale, *Book of Revelation*, 798–99.

Ps 97:2 LXX:

ἐγνώρισεν κύριος τὸ σωτήριον αὐτοῦ,	The Lord made known his salvation;
ἐναντίον τῶν ἐθνῶν ἀπεκάλυψεν τὴν δικαιοσύνην αὐτοῦ.	in the sight of the nations he revealed his righteousness.

Sandwiched between the words recorded here in 98:2 and a related clause in 98:3b—"All the ends of the earth have seen the salvation of our God"—comes the statement "He has remembered his *ḥsd* and his faithfulness to the house of Israel" in 98:3a (MT). Those words are fulfilled to an even greater extent in the experience of the ones who have conquered the beast, its image, and the number of its name. All the nations will come, for the Lord's righteous deeds have been revealed (Rev 15:2–4).[45] The one who alone is *hosios* (cf. *ḥsyd*) apparently has remembered his *ḥsd* to the house of Israel once again. The combination of allusions to texts containing *ḥsd* or *ḥsyd* outlined here indicates that the occurrence of *hosios* in Rev 15:4 denotes an instance of the category *ḤSYD*.

12.1.2.2. Corollary: Revelation 16:5

Revelation 16 opens with a loud voice telling seven angels to pour out seven bowls of the wrath of God,[46] a scene probably modelled on the Egyptian plagues (cf. 15:1).[47] The first bowl causes sores on those who bear the mark of the beast and worship its image (v. 2), the second bowl causes the sea to become like the blood of a dead person (v. 3), and the third bowl turns rivers and springs to blood (v. 4).[48] Then an angel in charge of the waters (cf. 1 En. 66:1–2)[49] elaborates on the third bowl in "a sort of antiphon" to 15:3–4 (vv. 5–6).[50] The descriptions *dikaios* and *hosios* from 15:3–4 are recited and illustrated in 16:5–6:[51]

45. An allusion to Ps 98:2. NA[28], 769, 854.

46. The heavenly temple context (cf. Rev 15:8) indicates that God is the speaker here. Beale, *Book of Revelation*, 812; Keener, *Revelation*, 392; Smalley, *Revelation to John*, 400.

47. Harrington, *Revelation*, 163.

48. Cf. "the first plague of the Exodus" (Exod 7:14–21). So, e.g., Aune, *Revelation 6–16*, 884. Beale, *Book of Revelation*, 818. Pattemore detects in the judgments of God "the answer to the prayers of the saints" (5:8; 6:10); the present passage "functions as a progress report" (*People of God*, 99).

49. Aune, *Revelation 6–16*, 884–85.

50. Swete, *Apocalypse of St John*, 202.

51. Harrington, *Revelation*, 163 (referring to Swete, *Apocalypse of St John*, 202), and Keener, *Revelation*, 393.

Rev 16:5–6:

δίκαιος εἶ, ὁ ὢν καὶ ὁ ἦν, ὁ ὅσιος,	Righteous are you, who is and who was, the *hosios* one,[52]
ὅτι ταῦτα ἔκρινας,	for you passed judgment on these things,
ὅτι αἷμα ἁγίων καὶ προφητῶν ἐξέχεαν	for they have poured out [the] blood of saints and prophets
καὶ αἷμα αὐτοῖς δέδωκας πιεῖν,	and you have given them blood to drink;
ἄξιοί εἰσιν.	they are deserving [i.e., as they deserve].

The formula "who is and who was" in 16:5a may be understood in relation to 1:4, 8 and 4:8,[53] where the Lord God the Almighty is "the one who is and who was and who is coming," as distinguished from Jesus Christ (1:5).[54] On the other hand, in 11:17, where the clause "for you have taken your great power and begun to reign" follows directly after "who is and who was,"[55] Christ appears to be included in the reign. The preceding statement refers to "the kingdom of our Lord and of his Christ," who will reign forever (11:15).[56] Therefore, prior to 16:5, this formula was consistently associated with God Almighty, but "his Christ" also began to feature. Likewise, the Lord God the Almighty is the referent for *ho hosios* in 16:5a, but the place of "his Christ" in the scene remains uncertain.

Verse 5b begins with *hoti*, signaling the reason why *ho hosios* is referred to as *dikaios* ("righteous"): "For you passed judgment on these things." Verse 6, also beginning with *hoti*, provides further information about the judgments mentioned in verse 5b.[57] The angel in charge of the waters declares that the *hosios* has given "them" (possibly those who bore the mark of the beast)[58] blood to drink, because they have shed the blood of saints and prophets (cf. Ps 16:4 [15:4

52. The definite article is missing in P47. NA28, 770. Nevertheless, Swete reads "ὁ ὅσιος" because the "ο" would have dropped out, and "ὅσιος (anarthrous) cannot be taken as a predicate after ὁ ὢν καὶ ὁ ἦν" (*Apocalypse of St John*, 202).

53. In 4:8, the Lord God is described as *hagios*.

54. Concerning Rev 16:5, Beale sees the insertion of *kai* before *hosios* in some manuscripts as evidence that early tradition identified "who is and who was" in that text with the threefold formula from earlier in the book, implying that the judgment passed "is another demonstration of God's sovereignty over history" (*Book of Revelation*, 817–18).

55. I.e., "the one who is coming" (*ho erchomenos*) is omitted.

56. Cf. 19:6–7 (the multitude give glory to the Lord God the Almighty because the marriage of the Lamb has come); 21:22 (the temple is both the Lord God the Almighty and the Lamb).

57. Cf. Beale, *Book of Revelation*, 818.

58. The identity of the *autois* in verse 6b is an "exegetical problem." Aune, *Revelation 6–16*, 887–88. Smalley connects those who somehow drink blood with "the murderers of the faithful" (*Revelation to John*, 403–4).

LXX]; 2 Tim 4:6). The principle recorded in Wis 11:16 seems to be at work here: "One is punished by the very things by which one sins."[59] This judgment also reflects the retribution evident in the exodus account (Exod 4:22–23)[60] and the connection between the Lord's *ḥsd* and repayment of a person according to what he does (Ps 62:12 [62:13 MT; 61:13 LXX]).[61]

Shared themes of righteousness and judgment link verses 5 and 7. The response in verse 7 provides another indication that *ho hosios* refers to the Lord God the Almighty:

Rev 16:7:	
Καὶ ἤκουσα τοῦ θυσιαστηρίου λέγοντος·	And I heard the altar saying,
ναὶ κύριε ὁ θεὸς ὁ παντοκράτωρ,	"Yes, O Lord God the Almighty,
ἀληθιναὶ καὶ δίκαιαι αἱ κρίσεις σου.	faithful and righteous are your judgments."

The *inclusio* formed by *kyrie ho theos ho pantokratōr* ("the Lord God the Almighty") and *dikaios/alēthinos* in 15:3 and 16:7, together with the development of themes from 15:3–4 in 16:5–7,[62] suggests that the one who is *hosios* in 15:4 is also the *hosios* in 16:5 and that therefore *hosios* in 16:5 denotes another instance of the category *ḤSYD*.

12.2. The Category *ḤSYD* in Revelation 15–16

Engagement with the category *ḤSYD* in Rev 15–16 is through free and creative use of allusions to scriptural texts that include *hosios* (cf. *ḥsyd*), so there is no single Hebrew Bible or LXX instance of that category to compare with the New Testament instances. I simply analyze elements involved in the two instances in Rev 15–16.

12.2.1. ḤSYD *in Revelation 15:4*

Those who have conquered the beast, its image, and the number of its name (time; context; perceivers) sing the song of Moses, the servant of God, and the song of the Lamb,[63] as they stand beside the sea of glass holding harps of God

59. NRSV translation, and Harrington, *Revelation*, 163.

60. I.e., death of Pharaoh's firstborn because YHWH's firstborn is not released. Ford, *Revelation*, 271–72.

61. Cf. "according to his/your works" in Rev 2:23; 20:12–13; 22:12.

62. See §12.1.2, n. 9.

63. The title "song of the Lamb" may reflect the victory won "by the blood of the Lamb (7:14; 12:11)" (Harrington, *Revelation*, 159) and/or the allusion to Ps 85 LXX (Fenske, "'Das Lied

(communication; Rev 15:2). This song praises the Lord God the Almighty, King of the Nations ([DEVOTED_PARTY]),[64] for his great and wonderful works, his righteous and faithful ways (response of perceivers; v. 3). Presumably, then, the relationship exists between the Lord and those who sing this song. With the pronoun/verb understood, *hosios* becomes the Complement in the Causal Nominal Clause *hoti monos hosios* ("for [you] alone [are] *hosios*"). It is expected that everyone will fear and glorify the Lord's name (universal [RESPONSE]) because he alone ([QUANTITY]/[QUALITY]) is *hosios* ([DEVOTED_PARTY]). All the nations ([OTHER_PARTY]) will come and worship before him ([RESPONSE_OF_OTHER_PARTY]; cf. Ps 86:8–10 [85:8–10 LXX]) because his righteous acts have been revealed ([JUSTIFICATION/REASONS]; v. 4).

12.2.2. ḤSYD *in Revelation 16:5*

In Rev 16, the third angel pours out his bowl, the rivers and springs of water become blood (v. 4; [context]), and then the angel in charge of the waters ([PERCEIVER]) describes the *hosios* ([DEVOTED_PARTY]) as righteous ([QUALITY]; [RESPONSE_OF_PERCEIVER]) because he made the judgments ([REASON]; communication; v. 5). Thus, *ho hosios* is a Vocative Phrase associated with the Nominal Clause *dikaios ei* ("you are righteous"). The relationship is between the Lord God the Almighty (*ho hosios*) and the "saints" (*hagioi*) and prophets whose blood has been shed. The *hosios* gives those who shed blood what they deserve: blood to drink (vv. 2, 6; [RESPONSE/ACTIVITY_OF_DEVOTED_PARTY]). The "altar"[65] declares (communication) that the Lord God's judgments are faithful and righteous (response of other party; v. 7).

12.2.3. General Observations

The following themes emerge from reading the hymns in Rev 15:3–4 and 16:5–7 as one unit.

---

des Mose,'" 259–60). In either case, the Lord God the Almighty's abundant *ḥsd* (cf. Exod 15:13; Ps 86:15) has been demonstrated by a new exodus (deliverance from the beast). Harrington, *Revelation*, 159. Cf. Osborne, *Revelation*, 562–64, and Smalley, *Revelation to John*, 382–85.

64. Smalley describes the hymn as "a song '*to or about*' the Lamb" (*Revelation to John*, 386; emphasis original). Given that several references to the Lamb elsewhere in Revelation speak of God and the Lamb as one unit (7:9–10; 14:4; 21:22, 23; 22:1, 3), and that at times the Lord / God and "his Christ" are mentioned together (11:15; 12:10), the Lamb may be addressed here along with the Lord God the Almighty. On the other hand, these examples illustrate that this author records explicitly when the Lamb / Christ is included, but he is not mentioned in the 15:3–4 hymn.

65. The "altar" probably represents the angel of the altar (and thus, the church's sacrifices and prayers) or a martyr from underneath the altar (cf. Rev 6:9–10). Smalley, *Revelation to John*, 404, and Swete, *Apocalypse of St John*, 203.

12.2.3.1. Righteous and Faithful Judgments of the Almighty

The faithful people who have suffered but also gained victory (context) have received help from the righteous Lord God the Almighty who alone is *hosios* ([DEVOTED_PARTY]; [QUANTITY]/[QUALITY]).[66] He gives the people who caused this innocent suffering what they deserve ([RESPONSE/ACTIVITY_OF_DEVOTED_PARTY]; v. 6).

12.2.3.2. Praise and Worship

The perceivers are those who have conquered the beast, its image, and the number of its name and the angel in charge of the waters. They praise the [DEVOTED_PARTY] for his great and wonderful works, his righteous character and acts, his righteous and faithful ways, and his judgments (response of perceivers; [JUSTIFICATION/REASONS]). Other [RESPONSES] include coming to worship before him, fearing, and glorifying his name.

12.3. Exegetical Value of Recognizing Engagement with the Category *ḤSYD* in Revelation 15–16

There could be at least two reasons for John's use of *hosios* in descriptions of the Lord God the Almighty when *hagios* would be the more likely choice if the idea of holiness were intended. The association between *hosios* and the category *ḤSYD* makes *hosios* suitable for both indicating that the Lord's judgments are an expression of his incomparable devotion toward his people and encouraging sustained allegiance to the faith in the midst of oppression.[67]

12.3.1. ḤSYD *and the Devoted God*

If Rev 15:4 is inspired by Ps 144:17 LXX,[68] where the Lord is referred to as "*dikaios* [MT: *ṣdyq*] in all his ways" and "*hosios* [MT: *ḥsyd*] in all his deeds,"[69] then by implication, the Lord God the Almighty is considered unique among

66. There is some speculation that the Lamb is also included in this description.

67. Beale, *Book of Revelation*, 28–33, and Mounce, *Book of Revelation*, 32.

68. See §12.1.2.1.2.

69. Cf. Pss. Sol. 10:5–7: "Our Lord is righteous [*dikaios*] and *hosios* in his judgments [pl. of *krima*] forever, . . . and the assemblies of Israel will glorify [fut. of *doxazō*; cf. Rev 15:4] the name of the Lord." (This psalm also speaks about the *eleos* [cf. *ḥsd*] of the Lord, and loving him in truth [*alētheia*; cf. *ʾmt*].) In Neh 9:32–33, the righteousness (*ṣdyq*; *dikaios*) and faithfulness (*ʾmt*; *alētheia*) of the great, mighty, and fearsome (*yrʾ*; *phoberos*) God are in the context of God keeping covenant and *ḥsd*.

the "deities" (cf. Ps 86:8–10),[70] and incomparably superior to the beast,[71] on account of being *ḥsyd* ("devoted to covenant relationship"; cf. *monos hosios*). Intertextual allusions (e.g., Ps 86:5–13) also indicate that other reasons given in Rev 15:3–4 for praising the Lord God are probably manifestations of his enduring covenant devotion (cf. *ḥsd*).[72] Thus, the ultimate acts of *ḥsd* performed by the divine *hosios* (cf. *ḥsyd*) will be "faithful" (*alēthinos*) and "righteous" (*dikaios*) judgments[73] against those who poured out the blood of saints and prophets (16:5; cf. the great prostitute in 17:5–6; 19:2). Indeed, the Lord God demonstrates his incomparable devotion to his covenant people by repaying Babylon according to what she has done (cf. Ps 62:12 [62:13 MT; 61:13 LXX]).

12.3.2. ḤSYD *and the Devoted People*

Although Christians are not referred to as *hoi hosioi* in Revelation,[74] the loyalty and solidarity normally associated with *ḥsd* are themes in this book. Addressing congregations who were probably experiencing pressures from external opposition, diverse influences, and/or divided loyalties (Rev 2–3),[75] John indicates that those who follow the faithful example of the one who "conquered" (*nikaō*) will also be similarly rewarded (Rev 2:10–11; 3:21; 12:10–11).[76]

For Christians who perceived a discrepancy between the forces of evil that oppressed them and their beliefs about the kingdom and sovereignty of God and the return of Christ,[77] the transumed tradition signaled by John's choice of vocabulary would also be a reminder not to give up. Psalm 106:7 (105:7 LXX) reads, "Our ancestors in Egypt did not consider your wonderful works [*niphal* pl. ptc. of *pl'*; LXX: *thaumasios*]; they did not remember the abundance of

70. Cf. "among the gods." Goldingay, *Psalms 42–89*, 624. Aune refers to inscriptional evidence for "a cult of Hosios and Dikaios (Holiness and Justice), often associated with other deities" (*Revelation 6–16*, 886). Also see Sheppard, "Pagan Cults of Angels," 87–92.

71. Beale, *Book of Revelation*, 796–97.

72. Verses in Ps 86 MT about the incomparable and wondrous things that YHWH does (*pl'*; LXX: *thaumasios*; v. 10; cf. Rev 15:3) and the expected responses to YHWH's incomparable nature (e.g., all the nations will come; v. 9; Rev 15:4) are preceded and followed by references to YHWH's abounding *ḥsd* (vv. 5, 15; cf. Ps 98:2–3 MT). Brueggemann, *Message of the Psalms*, 61, and Tate, *Psalms 51–100*, 381.

73. The order of these terms in Rev 16:7 is inverted in comparison to Rev 15:3. Cf. Ps 19:9 (19:10 MT; 18:10 LXX). References to *ḥsydym* in the context of judgment include Pss 50:5–6 (49:5–6 LXX); 149:9.

74. They are called *(hoi) hagioi* ("[the] saints"; esp. in gen. form [e.g., 14:12; 16:6]), which possibly alludes to those who receive the kingdom in Dan 7:18. Trebilco, "What Shall We Call Each Other?" 61–64.

75. Smalley, *Revelation to John*, 3–5. Cf. Osborne, *Revelation*, 10–12.

76. Beale, *Book of Revelation*, 171, and Michaels, *Revelation*, 36.

77. According to Beale, most commentators think this is a reason for John writing (*Book of Revelation*, 28).

your *ḥsd*." Concerning that verse among others, Walter Brueggemann notes, "The forgetting of impossibilities means to settle for what is possible, to give up hope, . . . and to define the world in terms of what is and can be managed."[78] In contrast, John's allusions to the exodus tradition and other texts that speak of the Lord's wonders should bring confidence to John's audience and inspire their commitment.[79] In Ps 86, the psalmist (a *ḥsyd*; LXX: *hosios*) indicates that YHWH's great *ḥsd* is demonstrated by preserving (requested) and delivering the psalmist's *npš* (vv. 2, 13). The psalmist also declares that all the nations will come and bow down before the Lord, for he does "wonderful things" (*pl'* as above; LXX: *thaumasios*; vv. 9–10). According to Ps 145, YHWH's *ḥsydym* (LXX: *hosioi*) bless YHWH, the divine *ḥsyd* (LXX: *hosios*), who saves all those who "fear" (*yr'*; LXX: *phobeō*) him, and the psalmist meditates on the "wonderful" (*pl'*; LXX: *thaumasios*) acts of YHWH (vv. 5, 10, 17, 19). As members of John's original audience recognized allusions to these texts in the Apocalypse, their hope, founded in the one who is incomparably *hosios* and will perform more "wonderful" (*thaumastos*; Rev 15:3) works of deliverance/judgment on behalf of those who fear him (*phobeō*; 15:4), might be renewed.

12.4. Conclusions

There appears to be a mixture of Greek and Hebrew ideas evoked by the occurrences of *hosios* in 1 Tim 2:8; Titus 1:8; Heb 7:26; and Rev 15:4; 16:5. The verses most likely to include instances of the category *ḤSYD* are Rev 15:4 and 16:5. The author of Revelation evidently had a strong grasp of the Hebrew Scriptures and made intertextual connections with the exodus tradition and relevant psalms.

While the redemptive work of the Lamb has brought about the triumphal deliverance of the overcomers, the Lord God the Almighty is the most obvious referent of *hosios* (cf. *ḥsyd*; [DEVOTED_PARTY]) in Rev 15–16. Intertextual connections indicate that the declaration *hoti monos hosios* in Rev 15:4 draws more attention to God's incomparable covenant devotion ([QUANTITY]/[QUALITY]; cf. Ps 86:5, 15) than to God's holiness. The [DEVOTED_PARTY] responds to the innocent suffering of his faithful people ([RESPONSE_OF_THE_DEVOTED_PARTY]; context) by giving those who caused that suffering a punishment that matches their crime. Though not stated explicitly, the faithful and righteous

78. Brueggemann, "'Impossibility' and Epistemology," 625.

79. *Ḥsd/ḥsyd* and *pl'* (noun or verb) sometimes appear together in texts about the exodus (e.g., Jer 32:16–23; Ps 77:9, 12, 15–16 MT; cf. Exod 15:11–13; 34:6–10). Cf. Beale, *Book of Revelation*, 798 (exodus texts), and Tate, *Psalms 51–100*, 381. See also Ps 107:8, 15, 21, 31 MT, and Brueggemann's description of *pela'* in "Israel's 'historical recitals'" ("'Impossibility' and Epistemology," 623).

judgments of the divine *hosios* (cf. *ḥsyd*) could be considered God's ultimate acts of *ḥsd*. They inspire fear, glorification, sung praise, and the worship of the nations ([RESPONSES_OF_OTHER_PARTIES/perceivers]; communication).

In addition, the Lord's devotion and the example of those who remained loyal to their God in the midst of opposition would be inspirational for John's audience.

CHAPTER 13

ḤSD, *ḤSYD*, *Eleos*, and *Hosios* in the New Testament

Drawing from the material in chapters 4–5 and 7–12, I now make comparisons between Hebrew Bible data and New Testament instances of the categories *ḤSD* and *ḤSYD* (§13.1). I also make generalizations about *eleos* (§13.2) and *hosios* (§13.3) in the New Testament as a whole. At least some New Testament occurrences of *eleos* and *hosios* evoke the senses of *ḥsd/ḥsyd* from the Hebrew Bible, more than the senses of "mercy" or "holy."

13.1. The Categories *ḤSD* and *ḤSYD* in the New Testament

My observations about New Testament engagement with the categories *ḤSD* and *ḤSYD* are drawn from those texts containing *eleos* or *hosios* with the strongest intertextual connections to Hebrew Bible texts containing *ḥsd* or *ḥsyd* (Matt 9:13; 12:7; Luke 1:50, 54, 58, 72, 78; Acts 2:27; 13:34, 35; Rom 15:9; 1 Pet 1:3; Rev 15:4) and corollaries built on those connections (Matt 23:23; Luke 10:37; Rom 9:23; 11:31; Gal 6:16; Rev 16:5).

There are five subcategories of *ḤSD* and *ḤSYD* represented among the occurrences of *eleos* and *hosios* in the texts listed above: ARTICLE_OF_TRANSACTION, CHARACTERISTIC, SPECIFIC_DEMONSTRATION, ENTITY, and ONE_DEVOTED_TO_COVENANT_RELATIONSHIP. ONE_DEVOTED is not represented. There are more New Testament instances of the CHARACTERISTIC and ENTITY subcategories than the other *ḤSD* subcategories. Some New Testament instances of the category *ḤSD* belong in more than one subcategory, but I analyze each instance in only the subcategory to which it belongs that has the fewest instances.

13.1.1. ARTICLE_OF_TRANSACTION

The occurrences of *eleos* in Luke 1:58, 72 and 10:37 involve transactions between two parties, one more (situationally) powerful/superior than the other. The Lord

God of Israel does *eleos* with the Israelite ancestors and abundantly/lavishly demonstrates his *eleos* with Elizabeth, a righteous but barren woman. A Samaritan does *eleos* with a man lying half-dead on the road. In each case, *meta* signals the relationship, and *eleos* (or "his *eleos*," or "the *eleos*") is the Direct Object of the aorist verb in its clause. In two cases, the verb is *poieō*, reflecting the construction *ʿśh ḥsd ʿm* ("do *ḥsd* with"). I deal with the occurrences of *eleos* in 1:58, 72 here, but *eleos* in 10:37 also denotes a [SPECIFIC_DEMONSTRATION], so it is dealt with in that section.

Given that the most common relational context for [ARTICLE_OF_TRANSACTION] *ḥsd* is between YHWH/God and YHWH/God's covenant partners, it is not surprising that a remembered covenant is also a relational context for [ARTICLE_OF_TRANSACTION] *eleos* in the New Testament. The [AGENT] of [ARTICLE_OF_TRANSACTION] *eleos* is the Lord God, who "does" and "makes great / lavishes" *eleos* ([AGENT'S_ACTIVITIES]). A righteous woman (Elizabeth) and Israel's ancestors are [PATIENTS] of the Lord's *eleos* (cf. the frequent mention of Israel and the patriarchs, and the naming of individual women, as [PATIENTS] of *ḥsd*).

True to the scriptural precedent, the Lord God of Israel is the [POSSESSOR] of the [ARTICLE_OF_TRANSACTION] *eleos* in the New Testament. Themes associated with the possible [MANIFESTATIONS] of God's *eleos* include the birth of a son, redemption, salvation coming from the house of David, and deliverance/salvation from enemies. Thus, of the common [MANIFESTATIONS] of [ARTICLE_OF_TRANSACTION] *ḥsd*, deliverance, salvation, and an enduring throne are themes extended into the New Testament era.

Where the [ARTICLE_OF_TRANSACTION] *ḥsd* was often associated with [CONTEXTS] of dislocation/distress, the Lord has now visited his people and fulfilled promise/s at an appointed time. With this evidence that the Lord's *ḥsd* (cf. *eleos*) is indeed "to the thousandth generation" (Hebrew Bible [DURATION]), the [OUTCOMES] no longer include additional requests, but rather righteous service and significant events in the growth of a child that will become a prophet who goes before the Lord. Like the Hebrew Bible [PERCEIVERS] of *ḥsd*, New Testament [PERCEIVERS] of [ARTICLE_OF_TRANSACTION] *eleos* rejoice and bless the Lord ([RESPONSES]).

13.1.2. CHARACTERISTIC

[CHARACTERISTIC] *eleos* is signaled in the New Testament by a genitive form of *eleos* (Rom 9:23), a genitive term (e.g., *autou*) positioned before or after *eleos* (Luke 1:50, 58, 78; 1 Pet 1:3; cf. Hebrew pronominal suffixes), or the adjective *hymeteros* positioned before *eleos* (Rom 11:31). Like [CHARACTERISTIC] *ḥsd*, [CHARACTERISTIC] *eleos* can be part of an Adverbial/Prepositional Phrase, explaining the basis for an action or experience. I deal with *eleos* in Luke 1:58 in the ARTICLE_OF_TRANSACTION subcategory section, although it also behaves like a [CHARACTERISTIC].

The Lord God of Israel is the most frequent [POSSESSOR] of [CHARACTERISTIC] *eleos* and the only [POSSESSOR] of abundant and enduring *eleos* (as for *ḥsd*). There is a new emphasis on Gentiles becoming [POSSESSORS] of *eleos*. God, the only [AGENT] of [CHARACTERISTIC] *eleos*, prepared beforehand ([AGENT'S_ACTIVITY]) vessels for glory. Those who benefit from [CHARACTERISTIC] *eleos* include the Lord's people Israel, those who fear the Lord, and the elect exiles of Asia Minor. The relationship between God and God's elect people is now on the basis of promises made to their ancestors. As in the scriptural tradition, those [JUSTIFIED] to receive *eleos* (cf. *ḥsd*) are contrasted with those who are not. [JUSTIFICATIONS] include God's will/calling and fear of the Lord.

The differences between Hebrew Bible [MANIFESTATIONS] of YHWH's *ḥsd* and New Testament [MANIFESTATIONS] of the Lord's *eleos* signal a new season in salvation history. New Testament [MANIFESTATIONS] include the regeneration of God's people and "compassion/mercy." The Lord's *eleos* is also associated with great things that the Lord has done, forgiveness of sins, and the visitation of a messianic figure. Actual or recommended [OUTCOMES] are thoroughly positive. Outcomes already predicted in the Hebrew Bible include the birth of Christ, light for those in darkness, and guidance into the way of peace.

New Testament writers/perceivers no longer appeal to God on the basis of God's *eleos* (cf. *ḥsd*); they praise God for the benefits they have now received. As with the Hebrew Bible [RESPONSES], New Testament [RESPONSES] are usually positive and either cognitive or vocal, but positive behavior changes are also recommended. A new response is praying for the salvation of Israel.

As in the scriptural tradition, various elements are [CONTRASTED]: the Lord's responses to the rich, proud, and powerful and to the lowly and needy; the vessels of *eleos* ([POSSESSORS]) and of *orgē*; Israel and the Gentiles; the abundant *eleos* of the Lord, associated with an imperishable inheritance, and the *doxa* of all flesh, which perishes ([QUANTITY]; [DURATION]; [OUTCOME]).

13.1.3. SPECIFIC_DEMONSTRATION

According to Luke 10:37, a Samaritan did a [SPECIFIC_DEMONSTRATION] of *eleos* with another man who fell among robbers. [SPECIFIC_DEMONSTRATIONS] of *hosios* are also featured in a quotation of Isa 55:3b in Acts 13:34 ("I will give you the faithful *hosia* of David"). Both instances are signaled by the definite article. As is common in the scriptural tradition, these [SPECIFIC_DEMONSTRATIONS] are Direct Objects of verbs.

In this subcategory, David and a particular generation of Abraham's descendants are [POSSESSORS] of *hosios*. The most frequent Hebrew Bible [AGENT] in this subcategory is God. God is also a New Testament [AGENT], along with a Samaritan man. On the other hand, a priest and a Levite are not [AGENTS] of *eleos*. Key Hebrew Bible [PATIENTS] of *ḥsd* are Israelites in need (patriarchs, kings, and people). Likewise, the New Testament [PATIENTS] of [SPECIFIC_DEMONSTRATIONS] of *eleos* or *hosios* are a wounded man (presumed to be Judean)[1] and Jesus (David's descendant), who had been executed.

The mutual-aid and covenant-relational contexts for [SPECIFIC_DEMONSTRATIONS] of *ḥsd* are also reflected (or expected) in the New Testament [SPECIFIC_DEMONSTRATIONS] of *eleos/hosios*. According to the Lucan parable and its frame, the relationship between the Samaritan man and the wounded man is initiated by aid provided in a crisis. By implication, such a wounded man would be expected to love a Samaritan (his neighbor, in this case) as himself. In addition, the lawyer should become a neighbor by doing *eleos*.[2] In Acts, the covenantal relationships are between God and Abraham, God and David, and God and the current generation of God's people (justification).

[SPECIFIC_DEMONSTRATIONS] of *eleos/hosios* are found in the generation when Jesus is resurrected from death (time), distant from corruption, and at a crisis on the road from Jerusalem to Jericho (locations/contexts) (cf. *ḥsd* in Israel; *ḥsd* associated with particular events). Thus, the [MANIFESTATIONS] of *eleos* and *hosios* involve preventing or raising from death.

The experience of Paul's audience (Acts 13) resembles some outcomes[3] and responses[4] promised/presented to Deutero-Isaiah's audience. Through Jesus, there is forgiveness of sins and justification. Appropriate responses include knowing and belief but not driving away the messengers, as some do.

13.1.4. ENTITY

New Testament instances of the ENTITY subcategory of *ḤSD* are proportionally higher than Hebrew Bible instances. The [ENTITY] *eleos* is something the Lord desires (Jesus cites Hos 6:6a in Matt 9:13; 12:7), one of three weighty matters of the law that religious leaders have neglected (Matt 23:23), something the Lord remembers to Israel's benefit (Luke 1:54) and for which the Gentiles are to glorify God (Rom 15:9), and part of a blessing upon those who follow the rule of new creation, the Israel of God (Gal 6:16). As expected, New Testament

1. See §9.2.5, n. 51.
2. [AGENT'S_ACTIVITIES] are doing (cf. *ʿśh ḥsd*) and giving.
3. Including nations (cf. Gentiles) running to Israel, mercy and forgiveness, being led forth in peace.
4. Including coming, seeking, returning, and creation rejoicing.

instances of the ENTITY subcategory are distinguished by the lack of any indicator of relationship, genitive noun, definite article, or common grammatical unit in the clauses to which *eleos* belongs.

Perceivers of the presence or absence of [ENTITY] *eleos* include YHWH (cf. the [ENTITY] *ḥsd*), Jesus, Mary, Paul, and the Gentiles. Actual or recommended [PERCEIVERS'_RESPONSES] to this [ENTITY] are mostly positive (e.g., desiring, glorifying, rejoicing). On the other hand, the Pharisees do not perceive the [ENTITY] *eleos*. They condemn the innocent and challenge the agent ([OUTCOMES]). Jesus reacts to their neglect of *eleos* with a statement of woe and a declaration of hypocrisy. He instructs his disciples to do as the Pharisees say and not as they do.

Where YHWH was the main [AGENT] of the [ENTITY] *ḥsd*, the Lord / God and (by implication) Jesus are [AGENTS] of the [ENTITY] *eleos*. Broadly interpreted, "patients" include Christ Jesus (Abraham's offspring) and the Lord's servant Israel (as spoken to Abraham and his offspring), Jesus's disciples, those who follow the rule of new creation, and sinners. In contrast, despite *appearing* to keep the law meticulously, the Pharisees neglect *eleos* (non-[AGENTS]; along with the scribes) and plot how they might kill Jesus (outcome).

Consistent with the most frequent relational context for the [ENTITY] *ḥsd* (YHWH and YHWH's people), some relational contexts for the [ENTITY] *eleos* are between God and the descendants of those to whom God made promises. Justifications for the [ENTITY] *eleos* include recognizing one's need, fulfilling scriptural declarations or covenantal promises, and the cross of Christ.

In a medical analogy associated with the [ENTITY] *eleos*, Jesus contrasts those who have need (patients) with those who do not have need. The [ENTITY] *eleos* should be evident whenever and wherever needs are recognized, even at the house of a tax collector or on the Sabbath (times; locations). Together with some manifestations of this [ENTITY] (e.g., calling sinners to discipleship), these notions challenge expectations.

The greater priority of the [ENTITY] *ḥsd/eleos* as a matter of the law is [CONTRASTED] with the lesser priorities of sacrifice and tithing herbs. The Pharisees, who do not understand that *eleos* is a priority for the Sabbath, are contrasted with Jesus, the Lord of the Sabbath. The rule of new creation and the circumstances of the Gentiles are [CONTRASTED] with the rule and circumstances of the circumcision.

13.1.5. ONE_DEVOTED_TO_COVENANT_RELATIONSHIP

The four New Testament occurrences of *hosios* that denote instances of the category *ḤSYD* are associated with the subcategory ONE_DEVOTED_TO_COVENANT_RELATIONSHIP. Acts 2:27 and 13:35 include quotations from Ps 15:10

LXX, where the psalmist says to the Lord, "You will not give/permit your *hosios* [MT: *ḥsyd*] to see corruption." In Rev 15:4 and 16:5, the Lord God the Almighty is referred to as *monos hosios* and *ho hosios*. As with the Hebrew Bible instances of this subcategory, there is no particular grammatical construction or unit common to the New Testament instances.

In the Hebrew Bible, *ḥsydym* (pl.) is more frequent than *ḥsyd* (sg.), indicating that God's covenant people are in mind, but in these New Testament texts, only singular forms of *hosios* are used, because the only [DEVOTED_PARTIES] are the Lord God the Almighty and Jesus Christ, a descendant of "David the son of Jesse."[5] David himself could not have been the [DEVOTED_PARTY] referred to in Ps 16 because he died, was buried, and saw corruption. But Jesus ("the Christ") is "he whom God raised." Thus, justifications/[REASONS] for the title *hosios* include the Davidic covenant and the works, character, acts, ways, and judgments of the Lord God. The Lord / God is also the only [POSSESSIVE_PARTY].[6] God did not abandon Christ to Hades or permit his flesh to see corruption but raised him, exalted him, and made known to him the paths of life (responses of possessive party).

In a Hebrew Bible exemplar for this subcategory (Ps 30:5–6 MT), the *ḥsydym* praise YHWH because suffering lasts only a short while and then rejoicing comes. New Testament contexts involving God's *hosios* or the Lord God himself as *hosios* are after suffering and death have occurred, although victory follows. The [RESPONSES_OF_DEVOTED_PARTIES] are then a glad heart, a rejoicing tongue, hopeful flesh (Jesus), and a deserved judgment (from the Lord God) for those who caused innocent suffering.

When David (potential [DEVOTED_PARTY]) had served the purpose of God in his generation, he fell asleep and saw corruption. In contrast, God raised Jesus (actual [DEVOTED_PARTY]) from death and burial and exalted him. Jesus did not see corruption. Through Jesus sins can be forgiven, and by him people can be justified from that which could not be justified under the law of Moses (outcomes; contrast).

Perceivers respond in song, declarations of praise, and calling others to believe. [REASONS] for the verbal declarations are even more dramatic and transforming than in the Hebrew Bible. They include revelation of final judgments and forgiveness/justification previously not available. Actual or recommended responses of other parties engage the heart but are expressed vocally or demonstrably. Some people in Paul's audience follow or believe, while others contradict what Paul says and stir up persecution (responses; outcomes; contrast).[7]

5. Note that, beyond the limited sample of texts listed, the plural form also occurs in 1 Tim 2:8 and being *hosios* is a qualification of an overseer in Titus 1:8.

6. But *hosious cheiras* ("*hosios* hands") occurs in 1 Tim 2:8.

7. Cf. the contrast between the *ḥsydym* and those opposed to YHWH's ways in the Hebrew Bible.

13.2. *Eleos* in the New Testament

Intertextual evidence indicates that the relationship between *ḥsd* and *eleos* in the scriptural tradition influences the connotations of at least some of the twenty-seven New Testament occurrences of *eleos*.[8] The following generalizations are based on the fourteen occurrences most likely to denote instances of the category *ḤSD*: those in Matt 9:13; 12:7; 23:23; Luke 1:50, 54, 58, 72, 78; 10:37; Rom 9:23; 11:31; 15:9; Gal 6:16; and 1 Pet 1:3.

13.2.1. Intertextual Connections, Grammatical Constructions, and Syntactic/Clause Roles

Intertextual connections between *eleos* and *ḥsd* include (1) quotations from Hos 6:6 in Matt 9:13 and 12:7; (2) indirect allusions to Exod 34:6–7 in Luke 1:50, 54, 58, 72, 78; (3) allusions to Pss 18:51 (17:51 LXX); 117:2 (116:2 LXX) (by quoting the verses directly before these); and Mic 7:20 in Rom 15:7–13; and (4) an echo of the tradition associated with YHWH's attribute (cf. Exod 34:6) in 1 Pet 1:3. The allusions and echo are signaled by New Testament use of vocabulary, themes, names, and grammatical constructions associated with *eleos* (rendering *ḥsd*) in the LXX.[9] In the New Testament, *eleos* is most frequently the Direct Object of a Transitive Verb, part of an Adverbial Prepositional Phrase, and/or part of a Causal/Purpose Clause, because significant events are explained in relation to God remembering/doing *eleos* or because people should possess/demonstrate *eleos* more often.

13.2.2. YHWH/God and Eleos

As with *ḥsd* in the Hebrew Bible, God is the primary [POSSESSOR] of *eleos* in the New Testament. God's *eleos* is still abundant ([QUANTITY]), enduring ([DURATION]), and demonstrated on the basis of covenant relationships (cf. YHWH's *ḥsd*, usually rendered by *eleos*), but it is now also [JUSTIFIED] by scriptural fulfillment, God's will/calling, and the cross of Jesus Christ. [MANIFESTATIONS] of God's *eleos* are consistent with [MANIFESTATIONS] of God's *ḥsd* throughout salvation history, yet they also signal radical developments. God's abundant *eleos* is the basis for regeneration, resulting in a living hope; an imperishable, undefiled, unfading inheritance; and a salvation yet to be revealed ([QUANTITY]; [OUTCOMES]).

8. Mounce, *Pastoral Epistles*, 10.

9. E.g., variations on "do [*poieō*] *eleos* with [*meta*]" (cf. *ʿśh ḥsd ʿm*) in Luke 1:72 and 10:37, parallel use of *eleos* and *alētheia* (cf. *ḥsd wʾmt*) in Rom 15:8–9, and *kata to poly autou eleos* (cf. *krb ḥsdw*) in 1 Pet 1:3.

13.2.3. *Jesus and* Eleos

A uniquely New Testament [MANIFESTATION] of God's *eleos* (cf. YHWH's *ḥsd*) is the coming of Messiah Jesus. Jesus is an exemplary perceiver and implied agent of *eleos*, in contrast to the Pharisees, who have inaccurate perceptions and misplaced priorities, and whose actions are inconsistent with their words. Jesus meets physical and spiritual needs, including calling sinners to discipleship (manifestation). His explanations infer that he demonstrates *eleos* in the house of a tax collector on one occasion, and during the Sabbath on another (location; time). And, just as YHWH [CONTRASTS] *ḥsd* with sacrifice, Jesus [CONTRASTS] doing *eleos* with observing legal minutiae like tithing herbs.

13.2.4. *The Reconstituted People of* Eleos

Another development in the [MANIFESTATIONS] of God's *eleos* (cf. YHWH's *ḥsd*) is the reconstitution of God's people. *Eleos* is now received by sinners, tax collectors, a barren woman, and Gentiles, among others ([PATIENTS]). Jews and Gentiles [PERCEIVE][10] and [POSSESS] God's *eleos*, and in this sample of texts, the only [AGENT] of *eleos*, apart from God and Jesus, is a Samaritan man. In Jesus's parable, the Samaritan's *eleos* is worked out in acts of compassion for another man in dire need (manifestation), initiating a relationship based on mutual aid. In contrast, a priest, a Levite, and Pharisees are not agents of *eleos*. The New Testament people of *eleos* (cf. Hebrew Bible *ḥsydym*) are people of belief and action, who walk according to the rule of new creation, love one another, praise God, and rejoice.

13.2.5. *Continuity, Change, and* Eleos

Certain notions are associated with *eleos* through its LXX function rendering *ḥsd*. The notions emphasized in each New Testament Gospel or letter depend on the target audience and the circumstances being described. Matthew, writing to a largely Jewish-Christian audience, establishes the validity of the new kingdom movement and Jesus's ministry in terms of the scriptural tradition. He emphasizes the priority of doing *eleos* (cf. *ḥsd*) in terms of genuine law observance, restoring covenant relationships, and meeting essential needs. For Paul, who seeks to show that salvation has come first to the Jew and also to the Greek, Scriptures that associate *eleos* (cf. *ḥsd*) with covenants and the nations are important. Luke writes to a predominantly Gentile audience but still emphasizes God's remembrance of covenant promises, what it means

10. Cf. predictions in Rom 15:9, 11.

to be God's covenant people, and the importance of meeting essential needs of neighbors, because Gentiles are becoming part of a movement that originated amongst Jews. And Peter addresses dispersed Christians suffering for their faith as if they were Israel. He emphasizes the association between *eleos* (cf. *ḥsd*) and God's motivation for helpful action, God's relationship with God's chosen people, and the expectation of enduring commitment/solidarity. Together they present a rich picture involving both assuring continuity and positive change.

13.2.6. **Ḥsd** ***and*** **Eleos**

Several New Testament occurrences of *eleos* are more about *ḥesed* than showing mercy to sinners or pity in situations of affliction. They are about being motivated to act, meeting essential needs, maintaining mutual relationships, remembering promises, sustaining covenantal devotion, belonging to God's people, and/or demonstrating solidarity with one's community. Though the boundaries between *eleos* and *eleeō* are fuzzy, the general distinction between the sense of the noun and the sense of the verb in the LXX (cf. *ḥsd* and *ḥnn* or *rḥm*, respectively) is often maintained in the New Testament.

13.3. *Hosios* in the New Testament

There is a mixture of general Greek and LXX / Hebrew Bible influences on the New Testament sense/s of *hosios*. Of the eight New Testament occurrences of *hosios*, the following generalizations are based on the five occurrences most likely to denote instances of the categories *ḤSD* and *ḤSYD*: Acts 2:27; 13:34, 35; and Rev 15:4; 16:5.

Syntactic functions of *hosios* and types of clauses to which it belongs—Object-Verbal, Complement/Vocative-Nominal—reflect the New Testament use of *hosios* to describe what God gives or does not give (a new emphasis in *ḤSD*/*ḤSYD* categories) or Godself.

Acts 13:34 is the only New Testament text in which *hosios* evokes an instance of the category *ḤSD*. That verse cites Isa 55:3b, the only instance of the category *ḤSD* where *hosios* in the LXX renders *ḥsd* in the Hebrew Bible. According to Acts 13:32–34, the resurrection of Jesus fulfills God's promise to give the faithful *hosia* associated with the Davidic covenant (*ta hosia Dauid ta pista*) to a new generation of covenant people ([AGENT]; [AGENT'S_ACTIVITY]; [QUALITY]; [JUSTIFICATION]; [POSSESSORS]; time). This demonstrates the enduring nature of God's covenant devotion. [SPECIFIC_DEMONSTRATIONS] of *hosios* (cf. *ḥsd*) in the New Testament context include God "raising up" David's offspring, Jesus

([MANIFESTATION]), and by intertextual association, the good things promised to those who respond to the Lord's invitation to "come."

Engagement with the category ḤSYD in Acts 2:27 and 13:35 (and literary contexts) emphasizes various contrasts: Jesus (the Lord's *hosios*; [DEVOTED_PARTY]) and his ancestor David ([PERCEIVER]),[11] life and death, those who receive the word and those who reject it. Jesus's resurrection is viewed as fulfillment of the promise quoted from Ps 15:10b LXX, where *hosios* renders *ḥsyd*. Intertextual connections between Rev 15–16, the exodus tradition, and psalms about the saving acts of YHWH indicate that the occurrences of *hosios* in Rev 15:4 and 16:5 also denote instances of the category ḤSYD. In Revelation, the Lord God the Almighty is the *hosios* ([DEVOTED_PARTY]), but the redemptive work of the Lamb has also brought victory. Each declaration of good news in the Rev 15–16 hymns takes place after a significant act of God's deliverance or righteous judgment (contexts; [JUSTIFICATION]). Whether the [POSSESSIVE_PARTY] (Acts) or the [DEVOTED_PARTY] (Revelation), God is proactive. Vocal [RESPONSES] to God's intervention include praise, worship, and rejoicing. Other positive responses/outcomes include forgiveness and justification, belief and baptism.

These New Testament occurrences of *hosios* evoke the relational and covenantal senses of *ḥsd/ḥsyd* from the Hebrew Bible, as distinct from the sense of *hagios* ("holy"). Instances of the categories ḤSD and ḤSYD are associated with God's incomparable devotion, evident throughout salvation history, and continuous with God's ongoing purposes. Scriptural quotations and allusions involving *hosios* are understood in light of the coming and resurrection of the Messiah, and now hold significance for a wider group of people, including those who suffer trials.

11. David saw corruption ([CONTEXT]).

CHAPTER 14

Ḥesed and the New Testament: Conclusions and Outlook

The following conclusions about the relationship between *ḥesed* and the New Testament as a whole are based on fourteen occurrences of *eleos* and five occurrences of *hosios*—those with the most intertextual evidence that they denote members of the categories ḤSD and ḤSYD or those associated as corollaries. Even this limited sample illustrates that New Testament authors engage with the concept corresponding to *ḥesed* to highlight consistency with and developments within the scriptural tradition, to highlight the enduring devotion of God and the exemplary ministry of Jesus, to critique the contemporary socioreligious situation, and to encourage belief, relationship, appropriately changed lifestyles, and enduring commitment. Furthermore, texts with occurrences of *eleos* or *hosios* that evoke *ḥesed* should be interpreted within a framework of interpersonal relationships.

The three guiding issues of this project have been: (1) *whether* there is evidence of New Testament engagement with the concept corresponding to *ḥesed*, and if so, (2) *how* that engagement occurs and (3) the *exegetical value* of recognizing that engagement. Sections 14.1, 14.2, 14.3 (respectively), and 14.4 (in summary) present conclusions about these issues, drawing on material from relevant sections in chapters 7–13 and reflecting on matters of intertextual categorization raised in chapter 2. However, the occurrences of *eleos* and *hosios* are dealt with in canonical order, not the order presented in earlier chapters. In section 14.5, I consider the value of this research for life and scholarship by outlining both its limitations and its implications and by revisiting issues raised in the opening chapters.

14.1. Evidence of New Testament Engagement with the Concept Corresponding to *Ḥesed*

The intertextual evidence for New Testament engagement with the concept corresponding to *ḥesed* highlighted in this monograph is a collection of quotations and allusions to particular texts in the Hebrew Bible containing *ḥsd* or *ḥsyd*, along with echoes of the *ḥesed* tradition.

Two occurrences of *eleos* in Matthew's Gospel (9:13; 12:7) are within identical citations from Hos 6:6a, where LXX *eleos* renders MT *ḥsd*. The description of *eleos* in Matt 23:23 (the only other occurrence of *eleos* in this Gospel) brings **thematic coherence** to Matthew's argument: *eleos* is one of the weighty matters of the law. This occurrence is treated as a corollary (an illustration of **volume** with respect to Hays's tests for allusions/echoes).

The first five occurrences of *eleos* in Luke's Gospel—1:50, 54, 58, 72, and 78—allude indirectly to *ḥsd* in YHWH's attribute formula (Exod 34:6–7), giving that precursor text prominence (**volume**). The concentrated repetition of *eleos* suggests that events associated with the incarnation of Christ provide ample evidence that the Lord God has remembered his *eleos* (cf. *ḥsd*) throughout the generations. LXX renderings of prototypical grammatical constructions involving *ḥsd* are also reflected among these occurrences of *eleos*. I treat the only other occurrence of *eleos* in this Gospel (10:37) as a corollary. Jesus's parable illustrates that doing *eleos* with a person in dire need is the essence of becoming a neighbor.

Two of the three occurrences of *hosios* in Acts—2:27 and 13:35—are within quotations of Ps 15:10 LXX, where *hosios* renders MT *ḥsyd*. Interpretations of that verse in the speeches of Peter and Paul indicate that God raising Jesus from the dead fulfilled the hopeful declaration of the psalmist David that the Lord would not give/permit his *hosios* to see corruption. The neuter plural of *hosios* occurs in Acts 13:34 within a quotation of Isa 55:3b, where LXX *ta hosia* renders MT *ḥsdym*. The contextual frame of this quotation indicates that the resurrection of Jesus fulfills a promise made about the *hosia* of David, which the tradition associates with the Davidic covenant. The word *hosios*, shared by Acts 13:34 and 13:35, provides **thematic coherence**.

Two scriptural quotations (Pss 18:49 [18:50 MT; 17:50 LXX]; 117:1 [116:1 LXX]) recorded in the Rom 15:9–12 series are followed, in their LXX contexts, by verses where LXX *eleos* translates MT *ḥsd*. The parallel terms *alētheia* and *eleos* in Rom 15:8–9 also allude to *ʾmt* and *ḥsd*, their order probably reflecting Mic 7:20. The combined intertextual evidence indicates that Gentiles are among those who glorify God for *ḥsd/eleos*. Romans 15:7–13 features multiple allusions to *ḥsd* (**recurrence**), and the assertion involving *eleos* (vv. 8–9) introduces in a satisfying way the quotations that follow (**satisfaction / thematic coherence**). I consider the occurrences of *eleos* in Rom 9:23; 11:31; and Gal 6:16 as corollaries to this argument.

Ho kata to poly autou eleos in 1 Pet 1:3 echoes the Hebrew Bible phrase *krb ḥsdw*. The unit from 1:3 to 2:10 also includes a quotation from Isa 40:6, 8 (40:6–8 LXX), where LXX *doxa* renders MT *ḥsd* (1:24). All the *doxa* of "all flesh" perishes like a flower of the field/grass, but God's abundant *eleos* (cf. *ḥsd*) bears imperishable fruit. Members of the covenant community are regenerated into a living hope. The **recurrence** of quotations and allusions to material from Isaiah provides **thematic coherence** for Peter's argument.

Phrases from Rev 15:3–4 allude to Pss 86 (85 LXX); 98 (97 LXX); and 145 (144 LXX), which include *ḥsd/ḥsyd* in the Hebrew texts. *Ḥsyd* in Pss 86 and 145 MT is rendered by *hosios* in the LXX. Owing to strong connections between the hymns in Rev 15:3–4 and 16:5–7 and the prominence of *hosios* there but nowhere else in Revelation (cf. **volume**), I consider *hosios* in Rev 16:5 as a corollary to the argument concerning *hosios* in 15:4. In this context, the Lord God the Almighty is the *hosios* (cf. *ḥsyd*) who makes faithful and righteous judgments.

Thus, New Testament quotations, allusions, and echoes of texts that include *ḥsd* or *ḥsyd* in the MT are most often associated with the Exod 34 attribute formula, Psalms, Deutero-Isaiah, Hosea, and Micah. Among Hays's tests for intertextual allusions/echoes, **volume**, **recurrence**, and **thematic coherence** are strong indicators that *ḥesed* is evoked in the New Testament.

14.2. Aspects of New Testament Engagement with the Concept Corresponding to *Ḥesed*

The concept corresponding to *ḥesed* is central to the tradition that New Testament authors consider authoritative. This concept brings cohesion between the story presented in their Scriptures and the sequel they are writing,[1] and its fundamental principles are significant for their arguments. It is evoked within proofs, clarifications, critiques, and exhortations, often concerning the transformation brought about by the incarnation, ministry, resurrection, and/or exaltation of Jesus.

The most common LXX translations for *ḥsd* and *ḥsyd*,[2] sometimes within LXX equivalents for prototypical grammatical constructions,[3] signal likely New Testament engagement with the concept corresponding to *ḥesed*. But the emphases in each context depend on the audience and circumstances addressed. *Eleos* (evoking *ḥsd*) is a weighty matter of the law, the basis for remembered promises, the motivation for a neighbor to act compassionately, the reason for

1. "The inevitable sequel": Bruce, *Book of Acts*, 254.
2. This reflects the particular intertextual connections involved.
3. The behavior of *eleos* in the New Testament seems closer to *ḥsd* in the Hebrew Bible than to *ḥsd* in the nonbiblical DSS texts, except that ENTITY is proportionally more frequent than other ḤSD subcategories, but the grammatical constructions involving *eleos* in the New Testament are less predictable than those involving *ḥsd* in the Hebrew Bible.

Gentiles glorifying God and for hope, and an enduring characteristic of God. The *hosia Dauid* (evoking *ḥsdym*) become a gift associated with the Davidic covenant, and the *hosios* (evoking *ḥsyd*) is a descendant of David or the one who makes faithful and righteous judgments.

Nevertheless, there are some general trends in the ways that New Testament authors engage with the concept corresponding to *ḥesed*, as evoked characteristically by those occurrences of *eleos* and *hosios* that belong to the categories *ḤSD* and/or *ḤSYD*. I outline these trends in sections 14.2.1–14.2.4 below.

14.2.1. Highlighting Both Consistency With and Developments Within the Scriptural Tradition

New Testament authors indicate how the events they report are consistent with the scriptural tradition. Thus, New Testament [PERCEPTIONS] of *eleos/hosios* and the experiences to which they relate are often communicated in or together with quotations, allusions, and echoes from the Scriptures. In the New Testament, God is still the most reliable [POSSESSOR] of *eleos* (cf. *ḥsd*) and [PATIENTS] are still the situationally less powerful parties in situations of dire need. They may have personal qualities that set them apart from others, but usually they receive *eleos/hosios* because of what was promised or declared to their ancestors, especially in covenants ([JUSTIFICATIONS]). [MANIFESTATIONS] of *eleos/hosios* not only remain consistent with the scriptural tradition, but fulfill that which was predicted.

On the other hand, New Testament authors report remarkable new events in ways that highlight developments within the tradition. For these writers, the Scriptures provide "proof" for the new developments. [MANIFESTATIONS] of *eleos/hosios* reach a new level. The Messiah has now come, and instead of being kept from death, he is raised from death and kept from corruption ([CONTEXTS]) by the transforming and life-giving activity of God ([POSSESSIVE_PARTY]). Contrasts highlight the unexpected new participants in some scenes involving *eleos*. In particular, where the traditional people of *ḥsd* were primarily God's covenant people,[4] Gentiles are now included more often among those who [PERCEIVE] and/or [POSSESS] *eleos*. [PATIENTS] of *eleos* are now part of a new movement, continuous with the old but also associated with the cross of Christ and the rule of new creation. God's will and calling are emphasized as [JUSTIFICATIONS] for possessing/receiving *eleos*. And Jesus is the only [DEVOTED_PARTY], apart from God.[5]

4. Some Gentiles were included among the people of *ḥsd* (e.g., Ruth and Orpah; Ruth 1:8).

5. I.e., within the specified sample of texts.

14.2.2. Highlighting the Enduring Devotion of God and the Exemplary Ministry of Jesus

New Testament appropriation of texts evoking *ḥsd* often in itself highlights the enduring nature of God's *ḥsd*. In addition, the Lord God is a proactive party in interactions involving *eleos/hosios*, the primary [AGENT] and most reliable [POSSESSOR] of *eleos*, the only [POSSESSOR] of abundant *eleos*, and the incomparable *hosios*. In contrast to the perishing *doxa* of all flesh, God's *eleos* endures for many generations.

But there is also another prominent figure featured in scenes involving *eleos/hosios*. Jesus is the first [DEVOTED_PARTY] not to see corruption ([CONTEXT]) but to be raised from death, the long-awaited *hosios*/Messiah through whom covenant promises have been fulfilled, the exemplary agent and discerning perceiver of *eleos*. Also, key imagery in pericopes involving *eleos* is associated with Jesus. He is the physician, the sunrise, and the root. Thus, Jesus is central to an understanding of New Testament engagement with the concept corresponding to *ḥesed*.

14.2.3. Critiquing the Contemporary Socioreligious Situation

The categories *ḤSD* and *ḤSYD* are also associated with New Testament critique of social and religious incongruities. Despite their meticulous attention to maintaining the outward appearance of righteousness, hypocritical religious leaders neglect *eleos* (non-[AGENTS]). They do not perceive the presence of *eleos*, nor do they understand its importance for keeping the law, so they challenge Jesus's decisions and condemn the innocent. Rejection of the gospel by some of God's chosen people is cause for distress (negative responses/outcomes), but also leads to an opportunity for Gentiles to engage with *eleos*. Demonstrations of *eleos* are also associated with other "unlikely" people (e.g., a barren woman, a Samaritan). In contrast to other religious leaders, Jesus teaches/demonstrates that any time (including the Sabbath) or location (including the house of a tax collector) when/where the need arises is appropriate for doing *eleos*.

14.2.4. Encouraging Belief, Relationship, Appropriately Changed Lifestyles, and Enduring Commitment

Demonstrations of *eleos/hosios* (cf. *ḥsd*) and positive responses to *eleos/hosios* lead to positive and sometimes permanent outcomes, some of which are the fulfillment of scriptural predictions. Positive [RESPONSES] to *eleos/hosios* (cf. *ḥsd* or *ḥsyd*) still relate to the heart/mind (e.g., belief), the tongue (e.g., glorifying), and behavior (e.g., baptism), but there is new emphasis on receiving the benefits of the new covenant and changing lifestyles to reflect what God has now brought to pass (e.g., loving one another). On the other hand, neglect of *eleos/hosios* and negative responses to *eleos/hosios* lead to negative outcomes.

There is also a focus on remaining loyal to the faith amid trials. *Eleos/Hosios* may occur at an appointed time or after a season of suffering or an acute crisis. Thankfully, God's *eleos/hosios* can be depended on in the long term, and the new transformations associated with it are even more "wonderful" than those associated with *ḥsd* in the Hebrew Bible. God has prepared vessels of *eleos* for glory ([AGENT'S_ACTIVITIES]). Furthermore, the Lord God the Almighty, who is incomparably *hosios* (cf. *ḥsyd*), will respond with righteous judgments to the innocent suffering of those who remain faithful.

14.3. Exegetical Value of Recognizing New Testament Engagement with the Concept Corresponding to *Ḥesed*

The main exegetical value in recognizing New Testament engagement with the concept corresponding to *ḥesed* is that it signals a particular interpretive framework for the issues considered in texts where *ḥsd* or *ḥsyd* is evoked—the author is likely to be discussing issues pertaining to interpersonal/covenantal relationships, such as mutuality, solidarity, need, responsible use of power, ongoing commitment, what it means to be God's special people, and/or God's devotion to them. As the concept is recognized, a wealth of transumed insights that could enhance the interpretation of New Testament texts becomes available to readers who follow the intertextual connections.

At least five key understandings (outlined in §§14.3.1–14.3.5 below) are significant for interpreting New Testament pericopes where *ḥsd* or *ḥsyd* is evoked. Different understandings about *ḥesed* are emphasized in different New Testament examples, according to the particular intertextual links involved and other contextual factors.

14.3.1. Ḥesed *Is Done in Relationships with Mutual Responsibilities*

Ḥesed is done in relationships where each party has responsibilities/obligations. Thus, YHWH speaks of Godself as doing *ḥsd* to the thousands of those who love YHWH and keep YHWH's commandments (Exod 20:5–6). And in light of this principle, New Testament authors portray God as the exemplary keeper of commitments and Jesus as having an exemplary understanding of the heart of the law. They also critique those who do not fulfill their obligations.

God assists, visits, redeems, and saves Israel as an expression of the *eleos* committed to their ancestors and now remembered. God fulfills promises regarding the *hosia* of David and the Lord's *hosios* (cf. *ḥsdym*/*ḥsyd*) when God raises Jesus. God fulfills promises regarding *eleos* (cf. *ḥsd*) to the descendants of Abraham and David in the great salvation/victory of one descendant, and in the experience of the current generation of God's people/believers, who are blessed with *eleos* "in Christ." God is not only moved by the circumstances of his people; God is true to his covenant obligations.

Jesus's exposition of the command to love one's neighbor as oneself also resonates with the relationship between love and *ḥsd* evident in Exod 20:5–6. The neighbor is one who does *eleos* (cf. *ḥsd*) with another in need. But Jesus must instruct a so-called "expert in the law" to do likewise. Similarly, when Jesus cites Hos 6:6a, he highlights the comparison between Hosea's contemporaries who prioritize sacrifice over *ḥsd/eleos* and the contemporary religious leaders who prioritize external ritualism and legal minutiae over *eleos*. According to Jesus's authoritative interpretation of the law, both groups have neglected their weighty covenant obligation.

14.3.2. **Ḥesed** ***Is Done by Meeting Dire Needs***

Ḥesed is done when one party freely offers help to another party in dire need. Thus, when *ḥesed* is evoked in the New Testament, this signals that there are dire needs to be met, whether or not they are recognized as such. The divine physician meets not only the physical but also the spiritual needs of all those who seek first God's kingdom and righteousness, including sinners and tax collectors! But the pretentiously "righteous" neither recognize their own need nor address the needs of others.

In the New Testament, there is a noticeable lack of requests made on the basis of God's *eleos/hosios* (cf. *ḥsd*), perhaps because many desperate prayers from the psalmists have now been answered. Owing to enduring *hosia* (cf. *ḥsdym*), needs that were not met under the law of Moses are now met. The Savior-Messiah has come, death is overcome, and everyone who believes can be forgiven their sins and justified. One day, those who cause the innocent suffering of faithful saints will be judged by the God who is incomparably *hosios*.

14.3.3. **Ḥesed** ***Is Done by a Situationally More Powerful Party Who Alone Can Provide Help***

Ḥesed is done when a situationally more powerful party (normally the only available source of assistance) helps a situationally less powerful party.[6] Given that God is always the more powerful party, it is not surprising that Hebrew

6. Sakenfeld, *Meaning of Hesed*, 234.

Bible and New Testament texts alike portray God as the primary [AGENT] of *ḥsd/eleos*, the sole [POSSESSOR] of abundant *ḥsd*, the proactive party in salvific events, and the incomparable *ḥsyd/hosios*. But knowing this principle also sheds light on certain New Testament developments. First, apart from God, Jesus, the new exemplary agent of *eleos*, is the only one who can save sinners. Second, a priest and a Levite, who could have used their situational power to provide necessary assistance, exercised their prerogative to decline. Thus, the only other human reported to have done *eleos* is someone despised—a Samaritan (hypothetical [AGENT]).[7] Third, though God is always the more powerful party, one way that humans can reciprocate God's *eleos* is by meeting the needs of Jesus's brothers and sisters.

14.3.4. **Ḥesed** ***Is a Hallmark of God's People***

In the Hebrew Bible, the relationship between YHWH and YHWH's covenant people is marked by *ḥesed*, to the extent that these people are known as the *ḥsydym*.[8] This explains why, in the New Testament, it is on the basis of covenant relationships associated with *eleos/hosios* that the Lord visits and redeems his people/servant Israel and God raises Jesus.

But the presence of *eleos/hosios* in certain New Testament scenarios also signals the realization of a "widening call" that had always been in view[9] and a redefinition of what it means to be the special people of God. God exalts the lowly, fills the hungry, and lavishes his *eleos* upon an elderly barren woman, and his abundant *eleos* is the basis for a work of regeneration. While other religious leaders are careful to retain separatist boundaries and ritual purity, Jesus shares table fellowship with tax collectors and sinners, calls them to discipleship, and indicates that genuine righteousness/neighborliness is more about doing *eleos* than having the right ancestry, role, or status. Vessels of *eleos* are those whom God has called and prepared for glory, from among the Jews and the Gentiles. Gentiles are also among those who glorify God for *eleos*. The "Israel of God," upon whom Paul invokes a blessing of peace and *eleos*, includes as many as will follow the rule of new creation, and the "elect exiles," who were once not a people, have become God's people, according to God's *eleos*. Finally, as promised, all the nations are coming to worship the one who is incomparably *hosios*.

Regarding the relationship between *ḥsydym* and the *Asidaioi* (§5.2.2), I see no evidence in the New Testament of any militancy or nationalism associated

7. Onesiphorus helped Paul, but Onesiphorus is not described as doing *eleos*.

8. There is also a relationship between the *ḥsydym* and covenant fidelity in the nonbiblical DSS texts.

9. See §8.3.2, including n. 105.

with the people of *eleos* or the long-awaited *hosios*. Instead, these terms are associated with Christ or those "in Christ," and it is the Lord God the Almighty, the *monos hosios*, who carries out judgments.

14.3.5. Ḥesed *Is Meant to Be Ongoing*

By its very nature, *ḥesed* is also meant to endure. The presence of God's *eleos/hosios* (cf. *ḥsd*) in the New Testament is evidence that, despite suspicions to the contrary (e.g., Ps 89:49 [89:50 MT; 88:50 LXX]), the refrain of Hebrew Bible thanksgiving liturgies is true: "His [YHWH's] *ḥsd* is forever." God's *eleos* (cf. *ḥsd*) is for those who fear God throughout the generations, and it is still the motivation for God's interventions in the present generation. *Eleos/hosia* (cf. *ḥsd/ḥsdym*) have not departed from the house of David, but God has sent God's anointed one as a Savior for Israel.

Unfortunately, the *doxa* (MT: *ḥsd*) of all flesh remains as perishable as a flower in the field. Nevertheless, believers who have been rebegotten according to God's abundant *eleos* (cf. *ḥsd*) are encouraged to demonstrate commitment to God and fellow believers, even in the midst of trials, knowing that an imperishable inheritance is kept in heaven for those whose faith proves genuine. The Lord God the Almighty, who is incomparably *hosios* (cf. *ḥsyd*), does "wonderful works" of deliverance for those who overcome and will eventually repay each one according to what he/she has done.

14.4. Conclusion

Common English translations for *eleos* or *hosios* have disguised New Testament engagement with the concept corresponding to *ḥesed.* Thinking that texts containing *eleos* or *hosios* are about mercy and holiness, respectively, readers have missed points about ongoing devotion to kinship/covenantal relationships made in many of those contexts. The incarnation, resurrection, and exaltation of Christ are evidence that God keeps his covenant promises throughout the generations. As a result of this great faithfulness, any repentant sinners who believe (Jews and Gentiles, women and men,[10] religious leaders and tax collectors) can belong to the reconstituted people of God. Rather than pretentious displays of religious observance, God delights in enduring devotion to covenant relationship and active attention to the needs of others. To this end, believers can follow the example of Jesus, who embodies genuine covenantal fidelity and communal solidarity.

10. Cf. Ben Sira's "men of *ḥsd*" (§4.2.2).

Indeed, a closer reading reveals that several New Testament occurrences of *eleos* and *hosios* evoke the concept corresponding to *ḥesed.* Quotations, allusions, and echoes of texts originally containing *ḥsd* or *ḥsyd* signal New Testament engagement with that concept and provide links to the domain of ancient Israelite interpersonal relationships, with their characteristic customs and expectations. Calling attention to these intertextual connections is an important step toward enhancing the interpretation of relevant texts and helping "words like 'faithfulness' and 'loyalty'" to regain their power in this generation.[11]

14.5. Limitations and Implications

14.5.1. For Research

This investigation has proven more complex than anticipated, and yet worthwhile. Despite the degree of subjectivity involved in assigning instances of the categories *ḤSD* and *ḤSYD* to subcategories, the improbability of attaining precise equivalence between terms in different languages, the fuzzy boundary between *eleos* and *eleeō*, and the impossibility of identifying every instance of the categories *ḤSD* and *ḤSYD* present in the New Testament, patient and exacting analysis has enabled me to recognize some New Testament engagement with the concept corresponding to *ḥesed.*

Thus, it would be worth adapting the hybrid methodological approach, Intertextual Categorization, for use by biblical scholars studying other monosemous Hebrew words. Quotations, allusions, and echoes of scriptural texts that originally contained a particular Hebrew word are the most reliable indicators of New Testament engagement with the corresponding concept. Categorization focuses intertextual interpretation onto that single concept, and prototypes provide a secondary control for identifying examples. Communicating analyses using linguistic terminology sharpens the results and provides precise criteria for comparing Hebrew Bible and New Testament sets of data. Moreover, recovering insights transumed by metalepsis enhances the interpretation of associated New Testament texts.

In addition, this study highlights several topics for further investigation. The vast amount of data generated by occurrences of *ḥsd, ḥsyd, eleos, hosios,* and related terms within biblical texts and associated literature meant limiting the number/scope of comparative analyses. But those limitations, along with the results of my research, suggest the following supplementary research projects: additional consideration of the subcategories of *ḤSD* and *ḤSYD* for

11. Sakenfeld, *Faithfulness in Action,* 1.

Hebrew lexicons; more comprehensive comparative analysis of the domains and subcategories associated with *ḥsd*, *ḥsyd*, related Hebrew terms, and their Greek/other renderings in the Hebrew Bible, LXX, Dead Sea Scrolls, targumim, and other extrabiblical literature; thorough reexamination of the assertions of other scholars about the equivalence of *agapē* or *charis* to *ḥsd*; further investigation of the relationship between *eleos*, *eleeō*, *eleaō*, *eleēmōn*, and *eleēmosynē* in the New Testament in light of their distinctive nuances in the LXX; and research into reasons for the divergence between Qumran community and New Testament engagement with the concept corresponding to *ḥesed*.

14.5.2. For Translation and Interpretation

The outcomes of this investigation are both linguistic and theological, since finding evidence of New Testament engagement with the concept corresponding to *ḥesed* has implications for the translation of particular Greek words and the interpretation of pericopes in which the concept is evoked.

I have focused on occurrences of *eleos* and *hosios*, the most frequent LXX renderings of *ḥsd* and *ḥsyd*, respectively, and thus the *most likely* terms to evoke *ḥesed* in the New Testament. This focus does not imply that entities/experiences/individuals denoted by other Greek words in the New Testament must be excluded from the categories *ḤSD* and *ḤSYD*, but rather that the intertextual evidence for proposed alternatives (including *charis* and *agapē*) is not as clear/substantial as for *eleos* and *hosios*.[12]

Knowing that any process of translation inevitably results in distortion, I cannot claim that *eleos* and *hosios* have become "Greek words with Hebrew meanings" when used in the New Testament.[13] Rather, I assign to each of these words the connotations they have assumed through their use in the LXX only where intertextual and linguistic evidence indicates that this is appropriate. Nevertheless, my research does show that, within at least some New Testament contexts, the "primary connotations" of *eleos* and *hosios* reflect their function in the LXX: to render *ḥsd* or *ḥsyd*.[14] The implications of this conclusion follow.

First, *eleos* is not always associated with the mercy for sinners or pity/compassion for those who are afflicted, typical of *eleeō* (cf. *ḥnn*). In at least some New Testament contexts, *eleos* shares the communal solidarity, ongoing covenant loyalty, Decalogue-in-one-word,[15] power imbalance, mutual/reciprocal, and/or anthropomorphic connotations of *ḥsd*. This broadens the scope of *eleos*

12. *Doxa* does render *ḥsd* in one LXX verse that happens to be cited in the New Testament, but that is an exceptional use of *doxa*. Also see §6.1.1, regarding *charis* and *agapē*.

13. The quoted phrase comes from McLay, *Use of the Septuagint*, 146.

14. See Janzen, *When Prayer Takes Place*, 294.

15. Sakenfeld, *Meaning of Hesed*, 181.

from extrabiblical Greek usage. Second, *hosios* should be distinguished from the much more frequent term *hagios*. They are both usually translated "holy" or "holy one," but at least some New Testament uses of *hosios* evoke *ḥsyd* ("one devoted to covenant relationship"). This generates a more specific sense of the term than the general Greek notions of piety and moral judgment.

Therefore, it seems appropriate to signal the presence of *eleos* and *hosios* in some New Testament contexts with distinctive English translations that bring to mind the relevant expectations and practices/customs associated with kinship and other covenantal relationships in ancient Israel. While I have been reluctant to use English translations of *ḥsd* and *ḥsyd*, I have resorted to "devotion" and "devoted one" where translation has been unavoidable. Although "devotion" can be directed toward a cause or express a degree of intimacy not appropriate for some *ḥesed* relationships, it does incorporate aspects of loving-kindness, pious relationship with God, and loyal commitment to people, which are also associated with the concept corresponding to *ḥesed*. In many contexts, "devotion" denotes that concept better than "mercy," but the extent to which the semantic ranges of "devotion" and *eleos* intersect is an issue for further consideration. On the other hand, "devoted (one)" does seem preferable to "holy (one)" as a translation for *hosios* within some New Testament contexts.

These insights should sharpen not only the translation of words but also the interpretation of relevant New Testament pericopes. However, I welcome the additional insights of those from cultural backgrounds/worldviews closer to the biblical contexts and with personal experience of the kinship relations from which *ḥsd* is derived.

14.5.3. For Life

Given that faithful interpretation of Scripture is meant to be demonstrated in life,[16] what can my research contribute to a society where people sometimes let others down and the power of "words like 'faithfulness' and 'loyalty'" seems to be shifting and/or diminishing?[17] First, while the reasons for individuals' reluctance to enter into long-term commitments or relationships involving mutual aid and hospitality are complex (e.g., past disappointments, abuse, "stranger danger") and I cannot recommend initiating or remaining in relationships that will be or are seriously detrimental to those involved, genuine *ḥesed* is still an ideal that people can aspire to and strive toward. We can do *ḥsd* with others and love as ourselves those who do *ḥsd* with us. That is how relationships are meant to work well.

16. Rae, "Response," 260.
17. Sakenfeld, *Faithfulness in Action*, 1.

Second, according to God's great *ḥsd*, the more permanent benefits of a new covenant predicted in the Hebrew Bible are now made available through/by Jesus: forgiveness, justification, spiritual healing, living hope, and eternal salvation. According to New Testament authors, the appropriate responses are belief, repentance, and baptism.

Third, life "in Christ" is not about maintaining an outward appearance of righteousness and enforcing separatist boundaries. It is about demonstrating *ḥsd* and restoring others to covenant relationship.

Finally, the transformative events to which the New Testament bears witness are evidence that, while human *ḥsd* cannot be relied on for long, God's *ḥsd* endures throughout the generations, despite how circumstances may appear. God's people can count on God's consistent *ḥsd*, even in the midst of trials. They can follow the example of Jesus, assured that an imperishable inheritance is kept in heaven for those who remain loyal to God and God's purpose for them.

The personal impact of this investigation goes beyond the awe-inspiring discovery that New Testament authors perceived God's enduring *eleos* (cf. *ḥsd*) as an underlying reason for events they recorded. Now an even more challenging yet rewarding task begins—putting into practice the lesson that the religious leaders of Jesus's time also had to learn: the true *ḥsyd* is not one who appears pious, one who teaches about *ḥesed*, or even one who writes a monograph on the topic, but one who *does ḥsd* . . . and that is a lifelong endeavor.

APPENDIX 1: HEBREW BIBLE OCCURRENCES OF חסד AND חסיד

In order to develop a comprehensive understanding of the concept corresponding to *ḥesed*, it has been helpful to identify typical patterns of behavior and usage for the words חסד and חסיד. There is not space within this monograph to document the entire semantic, syntactic, and grammatical analysis for each occurrence of חסד and חסיד on which my insights were based, but summaries of the key results are included in sections 4.1 and 5.1, respectively. The analysis included the following aspects:[1] Each MT clause containing חסד or חסיד was labeled according to the type of clause (e.g., Verbal, Nominal, Object), as defined in various resources about Hebrew grammar and syntax.[2] The items in the clause to which חסד or חסיד belongs were also analyzed according to their grammatical classes (e.g., Noun, Adjective, Pronominal Suffix) and syntactic functions (e.g., Subject, Direct Object, Indirect Object, Complement, Modifier).[3] An English translation of each MT clause or sentence was analyzed according to its semantic elements as they relate to חסד or חסיד (e.g., [AGENT], [PATIENT], [MANIFESTATION]). Definitions for all the elements in the semantic analysis are listed in table A1.1.

When an element was found in a clause involving חסד or חסיד, all other occurrences of חסד or חסיד were then analyzed in relation to that element, even if the information then had to be located in the wider literary context (i.e., outside of the clause or sentence to which חסד or חסיד belongs). Where appropriate,

1. Some aspects of the analysis were initially adapted from Megahan's table 4.8, "Example of a basic frame write-up" ("Some Lexemes," 187). E.g., among his summary headings, Megahan includes "Frame name," "Participants," "Location," "Temporal," and "Event description."

2. Principally, Gibson, *Davidson's Introductory Hebrew Grammar–Syntax*; *GKC*; Waltke and O'Connor, *Introduction to Biblical Hebrew Syntax*.

3. Words were assigned to grammatical classes with the help of morphology for respective texts on Logos Bible Software.

each occurrence was also analyzed for Communication (how חסד or information about חסד/חסיד is communicated) and the Relational Context that involves חסד or חסיד. If imagery is involved, the Figurative Expression (e.g., metaphor: חסד_IS_A_MESSENGER) was also noted.

Table A1.2 presents all Hebrew Bible (*BHS*) occurrences of חסד and חסיד included in the analysis. The table has three columns. The first column records the MT clause or sentence to which חסד or חסיד belongs, with verses presented in the Hebrew Bible order. The second column records my English translation of each MT clause or sentence. The third column records the LXX translation of the clause or sentence to which חסד or חסיד belongs. In each column, the clause to which חסד, חסיד, or the respective translation belongs is underlined with a single line. The LXX rendering of חסד or חסיד is underlined with two lines.

Tables A1.3 (חסד) and A1.4 (חסיד) present the instances of each particular LXX rendering grouped together. Unless stated otherwise, verse numbers in brackets indicate the MT/LXX numbering where that differs from the NRSV numbering.

TABLE A1.1. Definitions of Semantic Elements

[ACTIVITY]	What a party does (including passive or negated actions).
[AGENT]	The active party, the one who does or promises חסד in this instance.
[ARTICLE_OF_TRANSACTION]	חסד involved in a transaction.
[CHARACTERISTIC]	חסד that is characteristic of a possessor.
[CONTEXT]	The context in which חסד or חסיד is or should be present, exhibited, done, or perceived.
[CONTRAST]	Any contrast associated with חסד, חסיד, or others involved in the event.
[DEVOTED_PARTY]	The חסיד (one devoted [to covenant relationship]).
[DURATION]	The timeframe over which חסד or חסיד is present, exhibited, done, or perceived.
[ENTITY]	An abstract/schematic instance of חסד.
[JUSTIFICATION]	The reason why the perceiver, patient, or possessor is justified in appealing for or receiving חסד, or why a party is called חסיד.
[LOCATION]	The location where חסד or חסיד is or should be situated.
[MANIFESTATION]	The particular manifestation of חסד in this instance, as done, committed to, requested, or invoked.
[OBJECT_OF_DEVOTION]	The "object" to which the devoted party's devotion is directed.
[OUTCOME]	The outcome of the request for חסד, the manifestation/demonstration of חסד, or the situation involving חסיד.
[PATIENT]	The passive or receptive party, the one who is promised or receives חסד in this instance.

TABLE A1.1. Definitions of Semantic Elements (*continued*)

[PERCEIVER]	The party who observes, predicts, or appreciates the existence/presence (or critiques the nonexistence/absence) of חסד or חסיד.
[POSSESSIVE_PARTY]	The party to whom the חסיד belongs.
[POSSESSOR]	The party that possesses חסד,[4] including the one characterized by חסד, the one with a disposition to act according to חסד, and the one into whose possession חסד is transferred.
[POSSESSION_OF_DEVOTED_PARTY]	That which belongs to the חסיד.
[QUALITY]	The quality of חסד or חסיד.
[QUANTITY]	The quantity of חסד, חסדים, or חסידים.
[REASON]	The reason for the description, activity, or response.
[RESPONSE]	The requested or actual response of a specified party in an event or interaction involving חסד or חסיד.
[SPECIFIC_DEMONSTRATION]	The specific demonstration through which חסד is made manifest in this particular instance.
[TIME]	The time at which חסד or חסיד is present, exhibited, done, or perceived.

TABLE A1.2. Hebrew Bible Occurrences of חסד and חסיד

MT Clause(s)	English Translation of MT Clause(s)	LXX Translation of MT Clause(s)
Gen 19:19 ותגדל חסדך אשר עשית עמדי להחיות את נפשי	**Gen 19:19** And you [angels; those Lot refers to as "lords"] have magnified your חסד, that you have done with me [Lot] by reviving my נפש.	**Gen 19:19** καὶ ἐμεγάλυνας τὴν δικαιοσύνην σου, ὃ ποιεῖς ἐπ' ἐμέ, τοῦ ζῆν τὴν ψυχήν μου, Note: ἔλεος was used for חן in the previous colon.
Gen 20:13 זה חסדך אשר תעשי עמדי אל כל המקום אשר נבוא שמה אמרי לי אחי הוא	**Gen 20:13** This [is] your חסד that you [Sarah] will do with me [Abraham]: at every place to which we come, (there) say of me, "He [is] my brother."	**Gen 20:13** Ταύτην τὴν δικαιοσύνην ποιήσεις ἐπ' ἐμέ, εἰς πάντα τόπον, οὗ ἐὰν εἰσέλθωμεν ἐκεῖ, εἰπὸν ἐμὲ ὅτι Ἀδελφός μού ἐστιν.
Gen 21:23 כחסד אשר עשיתי עמך תעשה עמדי ועם הארץ אשר גרתה בה	**Gen 21:23** According to the חסד that I [Abimelech] have done with you [Abraham], you will do with me and with the land in which you have dwelt as an alien.	**Gen 21:23** ἀλλὰ κατὰ τὴν δικαιοσύνην, ἣν ἐποίησα μετὰ σοῦ, ποιήσεις μετ' ἐμοῦ καὶ τῇ γῇ, ᾗ σὺ παρῴκησας ἐν αὐτῇ.

4. This description is not necessarily linked to the nature of a genitive construction in which חסד features.

TABLE A1.2. Hebrew Bible Occurrences of חסד and חסיד (*continued*)

MT Clause(s)	English Translation of MT Clause(s)	LXX Translation of MT Clause(s)
Gen 24:12 יהוה אלהי אדני אברהם הקרה נא לפני היום ועשה חסד עם אדני אברהם	**Gen 24:12** O YHWH, God of my master, Abraham, please allow [it] to unfold before me today, and do חסד with my master, Abraham.	**Gen 24:12** Κύριε ὁ θεὸς τοῦ κυρίου μου Αβρααμ, εὐόδωσον ἐναντίον ἐμοῦ σήμερον καὶ ποίησον ἔλεος μετὰ τοῦ κυρίου μου Αβρααμ.
Gen 24:14 ובה אדע כי עשית חסד עם אדני	**Gen 24:14** By her [the girl YHWH has appointed for his servant, Isaac], I [Abraham's servant] will know that you [YHWH, God of his master] have done חסד with my master [Abraham].	**Gen 24:14** καὶ ἐν τούτῳ γνώσομαι ὅτι ἐποίησας ἔλεος τῷ κυρίῳ μου Αβρααμ.
Gen 24:27 ברוך יהוה אלהי אדני אברהם אשר לא עזב חסדו ואמתו מעם אדני	**Gen 24:27** Blessed be YHWH, God of my master, Abraham, who has not forsaken his [YHWH's] חסד or his אמת ["faithfulness"][5] (from) with my master.	**Gen 24:27** Εὐλογητὸς κύριος ὁ θεὸς τοῦ κυρίου μου Αβρααμ, ὃς οὐκ ἐγκατέλιπεν τὴν δικαιοσύνην αὐτοῦ καὶ τὴν ἀλήθειαν ἀπὸ τοῦ κυρίου μου,
Gen 24:49 ועתה אם ישכם עשים חסד ואמת את אדני הגידו לי	**Gen 24:49** And now, if you [Laban and Bethuel] are doing [i.e., going to do] חסד and faithfulness*** to my master [Abraham], tell me!	**Gen 24:49** εἰ οὖν ποιεῖτε ὑμεῖς ἔλεος καὶ δικαιοσύνην πρὸς τὸν κύριόν μου, ἀπαγγείλατέ μοι, Note: δικαιοσύνη is used for אמת.
Gen 32:11 קטנתי מכל החסדים ומכל האמת אשר עשית את עבדך	**Gen 32:10** I [Jacob] am too insignificant for all the חסדים and all the faithfulness*** that you have done to your servant.	**Gen 32:11** ἱκανοῦταί μοι ἀπὸ πάσης δικαιοσύνης καὶ ἀπὸ πάσης ἀληθείας, ἧς ἐποίησας τῷ παιδί σου,
Gen 39:21 ויט אליו חסד	**Gen 39:21** And he [YHWH] extended to him [Joseph] חסד	**Gen 39:21** καὶ κατέχεεν αὐτοῦ ἔλεος
Gen 40:14 ועשית נא עמדי חסד	**Gen 40:14** And please do with me [Joseph] חסד	**Gen 40:14** καὶ ποιήσεις ἐν ἐμοὶ ἔλεος
Gen 47:29 ועשית עמדי חסד ואמת	**Gen 47:29** And do with me [Israel] חסד and faithfulness***	**Gen 47:29** καὶ ποιήσεις ἐπ' ἐμὲ ἐλεημοσύνην καὶ ἀλήθειαν
Exod 15:13 נחית בחסדך עם זו גאלת	**Exod 15:13** You [YHWH] led in your חסד this people [whom] you redeemed	**Exod 15:13** ὡδήγησας τῇ δικαιοσύνῃ σου τὸν λαόν σου τοῦτον, ὃν ἐλυτρώσω,

5. אמת indicated hereafter by three asterisks.

TABLE A1.2. Hebrew Bible Occurrences of חסד and חסיד (*continued*)

MT Clause(s)	English Translation of MT Clause(s)	LXX Translation of MT Clause(s)
Exod 20:6 ועשה חסד לאלפים לאהבי ולשמרי מצותי	**Exod 20:6** But doing חסד to the thousands, to those who love me and (to those who) keep my commandments	**Exod 20:6** καὶ ποιῶν ἔλεος εἰς χιλιάδας τοῖς ἀγαπῶσίν με καὶ τοῖς φυλάσσουσιν τὰ προστάγματά μου.
Exod 34:6 Incomplete clause: יהוה יהוה אל רחום וחנון ארך אפים ורב חסד ואמת	**Exod 34:6** YHWH, YHWH, a God, compassionate and gracious, slow to anger, and abounding in חסד and faithfulness***	**Exod 34:6** Κύριος ὁ θεὸς οἰκτίρμων καὶ ἐλεήμων, μακρόθυμος καὶ πολυέλεος καὶ ἀληθινὸς
Exod 34:7 נצר חסד לאלפים	**Exod 34:7** Keeping חסד to the thousands	**Exod 34:7** καὶ δικαιοσύνην διατηρῶν καὶ ποιῶν ἔλεος εἰς χιλιάδας, (two possible equivalents)
Num 14:18 יהוה ארך אפים ורב חסד	**Num 14:18** YHWH [is] slow to anger and abounding in חסד	**Num 14:18** Κύριος μακρόθυμος καὶ πολυέλεος Supplied: καὶ ἀληθινός,
Num 14:19 סלח נא לעון העם הזה כגדל חסדך	**Num 14:19** Please forgive[6] the iniquity of this people according to the greatness of your חסד	**Num 14:19** ἄφες τὴν ἁμαρτίαν τῷ λαῷ τούτῳ κατὰ τὸ μέγα ἔλεός σου,
Deut 5:10 ועשה חסד לאלפים לאהבי ולשמרי מצותו[7]	**Deut 5:10** But doing חסד to the thousands, to those who love me [YHWH] and (to those who) keep my commandments.	**Deut 5:10** καὶ ποιῶν ἔλεος εἰς χιλιάδας τοῖς ἀγαπῶσίν με καὶ τοῖς φυλάσσουσιν τὰ προστάγματά μου.
Deut 7:9 וידעת כי יהוה אלהיך הוא האלהים האל הנאמן שמר הברית והחסד לאהביו ולשמרי מצותו[8] לאלף דור	**Deut 7:9** And know that YHWH, your God, he [is] the God, the faithful God, who keeps the covenant and (the) חסד to those who love him and (to those who) keep his commandments to a thousand generations!	**Deut 7:9** καὶ γνώσῃ ὅτι κύριος ὁ θεός σου, οὗτος θεός, θεὸς πιστός, ὁ φυλάσσων διαθήκην καὶ ἔλεος τοῖς ἀγαπῶσιν αὐτὸν καὶ τοῖς φυλάσσουσιν τὰς ἐντολὰς αὐτοῦ εἰς χιλίας γενεὰς

6. Or "be indulgent towards." *HALOT*, s.v. "סלח."
7. *Qere*: מצותי (*BHS*, 295).
8. *Qere*: מצותיו (*BHS*, 298).

TABLE A1.2. Hebrew Bible Occurrences of חסד and חסיד (*continued*)

MT Clause(s)	English Translation of MT Clause(s)	LXX Translation of MT Clause(s)
Deut 7:12 והיה עקב תשמעון את המשפטים האלה ושמ־רתם ועשיתם אתם ושמר יהוה אלהיך לך את הברית ואת החסד אשר נשבע לאבתיך	**Deut 7:12** And for the reason[9] that you [the people of Israel] heed these ordinances and you keep and do them, YHWH your God will keep for you, the covenant and the חסד that he swore to your ancestors	**Deut 7:12** Καὶ ἔσται ἡνίκα ἂν ἀκούσητε πάντα τὰ δικαιώματα ταῦτα καὶ φυλάξητε καὶ ποιήσητε αὐτά, καὶ διαφυλάξει κύριος ὁ θεός σού σοι τὴν διαθήκην καὶ τὸ ἔλεος, ὃ ὤμοσεν τοῖς πατράσιν ὑμῶν,
Deut 33:8 תמיך ואוריך לאיש חסידך[10]	**Deut 33:8** [Give][11] your Thumim and your Urim to (the man)[12] your חסיד	**Deut 33:8** Δότε Λευι δήλους αὐτοῦ καὶ ἀλήθειαν αὐτοῦ τῷ ἀνδρὶ τῷ ὁσίῳ,
Josh 2:12, 12 ועתה השבעו נא לי ביהוה כי עשיתי עמכם חסד ועשיתם גם אתם עם בית אבי חסד ונתתם לי אות אמת	**Josh 2:12, 12** And now please swear to me by YHWH that (a) [as] I [Rahab] have done חסד with you [spies], (b) you (emph.) also will do חסד with my father's house and give to me a sign of faithfulness.***	**Josh 2:12, 12** καὶ νῦν ὀμόσατέ μοι κύριον τὸν θεόν, ὅτι ποιῶ ὑμῖν ἔλεος καὶ ποιήσετε καὶ ὑμεῖς ἔλεος ἐν τῷ οἴκῳ τοῦ πατρός μου
Josh 2:14 אם לא תגידו את דברנו זה והיה בתת יהוה לנו את הארץ ועשינו עמך חסד ואמת	**Josh 2:14** If you do not tell this matter of ours, then,[13] when YHWH gives (to) us the land, we [Israelite spies] will do חסד and faithfulness*** with you [Rahab].	**Josh 2:14** καὶ αὐτὴ εἶπεν Ὡς ἂν παραδῷ κύριος ὑμῖν τὴν πόλιν, ποιήσετε εἰς ἐμὲ ἔλεος καὶ ἀλήθειαν.
Judg 1:24 הראנו נא את מבוא העיר ועשינו עמך חסד	**Judg 1:24** Show us please the entrance of the city, and we [spies] will do חסד with you [the man coming out of the city].	**Judg 1:24** Δεῖξον ἡμῖν τὴν εἴσοδον τῆς πόλεως, καὶ ποιήσομεν μετὰ σοῦ ἔλεος.
Judg 8:35 ולא עשו חסד עם בית ירבעל גדעון ככל הטובה אשר עשה עם ישראל[14]	**Judg 8:35** And they [the Israelites] did not do חסד with the house of Jerubbaal (Gideon) according to all the goodness that he had done with Israel.	**Judg 8:35** καὶ οὐκ ἐποίησαν ἔλεος μετὰ τοῦ οἴκου Ιεροβααλ Γεδεων κατὰ πᾶσαν τὴν ἀγαθωσύνην, ἣν ἐποίησεν μετὰ Ισραηλ.

9. *HALOT*, s.v. "עָקֵב."
10. חסידיך in a number of MSS (*BHS*, 350).
11. NRSV; ESV.
12. I render איש using "man"/"person" throughout to distinguish it from אדם ("humanity").
13. Harstad writes, "In a temporal expression formed by an infinitive (בְּתֵת, from נָתַן), future time is sometimes emphasized by the addition of הָיָה (. . .)" (*Joshua*, 131).
14. Some manuscripts read לישראל (*BHS*, 416).

TABLE A1.2. Hebrew Bible Occurrences of חסד and חסיד (*continued*)

MT Clause(s)	English Translation of MT Clause(s)	LXX Translation of MT Clause(s)
1 Sam 2:9 רגלי חסידו ישמר ורשעים בחשך ידמו כי לא בכח יגבר איש	**1 Sam 2:9** He [YHWH] will keep/guard the feet of his חסיד, but the wicked ones will perish in darkness, for not by might/power does a person achieve.[15]	**1 Kgdms 2:9** This seems mostly unrelated to the MT: διδοὺς εὐχὴν τῷ εὐχομένῳ καὶ εὐλόγησεν ἔτη δικαίου, ὅτι οὐκ ἐν ἰσχύι δυνατὸς ἀνήρ,
1 Sam 15:6 ואתה עשיתה חסד עם כל בני ישראל בעלותם ממצרים	**1 Sam 15:6** [For] you (emph.) [the Kenite] did חסד with all the sons of Israel when they came up from Egypt.	**1 Kgdms 15:6** καὶ σὺ ἐποίησας ἔλεος μετὰ τῶν υἱῶν Ισραηλ ἐν τῷ ἀναβαίνειν αὐτοὺς ἐξ Αἰγύπτου,
1 Sam 20:8 ועשית חסד על עבדך כי בברית יהוה הבאת את עבדך עמך	**1 Sam 20:8** And do חסד toward your servant [David] for you [Jonathan] have brought your servant into a covenant of YHWH with you	**1 Kgdms 20:8** καὶ ποιήσεις ἔλεος μετὰ τοῦ δούλου σου, ὅτι εἰσήγαγες εἰς διαθήκην κυρίου τὸν δοῦλόν σου μετὰ σεαυτοῦ,
1 Sam 20:14 ולא אם עודני חי ולא תעשה עמדי חסד יהוה ולא אמות	**1 Sam 20:14** And will you [David] not[16] do with me [Jonathan] the חסד of YHWH[17]	**1 Kgdms 20:14** καὶ μὲν ἔτι μου ζῶντος καὶ ποιήσεις ἔλεος μετ' ἐμοῦ, καὶ ἐὰν θανάτῳ ἀποθάνω,
1 Sam 20:15 ולא תכרת את חסדך מעם ביתי עד עולם	**1 Sam 20:15** Do not cut off your [David's] חסד, from (with) my [Jonathan's] house forever	**1 Kgdms 20:15** οὐκ ἐξαρεῖς ἔλεος σου ἀπὸ τοῦ οἴκου μου ἕως τοῦ αἰῶνος,
2 Sam 2:5 ברכים אתם ליהוה אשר עשיתם החסד הזה עם אדניכם עם שאול	**2 Sam 2:5** May you [the men of Jabesh-Gilead] be blessed by YHWH because you did this חסד with your master, Saul	**2 Kgdms 2:5** Εὐλογημένοι ὑμεῖς τῷ κυρίῳ, ὅτι πεποιήκατε τὸ ἔλεος τοῦτο ἐπὶ τὸν κύριον ὑμῶν ἐπὶ Σαουλ
2 Sam 2:6 ועתה יעש יהוה עמכם חסד ואמת	**2 Sam 2:6** And now, may YHWH do with you [the men of Jabesh-Gilead], חסד and faithfulness***	**2 Kgdms 2:6** καὶ νῦν ποιήσαι κύριος μεθ' ὑμῶν ἔλεος καὶ ἀλήθειαν,

15. *HALOT*, s.v. "גבר."

16. Firth, *1 & 2* Samuel, 221.

17. The Hebrew here is difficult. There are two aspects of Tsumura's explanation for v. 14: (1) being willing to accept the Lord's decision, "Jonathan asks David not to *show the Lord's kindness to* him if he should have to die," but (2) belonging to a previous dynasty that will be at risk when another succeeds it, Jonathan asks "for David's 'kindness' to his descendants 'forever' (v. 15)" (*First Book of Samuel*, 507, 509; emphasis original). On the other hand, Sakenfeld proposes that vv. 14–15 are "Jonathan's request that David do *ḥesed* with him by preserving his lineage whether he be alive or dead when David comes to power" (*Meaning of Hesed*, 85, 88).

TABLE A1.2. Hebrew Bible Occurrences of חסד and חסיד (*continued*)

MT Clause(s)	English Translation of MT Clause(s)	LXX Translation of MT Clause(s)
2 Sam 3:8 היום אעשה חסד עם בית שאול אביך אל אחיו ואל מרעהו ולא המציתך ביד דוד	**2 Sam 3:8** Today, I keep doing[18] חסד with the house of Saul, your father, to his brothers and to his friends, and have not let him fall into the hand of David.	**2 Kgdms 3:8** ἐποίησα ἔλεος σήμερον μετὰ τοῦ οἴκου Σαουλ τοῦ πατρός σου καὶ περὶ ἀδελφῶν καὶ γνωρίμων καὶ οὐκ ηὐτομόλησα εἰς τὸν οἶκον Δαυιδ,
2 Sam 7:15 וחסדי לא יסור ממנו כאשר הסרתי מעם שאול אשר הסרתי מלפניך	**2 Sam 7:15** And my [YHWH's] חסד shall not depart from him [David's off-spring] as I removed [it] from (with) Saul, whom I removed from before you.	**2 Kgdms 7:15** τὸ δὲ ἔλεός μου οὐκ ἀποστήσω ἀπ' αὐτοῦ, καθὼς ἀπέστησα ἀφ' ὧν ἀπέστησα ἐκ προσώπου μου. (Saul is not mentioned by name.)
2 Sam 9:1 הכי יש עוד אשר נותר לבית שאול ואעשה עמו חסד בעבור יהונתן	**2 Sam 9:1** Is there anyone (who is) left from the house of Saul that I [David] may do with him חסד for the sake of Jonathan?	**2 Kgdms 9:1** Εἰ ἔστιν ἔτι ὑπολελειμμένος τῷ οἴκῳ Σαουλ καὶ ποιήσω μετ' αὐτοῦ ἔλεος ἕνεκεν Ιωναθαν;
2 Sam 9:3 האפס עוד איש לבית שאול ואעשה עמו חסד אלהים	**2 Sam 9:3** Is there not still a man from the house of Saul that I [David] may do with him the חסד of God?	**2 Kgdms 9:3** Εἰ ὑπολέλειπται ἐκ τοῦ οἴκου Σαουλ ἔτι ἀνὴρ καὶ ποιήσω μετ' αὐτοῦ ἔλεος θεοῦ;
2 Sam 9:7 אל תירא כי עשה אעשה עמך חסד בעבור יהונתן אביך	**2 Sam 9:7** Do not fear for I [David] will certainly do with you [Mephibosheth] חסד for the sake of Jonathan, your father.	**2 Kgdms 9:7** Μὴ φοβοῦ, ὅτι ποιῶν ποιήσω μετὰ σοῦ ἔλεος διὰ Ιωναθαν τὸν πατέρα σου
2 Sam 10:2, 2 אעשה חסד עם חנון בן נחש כאשר עשה אביו עמדי חסד	**2 Sam 10:2, 2** (a) I [David] will do חסד with Hanun, son of Nahash, (b) as his father [Nahash] did חסד with me.	**2 Kgdms 10:2, 2** Ποιήσω ἔλεος μετὰ Αννων υἱοῦ Ναας, ὃν τρόπον ἐποίησεν ὁ πατὴρ αὐτοῦ μετ' ἐμοῦ ἔλεος,
2 Sam 15:20 חסד ואמת	**2 Sam 15:20** Blessing: חסד and faithfulness***	**2 Kgdms 15:20** καὶ κύριος ποιήσει μετὰ σοῦ (LXX addition) ἔλεος καὶ ἀλήθειαν.
2 Sam 16:17 זה חסדך את רעך	**2 Sam 16:17** [Is] this your [Hushai's] חסד toward your friend [David]?	**2 Kgdms 16:17** Τοῦτο τὸ ἔλεός σου μετὰ τοῦ ἑταίρου σου;

18. NRSV; ESV.

TABLE A1.2. Hebrew Bible Occurrences of חסד and חסיד (*continued*)

MT Clause(s)	English Translation of MT Clause(s)	LXX Translation of MT Clause(s)
2 Sam 22:26 עם חסיד תתחסד עם גבור תמים תתמם	**2 Sam 22:26** With חסיד, you [YHWH] will prove-yourself-חסיד,[19] with a devout person, you will prove-yourself-devout.	**2 Kgdms 22:26** μετὰ ὁσίου ὁσιωθήσῃ καὶ μετὰ ἀνδρὸς τελείου τελειωθήσῃ
2 Sam 22:51 ועשה חסד למשיחו לדוד ולזרעו עד עולם	**2 Sam 22:51** And he [YHWH] does חסד to his anointed, to David and to his offspring forever.	**2 Kgdms 22:51** καὶ ποιῶν ἔλεος τῷ χριστῷ αὐτοῦ, τῷ Δαυιδ καὶ τῷ σπέρματι αὐτοῦ ἕως αἰῶνος.
1 Kgs 2:7 ולבני ברזלי הגלעדי תעשה חסד	**1 Kgs 2:7** And to the sons of Barzillai the Gileadite do חסד	**3 Kgdms 2:7** καὶ τοῖς υἱοῖς Βερζελλι τοῦ Γαλααδίτου ποιήσεις ἔλεος,
1 Kgs 3:6, 6 אתה עשית עם עבדך דוד אבי חסד גדול . . . ותשמר לו את החסד הגדול הזה	**1 Kgs 3:6, 6** (a) You (emph.) [YHWH] did with your servant David, my father, great חסד . . . (b) And you [YHWH] have kept for him [David] this great חסד	**3 Kgdms 3:6, 6** Σὺ ἐποίησας μετὰ τοῦ δούλου σου Δαυιδ τοῦ πατρός μου ἔλεος μέγα, . . . καὶ ἐφύλαξας αὐτῷ τὸ ἔλεος τὸ μέγα τοῦτο
1 Kgs 8:23 יהוה אלהי ישראל אין כמוך אלהים בשמים ממעל ועל הארץ מתחת שמר הברית והחסד לעבדיך ההלכים לפניך בכל לבם	**1 Kgs 8:23** YHWH, God of Israel, there is no God like you in heaven above or on the earth below keeping the covenant and (the) חסד to your servants who walk before you with all their heart	**3 Kgdms 8:23** Κύριε ὁ θεὸς Ισραηλ, οὐκ ἔστιν ὡς σὺ θεὸς ἐν τῷ οὐρανῷ ἄνω καὶ ἐπὶ τῆς γῆς κάτω φυλάσσων διαθήκην καὶ ἔλεος τῷ δούλῳ σου τῷ πορευομένῳ ἐνώπιόν σου ἐν ὅλῃ τῇ καρδίᾳ αὐτοῦ,
1 Kgs 20:31 הנה נא שמענו כי מלכי בית ישראל כי מלכי חסד הם	**1 Kgs 20:31** Surely, we [Ben-Hadad's servants] have heard that the kings of the house of Israel, (that they) [are] kings of חסד	**3 Kgdms 21:31** Οἶδα ὅτι βασιλεῖς Ισραηλ βασιλεῖς ἐλέους εἰσίν,
Isa 16:5 והוכן בחסד כסא	**Isa 16:5** And a throne will be firmly established in/on the חסד	**Isa 16:5** καὶ διορθωθήσεται μετ' ἐλέους θρόνος,
Isa 40:6 וכל חסדו[20] כציץ השדה	**Isa 40:6** And all its [all flesh's] חסד [is] as a flower of the field	**Isa 40:6** καὶ πᾶσα δόξα ἀνθρώπου ὡς ἄνθος χόρτου,

19. "Prove yourself": Stoebe, "חֶסֶד *ḥesed*," 2:463.
20. DSS^Isa^ חסדיו.

TABLE A1.2. Hebrew Bible Occurrences of חסד and חסיד (*continued*)

MT Clause(s)	English Translation of MT Clause(s)	LXX Translation of MT Clause(s)
Isa 54:8 ובחסד עלום רחמתיך	**Isa 54:8** But in everlasting חסד I [YHWH, her redeemer] have[21] compassion on you [the barren one who did not bear]	**Isa 54:8** καὶ ἐν ἐλέει αἰωνίῳ ἐλεήσω σε,
Isa 54:10 כי ההרים ימושו והגבעות תמוטנה וחסדי מאתך לא ימוש וברית שלומי לא תמוט	**Isa 54:10** For the mountains may withdraw and the hills may sway but my [YHWH's] חסד shall not withdraw from you [the barren one who did not bear] and my covenant of peace will not sway	**Isa 54:10** τὰ ὄρη μεταστήσεσθαι οὐδὲ οἱ βουνοί σου μετακινηθήσονται, οὕτως οὐδὲ τὸ παρ᾽ ἐμοῦ σοι ἔλεος ἐκλείψει οὐδὲ ἡ διαθήκη τῆς εἰρήνης σου οὐ μὴ μεταστῇ,
Isa 55:3 ואכרתה לכם ברית עולם חסדי דוד הנאמנים	**Isa 55:3** And I [YHWH] will make for you [those called to come] an everlasting covenant, the faithful חסדים of David.	**Isa 55:3** καὶ διαθήσομαι ὑμῖν διαθήκην αἰώνιον, τὰ ὅσια Δαυιδ τὰ πιστά.
Isa 57:1 ואנשי חסד נאספים באין מבין	**Isa 57:1** And men of חסד are taken away while no one considers [it].	**Isa 57:1** καὶ ἄνδρες δίκαιοι αἴρονται, καὶ οὐδεὶς κατανοεῖ.
Isa 63:7, 7 חסדי יהוה אזכיר תהלת יהוה כעל כל אשר גמלנו יהוה ורב טוב לבית ישראל אשר גמלם כרחמיו וכרב חסדיו	**Isa 63:7, 7** (a) I [the prophet] will remember the חסדים of YHWH, the praiseworthy acts of YHWH, according to everything that YHWH showed us; and [the] great goodness to the house of Israel, (b) which he showed them according to his compassions and according to the abundance of his חסדים.	**Isa 63:7, 7** Τὸν ἔλεον κυρίου ἐμνήσθην, τὰς ἀρετὰς κυρίου ἐν πᾶσιν, οἷς ὁ κύριος ἡμῖν ἀνταποδίδωσιν, κύριος κριτὴς ἀγαθὸς τῷ οἴκῳ Ισραηλ, ἐπάγει ἡμῖν κατὰ τὸ ἔλεος αὐτοῦ καὶ κατὰ τὸ πλῆθος τῆς δικαιοσύνης αὐτοῦ.
Jer 2:2 זכרתי לך חסד נעוריך אהבת כלולתיך	**Jer 2:2** I [YHWH] have remembered to your [Jerusalem/Israel's] credit the חסד of your youth, the love of your betrothal time.	**Jer 2:2** Ἐμνήσθην ἐλέους νεότητός σου καὶ ἀγάπης τελειώσεώς σου

21. This tense: Watts, *Isaiah 34–66*, 234.

TABLE A1.2. Hebrew Bible Occurrences of חסד and חסיד (*continued*)

MT Clause(s)	English Translation of MT Clause(s)	LXX Translation of MT Clause(s)
Jer 3:12 לוא אפיל פני בכם כי חסיד אני	**Jer 3:12** My [YHWH's] face(s) will not look ungraciously on you [Israel], for I [am] חסיד.	**Jer 3:12** καὶ οὐ στηριῶ τὸ πρόσωπόν μου ἐφ' ὑμᾶς, ὅτι ἐλεήμων ἐγώ εἰμι,
Jer 9:23 כי אני יהוה עשה חסד משפט וצדקה בארץ כי באלה חפצתי	**Jer 9:24** For I [am] YHWH, who does חסד, justice, and righteousness in the earth, for in these things I delight	**Jer 9:23** ὅτι ἐγώ εἰμι κύριος ποιῶν ἔλεος καὶ κρίμα καὶ δικαιοσύνην ἐπὶ τῆς γῆς, ὅτι ἐν τούτοις τὸ θέλημά μου,
Jer 16:5 כי אספתי את שלומי מאת העם הזה נאם יהוה את החסד ואת הרחמים	**Jer 16:5** For I have withdrawn my peace from this people, says YHWH, the חסד and the compassions.	**Jer 16:5** ὅτι ἀφέστακα τὴν εἰρήνην μου ἀπὸ τοῦ λαοῦ τούτου. A translation for חסד is not included.
Jer 31:3 ואהבת עולם אהבתיך על כן משכתיך חסד	**Jer 31:3** And I loved you [with] an everlasting love, therefore, I [have] extended (stretched) to you [virgin Israel] חסד.	**Jer 38:3** Ἀγάπησιν αἰωνίαν ἠγάπησά σε, διὰ τοῦτο εἵλκυσά σε εἰς οἰκτίρημα.
Jer 32:18 עשה חסד לאלפים	**Jer 32:18** Doing חסד to the thousands	**Jer 39:18** ποιῶν ἔλεος εἰς χιλιάδας
Jer 33:11 הודו את יהוה צבאות כי טוב יהוה כי לעולם חסדו	**Jer 33:11** Give thanks to YHWH of hosts, for YHWH is good, for his חסד [is] forever.	**Jer 40:11** Ἐξομολογεῖσθε κυρίῳ παντοκράτορι, ὅτι χρηστὸς κύριος, ὅτι εἰς τὸν αἰῶνα τὸ ἔλεος αὐτοῦ,
Hos 2:21 וארשתיך לי בצדק ובמשפט ובחסד וברחמים	**Hos 2:19** And I [YHWH] will betroth you [Israel] to me with righteousness and with justice and with חסד and with compassion	**Hos 2:21** καὶ μνηστεύσομαί σε ἐμαυτῷ ἐν δικαιοσύνῃ καὶ ἐν κρίματι καὶ ἐν ἐλέει καὶ ἐν οἰκτιρμοῖς
Hos 4:1 כי ריב ליהוה עם יושבי הארץ כי אין אמת ואין חסד ואין דעת אלהים בארץ	**Hos 4:1** For YHWH [has] an indictment with the inhabitants of the land; for there is no faithfulness*** and no חסד and no knowledge of God in the land.	**Hos 4:1** διότι κρίσις τῷ κυρίῳ πρὸς τοὺς κατοικοῦντας τὴν γῆν, διότι οὐκ ἔστιν ἀλήθεια οὐδὲ ἔλεος οὐδὲ ἐπίγνωσις θεοῦ ἐπὶ τῆς γῆς,

TABLE A1.2. Hebrew Bible Occurrences of חסד and חסיד (*continued*)

MT Clause(s)	English Translation of MT Clause(s)	LXX Translation of MT Clause(s)
Hos 6:4 וחסדכם כענן בקר וכטל משכים הלך	**Hos 6:4** Your [Ephraim and Judah's] חסד [is] like the morning cloud and like the dew that goes away quickly.	**Hos 6:4** τὸ δὲ ἔλεος ὑμῶν ὡς νεφέλη πρωινὴ καὶ ὡς δρόσος ὀρθρινὴ πορευομένη.
Hos 6:6 כי חסד חפצתי ולא זבח	**Hos 6:6** For I [YHWH] delighted in חסד and not sacrifice	**Hos 6:6** διότι ἔλεος θέλω καὶ οὐ θυσίαν
Hos 10:12 זרעו לכם לצדקה קצרו לפי חסד	**Hos 10:12** Sow for yourselves (to) righteousness; reap according to the measure of חסד	**Hos 10:12** σπείρατε ἑαυτοῖς εἰς δικαιοσύνην, τρυγήσατε εἰς καρπὸν ζωῆς,
Hos 12:7 ואתה באלהיך תשוב חסד ומשפט שמר	**Hos 12:6** And you (emph.) [Judah and Jacob] should return[22] to your God; keep חסד and justice	**Hos 12:7** καὶ σὺ ἐν θεῷ σου ἐπιστρέψεις, ἔλεον καὶ κρίμα φυλάσσου
Joel 2:13 ושובו אל יהוה אלהיכם כי חנון ורחום הוא ארך אפים ורב חסד ונחם על הרעה	**Joel 2:13** And return to YHWH, your God, for he [is] gracious and compassionate, slow to anger and abounding in חסד, and relents concerning the calamity.	**Joel 2:13** καὶ ἐπιστράφητε πρὸς κύριον τὸν θεὸν ὑμῶν, ὅτι ἐλεήμων καὶ οἰκτίρμων ἐστίν, μακρόθυμος καὶ πολυέλεος καὶ μετανοῶν ἐπὶ ταῖς κακίαις.
Jonah 2:9 משמרים הבלי שוא חסדם יעזבו	**Jonah 2:8** Those who are followers of worthless idols forsake their חסד.	**Jonah 2:9** φυλασσόμενοι μάταια καὶ ψευδῆ ἔλεος αὐτῶν ἐγκατέλιπον.
Jonah 4:2 על כן קדמתי לברח תרשישה כי ידעתי כי אתה אל חנון ורחום ארך אפים ורב חסד ונחם על הרעה	**Jonah 4:2** Therefore, I [Jonah] went up to flee [to] Tarshish, for I knew that you [YHWH] [are] a God, gracious and compassionate, slow to anger and abounding in חסד and relenting concerning the calamity.	**Jonah 4:2** διὰ τοῦτο προέφθασα τοῦ φυγεῖν εἰς Θαρσις, διότι ἔγνων ὅτι σὺ ἐλεήμων καὶ οἰκτίρμων, μακρόθυμος καὶ πολυέλεος καὶ μετανοῶν ἐπὶ ταῖς κακίαις.

22. Dearman, *Book of Hosea*, 296.

TABLE A1.2. Hebrew Bible Occurrences of חסד and חסיד (*continued*)

MT Clause(s)	English Translation of MT Clause(s)	LXX Translation of MT Clause(s)
Mic 6:8	**Mic 6:8**	**Mic 6:8**
ומה יהוה דורש ממך כי אם עשות משפט ואהבת חסד והצנע לכת עם אלהיך	And what does YHWH require from you but to do justice and to love חסד and to walk humbly with your God?	ἢ τί κύριος ἐκζητεῖ παρὰ σοῦ ἀλλ’ ἢ τοῦ ποιεῖν κρίμα καὶ ἀγαπᾶν ἔλεον καὶ ἕτοιμον εἶναι τοῦ πορεύεσθαι μετὰ κυρίου θεοῦ σου;
Mic 7:2	**Mic 7:2**	**Mic 7:2**
אבד חסיד מן הארץ וישר באדם אין	חסיד has been carried off from the land, and there is no upright one among humanity;	ὅτι ἀπόλωλεν εὐλαβὴς ἀπὸ τῆς γῆς, καὶ κατορθῶν ἐν ἀνθρώποις οὐχ ὑπάρχει,
Mic 7:18	**Mic 7:18**	**Mic 7:18**
לא החזיק לעד אפו כי חפץ חסד הוא	He does not hold on to his anger forever, for he delights in[23] חסד.	καὶ οὐ συνέσχεν εἰς μαρτύριον ὀργὴν αὐτοῦ, ὅτι θελητὴς ἐλέους ἐστίν.
Mic 7:20	**Mic 7:20**	**Mic 7:20**
תתן אמת ליעקב חסד לאברהם	You [God] will give faithfulness*** to Jacob, חסד to Abraham.	δώσεις ἀλήθειαν τῷ Ιακωβ, ἔλεον τῷ Αβρααμ,
Zech 7:9	**Zech 7:9**	**Zech 7:9**
משפט אמת שפטו וחסד ורחמים עשו איש את אחיו	Render faithful*** judgments and do חסד and compassion, a man toward his brother.	Κρίμα δίκαιον κρίνατε καὶ ἔλεος καὶ οἰκτιρμὸν ποιεῖτε ἕκαστος πρὸς τὸν ἀδελφὸν αὐτοῦ
Ps 4:4	**Ps 4:3**	**Ps 4:4**
ודעו כי הפלה יהוה חסיד לו	And know that YHWH has treated specially חסיד to him[24]	καὶ γνῶτε ὅτι ἐθαυμάστωσεν κύριος τὸν ὅσιον αὐτοῦ,
Ps 5:8	**Ps 5:7**	**Ps 5:8**
ואני ברב חסדך אבוא ביתך	But I (emph.) [the psalmist], in the abundance of your [YHWH’s] חסד, will enter your house	ἐγὼ δὲ ἐν τῷ πλήθει τοῦ ἐλέους σου εἰσελεύσομαι εἰς τὸν οἶκόν σου,
Ps 6:5	**Ps 6:4**	**Ps 6:5**
הושיעני למען חסדך	Save me [the psalmist], for the sake of your [YHWH’s] חסד.	σῶσόν με ἕνεκεν τοῦ ἐλέους σου.
Ps 12:2	**Ps 12:1**	**Ps 11:2**
הושיעה יהוה כי גמר חסיד כי פסו אמונים מבני אדם	Save, O YHWH, for חסיד has come to an end, for the faithful have disappeared from humanity.	Σῶσόν με, κύριε, ὅτι ἐκλέλοιπεν ὅσιος, ὅτι ὠλιγώθησαν αἱ ἀλήθειαι ἀπὸ τῶν υἱῶν τῶν ἀνθρώπων.

23. Cf. Waltke, “Micah,” 762.

24. NRSV and ESV translate לו “for himself,” but I translate it “to him,” in the sense of “one devoted to him” (i.e., “his חסיד”), following Dahood, *Psalms I*, 22, 24.

TABLE A1.2. Hebrew Bible Occurrences of חסד and חסיד (*continued*)

MT Clause(s)	English Translation of MT Clause(s)	LXX Translation of MT Clause(s)
Ps 13:6 ואני בחסדך בטחתי	**Ps 13:5** But I (emph.) [the psalmist] trusted in your [YHWH's] חסד	**Ps 12:6** ἐγὼ δὲ ἐπὶ τῷ ἐλέει σου ἤλπισα,
Ps 16:10 כי לא תעזב נפשי לשאול לא תתן חסידך לראות שחת	**Ps 16:10** For you [YHWH] will not forsake my [the psalmist's] נפש to Sheol; you will not permit your חסיד to see the Pit.	**Ps 15:10** ὅτι οὐκ ἐγκαταλείψεις τὴν ψυχήν μου εἰς ᾅδην οὐδὲ δώσεις τὸν ὅσιόν σου ἰδεῖν διαφθοράν.
Ps 17:7 הפלה חסדיך מושיע חוסים ממתקוממים בימינך	**Ps 17:7** Wondrously do your חסדים, O Savior of those who seek refuge from their opponents at your right hand.	**Ps 16:7** Θαυμάστωσον τὰ ἐλέη σου, ὁ σῴζων τοὺς ἐλπίζοντας ἐπὶ σὲ ἐκ τῶν ἀνθεστηκότων τῇ δεξιᾷ σου.
Ps 18:26 עם חסיד תתחסד עם גבר תמים תתמם	**Ps 18:25** With חסיד, you [YHWH] will prove-yourself-חסיד, with a devout person, you will prove-yourself-devout.	**Ps 17:26** μετὰ ὁσίου ὁσιωθήσῃ καὶ μετὰ ἀνδρὸς ἀθῴου ἀθῷος ἔσῃ
Ps 18:51 ועשה חסד למשיחו לדוד ולזרעו עד עולם	**Ps 18:50** And he [YHWH] does חסד to his anointed, to David and to his offspring forever.	**Ps 17:51** καὶ ποιῶν ἔλεος τῷ χριστῷ αὐτοῦ, τῷ Δαυιδ καὶ τῷ σπέρματι αὐτοῦ ἕως αἰῶνος.
Ps 21:8 ובחסד עליון בל ימוט	**Ps 21:7** And in [the] חסד of the Most High, he [the king] shall not be moved / made to stagger.	**Ps 20:8** καὶ ἐν τῷ ἐλέει τοῦ ὑψίστου οὐ μὴ σαλευθῇ.
Ps 23:6 אך טוב וחסד ירדפוני כל ימי חיי	**Ps 23:6** Surely goodness and חסד shall pursue/follow me [the psalmist] all the days of my life.	**Ps 22:6** καὶ τὸ ἔλεός σου καταδιώξεταί με πάσας τὰς ἡμέρας τῆς ζωῆς μου,
Ps 25:6 זכר רחמיך יהוה וחסדיך	**Ps 25:6** Remember your compassions, O YHWH, and your חסדים	**Ps 24:6** μνήσθητι τῶν οἰκτιρμῶν σου, κύριε, καὶ τὰ ἐλέη σου,
Ps 25:7 כחסדך זכר לי אתה למען טובך יהוה	**Ps 25:7** According to your חסד, (you) remember (to) me, for the sake of your goodness, O YHWH.	**Ps 24:7** κατὰ τὸ ἔλεός σου μνήσθητί μου σὺ ἕνεκα τῆς χρηστότητός σου, κύριε.

TABLE A1.2. Hebrew Bible Occurrences of חסד and חסיד (*continued*)

MT Clause(s)	English Translation of MT Clause(s)	LXX Translation of MT Clause(s)
Ps 25:10 כל ארחות יהוה חסד ואמת לנצרי בריתו ועדתיו	**Ps 25:10** All the paths of YHWH [are] חסד and faithfulness*** for those who keep his covenant and his testimonies.	**Ps 24:10** πᾶσαι αἱ ὁδοὶ κυρίου ἔλεος καὶ ἀλήθεια τοῖς ἐκζητοῦσιν τὴν διαθήκην αὐτοῦ καὶ τὰ μαρτύρια αὐτοῦ.
Ps 26:3 כי חסדך לנגד עיני והתהלכתי באמתך	**Ps 26:3** For your [YHWH's] חסד [is] before my [the psalmist's] eyes, and I walk in your faithfulness.***	**Ps 25:3** ὅτι τὸ ἔλεός σου κατέναντι τῶν ὀφθαλμῶν μού ἐστιν, καὶ εὐηρέστησα ἐν τῇ ἀληθείᾳ σου.
Ps 30:5 זמרו ליהוה חסידיו והודו לזכר קדשו	**Ps 30:4** Sing praises to YHWH, his חסידים, and give thanks to/for the memorial of his holiness.[25]	**Ps 29:5** ψάλατε τῷ κυρίῳ, οἱ ὅσιοι αὐτοῦ, καὶ ἐξομολογεῖσθε τῇ μνήμῃ τῆς ἁγιωσύνης αὐτοῦ,
Ps 31:8 אגילה ואשמחה בחסדך	**Ps 31:7** I [the psalmist] will exult, and I will rejoice in your [YHWH's] חסד	**Ps 30:8** ἀγαλλιάσομαι καὶ εὐφρανθήσομαι ἐπὶ τῷ ἐλέει σου,
Ps 31:17 הושיעני בחסדך	**Ps 31:16** Save me [the psalmist], in your [YHWH's] חסד	**Ps 30:17** σῶσόν με ἐν τῷ ἐλέει σου.
Ps 31:22 ברוך יהוה כי הפליא חסדו לי בעיר מצור	**Ps 31:21** Blessed be YHWH, for he has wondrously done his חסד to me [the psalmist] in a besieged city.	**Ps 30:22** εὐλογητὸς κύριος, ὅτι ἐθαυμάστωσεν τὸ ἔλεος αὐτοῦ ἐν πόλει περιοχῆς.
Ps 31:24 אהבו את יהוה כל חסידיו אמונים נצר יהוה ומשלם על יתר עשה גאוה	**Ps 31:23** Love YHWH, all his חסידים, YHWH keeps watch over the faithful ones; and repays to excess / abundantly the one who acts arrogantly.	**Ps 30:24** ἀγαπήσατε τὸν κύριον, πάντες οἱ ὅσιοι αὐτοῦ, ὅτι ἀληθείας ἐκζητεῖ κύριος καὶ ἀνταποδίδωσιν τοῖς περισσῶς ποιοῦσιν ὑπερηφανίαν.
Ps 32:6 על זאת יתפלל כל חסיד אליך לעת מצא רק לשטף מים רבים אליו לא יגיעו	**Ps 32:6** For this reason, let every חסיד make intercession to you [YHWH], at a time when you may be found,[26] at the flood of mighty waters,[27] they will not reach (to) him.	**Ps 31:6** ὑπὲρ ταύτης προσεύξεται πᾶς ὅσιος πρὸς σὲ ἐν καιρῷ εὐθέτῳ, πλὴν ἐν κατακλυσμῷ ὑδάτων πολλῶν πρὸς αὐτὸν οὐκ ἐγγιοῦσιν.

25. ESV n.

26. ESV. "Literally in the moment of finding" (*HALOT*, s.v. "II רק").

27. This text is unclear. My translation combines the solutions of Craigie and Tate (*Psalms 1–50*, 264), and Goldingay (*Psalms 1–41*, 452).

TABLE A1.2. Hebrew Bible Occurrences of חסד and חסיד (*continued*)

MT Clause(s)	English Translation of MT Clause(s)	LXX Translation of MT Clause(s)
Ps 32:10 והבוטח ביהוה חסד יסובבנו	**Ps 32:10** But the one who trusts in YHWH, חסד will surround him.	**Ps 31:10** τὸν δὲ ἐλπίζοντα ἐπὶ κύριον ἔλεος κυκλώσει.
Ps 33:5 חסד יהוה מלאה הארץ	**Ps 33:5** The earth is full of the חסד of YHWH	**Ps 32:5** τοῦ ἐλέους κυρίου πλήρης ἡ γῆ.
Ps 33:18 הנה עין יהוה אל יראיו למיחלים לחסדו	**Ps 33:18** Behold, the eye of YHWH [is] toward those who fear him, toward those who wait for his חסד.	**Ps 32:18** ἰδοὺ οἱ ὀφθαλμοὶ κυρίου ἐπὶ τοὺς φοβουμένους αὐτὸν τοὺς ἐλπίζοντας ἐπὶ τὸ ἔλεος αὐτοῦ
Ps 33:22 יהי חסדך יהוה עלינו כאשר יחלנו לך	**Ps 33:22** Let your חסד, O YHWH, be upon us [the worshippers who wait],[28] as we wait for you.	**Ps 32:22** γένοιτο τὸ ἔλεός σου, κύριε, ἐφ' ἡμᾶς, καθάπερ ἠλπίσαμεν ἐπὶ σέ.
Ps 36:6 יהוה בהשמים חסדך אמונתך עד שחקים	**Ps 36:5** O YHWH, your חסד [is] in the heavens, your faithfulness [is] to the clouds.	**Ps 35:6** κύριε, ἐν τῷ οὐρανῷ τὸ ἔλεός σου, καὶ ἡ ἀλήθειά σου ἕως τῶν νεφελῶν,
Ps 36:8 מה יקר חסדך אלהים	**Ps 36:7** How precious [is] your חסד, O God	**Ps 35:8** ὡς ἐπλήθυνας τὸ ἔλεός σου, ὁ θεός,
Ps 36:11 משך חסדך לידעיך וצדקתך לישרי לב	**Ps 36:10** Stretch (i.e., continue) your חסד to those who know you [God] and your righteousness to the upright of heart!	**Ps 35:11** παράτεινον τὸ ἔλεός σου τοῖς γινώσκουσίν σε καὶ τὴν δικαιοσύνην σου τοῖς εὐθέσι τῇ καρδίᾳ.
Ps 37:28 כי יהוה אהב משפט ולא יעזב את חסידיו לעולם נשמרו וזרע רשעים נכרת	**Ps 37:28** For YHWH loves justice, and he will not forsake his חסידים; they are kept forever, but the offspring of [the] wicked are cut off.	**Ps 36:28** ὅτι κύριος ἀγαπᾷ κρίσιν καὶ οὐκ ἐγκαταλείψει τοὺς ὁσίους αὐτοῦ, εἰς τὸν αἰῶνα φυλαχθήσονται. ἄνομοι δὲ ἐκδιωχθήσονται, καὶ σπέρμα ἀσεβῶν ἐξολεθρευθήσεται,
Ps 40:11 לא כחדתי חסדך ואמתך לקהל רב	**Ps 40:10** I [the psalmist] have not con- cealed your [YHWH's] חסד or your faithfulness*** from the great assembly.	**Ps 39:11** οὐκ ἔκρυψα τὸ ἔλεός σου καὶ τὴν ἀλήθειάν σου ἀπὸ συναγωγῆς πολλῆς.

28. Goldingay, *Psalms 1–41*, 473.

TABLE A1.2. Hebrew Bible Occurrences of חסד and חסיד (*continued*)

MT Clause(s)	English Translation of MT Clause(s)	LXX Translation of MT Clause(s)
Ps 40:12 חסדך ואמתך תמיד יצרוני	**Ps 40:11** Your [YHWH's] חסד and your faithfulness*** will continually keep watch over me [the psalmist].	**Ps 39:12** τὸ ἔλεός σου καὶ ἡ ἀλήθειά σου διὰ παντὸς ἀντελάβοντό μου.
Ps 42:9 יומם יצוה יהוה חסדו ובלילה שירה עמי תפלה לאל חיי	**Ps 42:8** By day, YHWH will command his חסד and by night, his song [will be] with me, a prayer to the God of my life.	**Ps 41:9** ἡμέρας ἐντελεῖται κύριος τὸ ἔλεος αὐτοῦ, καὶ νυκτὸς ᾠδὴ παρ᾽ ἐμοί, προσευχὴ τῷ θεῷ τῆς ζωῆς μου.
Ps 43:1 שפטני אלהים וריבה ריבי מגוי לא חסיד מאיש מרמה ועולה תפלטני	**Ps 43:1** Vindicate me [the psalmist], O God, and defend my cause from a nation with no חסיד; from a person of deceit and injustice save me!	**Ps 42:1** Κρῖνόν με, ὁ θεός, καὶ δίκασον τὴν δίκην μου ἐξ ἔθνους οὐχ ὁσίου, ἀπὸ ἀνθρώπου ἀδίκου καὶ δολίου ῥῦσαί με.
Ps 44:27 ופדנו למען חסדך	**Ps 44:26** And redeem us [God's covenant people] for the sake of your [the Lord's] חסד	**Ps 43:27** καὶ λύτρωσαι ἡμᾶς ἕνεκεν τοῦ ὀνόματός σου.
Ps 48:10 דמינו אלהים חסדך בקרב היכלך	**Ps 48:9** We [the worshippers] have pondered, O God, your חסד, in the midst of your temple.	**Ps 47:10** ὑπελάβομεν, ὁ θεός, τὸ ἔλεός σου ἐν μέσῳ τοῦ ναοῦ σου.
Ps 50:5 אספו לי חסידי כרתי בריתי עלי זבח	**Ps 50:5** Gather to me [YHWH, their God] my חסידים, who made[29] a covenant with me by sacrifice	**Ps 49:5** συναγάγετε αὐτῷ τοὺς ὁσίους αὐτοῦ τοὺς διατιθεμένους τὴν διαθήκην αὐτοῦ ἐπὶ θυσίαις,
Ps 51:3 חנני אלהים כחסדך	**Ps 51:1** Have mercy on me [the psalmist], O God, according to your חסד	**Ps 50:3** Ἐλέησόν με,[30] ὁ θεός, κατὰ τὸ μέγα ἔλεός σου
Ps 52:3 חסד אל כל היום	**Ps 52:1** The חסד of God [is] all the day	**Ps 51:3** Not close to the Hebrew: ἀνομίαν ὅλην τὴν ἡμέραν;

29. NRSV.

30. Note the relationship between ἐλεέω and ἔλεος in this verse. In the LXX, ἔλεος usually translates חסד (see Table A2.1), but ἐλεέω usually translates חנן or רחם (see Table A2.2).

TABLE A1.2. Hebrew Bible Occurrences of חסד and חסיד (*continued*)

MT Clause(s)	English Translation of MT Clause(s)	LXX Translation of MT Clause(s)
Ps 52:10 בטחתי בחסד אלהים עולם ועד	**Ps 52:8** I [the psalmist] have put [my] trust[31] in the חסד of God for ever and ever.	**Ps 51:10** ἤλπισα ἐπὶ τὸ ἔλεος τοῦ θεοῦ εἰς τὸν αἰῶνα καὶ εἰς τὸν αἰῶνα τοῦ αἰῶνος.
Ps 52:11 ואקוה שמך כי טוב נגד חסידיך	**Ps 52:9** And I will wait for/on your name for it is good, in the presence of your חסידים.	**Ps 51:11** καὶ ὑπομενῶ τὸ ὄνομά σου, ὅτι χρηστὸν ἐναντίον τῶν ὁσίων σου.
Ps 57:4 ישלח אלהים חסדו ואמתו	**Ps 57:3** God will send forth his חסד and his faithfulness***	**Ps 56:4** ἐξαπέστειλεν ὁ θεὸς τὸ ἔλεος αὐτοῦ καὶ τὴν ἀλήθειαν αὐτοῦ
Ps 57:11 כי גדל עד שמים חסדך	**Ps 57:10** For great unto the heavens [is] your [God's] חסד	**Ps 56:11** ὅτι ἐμεγαλύνθη ἕως τῶν οὐρανῶν τὸ ἔλεός σου
Ps 59:11 אלהי חסדו[32] יקדמני	**Ps 59:10** My God, [in][33] his חסד, will meet me [the psalmist]	**Ps 58:11** ὁ θεός μου, τὸ ἔλεος αὐτοῦ προφθάσει με,
Ps 59:17 וארנן לבקר חסדך כי היית משגב לי	**Ps 59:16** But I [the psalmist] will cry out / rejoice in the morning [concern-ing] your [God's] חסד for you have been a place of ref-uge for me	**Ps 58:17** καὶ ἀγαλλιάσομαι τὸ πρωὶ τὸ ἔλεός σου, ὅτι ἐγενήθης ἀντιλήμπτωρ μου
Ps 59:18 עזי אליך אזמרה כי אלהים משגבי אלהי חסדי	**Ps 59:17** O my strength, I [the psalmist] will sing praises to you for God is my fortress, God of my חסד	**Ps 58:18** βοηθός μου, σοὶ ψαλῶ, ὅτι, ὁ θεός, ἀντιλήμπτωρ μου εἶ, ὁ θεός μου, τὸ ἔλεός μου.
Ps 61:8 חסד ואמת מן ינצרהו	**Ps 61:7** Appoint חסד and faithful-ness*** to watch over him [the king].	**Ps 60:8** ἔλεος καὶ ἀλήθειαν αὐτοῦ τίς ἐκζητήσει;
Ps 62:13 ולך אדני חסד כי אתה תשלם לאיש כמעשהו	**Ps 62:12** And to you, Lord, [is] חסד for you (emph.) repay (to) each person according to what he has done.	**Ps 61:13** καὶ σοί, κύριε, τὸ ἔλεος, ὅτι σὺ ἀποδώσεις ἑκάστῳ κατὰ τὰ ἔργα αὐτοῦ.

31. Goldingay, *Psalms 42–89*, 146.
32. *Qere*: חסדי (*BHS*, 1140).
33. NRSV; ESV.

TABLE A1.2. Hebrew Bible Occurrences of חסד and חסיד (*continued*)

MT Clause(s)	English Translation of MT Clause(s)	LXX Translation of MT Clause(s)
Ps 63:4 כי טוב חסדך מחיים שפתי ישבחונך	**Ps 63:3** Because your [God's] חסד [is] better than life, my [the psalmist's] lips will sing praises to you.	**Ps 62:4** ὅτι κρεῖσσον τὸ ἔλεός σου ὑπὲρ ζωάς, τὰ χείλη μου ἐπαινέσουσίν σε.
Ps 66:20 ברוך אלהים אשר לא הסיר תפלתי וחסדו מאתי	**Ps 66:20** Blessed be God, who did not turn away[34] my prayer nor his חסד from me [the psalmist].	**Ps 65:20** εὐλογητὸς ὁ θεός, ὃς οὐκ ἀπέστησεν τὴν προσευχήν μου καὶ τὸ ἔλεος αὐτοῦ ἀπ' ἐμοῦ.
Ps 69:14 עת רצון אלהים ברב חסדך ענני	**Ps 69:13** At a favorable time, O God, in the abundance of your חסד answer me [the psalmist]	**Ps 68:14** καιρὸς εὐδοκίας, ὁ θεός, ἐν τῷ πλήθει τοῦ ἐλέους σου, ἐπάκουσόν μου
Ps 69:17 ענני יהוה כי טוב חסדך	**Ps 69:16** Answer me [the psalmist], O YHWH, for your חסד [is] good	**Ps 68:17** εἰσάκουσόν μου, κύριε, ὅτι χρηστὸν τὸ ἔλεός σου,
Ps 77:9 האפס לנצח חסדו	**Ps 77:8** Has his [the Lord's] חסד come to an end forever?	**Ps 76:9** ἢ εἰς τέλος τὸ ἔλεος αὐτοῦ ἀποκόψει ἀπὸ γενεᾶς εἰς γενεάν; (whole verse)
Ps 79:2 נתנו את נבלת עבדיך מאכל לעוף השמים בשר חסידיך לחיתו ארץ	**Ps 79:2** They [the nations] have given the corpses of your [God's] servants [as] food for the birds of the air, the flesh of your חסידים for the beasts of the earth.	**Ps 78:2** ἔθεντο τὰ θνησιμαῖα τῶν δούλων σου βρώματα τοῖς πετεινοῖς τοῦ οὐρανοῦ, τὰς σάρκας τῶν ὁσίων σου τοῖς θηρίοις τῆς γῆς,
Ps 85:8 הראנו יהוה חסדך וישעך תתן לנו	**Ps 85:7** Show us [YHWH's people] your חסד, O YHWH, and grant us your salvation	**Ps 84:8** δεῖξον ἡμῖν, κύριε, τὸ ἔλεός σου καὶ τὸ σωτήριόν σου δῴης ἡμῖν.
Ps 85:9 אשמעה מה ידבר האל יהוה כי ידבר שלום אל עמו ואל חסידיו ואל ישובו לכסלה	**Ps 85:8** Let me [the psalmist] hear what God-YHWH will speak, for he will speak peace to his people, to his חסידים —they should not return to stupidity.	**Ps 84:9** ἀκούσομαι τί λαλήσει ἐν ἐμοὶ κύριος ὁ θεός, ὅτι λαλήσει εἰρήνην ἐπὶ τὸν λαὸν αὐτοῦ καὶ ἐπὶ τοὺς ὁσίους αὐτοῦ καὶ ἐπὶ τοὺς ἐπιστρέφοντας πρὸς αὐτὸν καρδίαν.

34. Goldingay, *Psalms 42–89*, 296.

TABLE A1.2. Hebrew Bible Occurrences of חסד and חסיד (*continued*)

MT Clause(s)	English Translation of MT Clause(s)	LXX Translation of MT Clause(s)
Ps 85:11 חסד ואמת נפגשו	**Ps 85:10** חסד and faithfulness*** have met	**Ps 84:11** ἔλεος καὶ ἀλήθεια συνήντησαν,
Ps 86:2 שמרה נפשי כי חסיד אני הושע עבדך אתה אלהי הבוטח אליך	**Ps 86:2** Preserve my נפש for I [the psalmist] [am] חסיד; save your servant (you are my God), the one who trusts in you.	**Ps 85:2** φύλαξον τὴν ψυχήν μου, ὅτι ὅσιός εἰμι, σῶσον τὸν δοῦλόν σου, ὁ θεός μου, τὸν ἐλπίζοντα ἐπὶ σέ.
Ps 86:5 כי אתה אדני טוב וסלח ורב חסד לכל קראיך	**Ps 86:5** For you, O Lord, [are] good and forgiving, And abounding in חסד to all who call on you.	**Ps 85:5** ὅτι σύ, κύριε, χρηστὸς καὶ ἐπιεικὴς καὶ πολυέλεος πᾶσι τοῖς ἐπικαλουμένοις σε.
Ps 86:13 כי חסדך גדול עלי והצלת נפשי משאול תחתיה	**Ps 86:13** For your [the Lord's] חסד [is] great toward me [the psalmist], and you have delivered my נפש from the depths of Sheol.	**Ps 85:13** ὅτι τὸ ἔλεός σου μέγα ἐπ' ἐμὲ καὶ ἐρρύσω τὴν ψυχήν μου ἐξ ᾅδου κατωτάτου.
Ps 86:15 ואתה אדני אל רחום וחנון ארך אפים ורב חסד ואמת	**Ps 86:15** And you, O Lord, [are] a God, compassionate and gracious, slow to anger and abounding in חסד and faithfulness.***	**Ps 85:15** καὶ σύ, κύριε ὁ θεός, οἰκτίρμων καὶ ἐλεήμων, μακρόθυμος καὶ πολυέλεος καὶ ἀληθινός.
Ps 88:12 היספר בקבר חסדך אמונתך באבדון	**Ps 88:11** Is your [YHWH's] חסד declared in the grave, your faithfulness in Abaddon?	**Ps 87:12** μὴ διηγήσεταί τις ἐν τάφῳ τὸ ἔλεός σου καὶ τὴν ἀλήθειάν σου ἐν τῇ ἀπωλείᾳ;
Ps 89:2 חסדי יהוה עולם אשירה	**Ps 89:1** [Of] the חסדים of YHWH, forever I [the psalmist] will sing	**Ps 88:2** Τὰ ἐλέη σου, κύριε, εἰς τὸν αἰῶνα ᾄσομαι,
Ps 89:3 כי אמרתי עולם חסד יבנה	**Ps 89:2** For I [the psalmist] declared, חסד will be built/established forever	**Ps 88:3** ὅτι εἶπας Εἰς τὸν αἰῶνα ἔλεος οἰκοδομηθήσεται,
Ps 89:15 חסד ואמת יקדמו פניך	**Ps 89:14** חסד and faithfulness*** go before your [YHWH's] face.	**Ps 88:15** ἔλεος καὶ ἀλήθεια προπορεύσεται πρὸ προσώπου σου.
Ps 89:20 אז דברת בחזון לחסידיך[35]	**Ps 89:19** Then you [YHWH] spoke in a vision to your חסידים	**Ps 88:20** τότε ἐλάλησας ἐν ὁράσει τοῖς ὁσίοις σου

35. Sg. in a number of MSS (*BHS*, 1171).

TABLE A1.2. Hebrew Bible Occurrences of חסד and חסיד (*continued*)

MT Clause(s)	**English Translation of MT Clause(s)**	**LXX Translation of MT Clause(s)**
Ps 89:25 ואמונתי וחסדי עמו	**Ps 89:24** And my [YHWH's] faithfulness and my חסד [will be] with him [YHWH's servant, David]	**Ps 88:25** καὶ ἡ ἀλήθειά μου καὶ τὸ ἔλεός μου μετ' αὐτοῦ,
Ps 89:29 לעולם אשמור לו חסדי	**Ps 89:28** Forever I [YHWH] will keep for him [David] my חסד	**Ps 88:29** εἰς τὸν αἰῶνα φυλάξω αὐτῷ τὸ ἔλεός μου,
Ps 89:34 וחסדי לא אפיר מעמו	**Ps 89:33** But my חסד I [YHWH] will not break (from) with him [David]	**Ps 88:34** τὸ δὲ ἔλεός μου οὐ μὴ διασκεδάσω ἀπ' αὐτοῦ
Ps 89:50 איה חסדיך הראשנים אדני נשבעת לדוד באמונתך	**Ps 89:49** Where [are] your former חסדים, Lord, you swore to David in your faithfulness?	**Ps 88:50** ποῦ εἰσιν τὰ ἐλέη σου τὰ ἀρχαῖα, κύριε, ἃ ὤμοσας τῷ Δαυιδ ἐν τῇ ἀληθείᾳ σου;
Ps 90:14 שבענו בבקר חסדך ונרננה ונשמחה בכל ימינו	**Ps 90:14** Satisfy us [YHWH's servants] in the morning [with] your [YHWH's] חסד, and we will rejoice and be glad (in) all our days.	**Ps 89:14** ἐνεπλήσθημεν τὸ πρωὶ τοῦ ἐλέους σου καὶ ἠγαλλιασάμεθα καὶ εὐφράνθημεν ἐν πάσαις ταῖς ἡμέραις ἡμῶν,
Ps 92:3 Verse 2: טוב . . . Verse 3: להגיד בבקר חסדך ואמונתך בלילות	**Ps 92:2** Verse 1: [It is] good . . . Verse 2: to declare your [YHWH, Most High's] חסד in the morning and your faithfulness by night	**Ps 91:3** Verse 2: Ἀγαθὸν . . . Verse 3: τοῦ ἀναγγέλλειν τὸ πρωὶ τὸ ἔλεός σου καὶ τὴν ἀλήθειάν σου κατὰ νύκτα
Ps 94:18 אם אמרתי מטה רגלי חסדך יהוה יסעדני	**Ps 94:18** If I [the psalmist] said, "My foot has slipped," your חסד, YHWH, held me up	**Ps 93:18** εἰ ἔλεγον Σεσάλευται ὁ πούς μου, τὸ ἔλεός σου, κύριε, βοηθεῖ μοι,
Ps 97:10 אהבי יהוה שנאו רע שמר נפשות חסידיו מיד רשעים יצילם	**Ps 97:10** Lovers of YHWH, hate evil! He keeps the נפשות of his חסידים; from the hand of the wicked ones, he delivers them.	**Ps 96:10** οἱ ἀγαπῶντες τὸν κύριον, μισεῖτε πονηρόν, φυλάσσει κύριος τὰς ψυχὰς τῶν ὁσίων αὐτοῦ, ἐκ χειρὸς ἁμαρτωλῶν ῥύσεται αὐτούς.
Ps 98:3 זכר חסדו ואמונתו לבית ישראל	**Ps 98:3** He [YHWH] has remembered his חסד and his faithfulness to the house of Israel.	**Ps 97:3** ἐμνήσθη τοῦ ἐλέους αὐτοῦ τῷ Ιακωβ καὶ τῆς ἀληθείας αὐτοῦ τῷ οἴκῳ Ισραηλ,

TABLE A1.2. Hebrew Bible Occurrences of חסד and חסיד (*continued*)

MT Clause(s)	English Translation of MT Clause(s)	LXX Translation of MT Clause(s)
Ps 100:5 כי טוב יהוה לעולם חסדו ועד דר ודר אמונתו	**Ps 100:5** For YHWH [is] good, his חסד [is] forever, and his faithfulness [is] to all generations.	**Ps 99:5** ὅτι χρηστὸς κύριος, εἰς τὸν αἰῶνα τὸ ἔλεος αὐτοῦ, καὶ ἕως γενεᾶς καὶ γενεᾶς ἡ ἀλήθεια αὐτοῦ.
Ps 101:1 חסד ומשפט אשירה לך יהוה אזמרה	**Ps 101:1** I [the psalmist] will sing of חסד and justice; to you, O YHWH, I will sing.	**Ps 100:1** Ἔλεος καὶ κρίσιν ᾄσομαί σοι, κύριε, Verse 2: ψαλῶ
Ps 103:4 Verse 2: ברכי נפשי את יהוה . . . Verse 4: המעטרכי חסד ורחמים	**Ps 103:4** Verse 2: Bless YHWH, my [the psalmist's] נפש . . . Verse 4: [the one] who crowns you with חסד and compassion	**Ps 102:4** Verse 2: εὐλόγει, ἡ ψυχή μου, τὸν κύριον . . . Verse 4: τὸν στεφανοῦντά σε ἐν ἐλέει καὶ οἰκτιρμοῖς,
Ps 103:8 רחום וחנון יהוה ארך אפים ורב חסד	**Ps 103:8** YHWH [is] compassionate and gracious, slow to anger and abounding in חסד.	**Ps 102:8** οἰκτίρμων καὶ ἐλεήμων ὁ κύριος, μακρόθυμος καὶ πολυέλεος,
Ps 103:11 כי כגבה שמים על הארץ גבר חסדו על יראיו	**Ps 103:11** For as high as the heavens are above the earth his [YHWH's] חסד is superior toward those who fear him.	**Ps 102:11** ὅτι κατὰ τὸ ὕψος τοῦ οὐρανοῦ ἀπὸ τῆς γῆς ἐκραταίωσεν κύριος τὸ ἔλεος αὐτοῦ ἐπὶ τοὺς φοβουμένους αὐτόν,
Ps 103:17 וחסד יהוה מעולם ועד עולם על יראיו	**Ps 103:17** But the חסד of YHWH [is] from everlasting unto everlasting upon those who fear him.	**Ps 102:17** τὸ δὲ ἔλεος τοῦ κυρίου ἀπὸ τοῦ αἰῶνος καὶ ἕως τοῦ αἰῶνος ἐπὶ τοὺς φοβουμένους αὐτόν,
Ps 106:1 הודו ליהוה כי טוב כי לעולם חסדו	**Ps 106:1** Give thanks to YHWH, for [he is] good, for his חסד [is] forever.	**Ps 105:1** Ἐξομολογεῖσθε τῷ κυρίῳ, ὅτι χρηστός, ὅτι εἰς τὸν αἰῶνα τὸ ἔλεος αὐτοῦ.
Ps 106:7 לא זכרו את רב חסדיך וימרו על ים בים סוף	**Ps 106:7** They [the ancestors of YHWH's people] did not remember the abundance of your [YHWH's] חסדים, and they rebelled by the sea, at the Sea of Reeds.	**Ps 105:7** οὐκ ἐμνήσθησαν τοῦ πλήθους τοῦ ἐλέους σου καὶ παρεπίκραναν ἀναβαίνοντες ἐν τῇ ἐρυθρᾷ θαλάσσῃ.

TABLE A1.2. Hebrew Bible Occurrences of חסד and חסיד (*continued*)

MT Clause(s)	English Translation of MT Clause(s)	LXX Translation of MT Clause(s)
Ps 106:45 וינחם כרב חסדו[36]	**Ps 106:45** And he [YHWH] relented according to the abundance of his חסד.	**Ps 105:45** καὶ μετεμελήθη κατὰ τὸ πλῆθος τοῦ ἐλέους αὐτοῦ
Ps 107:1 הדו ליהוה כי טוב כי לעולם חסדו	**Ps 107:1** Give thanks to YHWH, for [he is] good, for his חסד [is] forever.	**Ps 106:1** Ἐξομολογεῖσθε τῷ κυρίῳ, ὅτι χρηστός, ὅτι εἰς τὸν αἰῶνα τὸ ἔλεος αὐτοῦ
Ps 107:8 יודו ליהוה חסדו	**Ps 107:8** Let them [those who wandered about in the wilderness] give thanks to YHWH [for] his חסד	**Ps 106:8** ἐξομολογησάσθωσαν τῷ κυρίῳ τὰ ἐλέη αὐτοῦ
Ps 107:15 יודו ליהוה חסדו	**Ps 107:15** Let them [those who sat in darkness and gloom] give thanks to YHWH [for] his חסד	**Ps 106:15** ἐξομολογησάσθωσαν τῷ κυρίῳ τὰ ἐλέη αὐτοῦ
Ps 107:21 יודו ליהוה חסדו	**Ps 107:21** Let them [those who are fools because of their criminal way] give thanks to YHWH [for] his חסד	**Ps 106:21** ἐξομολογησάσθωσαν τῷ κυρίῳ τὰ ἐλέη αὐτοῦ
Ps 107:31 יודו ליהוה חסדו	**Ps 107:31** Let them [those who went down to the sea in ships] give thanks to YHWH [for] his חסד	**Ps 106:31** ἐξομολογησάσθωσαν τῷ κυρίῳ τὰ ἐλέη αὐτοῦ
Ps 107:43 מי חכם וישמר אלה ויתבוננו חסדי יהוה	**Ps 107:43** Who [is] wise and will observe these things? Let them consider the חסדים of YHWH.	**Ps 106:43** τίς σοφὸς καὶ φυλάξει ταῦτα καὶ συνήσουσιν τὰ ἐλέη τοῦ κυρίου;
Ps 108:5 כי גדול מעל שמים חסדך ועד שחקים אמתך	**Ps 108:4** For your [YHWH's] חסד [is] greater/higher than the heavens and your faithfulness,*** unto the clouds.	**Ps 107:5** ὅτι μέγα ἐπάνω τῶν οὐρανῶν τὸ ἔλεός σου καὶ ἕως τῶν νεφελῶν ἡ ἀλήθειά σου.
Ps 109:12 אל יהי לו משך חסד	**Ps 109:12** May there be no one to extend חסד to him [the psalmist]	**Ps 108:12** μὴ ὑπαρξάτω αὐτῷ ἀντιλήμπτωρ,
Ps 109:16 לא זכר עשות חסד	**Ps 109:16** He [allegedly the psalmist][37] did not remember to do חסד	**Ps 108:16** οὐκ ἐμνήσθη τοῦ ποιῆσαι ἔλεος

36. *Qere*: חסדיו (*BHS*, 1189).

37. In vv. 6–19, the psalmist may be expressing his "own negative wishes" or quoting his enemies' accusations (as interpreted here). Allen argues in favor of the latter option on the grounds of smoother development (form-critically), the consistent differentiation between plural and singular references, and the apparent "framework of repeated terms" (*Psalms 101–150*, 101–4).

TABLE A1.2. Hebrew Bible Occurrences of חסד and חסיד (*continued*)

MT Clause(s)	English Translation of MT Clause(s)	LXX Translation of MT Clause(s)
Ps 109:21 כי טוב חסדך הצילני	**Ps 109:21** Because your [YHWH's] חסד [is] good, deliver me [the psalmist]	**Ps 108:21** ὅτι χρηστὸν τὸ ἔλεός σου. Verse 22: ῥῦσαί με,
Ps 109:26 עזרני יהוה אלהי הושיעני כחסדך	**Ps 109:26** Help me [the psalmist], O YHWH, my God, save me, according to your חסד.	**Ps 108:26** βοήθησόν μοι, κύριε ὁ θεός μου, σῶσόν με κατὰ τὸ ἔλεός σου,
Ps 115:1 לא לנו יהוה לא לנו כי לשמך תן כבוד על חסדך על אמתך	**Ps 115:1** Not for us, O YHWH, not for us, [but] for your name give glory, on account of your חסד, on account of your faithfulness.***	**Ps 113:9** μὴ ἡμῖν, κύριε, μὴ ἡμῖν, ἀλλ' ἢ τῷ ὀνόματί σου δὸς δόξαν ἐπὶ τῷ ἐλέει σου καὶ τῇ ἀληθείᾳ σου,
Ps 116:15 יקר בעיני יהוה המותה לחסידיו	**Ps 116:15** Precious in the eyes of YHWH [is] the death of his חסידים.	**Ps 115:6** τίμιος ἐναντίον κυρίου ὁ θάνατος τῶν ὁσίων αὐτοῦ.
Ps 117:2 Verse 1: הללו את יהוה כל גוים שבחוהו כל האמים Verse 2: כי גבר עלינו חסדו ואמת יהוה לעולם הללו יה	**Ps 117:2** Verse 1: Praise YHWH all nations, laud him all (the) peoples, Verse 2: for his חסד toward us [Israel] is superior, and the faithfulness*** of YHWH [is] forever. Praise YHWH!	**Ps 116:2** Verse 1: Αλληλουια. Αἰνεῖτε τὸν κύριον, πάντα τὰ ἔθνη, ἐπαινέσατε αὐτόν, πάντες οἱ λαοί, Verse 2: ὅτι ἐκραταιώθη τὸ ἔλεος αὐτοῦ ἐφ' ἡμᾶς, καὶ ἡ ἀλήθεια τοῦ κυρίου μένει εἰς τὸν αἰῶνα.
Ps 118:1 הודו ליהוה כי טוב כי לעולם חסדו	**Ps 118:1** Give thanks to YHWH, for [he is] good, for his חסד [is] forever.	**Ps 117:1** Ἐξομολογεῖσθε τῷ κυρίῳ, ὅτι ἀγαθός, ὅτι εἰς τὸν αἰῶνα τὸ ἔλεος αὐτοῦ.
Ps 118:2 יאמר נא ישראל כי לעולם חסדו	**Ps 118:2** Let Israel say, "For his [YHWH's] חסד [is] forever."	**Ps 117:2** εἰπάτω δὴ οἶκος Ισραηλ [ὅτι ἀγαθός], ὅτι εἰς τὸν αἰῶνα τὸ ἔλεος αὐτοῦ,
Ps 118:3 יאמרו נא בית אהרן כי לעולם חסדו	**Ps 118:3** Let the house of Aaron say, "For his [YHWH's] חסד [is] forever."	**Ps 117:3** εἰπάτω δὴ οἶκος Ααρων [ὅτι ἀγαθός], ὅτι εἰς τὸν αἰῶνα τὸ ἔλεος αὐτοῦ,
Ps 118:4 יאמרו נא יראי יהוה כי לעולם חסדו	**Ps 118:4** Let those who fear YHWH say, "For his [YHWH's] חסד [is] forever."	**Ps 117:4** εἰπάτωσαν δὴ πάντες οἱ φοβούμενοι τὸν κύριον [ὅτι ἀγαθός], ὅτι εἰς τὸν αἰῶνα τὸ ἔλεος αὐτοῦ,

TABLE A1.2. Hebrew Bible Occurrences of חסד and חסיד (*continued*)

MT Clause(s)	English Translation of MT Clause(s)	LXX Translation of MT Clause(s)
Ps 118:29 הודו ליהוה כי טוב כי לעולם חסדו	**Ps 118:29** Give thanks to YHWH, for [he is] good, for his חסד [is] forever.	**Ps 117:29** ἐξομολογεῖσθε τῷ κυρίῳ, ὅτι ἀγαθός, ὅτι εἰς τὸν αἰῶνα τὸ ἔλεος αὐτοῦ,
Ps 119:41 ויבאני חסדך יהוה תשועתך כאמרתך	**Ps 119:41** And let your חסד come to me [the psalmist], YHWH, your salvation, according to your promise.	**Ps 118:41** Καὶ ἔλθοι ἐπ᾽ ἐμὲ τὸ ἔλεός σου, κύριε, τὸ σωτήριόν σου κατὰ τὸ λόγιόν σου.
Ps 119:64 חסדך יהוה מלאה הארץ חקיך למדני	**Ps 119:64** The earth, O YHWH, is full of your חסד; teach me [the psalmist] your precepts.	**Ps 118:64** τοῦ ἐλέους σου, κύριε, πλήρης ἡ γῆ, τὰ δικαιώματά σου δίδαξόν με.
Ps 119:76 יהי נא חסדך לנחמני כאמרתך לעבדך	**Ps 119:76** Please let your [YHWH's] חסד (be to) comfort me [the psalmist] according to your promise to your servant.	**Ps 118:76** γενηθήτω δὴ τὸ ἔλεός σου τοῦ παρακαλέσαι με κατὰ τὸ λόγιόν σου τῷ δούλῳ σου.
Ps 119:88 כחסדך חיני ואשמרה עדות פיך	**Ps 119:88** According to your [YHWH's] חסד, revive me [the psalmist], that I may keep the testimony of your mouth.	**Ps 118:88** κατὰ τὸ ἔλεός σου ζῆσόν με, καὶ φυλάξω τὰ μαρτύρια τοῦ στόματός σου.
Ps 119:124 עשה עם עבדך כחסדך וחקיך למדני	**Ps 119:124** Do with your [YHWH's] servant according to your חסד, and teach me [the psalmist] your statutes.	**Ps 118:124** ποίησον μετὰ τοῦ δούλου σου κατὰ τὸ ἔλεός σου καὶ τὰ δικαιώματά σου δίδαξόν με.
Ps 119:149 קולי שמעה כחסדך	**Ps 119:149** Hear my [the psalmist's] voice, according to your [YHWH's] חסד	**Ps 118:149** τῆς φωνῆς μου ἄκουσον, κύριε, κατὰ τὸ ἔλεός σου,
Ps 119:159 כחסדך חיני	**Ps 119:159** According to your [YHWH's] חסד, revive me [the psalmist].[38]	**Ps 118:159** ἐν τῷ ἐλέει σου ζῆσόν με.
Ps 130:7 יחל ישראל אל יהוה כי עם יהוה החסד והרבה עמו פדות	**Ps 130:7** Israel, wait for YHWH! For with YHWH [is] the חסד and with him is abundant redemption.	**Ps 129:6–7** Verse 6: ἐλπισάτω Ισραηλ ἐπὶ τὸν κύριον. Verse 7: ὅτι παρὰ τῷ κυρίῳ τὸ ἔλεος, καὶ πολλὴ παρ᾽ αὐτῷ λύτρωσις,

38. In the latter four occurrences from Ps 119, the word order and requests are mirrored.

TABLE A1.2. Hebrew Bible Occurrences of חסד and חסיד (*continued*)

MT Clause(s)	English Translation of MT Clause(s)	LXX Translation of MT Clause(s)
Ps 132:9 כהניך ילבשו צדק וחסידיך ירננו	**Ps 132:9** Let your [YHWH's] priests put on righteousness, and let your חסידים shout for joy.	**Ps 131:9** οἱ ἱερεῖς σου ἐνδύσονται δικαιοσύνην, καὶ οἱ ὅσιοί σου ἀγαλλιάσονται.
Ps 132:16 וכהניה אלביש ישע וחסידיה רנן ירננו	**Ps 132:16** And her [Zion's] priests I will clothe with salvation, and her חסידים will shout aloud for joy.	**Ps 131:16** τοὺς ἱερεῖς αὐτῆς ἐνδύσω σωτηρίαν, καὶ οἱ ὅσιοι αὐτῆς ἀγαλλιάσει ἀγαλλιάσονται,
Ps 136:1 הודו ליהוה כי טוב כי לעולם חסדו	**Ps 136:1** Give thanks to YHWH, for [he is] good, for his חסד [is] forever.	**Ps 135:1** Ἐξομολογεῖσθε τῷ κυρίῳ, ὅτι χρηστός, ὅτι εἰς τὸν αἰῶνα τὸ ἔλεος αὐτοῦ,
Ps 136:2–26 כי לעולם חסדו	**Ps 136:2–26** The refrain throughout this psalm about the work of YHWH in creation and salvation history is— For his [YHWH's] חסד [is] forever.	**Ps 135:2–26** ὅτι εἰς τὸν αἰῶνα τὸ ἔλεος αὐτοῦ,
Ps 138:2 אשתחוה אל היכל קדשך ואודה את שמך על חסדך ועל אמתך כי הגדלת על כל שמך אמרתך	**Ps 138:2** I [the psalmist] will bow down toward your [YHWH's] holy temple and I will give thanks to your name for the sake of your חסד and for the sake of your faithfulness,*** for you have magnified above all your name, your word.	**Ps 137:2** προσκυνήσω πρὸς ναὸν ἅγιόν σου καὶ ἐξομολογήσομαι τῷ ὀνόματί σου ἐπὶ τῷ ἐλέει σου καὶ τῇ ἀληθείᾳ σου, ὅτι ἐμεγάλυνας ἐπὶ πᾶν ὄνομα τὸ λόγιόν σου.
Ps 138:8 יהוה יגמר בעדי יהוה חסדך לעולם מעשי ידיך אל תרף	**Ps 138:8** YHWH will avenge on my behalf; your חסד, O YHWH, [is] forever. Do not desert the works of your hands.	**Ps 137:8** κύριος ἀνταποδώσει ὑπὲρ ἐμοῦ. κύριε, τὸ ἔλεός σου εἰς τὸν αἰῶνα, τὰ ἔργα τῶν χειρῶν σου μὴ παρῇς.
Ps 141:5 יהלמני צדיק חסד ויוכיחני	**Ps 141:5** The righteous may strike me [the psalmist] [on account of][39] חסד, and rebuke me;	**Ps 140:5** παιδεύσει με δίκαιος ἐν ἐλέει καὶ ἐλέγξει με,
Ps 143:8 השמיעני בבקר חסדך כי בך בטחתי	**Ps 143:8** Cause me [the psalmist] to hear in the morning of your חסד, for in you I have trusted.	**Ps 142:8** ἀκουστὸν ποίησόν μοι τὸ πρωὶ τὸ ἔλεός σου, ὅτι ἐπὶ σοὶ ἤλπισα,

39. Cf. Tg. Pss.: מטול חסדא.

TABLE AI.2. Hebrew Bible Occurrences of חסד and חסיד (*continued*)

MT Clause(s)	English Translation of MT Clause(s)	LXX Translation of MT Clause(s)
Ps 143:12 ובחסדך תצמית איבי והאבדת כל צררי נפשי כי אני עבדך	**Ps 143:12** And in your [YHWH's] חסד, destroy my [the psalmist's] enemies and exterminate all the adversaries of my נפש, for I [am] your servant.	**Ps 142:12** καὶ ἐν τῷ ἐλέει σου ἐξολεθρεύσεις τοὺς ἐχθρούς μου καὶ ἀπολεῖς πάντας τοὺς θλίβοντας τὴν ψυχήν μου, ὅτι δοῦλός σού εἰμι ἐγώ.
Ps 144:2 Verse 1: . . . ברוך יהוה Verse 2: חסדי ומצודתי	**Ps 144:2** Verse 1: Blessed be YHWH . . . Verse 2: My [the psalmist's] חסד and my fortress	**Ps 143:2** Verse 1: Εὐλογητὸς κύριος . . . Verse 2: ἔλεός μου καὶ καταφυγή μου,
Ps 145:8 חנון ורחום יהוה ארך אפים וגדל חסד	**Ps 145:8** YHWH [is] gracious and compassionate, slow to anger and great in חסד.	**Ps 144:8** οἰκτίρμων καὶ ἐλεήμων ὁ κύριος, μακρόθυμος καὶ πολυέλεος.
Ps 145:10 יודוך יהוה כל מעשיך וחסידיך יברכוכה	**Ps 145:10** All your works will give thanks to you, O YHWH, and your חסידים will bless you.	**Ps 144:10** ἐξομολογησάσθωσάν σοι, κύριε, πάντα τὰ ἔργα σου, καὶ οἱ ὅσιοί σου εὐλογησάτωσάν σε.
Ps 145:17 צדיק יהוה בכל דרכיו וחסיד בכל מעשיו	**Ps 145:17** YHWH [is] righteous in all his ways, and חסיד in all his doings/deeds.	**Ps 144:17** δίκαιος κύριος ἐν πάσαις ταῖς ὁδοῖς αὐτοῦ καὶ ὅσιος ἐν πᾶσιν τοῖς ἔργοις αὐτοῦ.
Ps 147:11 רוצה יהוה את יראיו את המיחלים לחסדו	**Ps 147:11** YHWH takes pleasure in those who fear him, those who wait for his חסד.	**Ps 146:11** εὐδοκεῖ κύριος ἐν τοῖς φοβουμένοις αὐτὸν καὶ ἐν τοῖς ἐλπίζουσιν ἐπὶ τὸ ἔλεος αὐτοῦ.
Ps 148:14 וירם קרן לעמו תהלה לכל חסידיו לבני ישראל עם קרבו הללו יה	**Ps 148:14** He [YHWH] has raised up a horn for his people, praise[40] for all his חסידים, for the sons of Israel, a people close to him. Hallelujah!	**Ps 148:14** καὶ ὑψώσει κέρας λαοῦ αὐτοῦ, ὕμνος πᾶσι τοῖς ὁσίοις αὐτοῦ, τοῖς υἱοῖς Ισραηλ, λαῷ ἐγγίζοντι αὐτῷ.

40. This "praise" could be the response of the devoted party or another party (i.e., this people becomes "an object of praise" by other "entities" mentioned in the psalm). The new reason for praise is the lifting up of the horn (Goldingay, *Psalms 90–150*, 734). Hossfeld and Zenger claim that the reason must be the "dignity and (. . .) gift of power" that YHWH gives to YHWH's people (*Psalms 3*, 638–39).

TABLE A1.2. Hebrew Bible Occurrences of חסד and חסיד (*continued*)

MT Clause(s)	English Translation of MT Clause(s)	LXX Translation of MT Clause(s)
Ps 149:1	**Ps 149:1**	**Ps 149:1**
הללו יה	Hallelujah!	Αλληλουια.
שירו ליהוה שיר חדש	Sing to YHWH a new song,	Ἄισατε τῷ κυρίῳ ᾆσμα καινόν,
תהלתו בקהל חסידים	his praise in the assembly of חסידים.	ἡ αἴνεσις αὐτοῦ ἐν ἐκκλησίᾳ ὁσίων.
Ps 149:5	**Ps 149:5**	**Ps 149:5**
יעלזו חסידים בכבוד	Let חסידים exult in glory,	καυχήσονται ὅσιοι ἐν δόξῃ
ירננו על משכבותם	let them cry out on their beds.	καὶ ἀγαλλιάσονται ἐπὶ τῶν κοιτῶν αὐτῶν,
Ps 149:9	**Ps 149:9**	**Ps 149:9**
הדר הוא לכל חסידיו	It[41] [is] splendor for all his [God's] חסידים.	δόξα αὕτη ἐστὶν πᾶσι τοῖς ὁσίοις αὐτοῦ.
הללו יה	Hallelujah!	
Job 6:14	**Job 6:14**	**Job 6:14**
למס מרעהו חסד	The one who withholds[42] חסד from his friend,[43]	ἀπείπατό με ἔλεος,
ויראת שדי יעזוב	he will forsake the fear of the Almighty.	ἐπισκοπὴ δὲ κυρίου ὑπερεῖδέν με.
Job 10:12	**Job 10:12**	**Job 10:12**
חיים וחסד עשית עמדי	You [God] have done life and חסד with me [Job]	ζωὴν δὲ καὶ ἔλεος ἔθου παρ' ἐμοί,
Job 37:13	**Job 37:13**	**Job 37:13**
אם לשבט	Whether for a rod,	ἐὰν εἰς παιδείαν,
אם לארצו	or for his land,	ἐὰν εἰς τὴν γῆν αὐτοῦ,
אם לחסד	or for חסד,	ἐὰν εἰς ἔλεος
ימצאהו	he [God] causes it to succeed.	εὑρήσει αὐτόν.
Prov 2:8	**Prov 2:8**	**Prov 2:8**
Verse 7: מגן להלכי תם	Verse 7: [He is] a shield for those who walk in integrity	Verse 7: ὑπερασπιεῖ τὴν πορείαν αὐτῶν
Verse 8: לנצר ארחות משפט	Verse 8: to keep watch over paths of justice	Verse 8: τοῦ φυλάξαι ὁδοὺς δικαιωμάτων
ודרך חסידו ישמר	and the way of his [YHWH's] חסידים he will keep.	καὶ ὁδὸν εὐλαβουμένων αὐτὸν διαφυλάξει.
Prov 3:3	**Prov 3:3**	**Prov 3:3**
חסד ואמת אל יעזבך	חסד and faithfulness*** will not forsake you [the child];	ἐλεημοσύναι καὶ πίστεις μὴ ἐκλιπέτωσάν σε,
קשרם על גרגרותיך	bind them around your neck;	ἄφαψαι δὲ αὐτὰς ἐπὶ σῷ τραχήλῳ,
כתבם על לוח לבך	write them on the tablet of your heart.	καὶ εὑρήσεις χάριν, (this clause relates to MT v. 4a)

41. This pronoun could also be applied to YHWH/God. So Hossfeld and Zenger, *Psalms 3*, 652.
42. Meaning uncertain. This translation is adapted from the NRSV and NIV models.
43. Lit.: "For the discouraged from his friend חסד."

TABLE A1.2. Hebrew Bible Occurrences of חסד and חסיד (*continued*)

MT Clause(s)	English Translation of MT Clause(s)	LXX Translation of MT Clause(s)
Prov 11:17 גמל נפשו איש חסד ועכר שארו אכזרי	**Prov 11:17** A person of חסד does [good] to his נפש, but a cruel one ruins his flesh.	**Prov 11:17** τῇ ψυχῇ αὐτοῦ ἀγαθὸν ποιεῖ ἀνὴρ ἐλεήμων, ἐξολλύει δὲ αὐτοῦ σῶμα ὁ ἀνελεήμων.
Prov 14:22 הלוא יתעו חרשי רע וחסד ואמת חרשי טוב	**Prov 14:22** Do they not err who plan/plough evil, and [are not] חסד and faithfulness*** [the reward of] those who plan/plough good?	**Prov 14:22** πλανώμενοι τεκταίνουσι κακά, ἔλεον δὲ καὶ ἀλήθειαν τεκταίνουσιν ἀγαθοί. Additions: οὐκ ἐπίστανται ἔλεον καὶ πίστιν τέκτονες κακῶν, ἐλεημοσύναι δὲ καὶ πίστεις παρὰ τέκτοσιν ἀγαθοῖς.
Prov 16:6 בחסד ואמת יכפר עון	**Prov 16:6** By חסד and faithfulness*** iniquity will be atoned for.	**Prov 15:27a** ἐλεημοσύναις καὶ πίστεσιν ἀποκαθαίρονται ἁμαρτίαι,
Prov 19:22 תאות אדם חסדו	**Prov 19:22** The longing of a human being [is] his חסד	**Prov 19:22** καρπὸς ἀνδρὶ ἐλεημοσύνη,
Prov 20:6 רב אדם יקרא איש חסדו ואיש אמונים מי ימצא	**Prov 20:6** Many a human will call upon a person of (his) חסד, but a person of trustworthy/faithful acts, who can find?	**Prov 20:6** μέγα ἄνθρωπος καὶ τίμιον ἀνὴρ ἐλεήμων, ἄνδρα δὲ πιστὸν ἔργον εὑρεῖν.
Prov 20:28, 28 חסד ואמת יצרו מלך וסעד בחסד כסאו	**Prov 20:28, 28** (a) חסד and faithfulness*** watch over [the] king (b) and his throne is upheld/supported by the חסד.	**Prov 20:28, 28** ἐλεημοσύνη καὶ ἀλήθεια φυλακὴ βασιλεῖ καὶ περικυκλώσουσιν ἐν δικαιοσύνῃ τὸν θρόνον αὐτοῦ.
Prov 21:21 רדף צדקה וחסד ימצא חיים צדקה וכבוד	**Prov 21:21** The one who pursues righteousness and חסד will find life, righteousness, and glory/honor.	**Prov 21:21** ὁδὸς δικαιοσύνης καὶ ἐλεημοσύνης εὑρήσει ζωὴν καὶ δόξαν.
Prov 31:26 פיה פתחה בחכמה ותורת חסד על לשונה	**Prov 31:26** She [the worthy woman] opens her mouth with wisdom and the teaching of חסד [is] on her tongue.	**Prov 31:25** στόμα αὐτῆς διήνοιξεν προσεχόντως καὶ ἐννόμως καὶ τάξιν ἐστείλατο τῇ γλώσσῃ αὐτῆς.

TABLE A1.2. Hebrew Bible Occurrences of חסד and חסיד (*continued*)

MT Clause(s)	English Translation of MT Clause(s)	LXX Translation of MT Clause(s)
Ruth 1:8 יעשה[44] יהוה עמכם חסד כאשר עשיתם עם המתים ועמדי	**Ruth 1:8** May YHWH do חסד with you [Ruth and Orpah], as you have done with the dead and with me [Naomi].	**Ruth 1:8** ποιήσαι κύριος μεθ' ὑμῶν ἔλεος, καθὼς ἐποιήσατε μετὰ τῶν τεθνηκότων καὶ μετ' ἐμοῦ,
Ruth 2:20 ברוך הוא ליהוה אשר לא עזב חסדו את החיים ואת המתים	**Ruth 2:20** Blessed be he by YHWH, who[45] has not forsaken his חסד[46] to the living or to the dead.	**Ruth 2:20** Εὐλογητός ἐστιν τῷ κυρίῳ, ὅτι οὐκ ἐγκατέλιπεν τὸ ἔλεος αὐτοῦ μετὰ τῶν ζώντων καὶ μετὰ τῶν τεθνηκότων.
Ruth 3:10 ברוכה את ליהוה בתי היטבת חסדך האחרון מן הראשין לבלתי לכת אחרי הבחורים אם דל ואם עשיר	**Ruth 3:10** May you [Ruth] be blessed by YHWH, my daughter, your latter חסד is better than the first, for you have not gone after young men, whether poor or rich.	**Ruth 3:10** Εὐλογημένη σὺ τῷ κυρίῳ θεῷ, θύγατερ, ὅτι ἠγάθυνας τὸ ἔλεός σου τὸ ἔσχατον ὑπὲρ τὸ πρῶτον, τὸ μὴ πορευθῆναί σε ὀπίσω νεανιῶν, εἴτοι πτωχὸς εἴτοι πλούσιος.
Lam 3:22 חסדי יהוה כי לא תמנו כי לא כלו רחמיו	**Lam 3:22** [Because of] the חסדים of YHWH—(for) we do not perish; (for) his compassions do not come to an end.	**No LXX equivalent**
Lam 3:32 כי אם הוגה ורחם כרב חסדו[47]	**Lam 3:32** For though he causes grief, he will have compassion, according to the abundance of his חסד.	**Lam 3:32** ὅτι ὁ ταπεινώσας οἰκτιρήσει κατὰ τὸ πλῆθος τοῦ ἐλέους αὐτοῦ,
Esth 2:9 ותיטב הנערה בעיניו ותשא חסד לפניו	**Esth 2:9** And the young woman [Esther] was pleasing in his [Hegai's] eyes, and she lifted up חסד before him.	**Esth 2:9** καὶ ἤρεσεν αὐτῷ τὸ κοράσιον καὶ εὗρεν χάριν ἐνώπιον αὐτοῦ,

44. *Qere*: יעש (*BHS*, 1320).

45. The agent of חסד in this context could be YHWH or Boaz. Sakenfeld, *Meaning of Hesed*, 104–7. If the ambiguity is intentional, this suggests the perception that both act "in concert" as agents of חסד. Hawk, *Ruth*, 86.

46. Schipper notes that "his kindness" could also be understood as the subject of the verb "abandoned" (*Ruth*, 134).

47. *Qere*: חסדיו (*BHS*, 1362).

TABLE A1.2. Hebrew Bible Occurrences of חסד and חסיד (*continued*)

MT Clause(s)	English Translation of MT Clause(s)	LXX Translation of MT Clause(s)
Esth 2:17 ויאהב המלך את אסתר מכל הנשים ותשא חן וחסד לפניו מכל הבתולת וישם כתר מלכות בראשה וימליכה תחת ושתי	**Esth 2:17** The king loved Esther more than all the women, and she lifted up grace and חסד before him more than all the virgins; (and) he set a royal crown on her head, and he made her queen instead of Vashti.	**Esth 2:17** καὶ ἠράσθη ὁ βασιλεὺς Εσθηρ, καὶ εὗρεν χάριν παρὰ πάσας τὰς παρθένους, καὶ ἐπέθηκεν αὐτῇ τὸ διάδημα τὸ γυναικεῖον.
Dan 1:9 ויתן האלהים את דניאל לחסד ולרחמים לפני שר הסריסים	**Dan 1:9** And God gave Daniel to חסד and to compassion[48] before the palace master.[49]	**Dan 1:9** καὶ ἔδωκε κύριος τῷ Δανιηλ τιμὴν καὶ χάριν ἐναντίον τοῦ ἀρχιευνούχου.
Dan 9:4 אנא אדני האל הגדול והנורא שמר הברית והחסד לאהביו ולשמרי מצותיו	**Dan 9:4** Ah[50] Lord, the great and awesome God, who keeps the covenant and the חסד to those who love him and (to those who) keep his commandments.	**Dan 9:4** Ἰδού, κύριε, σὺ εἶ ὁ θεὸς ὁ μέγας καὶ ὁ ἰσχυρὸς καὶ ὁ φοβερὸς τηρῶν τὴν διαθήκην καὶ τὸ ἔλεος τοῖς ἀγαπῶσί σε καὶ τοῖς φυλάσσουσι τὰ προστάγματά σου,
Ezra 3:11 ויענו בהלל ובהודת ליהוה כי טוב כי לעולם חסדו על ישראל	**Ezra 3:11** And they [priests, Levites, and sons of Asaph] sang responsively in praise and thanksgiving to YHWH, "For [he is] good, for his חסד [is] forever toward Israel."	**2 Esd 3:11** καὶ ἀπεκρίθησαν ἐν αἴνῳ καὶ ἀνθομολογήσει τῷ κυρίῳ, ὅτι ἀγαθόν, ὅτι εἰς τὸν αἰῶνα τὸ ἔλεος αὐτοῦ ἐπὶ Ισραηλ.
Ezra 7:28 Verse 27: ברוך יהוה אלהי אבותינו . . . Verse 28: ועלי הטה חסד לפני המלך ויועציו ולכל שרי המלך הגברים	**Ezra 7:28** Verse 27: Blessed be YHWH, the God of our ancestors . . . Verse 28: And he has extended חסד toward me [Ezra] before the king and his counselors and to all of the king's mighty officials.	**2 Esd 7:28** Verse 27: Εὐλογητὸς κύριος ὁ θεὸς τῶν πατέρων ἡμῶν, . . . Verse 28: καὶ ἐπ' ἐμὲ ἔκλινεν ἔλεος ἐν ὀφθαλμοῖς τοῦ βασιλέως καὶ τῶν συμβούλων αὐτοῦ καὶ πάντων τῶν ἀρχόντων τοῦ βασιλέως τῶν ἐπηρμένων.

48. ESV has "gave Daniel favor and compassion," but Sakenfeld's "made Daniel the object of *ḥesed* and mercy" communicates the transfer of agency from God to the palace master more clearly (*Meaning of Hesed*, 163).

49. "Palace master": NRSV.

50. NRSV.

TABLE A1.2. Hebrew Bible Occurrences of חסד and חסיד (*continued*)

MT Clause(s)	English Translation of MT Clause(s)	LXX Translation of MT Clause(s)
Ezra 9:9 ויט עלינו חסד לפני מלכי פרס לתת לנו מחיה לרומם את בית אלהינו ולהעמיד את חרבתיו ולתת לנו גדר ביהודה ובירושלם	**Ezra 9:9** And he [our God] has extended חסד toward us [Israelite remnant] before the kings of Persia, to give us new life, to set up the house of our God, and to repair its ruins, and to give us a wall in Judah and in Jerusalem.	**2 Esd 9:9** καὶ ἔκλινεν ἐφ' ἡμᾶς ἔλεος ἐνώπιον βασιλέων Περσῶν δοῦναι ἡμῖν ζωοποίησιν τοῦ ὑψῶσαι αὐτοὺς τὸν οἶκον τοῦ θεοῦ ἡμῶν καὶ ἀναστῆσαι τὰ ἔρημα αὐτῆς καὶ τοῦ δοῦναι ἡμῖν φραγμὸν ἐν Ιουδα καὶ ἐν Ιερουσαλημ.
Neh 1:5 אנא יהוה אלהי השמים האל הגדול והנורא שמר הברית וחסד לאהביו ולשמרי מצותיו	**Neh 1:5** Ah YHWH, God of heavens, the great and awesome God, who keeps the covenant and חסד to those who love him and (to those who) keep his commandments.	**2 Esd 11:5** Μὴ δή, κύριε ὁ θεὸς τοῦ οὐρανοῦ ὁ ἰσχυρὸς ὁ μέγας καὶ ὁ φοβερός, φυλάσσων τὴν διαθήκην καὶ τὸ ἔλεος τοῖς ἀγαπῶσιν αὐτὸν καὶ τοῖς φυλάσσουσιν τὰς ἐντολὰς αὐτοῦ,
Neh 9:17 ואתה אלוה סליחות חנון ורחום ארך אפים ורב וחסד ולא עזבתם	**Neh 9:17** But you [YHWH] [are] a God of pardons, gracious and compassionate, slow to anger and abounding in חסד and you did not forsake them [the ancestors].	**2 Esd 19:17** καὶ σὺ θεὸς ἐλεήμων καὶ οἰκτίρμων, μακρόθυμος καὶ πολυέλεος, καὶ οὐκ ἐγκατέλιπες αὐτούς.
Neh 9:32 ועתה אלהינו האל הגדול הגבור והנורא שומר הברית והחסד אל ימעט לפניך את כל התלאה אשר מצאתנו . . .	**Neh 9:32** And now, our God, the great and mighty and awesome God, who keeps the covenant and (the) חסד, do not belittle (before you) all the hardship that has come upon us [all God's people, including their kings, officials, priests, prophets, and ancestors] . . .	**2 Esd 19:32** καὶ νῦν, ὁ θεὸς ἡμῶν ὁ ἰσχυρὸς ὁ μέγας ὁ κραταιὸς καὶ ὁ φοβερὸς φυλάσσων τὴν διαθήκην σου καὶ τὸ ἔλεός σου, μὴ ὀλιγωθήτω ἐνώπιόν σου πᾶς ὁ μόχθος, ὃς εὗρεν ἡμᾶς . . .
Neh 13:14 זכרה לי אלהי על זאת ואל תמח חסדי אשר עשיתי בבית אלהי ובמשמריו	**Neh 13:14** Remember (to) me [Nehemiah] [i.e., to my credit], O my God, concerning this, and do not wipe out my חסדים that I have done in the house of my God and in his service.	**2 Esd 23:14** μνήσθητί μου, ὁ θεός, ἐν ταύτῃ, καὶ μὴ ἐξαλειφθήτω ἔλεός μου, ὃ ἐποίησα ἐν οἴκῳ κυρίου τοῦ θεοῦ.

TABLE A1.2. Hebrew Bible Occurrences of חסד and חסיד (*continued*)

MT Clause(s)	English Translation of MT Clause(s)	LXX Translation of MT Clause(s)
Neh 13:22 גם זאת זכרה לי אלהי וחוסה עלי כרב חסדך	**Neh 13:22** This also, remember to me [Nehemiah] [i.e., to my credit], O my God, and look compassionately upon me according to the abundance of your חסד.	**2 Esd 23:22** πρὸς ταῦτα μνήσθητί μου, ὁ θεός, καὶ φεῖσαί μου κατὰ τὸ πλῆθος τοῦ ἐλέους σου.
1 Chr 16:34 הודו ליהוה כי טוב כי לעולם חסדו	**1 Chr 16:34** Give thanks to YHWH, for [he is] good, for his חסד [is] forever.	**1 Chr 16:34** ἐξομολογεῖσθε τῷ κυρίῳ, ὅτι ἀγαθόν, ὅτι εἰς τὸν αἰῶνα τὸ ἔλεος αὐτοῦ.
1 Chr 16:41 ועמהם הימן וידותון ושאר הברורים אשר נקבו בשמות להדות ליהוה כי לעולם חסדו	**1 Chr 16:41** And with them [were] Heman and Jeduthun and the rest of those chosen who were marked by name to give thanks to YHWH for his חסד [is] forever.	**1 Chr 16:41** καὶ μετ᾽ αὐτοῦ Αιμαν καὶ Ιδιθων καὶ οἱ λοιποὶ ἐκλεγέντες ἐπ᾽ ὀνόματος τοῦ αἰνεῖν τὸν κύριον, ὅτι εἰς τὸν αἰῶνα τὸ ἔλεος αὐτοῦ,
1 Chr 17:13 וחסדי לא אסיר מעמו כאשר הסירותי מאשר היה לפניך	**1 Chr 17:13** And I [YHWH] will not remove my חסד from (with) him [David's descendant] as I removed [it] from he who was before you [Saul].	**1 Chr 17:13** καὶ τὸ ἔλεός μου οὐκ ἀποστήσω ἀπ᾽ αὐτοῦ ὡς ἀπέστησα ἀπὸ τῶν ὄντων ἔμπροσθέν σου.
1 Chr 19:2, 2 אעשה חסד עם חנון בן נחש כי עשה אביו עמי חסד	**1 Chr 19:2, 2** (a) I [David] will do חסד with Hanun, son of Nahash, (b) for his father did חסד with me	**1 Chr 19:2, 2** Ποιήσω ἔλεος μετὰ Αναν υἱοῦ Ναας, ὡς ἐποίησεν ὁ πατὴρ αὐτοῦ μετ᾽ ἐμοῦ ἔλεος,
2 Chr 1:8 אתה עשית עם דויד אבי חסד גדול והמלכתני תחתיו	**2 Chr 1:8** You (emph.) [God] have done with David, my father, great חסד and have made me [Solomon] succeed him as king.	**2 Chr 1:8** Σὺ ἐποίησας μετὰ Δαυιδ τοῦ πατρός μου ἔλεος μέγα καὶ ἐβασίλευσάς με ἀντ᾽ αὐτοῦ,
2 Chr 5:13 כי טוב כי לעולם חסדו	**2 Chr 5:13** For [he is] good, for his [YHWH's] חסד [is] forever.	**2 Chr 5:13** ὅτι ἀγαθόν, ὅτι εἰς τὸν αἰῶνα τὸ ἔλεος αὐτοῦ,
2 Chr 6:14 יהוה אלהי ישראל אין כמוך אלהים בשמים ובארץ שמר הברית והחסד לעבדיך ההלכים לפניך בכל לבם	**2 Chr 6:14** O YHWH, God of Israel, there is no God like you in the heavens and in the earth, who keeps the covenant and the חסד to your servants who walk before you with all their heart.	**2 Chr 6:14** Κύριε ὁ θεὸς Ισραηλ, οὐκ ἔστιν ὅμοιός σοι θεὸς ἐν οὐρανῷ καὶ ἐπὶ τῆς γῆς, φυλάσσων τὴν διαθήκην καὶ τὸ ἔλεος τοῖς παισίν σου τοῖς πορευομένοις ἐναντίον σου ἐν ὅλῃ καρδίᾳ.

TABLE A1.2. Hebrew Bible Occurrences of חסד and חסיד (*continued*)

MT Clause(s)	English Translation of MT Clause(s)	LXX Translation of MT Clause(s)
2 Chr 6:41 כהניך יהוה אלהים ילבשו תשועה וחסידיך ישמחו בטוב	**2 Chr 6:41** Let your priests, O YHWH God, put on salvation, and let your חסידים rejoice in goodness.	**2 Chr 6:41** οἱ ἱερεῖς σου, κύριε ὁ θεός, ἐνδύσαιντο σωτηρίαν, καὶ οἱ υἱοί σου εὐφρανθήτωσαν ἐν ἀγαθοῖς.
2 Chr 6:42 יהוה אלהים אל תשב פני משיחיך זכרה לחסדי דויד עבדך	**2 Chr 6:42** O YHWH God, do not turn away from (the faces of) your anointed ones; remember the חסדים of David, your servant!	**2 Chr 6:42** κύριε ὁ θεός, μὴ ἀποστρέψῃς τὸ πρόσωπον τοῦ χριστοῦ σου, μνήσθητι τὰ ἐλέη Δαυιδ τοῦ δούλου σου.
2 Chr 7:3 כי טוב כי לעולם חסדו	**2 Chr 7:3** For [he is] good, for his [YHWH's] חסד [is] forever.	**2 Chr 7:3** ὅτι ἀγαθόν, ὅτι εἰς τὸν αἰῶνα τὸ ἔλεος αὐτοῦ.
2 Chr 7:6 כי לעולם חסדו	**2 Chr 7:6** For his [YHWH's] חסד [is] forever	**2 Chr 7:6** ὅτι εἰς τὸν αἰῶνα τὸ ἔλεος αὐτοῦ
2 Chr 20:21 הודו ליהוה כי לעולם חסדו	**2 Chr 20:21** Give thanks to YHWH, for his חסד [is] forever.	**2 Chr 20:21** Ἐξομολογεῖσθε τῷ κυρίῳ, ὅτι εἰς τὸν αἰῶνα τὸ ἔλεος αὐτοῦ.
2 Chr 24:22 ולא זכר יואש המלך החסד אשר עשה יהוידע אביו עמו ויהרג את בנו	**2 Chr 24:22** And Joash, the king, did not remember the חסד that Jehoiada, his [Zechariah's] father, had done with him [Joash], and he [Joash] killed his [Jehoiada's] son.	**2 Chr 24:22** καὶ οὐκ ἐμνήσθη Ιωας τοῦ ἐλέους, οὗ ἐποίησεν μετ' αὐτοῦ Ιωδαε ὁ πατὴρ αὐτοῦ, καὶ ἐθανάτωσεν τὸν υἱὸν αὐτοῦ.
2 Chr 32:32 ויתר דברי יחזקיהו וחסדיו הנם כתובים בחזון ישעיהו בן אמוץ הנביא על ספר מלכי יהודה וישראל	**2 Chr 32:32** And the rest of the affairs of Hezekiah and his חסדים, see, they are written in the vision of Isaiah, son of Amoz, the prophet, on the scroll of the kings of Judah and Israel.	**2 Chr 32:32** καὶ τὰ κατάλοιπα τῶν λόγων Εζεκιου καὶ τὸ ἔλεος αὐτοῦ, ἰδοὺ γέγραπται ἐν τῇ προφητείᾳ Ησαιου υἱοῦ Αμως τοῦ προφήτου καὶ ἐπὶ βιβλίου βασιλέων Ιουδα καὶ Ισραηλ.
2 Chr 35:26 ויתר דברי יאשיהו וחסדיו ככתוב בתורת יהוה	**2 Chr 35:26** And the rest of the affairs of Josiah and his חסדים, according to what is written in the teaching of YHWH . . .	**2 Chr 35:26** καὶ ἦσαν οἱ λόγοι Ιωσια καὶ ἡ ἐλπὶς αὐτοῦ γεγραμμένα ἐν νόμῳ κυρίου,

TABLE A1.3. LXX Translations of Hebrew Bible Occurrences of חסד.
There are 245 occurrences of חסד in 239 Hebrew Bible (*BHS*) verses.*

LXX Equivalent	Reference
ἔλεος	205 occurrences:** Gen 24:12, 14, 49; 39:21; 40:14; Exod 20:6; 34:7 (one of two possible translations); Num 14:19; Deut 5:10; 7:9, 12; Josh 2:12, 12, 14; Judg 1:24; 8:35; 1 Sam (1 Kgdms LXX) 15:6; 20:8, 14, 15; 2 Sam (2 Kgdms LXX) 2:5, 6; 3:8; 7:15; 9:1, 3, 7; 10:2, 2; 15:20; 16:17; 22:51; 1 Kgs (3 Kgdms LXX) 2:7; 3:6, 6; 8:23; 20(21 LXX):31; Isa 16:5; 54:8, 10; 63:7; Jer 2:2; 9:24(23); 32(39 LXX):18; 33(40 LXX):11; Hos 2:19(21); 4:1; 6:4, 6; 12:6(7); Jonah 2:8(9); Mic 6:8; 7:18, 20; Zech 7:9; Pss 5:7(8); 6:4(5); 13(12 LXX):5(6); 17(16 LXX):7; 18(17 LXX):50(51); 21(20 LXX):7(8); 23(22 LXX):6; 25(24 LXX):6, 7, 10; 26(25 LXX):3; 31(30 LXX):7(8), 16(17), 21(22); 32(31 LXX):10; 33(32 LXX):5, 18, 22; 36(35 LXX):5(6), 7(8), 10(11); 40(39 LXX):10(11), 11(12); 42(41 LXX):8(9); 48(47 LXX):9(10); 51(50 LXX):1(3); 52(51 LXX):8(10); 57(56 LXX):3(4), 10(11); 59(58 LXX):10(11), 16(17), 17(18); 61(60 LXX):7(8); 62(61 LXX):12(13); 63(62 LXX):3(4); 66(65 LXX):20; 69(68 LXX):13(14), 16(17); 77(76 LXX):8(9); 85(84 LXX):7(8), 10(11); 86(85 LXX):13; 88(87 LXX):11(12); 89(88 LXX):1(2), 2(3), 14(15), 24(25), 28(29), 33(34), 49(50); 90(89 LXX):14; 92(91 LXX):2(3); 94(93 LXX):18; 98(97 LXX):3; 100(99 LXX):5; 101(100 LXX):1; 103(102 LXX):4, 11, 17; 106(105 LXX):1, 7, 45; 107(106 LXX):1, 8, 15, 21, 31, 43; 108(107 LXX):4(5); 109(108 LXX):16, 21, 26; 115:1 (113:9 LXX); 117(116 LXX):2; 118(117 LXX):1, 2, 3, 4, 29; 119(118 LXX):41, 64, 76, 88, 124, 149, 159; 130(129 LXX):7; 136(135 LXX):1, 2, 3, 4, 5, 6, 7, 8, 9, 10, 11, 12, 13, 14, 15, 16, 17, 18, 19, 20, 21, 22, 23, 24, 25, 26; 138(137 LXX):2, 8; 141(140 LXX):5; 143(142 LXX):8, 12; 144(143 LXX):2; 147(146 LXX):11; Job 6:14; 10:12; 37:13; Prov 14:22; Ruth 1:8; 2:20; 3:10; Lam 3:32; Dan 9:4; Ezra (2 Esd LXX) 3:11; 7:28; 9:9; Neh 1 (2 Esd 11 LXX):5; 9(19 LXX):32; 13(23 LXX):14, 22; 1 Chr 16:34, 41; 17:13; 19:2, 2; 2 Chr 1:8; 5:13; 6:14, 42; 7:3, 6; 20:21; 24:22; 32:32 ἔλεος in a LXX addition to Prov 14:22 could also be an equivalent for חסד.
πολυέλεος (for רב חסד or גדל חסד)	9 occurrences: Exod 34:6; Num 14:18; Joel 2:13; Jonah 4:2; Pss 86(85 LXX):5, 15; 103(102 LXX):8; 145(144 LXX):8; Neh 9 (2 Esd 19 LXX):17
δικαιοσύνη ("righteousness")	9 occurrences: Gen 19:19; 20:13; 21:23; 24:27; 32:10(11); Exod 15:13; 34:7 (one of two possible translations); Isa 63:7; Prov 20:28
ἐλεημοσύνη ("act of mercy/alms")	6 occurrences: Gen 47:29; Prov 3:3; 16:6 (15:27a LXX); 19:22; 20:28; 21:21 ἐλεημοσύνη in an LXX addition to Prov 14:22 could also be an equivalent for חסד.

TABLE A1.3. LXX Translations of Hebrew Bible Occurrences of חסד (*continued*)

LXX Equivalent	Reference
ἐλεήμων ("merciful")	2 occurrences: Prov 11:17; 20:6
δόξα ("glory")	Isa 40:6
ὅσιος	Isa 55:3
δίκαιος ("righteous/ upright")	Isa 57:1
οἰκτίρημα ("compassion")	Jer 31(38 LXX):3
ζωή ("life")	Hos 10:12
ὄνομα ("name")	Ps 44(43 LXX):26(27)
ἀντιλήμπτωρ ("helper")	Ps 109(108 LXX):12
τάξις ("order")	Prov 31:26(25 LXX)
χάρις ("grace/favor")	Esth 2:9; possibly also 2:17
τιμή ("honor/favor")	Dan 1:9
ἐλπίς ("hope")	2 Chr 35:26
No LXX equivalent	Jer 16:5; Ps 52(51 LXX):1(3); Lam 3:22 In Ps 51:3 LXX, ἀνομία ("lawlessness") is in place of חסד אל.

TABLE A1.4. LXX Translations of Hebrew Bible Occurrences of חסיד.
There are 32 occurrences of חסיד in 32 Hebrew Bible (*BHS*) verses.*

LXX Equivalent	Reference
ὅσιος	27 occurrences (25 in Psalms):** Deut 33:8; 2 Sam (2 Kgdms LXX) 22:26; Pss 4:3(4); 12(11 LXX):1(2); 16(15 LXX):10; 18(17 LXX):25(26); 30(29 LXX):4(5); 31(30 LXX):23(24); 32(31 LXX):6; 37(36 LXX):28; 43(42 LXX):1; 50(49 LXX):5; 52(51 LXX):9(11); 79(78 LXX):2; 85(84 LXX):8(9); 86(85 LXX):2; 89(88 LXX):19(20); 97(96 LXX):10; 116:15 (115:6 LXX); 132(131 LXX):9, 16; 145(144 LXX):10, 17; 148:14; 149:1, 5, 9
ἐλεήμων ("merciful")	Jer 3:12
εὐλαβής ("pious/devout")	Mic 7:2
εὐλαβέομαι ("be reverent")	Prov 2:8
υἱός ("son")	2 Chr 6:41
No LXX equivalent	1 Sam (1 Kgdms LXX) 2:9

APPENDIX 2: LXX OCCURRENCES OF ἜΛΕΟΣ, ἘΛΕΈΩ, AND ὍΣΙΟΣ

Tables A2.1, A2.2, and A2.3 present the LXX occurrences of ἔλεος, ἐλεέω, and ὅσιος, respectively. The occurrences of these words are grouped according to their Hebrew Bible equivalents. In these tables, the Greek word may be in the same position as its Hebrew "equivalent" within the corresponding clause, but it is not necessarily a direct translation of that "equivalent." The noun ἔλεος is the most frequent LXX rendering of חסד. The related verb ἐλεέω is included for comparison. ὅσιος is the most frequent LXX rendering of חסיד.

Unless stated otherwise, verse numbers in brackets indicate the MT/LXX numbering where that differs from the NRSV numbering.

TABLE A2.1. LXX Occurrences of ἔλεος.
There are 334 occurrences of ἔλεος in 322 LXX verses.*

Hebrew Equivalent	Reference
חסד	211 occurrences:** Gen 24:12, 14, 49; 39:21; 40:14; Exod 20:6; 34:7; Num 14:19; Deut 5:10; 7:9, 12; Josh 2:12, 12, 14; Judg 1:24; 8:35; Ruth 1:8; 2:20; 3:10; 1 Sam (1 Kgdms LXX) 15:6; 20:8, 14, 15; 2 Sam (2 Kgdms LXX) 2:5, 6; 3:8; 7:15; 9:1, 3, 7; 10:2, 2; 15:20; 16:17; 22:51; 1 Kgs (3 Kgdms LXX) 2:7; 3:6, 6; 8:23; 20(21 LXX):31; 1 Chr 16:34, 41; 17:13; 19:2, 2; 2 Chr 1:8; 5:13; 6:14, 42; 7:3, 6; 20:21; 24:22; 32:32; Ezra (2 Esd LXX) 3:11; 7:28; 9:9; Neh 1 (2 Esd 11 LXX):5; 9(19 LXX):32; 13(23 LXX):14, 22; Pss 5:7(8); 6:4(5); 13(12 LXX):5(6); 17(16 LXX):7; 18(17 LXX):50(51); 21(20 LXX):7(8); 23(22 LXX):6; 25(24 LXX):6, 7, 10; 26(25 LXX):3; 31(30 LXX):7(8), 16(17), 21(22); 32(31 LXX):10; 33(32 LXX):5, 18, 22; 36(35 LXX):5(6), 7(8), 10(11); 40(39 LXX):10(11), 11(12); 42(41 LXX):8(9); 48(47 LXX):9(10); 51(50 LXX):1(3); 52(51 LXX):8(10); 57(56 LXX):3(4), 10(11);

TABLE A2.1. LXX Occurrences of ἔλεος (*continued*)

Hebrew Equivalent	Reference
	59(58 LXX):10(11), 16(17), 17(18); 61(60 LXX):7(8); 62(61 LXX):12(13); 63(62 LXX):3(4); 66(65 LXX):20; 69(68 LXX):13(14), 16(17); 77(76 LXX):8(9); 85(84 LXX):7(8), 10(11); 86(85 LXX):13; 88(87 LXX):11(12); 89(88 LXX):1(2), 2(3), 14(15), 24(25), 28(29), 33(34), 49(50); 90(89 LXX):14; 92(91 LXX):2(3); 94(93 LXX):18; 98(97 LXX):3; 100(99 LXX):5; 101(100 LXX):1; 103(102 LXX):4, 11, 17; 106(105 LXX):1, 7, 45; 107(106 LXX):1, 8, 15, 21, 31, 43; 108(107 LXX):4(5); 109(108 LXX):16, 21, 26; 115:1 (113:9 LXX); 117(116 LXX):2; 118(117 LXX):1, 2, 3, 4, 29; 119(118 LXX):41, 64, 76, 88, 124, 149, 159; 130(129 LXX):7; 136(135 LXX):1, 2, 3, 4, 5, 6, 7, 8, 9, 10, 11, 12, 13, 14, 15, 16, 17, 18, 19, 20, 21, 22, 23, 24, 25, 26; 138(137 LXX):2, 8; 141(140 LXX):5; 143(142 LXX):8, 12; 144(143 LXX):2; 147(146 LXX):11; Odes 6:9 (cf. Jonah 2:9); Prov 14:22; Job 6:14; 10:12; 37:13; Sir 44:10 (MSS B, M); 46:7 (MS B); 47:22 (MS B); 50:24 (MS B); 51:3 (MS B); Hos 2:19(21); 4:1; 6:4, 6; 12:6(7); Mic 6:8; 7:18, 20; Jonah 2:8(9); Zech 7:9; Isa 16:5; 54:8, 10; 63:7; Jer 2:2; 9:24(23); 32(39 LXX):18; 33(40 LXX):11; Lam 3:32; Dan 9:4
תחנון, תחנה, חנה, חן ("grace, favor")	9 occurrences: Gen 19:19; Num 11:15; Josh 11:20; Jer 16:13; 36(43 LXX):7; 37(44 LXX):20; 38(45 LXX):26; 42(49 LXX):2; Dan 9:3
רחמים ("compassion")	11 occurrences: Deut 13:17(18); Sir 5:6 (MSS A, C); 16:11, 12 (MS A); 51:8 (MS B); Isa 47:6; 54:7; 63:7; Jer 42(49 LXX):12; Dan 9:9, 18
רחם ("have compassion")	2 occurrences (the same text repeated): Odes 4:2; Hab 3:2
צדקה ("righteousness")	3 occurrences: Isa 56:1; Ezek 18:19, 21
ישועה; ישע ("salvation")	2 occurrences: Sir 35:25 (MS B) (35:23 LXX); Isa 45:8
רצון ("pleasure/will")	2 occurrences: Sir 50:22 (MS B); Isa 60:10
שמש ("sun")	Ps 84(83 LXX):11(12)
מעה ("inner being")	Isa 63:15
ישיבה ("council")[1]	Sir 51:29 (MS B)
ו (PronSfx)	Isa 64:4(3)
Hebrew equivalent uncertain	4 occurrences: Gen 24:44; Ps 109(108 LXX):21; Sir 36:28 (MS B) (36:23 LXX); 44:23 (MS B) (45:1 LXX)
No Hebrew equivalent	86 occurrences: 1 Esd 8:78(75 LXX); Jdt 7:30; 13:14; Tob 8:16, 17, 17; 14:7; 1 Macc 2:57; 3:44; 4:24; 13:46; 16:3; 2 Macc 4:37; 6:16; 7:23, 29; 8:5, 27; 3 Macc 2:19; 4:4; 6:4, 39;

1. Trans. Parker and Abegg, *Book of Ben Sira*, B XXI Verso.

TABLE A2.1. LXX Occurrences of ἔλεος (*continued*)

Hebrew Equivalent	Reference
No Hebrew equivalent	4 Macc 9:4; Ps 136(135 LXX):16, 26; Odes 7:35, 38, 42 (cf. Dan 3:35, 38, 42); 9:50, 54, 72, 78 (cf. Luke 1:50, 54, 72, 78); 12:6, 14 (cf. Prayer of Manesseh 6, 14); 14:46;[2] Prov 3:16a; 14:22; Wis 3:9; 4:15; 6:6; 9:1; 11:9; 12:22; 15:1; 16:10; Sir 2:7, 9, 17(18 LXX); 18:5, 11, 13, 13; 28:4; 29:1; 35:26 (MS B) (35:24 LXX); Pss. Sol. 2:8, 33, 36; 4:25; 5:12, 15; 6:6; 8:27, 28; 9:8; 10:3, 4; 11:9; 13:12, 12; 14:9; 16:3, 6; 17:3, 15, 45; 18:1, 3, 5, 9; Bar 2:19; Dan 3:35, 38, 42, 89, 90

TABLE A2.2. LXX Occurrences of ἐλεέω.
There are 135 occurrences of ἐλεέω in 128 LXX verses.*

Hebrew Equivalent	Reference
חנן ("have pity/mercy")	44 occurrences:** Gen 33:5, 11; 43:29; Exod 33:19, 19; Num 6:25; Deut 7:2; 28:50; Judg 21:22; 2 Sam (2 Kgdms LXX) 12:22; 2 Kgs (4 Kgdms LXX) 13:23; Pss 6:2(3); 9:13(14); 25(24 LXX):16; 26(25 LXX):11; 27(26 LXX):7; 30(29 LXX):10(11); 31(30 LXX):9(10); 41(40 LXX):4(5), 10(11); 51(50 LXX):1(3); 56(55 LXX):1(2); 57(56 LXX):1(2), 1(2); 86(85 LXX):3, 16; 119(118 LXX):29, 58, 132; 123(122 LXX):3, 3; Prov 14:21; 19:17; 21:10; 28:8; Job 19:21, 21; Sir 12:13 (MS A); Amos 5:15; Isa 27:11; 30:19, 19; 33:2; Lam 4:16
רחם ("have compassion")	27 occurrences: Deut 13:17(18); 30:3; Sir 36:17 (MS B) (36:11 LXX); Hos 1:6, 6 (רחמה), 7, 8 (רחמה); 2:1(3) (רחמה), 4(6), 23(25); 14:3(4); Zech 1:12; Isa 9:17(16); 13:18; 14:1; 30:18; 49:15; 54:8; 55:7; Jer 6:23; 12:15; 30(37 LXX):18; 31(38 LXX):20, 20; 42(49 LXX):12; 50(27 LXX):42; Ezek 39:25
חמל ("spare")	9 occurrences: 2 Chr 36:17; Sir 16:9 (MS A); Isa 9:19(18); Ezek 5:11; 7:9(6 LXX), 4(8 LXX); 8:18; 9:5, 10
נחם ("comfort")	5 occurrences: Zech 1:17; Isa 12:1; 49:13; 52:9; Ezek 24:14
הדר ("be partial to")[3]	Exod 23:3
טוב עין ("a good eye")	Prov 22:9
יטב ("do good")	Job 24:21
בכה ("weep")	Job 27:15

2. This verse resembles Ps 35:11a LXX (36:11a MT) where ἔλεος renders חסד.
3. NRSV; ESV.

TABLE A2.2. LXX Occurrences of ἐλεέω (*continued*)

Hebrew Equivalent	Reference
חין (uncertain)	Job 41:12(4)
ישע ("save")	Sir 36:1 (MS B)
עשה ("do")	Isa 44:23
שוב ("return")	Isa 52:8
קבץ ("gather")	Isa 54:7
שמע ("hear")	Isa 59:2
בעד ("for the benefit of")[4]	Jer 7:16
No Hebrew equivalent	39 occurrences: Jdt 6:19; Tob 3:15; 6:18; 8:4, 7, 17; 11:14, 16; 13:5, 9(10 LXX); 14:5; 2 Macc 2:18; 3:21; 7:27; 8:3; 9:13; 11:10; 3 Macc 6:12; 4 Macc 8:20; 12:6; Odes 14:20, 24, 40; Prov 12:13a; 13:9a; 17:5; Wis 11:23; Pss. Sol. 2:35; 7:6, 10; 10:6; 11:1; 15:13; 16:15; 17:9, 34; Bar 3:2; 4:15; Ep Jer 37

TABLE A2.3. LXX Occurrences of ὅσιος.
There are 77 occurrences of ὅσιος in 76 LXX verses.*

Hebrew Equivalent	Reference
חסיד	28 occurrences (26 in Psalms):** Deut 33:8; 2 Sam (2 Kgdms LXX) 22:26; Pss 4:3(4); 12(11 LXX):1(2); 16(15 LXX):10; 18(17 LXX):25(26); 30(29 LXX):4(5); 31(30 LXX):23(24); 32(31 LXX):6; 37(36 LXX):28; 43(42 LXX):1; 50(49 LXX):5; 52(51 LXX):9(11); 79(78 LXX):2; 85(84 LXX):8(9); 86(85 LXX):2; 89(88 LXX):19(20); 97(96 LXX):10; 116:15 (115:6 LXX); 132(131 LXX):9, 16; 145(144 LXX):10, 13a (cf. 11Q5 XVII, 3), 17; 148:14; 149:1, 5, 9
תם, תָּם, or תמים ("innocent," "upright," "blameless," "complete")	5 occurrences: Prov 2:21; 10:29; 29:10; Sir 39:24 (MS B); Amos 5:10
ישר ("upright")	2 occurrences (the same text repeated): Deut 32:4; Odes 2:4
שלום ("safe")[5]	Deut 29:18
זך ("pure")	Prov 20:11
טהר ("clean")	Prov 22:11
תבונה ("understanding")	ἔννοια ὁσία in Prov 2:11
חסד	Isa 55:3

4. *HALOT*, s.v. "I בַּעַד."
5. NRSV.

TABLE A2.3. LXX Occurrences of ὅσιος (*continued*)

Hebrew Equivalent	Reference
No Hebrew equivalent	37 occurrences: 1 Macc 7:17; 2 Macc 12:45; Odes 8:87 (cf. Dan 3:87); Prov 17:26; 18:5; 21:15; Wis 4:15; 6:10; 7:27; 10:15, 17; 18:1, 5, 9; Sir 39:13; Pss. Sol. 2:36; 3:8; 4:1, 6, 8; 8:23, 34; 9:3; 10:5, 6; 12:4, 6; 13:10, 12; 14:3, 3, 10; 15:3, 7; 16:1; 17:16; Dan 3:87

APPENDIX 3: OCCURRENCES OF חסד AND חסיד IN THE DEAD SEA SCROLLS AND SIRACH

Table A3.1 presents all occurrences of חסד and חסיד in the nonbiblical texts among the Dead Sea Scrolls (excluding instances where חסד or חסיד is entirely reconstructed).[1] Symbols in the notation include אׄ ("probable letter" or "essentially certain reading of a damaged character"), א̊ ("possible letter" or "uncertain reading of a damaged character"), ∘ ("unreadable letter"), {{א}} (deletion), [א] ("reconstructed letter"), and ^א^ ("supralinear insertion").[2] Table A3.2 presents all occurrences of חסד and חסיד in Sirach.[3] This table also includes the Greek (LXX) renderings of the phrases/clauses containing these words. For both tables, each phrase/clause containing חסד or חסיד is translated into English.

I present the data in tables A3.1 and A3.2 for comparison: showing the extent to which the use of חסד and חסיד changed over time, and the extent to which New Testament engagement with Hebrew Bible texts containing חסד or חסיד differs from other engagement with these terms. The class, function, and element analyses of the data in these tables, along with associated definitions, were as for appendix 1.[4]

1. E.g., רׄוב] חסד[יׄכׄהׄ is reconstructed in 1QHᵃ XVII, 31, and בחסד צדקה וברוב] / [רחמים in 1QHᵃ XXVI, 17–18. Stegemann, Schuller, and Newsom, *Qumran Cave 1.III* (DJD XL in the following note), 227, 299. Hebrew texts and textual reconstructions for the Dead Sea Scrolls phrases/clauses containing חסד or חסיד are taken from Charlesworth, *Dead Sea Scrolls*, vols. 1–2 (CD, 1QS, 1QSb, 1QM), and relevant DJD volumes (I, III–V, VII, X–XI, XIX–XX, XXII–XXIII, XXV–XXVI, XXVIII–XXX, XXXIII–XXXVI, XL). I do not deal with biblical texts found at Qumran.

2. Based on *DSSC* 1:xix; DJD XL, xv, 323; or Charlesworth, *Rule of the Community* or *Damascus Document, War Scroll*, XI–XII (second options). The diamond above א in א̊ is in place of a dot in these sources. Texts listed in table A3.1 are numbered according to *DSSC*, except for 1QHᵃ texts, which are numbered according to DJD XL.

3. Hebrew texts, textual reconstructions, and symbols for the Sirach phrases/clauses containing חסד or חסיד are taken from relevant manuscripts presented in *Book of Ben Sira*, https://www.bensira.org.

4. Words were assigned to grammatical classes with the help of morphology for respective texts in Abegg, *Qumran Sectarian Manuscripts*.

TABLE A3.1. Occurrences of חסד and חסיד in the Dead Sea Scrolls

Reference	Phrase or Clause Containing חסד or חסיד	English Translation
CD XIII, 18 (MS A)	ובאהבׄת חסד֯	And with חסד love
CD XIX, 1 (MS B) (cf. Deut 7:9)	שומר הברית והחסד֯	He [God] keeps the covenant and (the) חסד [YHWH in Deut 7:9]
CD XX, 21 (MS B)	ו֯ע֯ש֯ה֯ ח֯ס֯ד֯	And he [God] does חסד
1QS I, 8	בברית חסד	In[to] the covenant of חסד
1QS I, 22	ו֯משמיעים כול חסדי֯ רחמים	And proclaim all the compassionate חסדים
1QS II, 1	ורחמי חסדו ג֯מל עלינו	And he [God][5] showed (toward) us the compassionate acts of his חסד
1QS II, 4	וישא פני חסדיו	And may he [God (2)] lift up the countenance(s) of his חסדים
1QS II, 24	ו֯אהבת חסד	And חסד love
1QS IV, 4	ברוב חסדו	In the abundance of his [God's] חסד
1QS IV, 5	ורוב חסדים	And an abundance of חסדים
1QS V, 4	ואהבת חסד	And חסד love
1QS V, 25	ואהבת חסד	And חסד love
1QS VIII, 2	ואהבת חסד	And חסד love
1QS X, 4	למפתח חסדיו עולם	For the opening of his [God's][6] everlasting חסדים
1QS X, 16	ועל חסדיו	And upon his [God's (11)] חסדים
1QS X, 26	אהבת חסד לנ֯וכנעים[7]	חסד love to those who are humbled
1QS XI, 12	חסדי אל ישועתי	The חסדים of God are my [the Master's][8] salvation
1QS XI, 13	ובחסדיו	And in his [God's (12)] חסדים
1QSb II, 24	ברו֯ח קודש וחס֯[ד	In a spirit[9] of holiness and [ד]חס
1QM III, 6	ומשוב חסדים	And return of חסדים
1QM XII, 3	וחסדי ברכו֯[תיכה]	The חסדים of [your] [God of Israel's (7; XIII, 13)] blessing[s]
1QM XIV, 4	השומר חסד	The one who keeps חסד

5. Reconstructed in I, 26. Qimron and Charlesworth, "Rule of the Community," 8–9.

6. Interpretation of X, 2. Ibid., 42–43.

7. ו֯ (Qimron and Charlesworth, "Rule of the Community") could be ׳, as in Abegg, *Qumran Sectarian Manuscripts*.

8. Trans. "master"—see IX, 21: Qimron and Charlesworth, "Rule of the Community," 41. The Hebrew term is משכיל. Church describes the "*maskil*" as "a community functionary" with the role of "admit[ting] candidates to the community" and regulating their lives (*Hebrews and the Temple*, 102n117).

9. Trans. Martínez and Tigchelaar, *Dead Sea Scrolls Study Edition*, 1:105.

TABLE A3.1. Occurrences of חסד and חסיד in the Dead Sea Scrolls (*continued*)

Reference	**Phrase or Clause Containing חסד or חסיד**	**English Translation**
1QM XIV, 8	ברוך] שמכה אל החסדים	[Blessed be] your name, O God of (the) חסדים
1QM XIV, 9	הפלתה חסדיכה	You [God (8)] have wondrously shown your חסדים
1QM XVIII, 11	יד חסדיכ[[ ]]ה[10]	The hand of your [God's (6, 8)] חסדים
1QH^a^ V, 16	[והמון ח]ס֯ד֯ך	[And the multitude] of your [ח]סד
1QH^a^ V, 22	וחסדי עולם	And everlasting חסדים
1QH^a^ VI, (34–)35	וגדול [החס]ד֯ים	And [the] great [חס]דים
1QH^a^ VIII, (26–)27	לעשו֯ת֯ ב֯י֯ ר֯[וב] חסד	To do in me an ab[undance of] חסד
1QH^a^ VIII, (29–)30	להשלים ח֯ס֯דיך	To carry out your [the Lord's (26)] חסדים
Two occurrences	כגדול חסדיך	According to the greatness of your [the Lord's] חסדים
1QH^a^ VIII, 34	ו֯ר֯ב֯ חסד ואמת	And abounding in חסד and faithfulness***
1QH^a^ IX, (33–)34	ברחמיכה וגדול חסדיכה	In your [God's (28)] compassion/s and the greatness of your חסדים
1QH^a^ X, 25	ובחסדיכה	And in your [the Lord's (22)] חסדים
1QH^a^ X, 27	בחסדכה	In your [the Lord's] חסד
1QH^a^ XII, 38	בחסדיכה	In your [God's (32)] חסדים
1QH^a^ XIII, 24	כול {נמה}[11] אביוני חסד	All {. . .} [the] poor of חסד
1QH^a^ XIV, 12	ובחסדיך	And in your [God's] חסדים
1QH^a^ XV, 21	ולהמון] חסדכה אוחיל	And for the multitude] of your [the psalmist's God's (13)] חסד, I [the psalmist] wait
1QH^a^ XV, 23	לבני חסד	For the sons of חסד
1QH^a^ XV, 30	ובחסדיכה לאיש	And in your [the Lord's (31)] חסדים toward a person
1QH^a^ XV, 38	לחסדיכה	To/For your [the Lord's (37)] חסדים
1QH^a^ XVII, 7	בחסדיכ֯ה֯	In your [the psalmist's God's (23)] חסדים
1QH^a^ XVII, 10	לחסדיכה	For your [the psalmist's God's (23)] חסדים
1QH^a^ XVII, 14	ב֯חסדיכה	In your [the psalmist's God's (23)] חסדים
1QH^a^ XVIII, 16	אל הרחמי֯ם֯ ו֯[רב ה]חסד	God of (the) compassion/s and (the) [abundant] חסד
1QH^a^ XVIII, 18	לחסדכה	For your [the Lord's (16)][12] חסד
1QH^a^ XIX, 8	בחסדיכה	In your [the psalmist's God's (6)] חסדים
1QH^a^ XIX, 20	ואביט ב֯[ ]∘∘י חסד	And I [the psalmist] have gazed upon[13] . . . חסד

10. [[ ]] means "join between fragments" in Charlesworth, *Damascus Document, War Scroll*, XI.

11. Erased by scribe. Stegemann, Schuller, and Newsom, *Qumran Cave 1.III*, xv.

12. Lord, God of compassion and abundant חסד.

13. Trans. "gazed upon" from Newsom in Stegemann, Schuller, and Newsom, *Qumran Cave 1.III*, 248.

TABLE A3.1. Occurrences of חסד and חסיד in the Dead Sea Scrolls (*continued*)

Reference	**Phrase or Clause Containing חסד or חסיד**	**English Translation**
1QH^{a} XIX, 21	ובחסדיכה	And in your [the psalmist's God's (18)] חסדים
1QH^{a} XIX, 31	ברוב חסדיכה	In the abundance of your [the Lord's][14] חסדים
1QH^{a} XIX, (32–)33	והמו[ן] חסדיכה	And the multi[tude] of your [God of compassion and grace's (32)] חסדים
1QH^{a} XIX, 34	ולחסדיכה	And for your [God of compassion and grace's (32)] חסדים
1QH^{a} XX, 17	לרוב חסד	For the abundance of חסד
1QH^{a} XX, 24	בחס֯ד֯]כה	In [your] [the Instructor's God's (14)][15] חסד
1QH^{a} XXIII, 25	כרוב חסדיכה	According to the abundance of your [probably God's] חסדים
1QH^{a} XXV, 11	חסדיכה	Your חסדים
1QH^{a} XXVI, 32	ברוב חסדי֯ו֯[	In the abundance of his [probably God's (33)] חסדים
1Q16 2, 2	]חסד[ו	[His] חסד
4Q175 14 (cf. Deut 33:8)	לאיש חסידך	To your [YHWH's (Deut 33:8)] חסיד man
4Q176 8–11, 10 (cf. Isa 54:8)	ובחסדי עולמ	And in everlasting חסדים
4Q176 8–11, 12 (cf. Isa 54:10)	וחס֯די מאתיכי לוא ימוש֯[	But my [YHWH's (Isa 54:8)] חסד shall not withdraw from you [the rejected wife (8)]
4Q185 1–2i10	ופרחׄ כציץ חסדו	And his [probably God's (cf. 14)] חסד blooms like a flower
4Q185 1–2ii1	כחסדיו הטבים	According to his [YHWH's (3)] good חסדים
4Q185 1–2ii13	וחסדיו ע֯למיה	His [probably YHWH's] חסדים are her [Wisdom's] youth
4Q215a 1ii4	בעבור חׄס[ד]י֯ו	On account of his [probably God's] חס[ד]ים
4Q256 IX, (3–)4	ואהבת] חׄסד והצנע לכת	And] חסד [love] and careful behavior
4Q256 XIX, (2–)3	ואות למפתח חׄס֯]די עו]ל֯[ם	And a sign for the opening of [ever]last[ing] [חס]דים
4Q258 II, 4	ואהבת חסד	And חסד love
4Q258 IX, 1 (cf. 4Q256 XIX, 2–3)	ואות למפתח חסדי עולם	And a sign for the opening of everlasting חסדים
4Q260 IV, 2 (cf. 1QS X, 16)	ועל חסד[יו	And upon [his] [God's (5)] חסד[ים]
4Q286 1ii(7–)8 Two occurrences	רב] חסדי֯ם֯ וענו֯ת טוב וחסדי אמת ורחמי עולמים	[Abounding] in חסדים and good humility and faithful*** חסדים and everlasting compassion/s
4Q286 14, 1	ח]ס֯דו	His [probably God's] [ח]סד

14. Reconstructed in the previous line by Stegemann (ibid.).
15. Trans. "Instructor" from Newsom (ibid., 259).

TABLE A3.1. Occurrences of חסד and חסיד in the Dead Sea Scrolls (*continued*)

Reference	Phrase or Clause Containing חסד or חסיד	English Translation
4Q298 3–4ii7	ואהבו חסד	And love חסד
4Q299 54, 3	כיא אהבת חסד]	For חסד love
4Q372 1, 19	וחסדיך גדלים	And your [Joseph's God's (16)] חסדים are great
4Q372 1, 25	ואגיד חסדי[ך	And I will declare [your] [Joseph's God's (16)] חסדים
4Q377 2i8	איש החסידים	A man of the חסידים
4Q377 2ii12	איש חסדים ויו∘∘]	A man [Moses (10)] of חסדים and . . .
4Q378 22i5	]חסד לאלפים	חסד to thousands
4Q378 26, 6	ה[ח]סדים	The חסדים
4Q380 1ii9	וחסדו	And his [probably God's] חסד
4Q380 2, 5	כי]ל[ח]ס‸י‸ד יחנן יהוה ∘∘]	[For] YHWH will be gracious to [ח]סיד
4Q381 33+35, 5	וחסדיך לעבד קרב לך	And your [God's (4)] חסדים to a servant [who is] near to you
4Q381 33+35, 6	וכחסדיך]	And according to your [the servant's God's] חסדים
4Q381 46a+b, 2	ר]ב חסדיך]	Your [probably God's] [abundant] חסדים
4Q385 2, 3	והיככה ישתלמו חסדם	And how will they [many from Israel who love YHWH's name (2)] be repaid for their חסד?
4Q385a 7, 2	וע]שה חסד]	[And he d]id חסד
4Q386 1i2 (cf. 4Q385 2, 3)	ו]הכה ישתלמו חסדם	[And] how will they [many from Israel who love YHWH's name] be repaid for their חסד?
4Q388 7, 5 (cf. 4Q385 2, 3; 4Q386 1i2)	וא[י]ככה ישתלמו חסד[ם	As above
4Q393 3, 2	האל הנאמן שומר [ה]ברית והחסד	The faithful God who keeps [the] covenant and (the) חסד
4Q398 14–17ii1	שהיא איש חסדים	Who was a man [David] of חסדים
4Q400 1i18	∘∘[ח]סדיו לסליחות רחמי עולמים	His [probably God's] [ח]סדים for everlasting, compassionate acts of forgiveness
4Q400 1ii20	חסדי אלו[הים	The חסדים of Go[d]
4Q403 1i23	ל[מ]שוב ר[חמי] חסדיו	For the [re]turn of his [God's][16] חסד com[passion(s)]
4Q405 3ii15 (cf. 4Q403 1i23)	רחמי חסדו	His [probably God's] חסד compassion/s
4Q408 3+3a, 6	הח[סיד במש]פטיך	The [ח[סיד [YHWH] [in] your [judg]ments
4Q413 1–2, 4	חסד [ ] ר‸א‸ישונים	חסד [ ] the former ones
4Q414 10, 1	ח]סדכה אש[ר	Your [probably God's] [ח]סד whi[ch] . . .

16. Trans. "of His gracious com[passion" from Newsom, *Songs of the Sabbath Sacrifice*, 194; Newsom, "Shirot 'Olat HaShabbat," 261.

TABLE A3.1. Occurrences of חסד and חסיד in the Dead Sea Scrolls (*continued*)

Reference	Phrase or Clause Containing חסד or חסיד	English Translation
4Q418 81+81a, 8	ובחסד {{עולם}}	And in {everlasting} חסד
4Q418 169+170, 3	ובאהב[ת ח]סד	And in ח]סד] love
4Q423 3a, 2	ובחסדיׄכׄ[ה	And in your [probably God's] חסדים
4Q427 7i22	בחסד צדקה וברוב רחמימ	In חסד, righteousness, and in an abundance of compassion/s
4Q427 7ii13	ברוב חס[דיו	In the abundance of [his] [probably God's] [חס[דים]
4Q434 1i4	למען חסדו	For the sake of his [the Lord's (1)] חסד
4Q434 2, 11	]חסדך עלי	Your [probably the Most High's (10)] חסד upon/toward me [the speaker]
4Q437 2i5	וחסדיך לי צנה סביב	And your [the Lord's (13, 14)] חסדים to me [the speaker] are a shield all around
4Q437 4, 4	בא]הׄבת חסד	[In] חסד [l]ove
4Q438 4ii4	באה]בׄתׄ חסד	[In] חסד [lo]ve
4Q463 1, 3 (cf. Lev 26:44: חסד added)	להפר בריתׄי וחסדׄי מהמה	To break my [God's (1)] covenant and my חסד from them [those who survive (Lev 26:36, 44)]
4Q491 8–10i2 (cf. 1QM XIV, 4)	ה]שׁומר חסד	[The] one who keeps חסד [the God of Israel]
4Q491 8–10i6 Two occurrences (cf. 1QM XIV, 9)	אל הׄ[ח]סׄדים הׄמ[פ]ליא חסדיך בנׄו	God of (the) ח]סדים] who has [won]drously shown your חסדים with us [the remnant][17]
4Q502 14, 5	ואהבׄת חסד]	And חסד love
4Q502 16, 2	]חסדים ע[ל	חסדים to[ward] . . .
4Q502 254, 1	] לחסדׄי[	To/For חסדים
4Q504 1–2ii10	וׄלמען דעת את כוחכה הגׄדול ואת רובׄ חסׄדכ[ה]	And in order to know your [the Lord's (7)] great power and an abundance of your חסד
4Q509 3, 5	ח]סׄדׄיׄכׄהׄ	Your [probably the Lord's (9)] ח]סדים]
4Q509 50, 2	] וחסׄיׄד]	And חסיד
4Q511 10, 10	[שומר חס]דׄ	[Keeps] חס]ד]
4Q511 26, 2	]חׄסדיו וכול מחׄשׄ[בותיו	His [probably God's] חסדים and all [his] though[ts]/pla[ns]
4Q511 36, 2	]חסדׄ[י]ו	His [probably God's] [חסד[ים
4Q511 52–59, 1	רׄב החסד	The abundant חסד
4Q511 148, 3	]חסׄדו]	His [probably God's] חסד
4Q512 56–58, 6	]יׄ חסד	חסד
4Q521 2ii+4, 5	כי אדני חסידים יבקר	For the Lord will attend to חסידים
4Q521 2ii+4, 7	כׄיׄ יכבד את חסידים	For he [the Lord (5)] will honor חסידים
4Q521 2ii+4, 9	ובחסדו יׄ[	And in his [the Lord's (5)] חסד

17. שארית ("remnant") is reconstructed (Baillet, *Qumrân Grotte 4.III [4Q482–4Q520]*, 21).

TABLE A3.1. Occurrences of חסד and חסיד in the Dead Sea Scrolls (*continued*)

Reference	Phrase or Clause Containing חסד or חסיד	English Translation
4Q521 2iii1	ואת חק חסד{{יד}}ך	And the law of your [probably the Lord's (3)] חסד
4Q525 30, 3	בחסד וֹ[	In חסד and . . .
5Q13 23, 2	]◦◦ חסדים [	חסדים
11Q5 XVIII, 10	ומקהל חסידים	From the assembly of חסידים
11Q5 XVIII, 14	יגדל חסדו	He [YHWH] makes great his חסד
11Q5 XIX, 1	ולוא תספר חסדכה תולעה	And a worm cannot tell of your [YHWH's (4)] חסד
11Q5 XIX, 3	חסדכה להמה	Your [YHWH's (4)] חסד to them [everyone whose foot stumbles (2)]
11Q5 XIX, 6	ולוא עזב חסדו מהמה	And he [YHWH] has not forsaken his חסד from them [those loving YHWH's name]
11Q5 XIX, 7	מעטר חסידיו	Who crowns his [YHWH's] חסידים
11Q5 XIX, 8	חסד ורחמים	חסד and compassion/s
11Q5 XIX, (8–)9	להודות ברנה חסדיכה	To give thanks in a cry of joy for your [YHWH's (7)] חסדים
11Q5 XIX, 13	ועל חסדיכה	And on your [YHWH's] חסדים
11Q5 XXII, 3	ודורות חסידים	And generations of חסידים
11Q5 XXII, 5	חסדי נביאיך	חסדים of your [Zion's] prophets
11Q5 XXII, 6	ובמעשי חסידיך	And in the deeds of your [Zion's] חסידים
11Q5 XXVI, 10	חסד ואמת סביב פניו	חסד and faithfulness*** surround his [YHWH's] face(s) (9–10)
11Q6 4–5, 5 (cf. 11Q5 XIX, 3)	בהודיעכה] חסדכה להם	[When you make known] your [YHWH's] חסד to them [everyone whose foot stumbles] (cf. 11Q5 XIX, 2, 4)
11Q6 4–5, 8 (cf. 11Q5 XIX, 6)	ולוא ע]זֹב חסדו מהם	[And he has not for]saken his [YHWH's] חסד from them [those loving YHWH's name] (cf. 11Q5 XIX, 6)
11Q6 4–5, 9 (cf. 11Q5 XIX, 8)	חסד ורחמים	חסד and compassion/s
11Q6 4–5, 10 (cf. 11Q5 XIX, [8–]9)	להודות]ברנה חסדיכה	[To give thanks] with a cry of joy for your [YHWH's] חסדים (cf. 11Q5 XIX, 7)
11Q11 VI, 6[18]	חסדֹ[ו ע]לֹיֹך צנה	[His] חסד [up]on you [will be] a shield
PAM 43.676 2ii2	ואֹהבי חֹסד ה[	And loving חסד
PAM 43.678 28, 1	]לחסדוֹ[	To/For his [probably God's] חסד

18. This is not included in the *DSSC* list (1:270–71).

TABLE A3.2. Occurrences of חסד and חסיד in Sirach

Reference (MSS)	Phrase or Clause Containing חסד or חסיד	English Translation	Greek Translation
7:33 (A) **(D)**	אל תמנע חסד [א]ל תמנע חסד	Do not withhold חסד	μὴ ἀποκωλύσῃς χάριν.
16:23 (A)	חסדי לב	חסדים of a heart	ἐλαττούμενος καρδίᾳ
37:11 (B) **(D)**	<על גימילות> חסד על גמילות חסד	concerning the charity/fruits[19] of חסד	περὶ εὐχαριστίας (one word equivalent to construct phrase)
40:17 (B) **(M)**	וחסד לעולם̊ לא ימוט חסד כעֹ̇ד לא תכרת	And חסד will never sway חסד, as eternity,[20] do not cut off	Different from the Hebrew texts: χάρις ὡς παράδεισος ἐν εὐλογίαις,
41:11 (B) **(M)**	שם חסד לא יכרת]שם ח̇ס̇ד ללא יכ̇ר̇ת	A name of חסד will not be cut off	Different from the Hebrew texts: ὄνομα δὲ ἁμαρτωλῶν οὐκ ἀγαθὸν ἐξαλειφθήσεται
41:22 (B) **(M)**	<דבר חסד> על דברי חסד	חסד word/s	41:25: λόγων ὀνειδισμοῦ (negative connotations)
44:1 (B) **(M)**	אהללה נא אנשי חסד]א̊ אנ̇[ ] חסד	Let me [the hymnist] now praise the men of חסד	Αἰνέσωμεν δὴ ἄνδρας ἐνδόξους
44:10 (B) **(M)**	ואולם אלה אנשי חסד אולם אלה אנשי חסד	But these were men of חסד	ἀλλ’ ἢ οὗτοι ἄνδρες ἐλέους,
46:7 (B)	עשה חסד	He [Joshua son of Nun (1)] did חסד [also Caleb son of Jephunneh]	ἐποίησεν ἔλεος αὐτὸς
47:22 (B)	[א]ל[21] לא יטוש חסד	[Go]d will not give up חסד	ὁ δὲ κύριος οὐ μὴ καταλίπῃ τὸ ἔλεος αὐτοῦ
49:3 (B)	עשה חסד	He [Josiah (1)] did חסד	κατίσχυσεν τὴν εὐσέβειαν
50:24 (B)	יאמן עם שמעון חסדו	Let his [YHWH, the God of Israel’s (22)] חסד be established with Simeon	ἐμπιστεύσαι μεθ’ ἡμῶν τὸ ἔλεος αὐτοῦ
51:3 (B)	כרוב חסדך	According to [the] abundance of your [God’s (1)] חסד	κατὰ τὸ πλῆθος ἐλέους Adds: καὶ ὀνόματός σου

19. Trans. “concerning,” “charity,” and “fruits” from Parker and Abegg, *Book of Ben Sira*, B VII Verso, D II Recto.

20. Trans. “eternity” from Reymond, *Book of Ben Sira*, Masada II.

21. Reconstructed: B XVII Recto. Transcribed by Abegg, *Book of Ben Sira*.

TABLE A3.2. Occurrences of חסד and חסיד in Sirach (*continued*)

Reference (MSS)	Phrase or Clause Containing חסד or חסיד	English Translation	Greek Translation
51:8 (B)	וחסדיו	And his [YHWH's] חסדים	καὶ τῆς ἐργασίας σου
51:12a–n (B)	Repeated refrain: כי לעולם חסדו	For his [YHWH's] חסד is forever	Hebrew only
51:12o (B) (cf. Ps 148:14)	תהלה לכל חסידיו	Praise for all his [YHWH's] חסידים	Hebrew only

BIBLIOGRAPHY

Abegg, Martin G., Jr., transcriber. *The Book of Ben Sira*. B XVII Recto. https://www.bensira.org.

———. "Hebrew Language." *DNTB,* 459–63.

———. *Qumran Sectarian Manuscripts*. Bellingham, WA: Logos Bible Software, 2003.

Abel, Douglas Stephen. "The Marriage Metaphor in Hosea 4 and Jeremiah 2: How Prophetic Speech 'Kills Two Birds with One Stone.'" *Proceedings* 29 (2009): 15–27.

Abma, R. *Bonds of Love: Methodic Studies of Prophetic Texts with Marriage Imagery (Isaiah 50:1–3 and 54:1–10, Hosea 1–3, Jeremiah 2–3)*. Studia Semitica Neerlandica. Assen: Van Gorcum, 1999.

Achtemeier, Paul J. *1 Peter: A Commentary on First Peter*. Hermeneia. Minneapolis: Fortress, 1996.

Allen, Leslie C. *Psalms 101–150*. Rev. ed. WBC 21. Nashville: Thomas Nelson, 2002.

Andersen, Francis I., and David Noel Freedman. *Hosea: A New Translation with Introduction and Commentary*. AB 24. Garden City, NY: Doubleday, 1980.

———. *Micah: A New Translation with Introduction and Commentary*. AB 24E. New York: Doubleday, 2000.

Arnold, Clinton E. "Letter to the Ephesians." *DPL,* 238–49.

Ashby, Godfrey. *Go Out and Meet God: A Commentary on the Book of Exodus*. Grand Rapids: Eerdmans; Edinburgh: Handsel, 1998.

Aune, David E. *Revelation 1–5*. WBC 52A. Nashville: Thomas Nelson, 1997.

———. *Revelation 6–16*. WBC 52B. Nashville: Thomas Nelson, 1998.

Baer, D. A., and R. P. Gordon. "חסד." *NIDOTTE* 2:211–18.

Bailey, Kenneth E. *Through Peasant Eyes*. In *Poet and Peasant and Through Peasant Eyes: A Literary-Cultural Approach to the Parables in Luke*. Combined ed. Grand Rapids: Eerdmans, 1983.

Baillet, Maurice. *Qumrân Grotte 4.III (4Q482–4Q520)*. DJD VII. Oxford: Clarendon, 1982.

Baltzer, Klaus. *Deutero-Isaiah: A Commentary on Isaiah 40–55*. Hermeneia. Minneapolis: Augsburg Fortress, 2001.

Barr, James. *The Semantics of Biblical Language*. London: Oxford University Press, 1961.

Barrett, C. K. *Introduction and Commentary on Acts XV–XXVIII*. Vol. 2 of *A Critical and Exegetical Commentary on the Acts of the Apostles*. ICC. London: T&T Clark, 1998.

———. *Preliminary Introduction and Commentary on Acts I–XIV*. Vol. 1 of *A Critical and Exegetical Commentary on the Acts of the Apostles*. ICC. Edinburgh: T&T Clark, 1994.

Barth, Markus. *Ephesians: Introduction, Translation, and Commentary on Chapters 1–3*. AB 34. Garden City, NY: Doubleday, 1974.

Bauer, Walter. "An Introduction to the Lexicon of the Greek New Testament." BDAG, xiii–xxix.

Beale, G. K. *The Book of Revelation: A Commentary on the Greek Text*. NIGTC. Grand Rapids: Eerdmans; Carlisle: Paternoster, 1999.

Beale, G. K., and Sean M. McDonough. "Revelation." Pages 1081–161 in *Commentary on the New Testament Use of the Old Testament*. Edited by G. K. Beale and D. A. Carson. Grand Rapids: Baker Academic; Nottingham: Apollos, 2007.

Best, Ernest. *A Critical and Exegetical Commentary on Ephesians*. ICC. Edinburgh: T&T Clark, 1998.

Bibb, C. Wade. "The Characterization of God in the Opening Scenes of Luke and Acts." *Proceedings* 13 (1993): 275–92.

Bier, Miriam J. *"Perhaps There is Hope": Reading Lamentations as a Polyphony of Pain, Penitence, and Protest*. The Library of the Hebrew Bible / Old Testament Studies 603. New York: Bloomsbury T&T Clark, 2015.

Bigg, Charles. *A Critical and Exegetical Commentary on the Epistles of St. Peter and St. Jude*. 2nd ed. ICC. Edinburgh: T&T Clark, 1902.

Blenkinsopp, Joseph. "The Family in First Temple Israel." Pages 48–103 in *Families in Ancient Israel*. Edited by Leo G. Perdue, Joseph Blenkinsopp, John J. Collins, and Carol Meyers. The Family, Religion, and Culture. Louisville: Westminster John Knox, 1997.

———. *Isaiah 40–55: A New Translation with Introduction and Commentary*. AB 19A. New York: Doubleday, 2002.

Blomberg, Craig L. "Matthew." Pages 1–109 in *Commentary on the New Testament Use of the Old Testament*. Edited by G. K. Beale and D. A. Carson. Grand Rapids: Baker Academic; Nottingham: Apollos, 2007.

Blount, Brian K. *Revelation: A Commentary*. New Testament Library. Louisville: Westminster John Knox, 2009.

Bock, Darrell L. "Gospel of Luke." *DJG*, 495–510.

———. *Luke*. NIVAC. Grand Rapids: Zondervan, 1996.

———. *Proclamation from Prophecy and Pattern: Lucan Old Testament Christology*. JSNTSup 12. Sheffield: JSOT Press, 1987.

Boman, Thorleif. *Hebrew Thought Compared with Greek*. London: SCM, 1960.

Borgen, Peder, Kåre Fuglseth, and Roald Skarsten, eds. *The Works of Philo: Greek Text with Morphology*. Bellingham, WA: Logos Bible Software, 2005.

Bovon, François. *Luke 1: A Commentary on the Gospel of Luke 1:1–9:50*. Translated by Christine M. Thomas. Hermeneia. Minneapolis: Augsburg Fortress, 2002.

Brands, Monica. "Vessels of Mercy: Aquinas and Barth on Election and Romans Chapters 9–11." *Journal of Theta Alpha Kappa* 37 (2013): 23–39.

Braude, William G., trans. *The Midrash on Psalms*. 2 vols. Yale Judaica 13. New Haven: Yale University Press, 1959.

Brockington, L. H. "The Greek Translator of Isaiah and His Interest in ΔΟΞΑ." *Vetus Testamentum* 1 (1951): 23–32.
Bruce, F. F. *The Acts of the Apostles: The Greek Text with Introduction and Commentary*. 3rd rev. and enl. ed. Grand Rapids: Eerdmans; Leicester: Apollos, 1990.
———. *The Book of Acts*. Rev. ed. NICNT. Grand Rapids: Eerdmans, 1988.
———. "Paul in Acts and Letters." *DPL*, 679–92.
Brueggemann, Walter. "'Impossibility' and Epistemology in the Faith Tradition of Abraham and Sarah (Gen 18:1–15)." *Zeitschrift für die alttestamentliche Wissenschaft* 94 (1982): 615–34.
———. *Isaiah 40–66*. Westminster Bible Companion. Louisville: Westminster John Knox, 1998.
———. *The Message of the Psalms: A Theological Commentary*. Minneapolis: Augsburg, 1984.
Bultmann, Rudolf. *Das Evangelium des Johannes*. 11th ed. Kritisch-exegetischer Kommentar über das Neue Testament. Göttingen: Vandenhoeck & Ruprecht, 1950.
———. "ἔλεος, ἐλεέω, ἐλεήμων, ἐλεημοσύνη, ἀνέλεος, ἀνελεήμων." *TDNT* 2:477–87.
Buth, Randall J. "Aramaic Language." *DNTB*, 86–91.
Byrne, Brendan. *Romans*. SP 6. Collegeville, MN: Liturgical Press, 1996.
Caquot, André. "Les 'Graces de David': A Propos D'Isaie 55/3b." *Semitica* 15 (1965): 45–59.
Carson, D. A. *The Gospel According to John*. Leicester: Apollos; Grand Rapids: Eerdmans, 1991.
Cathcart, Kevin J., and Robert P. Gordon. *The Targum of the Minor Prophets: Translated, with a Critical Introduction, Apparatus, and Notes*. The Aramaic Bible 14. Edinburgh: T&T Clark, 1989.
Chance, J. Bradley. *Acts*. Smyth & Helwys Bible Commentary. Macon, GA: Smyth & Helwys, 2007.
Charles, R. H. *A Critical and Exegetical Commentary on the Revelation of St. John*. 2 vols. ICC. Edinburgh: T&T Clark, 1920.
Charlesworth, James H., ed. *Damascus Document, War Scroll, and Related Documents*. Vol. 2 of *The Dead Sea Scrolls: Hebrew, Aramaic, and Greek Texts with English Translations*. Tübingen: Mohr Siebeck; Louisville: Westminster John Knox, 1995.
———. *Rule of the Community and Related Documents*. Vol. 1 of *The Dead Sea Scrolls: Hebrew, Aramaic, and Greek Texts with English Translations*. Tübingen: Mohr Siebeck; Louisville: Westminster John Knox, 1994.
Childs, Brevard S. *Isaiah*. Old Testament Library. Louisville: Westminster John Knox, 2001.
Chilton, Bruce D. *The Isaiah Targum: Introduction, Translation, Apparatus and Notes*. The Aramaic Bible 11. Edinburgh: T&T Clark, 1987.
———. "Targums." *DJG*, 800–804.
Church, Philip A. F. *Hebrews and the Temple: Attitudes to the Temple in Second Temple Judaism and in Hebrews*. Supplements to Novum Testamentum 171. Leiden: Brill, 2017.
———. "Jesus and His People: Covenant, Christology and the Community in Matthew's Gospel." Master's thesis, Australian College of Theology, 1995.
Cicero. *De officiis*. Translated by Walter Miller. LCL. Cambridge: Harvard University Press, 1913.

Clark, Gordon R. *The Word Hesed in the Hebrew Bible*. Journal for the Study of the Old Testament Supplement Series 157. Sheffield: JSOT Press, 1993.
Craigie, Peter C., and Marvin E. Tate. *Psalms 1–50*. 2nd ed. WBC 19. Nashville: Thomas Nelson, 2004.
Cranfield, C. E. B. *Commentary on Romans IX–XVI and Essays*. Vol. 2 of *A Critical and Exegetical Commentary on the Epistle to the Romans*. ICC. Edinburgh: T&T Clark, 1979.
———. *Introduction and Commentary on Romans I–VIII*. Vol. 1 of *A Critical and Exegetical Commentary on the Epistle to the Romans*. ICC. Edinburgh: T&T Clark, 1975.
Croft, William, and D. Alan Cruse. *Cognitive Linguistics*. Cambridge Textbooks in Linguistics. Cambridge: Cambridge University Press, 2004.
Cross, Frank Moore, Jr. *From Epic to Canon: History and Literature in Ancient Israel*. Baltimore: Johns Hopkins University Press, 1998.
Crossan, John Dominic. "Parable and Example in the Teaching of Jesus." *Semeia* 1 (1974): 63–104.
Culy, Martin M., Mikael C. Parsons, and Joshua J. Stigall. *Luke: A Handbook on the Greek Text*. Baylor Handbook on the Greek New Testament 4. Waco, TX: Baylor University Press, 2010.
Dahood, Mitchell. *Psalms I: 1–50*. AB 16. Garden City, NY: Doubleday, 1965–66.
Das, A. Andrew. " 'Praise the Lord, All You Gentiles': The Encoded Audience of Romans 15.7–13." *Journal for the Study of the New Testament* 34 (2011): 90–110.
Davids, Peter H. *The First Epistle of Peter*. NICNT. Grand Rapids: Eerdmans, 1990.
Davies, Philip. "*Ḥasidim* in the Maccabean Period." *Journal of Jewish Studies* 28 (1977): 127–40.
Davies, W. D., and Dale C. Allison Jr. *Commentary on Matthew VIII–XVIII*. Vol. 2 of *A Critical and Exegetical Commentary on the Gospel According to Saint Matthew*. ICC. Edinburgh: T&T Clark, 1991.
———. *Commentary on Matthew XIX–XXVIII*. Vol. 3 of *A Critical and Exegetical Commentary on the Gospel According to Saint Matthew*. ICC. London: T&T Clark, 1997.
———. *Introduction and Commentary on Matthew I–VII*. Vol. 1 of *A Critical and Exegetical Commentary on the Gospel According to Saint Matthew*. ICC. Edinburgh: T&T Clark, 1988.
Dearman, J. Andrew. *The Book of Hosea*. NICOT. Grand Rapids: Eerdmans, 2010.
Deist, Ferdinand E. *The Material Culture of the Bible: An Introduction*. The Biblical Seminar 70. Sheffield: Sheffield Academic Press, 2000.
Dickey, Franz L., Jr. "The Development of the Hebrew Idea of Hesed in the Biblical Literature." DMin diss., Claremont School of Theology, 1976.
Donelson, Lewis R. *I and II Peter and Jude: A Commentary*. New Testament Library. Louisville: Westminster John Knox, 2010.
Dunn, James D. G. *Romans 1–8*. WBC 38A. Dallas: Word, 1988.
———. *Romans 9–16*. WBC 38B. Dallas: Word, 1988.
Durham, John I. *Exodus*. WBC 3. Waco, TX: Word, 1987.
Eastman, Susan Grove. "Israel and the Mercy of God: A Re-reading of Galatians 6.16 and Romans 9–11." *New Testament Studies* 56 (2010): 367–95.
Edin, Mary Hinkle. "Learning What Righteousness Means: Hosea 6:6 and the Ethic of Mercy in Matthew's Gospel." *Word and World* 18 (1998): 355–63.

Edwards, James R. *The Gospel According to Luke*. The Pillar New Testament Commentary. Grand Rapids: Eerdmans; Nottingham: Apollos, 2015.
Eerdmans, B. D. "The Chasidim." *Old Testament Studies* 1 (1942): 176–257.
Elliott, John H. *I Peter: A New Translation with Introduction and Commentary*. AB 37B. New York: Doubleday, 2000.
———. "Temple Versus Household in Luke-Acts: A Contrast in Social Institutions." Pages 211–40 in *The Social World of Luke-Acts: Models for Interpretation*. Edited by Jerome H. Neyrey. Peabody, MA: Hendrickson, 1991.
Enns, Peter. *Exodus*. NIVAC. Grand Rapids: Zondervan, 2000.
Evans, C. F. *Saint Luke*. TPI New Testament Commentaries. London: SCM; Philadelphia: Trinity, 1990.
Evans, Craig A. "Listening for Echoes of Interpreted Scripture." Pages 47–51 in *Paul and the Scriptures of Israel*. Edited by Craig A. Evans and James A. Sanders. JSNTSup 83. Studies in Scripture in Early Judaism and Christianity 1. Sheffield: JSOT Press, 1993.
Fairclough, Norman. *Analysing Discourse: Textual Analysis for Social Research*. London: Routledge, 2003.
Fenske, Wolfgang. "'Das Lied des Mose, des Knechtes Gottes, und das Lied des Lammes' (Apokalypse des Johannes 15,3 f.): Der Text und seine Bedeutung für die Johannnes-Apokalypse." *Zeitschrift für die neutestamentliche Wissenschaft und die Kunde der älteren Kirche* 90 (1999): 250–64.
Fernando, Ajith. *Acts*. NIVAC. Grand Rapids: Zondervan, 1998.
Firth, David G. *1 and 2 Samuel*. Apollos Old Testament Commentary 8. Nottingham: Apollos; Downers Grove, IL: InterVarsity Press, 2009.
Fishbane, Michael. *Biblical Interpretation in Ancient Israel*. Oxford: Clarendon, 1985.
Fitzgerald, John T. "Virtue/Vice Lists." *ABD* 6:857–59.
Fitzmyer, Joseph A. *The Acts of the Apostles: A New Translation with Introduction and Commentary*. AB 31. New York: Doubleday, 1998.
———. *The Gospel According to Luke (I–IX): Introduction, Translation, and Notes*. AB 28. New York: Doubleday, 1970.
———. *The Gospel According to Luke (X–XXIV): Introduction, Translation, and Notes*. AB 28A. New York: Doubleday, 1985.
———. *Romans: A New Translation with Introduction and Commentary*. AB 33. New York: Doubleday, 1993.
Ford, J. Massyngberde. *Revelation: Introduction, Translation and Commentary*. AB 38. Garden City, NY: Doubleday, 1975.
Fox, Michael V. "Jeremiah 2:2 and the 'Desert Ideal.'" *CBQ* 35 (1973): 441–50.
France, R. T. *The Gospel According to Matthew: An Introduction and Commentary*. TNTC. Leicester: Inter-Varsity Press; Grand Rapids: Eerdmans, 1985.
———. *The Gospel of Matthew*. NICNT. Grand Rapids: Eerdmans, 2007.
Friedman, Mordechai Akiva. *The Ketubba Traditions of Eretz Israel*. Vol. 1 of *Jewish Marriage in Palestine: A Cairo Geniza Study*. Tel-Aviv: Tel-Aviv University, the Chaim Rosenberg School of Jewish Studies, and the Jewish Theological Seminary of America Press, 1980.
Fung, Ronald Y. K. *The Epistle to the Galatians*. NICNT. Grand Rapids: Eerdmans, 1988.
García Martínez, Florentino, and Eibert J. C. Tigchelaar. *The Dead Sea Scrolls Study Edition*. 2 vols. Leiden: Brill; Grand Rapids: Eerdmans, 1997–98.

Geldenhuys, Norval. *Commentary on the Gospel of Luke: The English Text with Introduction, Exposition and Notes*. NICNT. Grand Rapids: Eerdmans, 1988.
Gentry, Peter J. "Rethinking the 'Sure Mercies of David' in Isaiah 55:3." *Westminster Theological Journal* 69 (2007): 279–304.
Gibson, J. C. L. *Davidson's Introductory Hebrew Grammar–Syntax*. 4th ed. Edinburgh: T&T Clark, 1994.
Glueck, Nelson. *Ḥesed in the Bible*. Edited by Elias L. Epstein. Translated by Alfred Gottschalk. Eugene, OR: Wipf & Stock, 2011.
———. *Das Wort ḥesed im alttestamentlichen Sprachgebrauche als menschliche und göttliche gemeinschaftgemässe Verhaltungsweise*. Beihefte zur Zeitschrift für die alttestamentliche Wissenschaft 47. Berlin: Alfred Töpelmann, 1961.
Goldingay, John. *The Message of Isaiah 40–55: A Literary-Theological Commentary*. London: T&T Clark, 2005.
———. *Psalms 1–41*. Vol. 1 of *Psalms*. BCOTWP. Grand Rapids: Baker Academic, 2006.
———. *Psalms 42–89*. Vol. 2 of *Psalms*. BCOTWP. Grand Rapids: Baker Academic, 2007.
———. *Psalms 90–150*. Vol. 3 of *Psalms*. BCOTWP. Grand Rapids: Baker Academic, 2008.
Goldingay, John, and David Payne. *Isaiah 40–55*. 2 vols. ICC. London: T&T Clark, 2006.
Gourgues, Michel. "The Priest, the Levite, and the Samaritan Revisited: A Critical Note on Luke 10:31–35." *Journal of Biblical Literature* 117 (1998): 709–13.
Green, Joel B. *The Gospel of Luke*. NICNT. Grand Rapids: Eerdmans, 1997.
Greenberg, Moshe. *Ezekiel, 1–20: A New Translation with Introduction and Commentary*. AB 22. New York: Doubleday, 1983.
Greenspoon, Leonard J. "Old Testament Versions, Ancient." *DNTB*, 752–55.
Grudem, Wayne. *The First Epistle of Peter: An Introduction and Commentary*. TNTC. Leicester: Inter-Varsity Press; Grand Rapids: Eerdmans, 1988.
Gundry, Robert H. *Matthew: A Commentary of His Literary and Theological Art*. 2nd ed. Grand Rapids: Eerdmans, 1982.
———. *The Use of the Old Testament in St. Matthew's Gospel, with Special Reference to the Messianic Hope*. Supplements to Novum Testamentum 18. Leiden: Brill, 1967.
Hagner, Donald A. *Matthew 1–13*. WBC 33A. Dallas: Word, 1993.
———. *Matthew 14–28*. WBC 33B. Dallas: Word, 1995.
Hare, Douglas R. A. *Matthew*. IBC. Louisville: John Knox, 1993.
Harrington, Wilfrid J. *Revelation*. SP 15. Collegeville, MN: Liturgical Press, 1993.
Harstad, Adolph L. *Joshua*. Concordia Commentary. St. Louis: Concordia, 2004.
Hauck, Friedrich. "ὅσιος, ὁσίως, ἀνόσιος, ὁσιότης." *TDNT* 5:489–93.
Hawk, L. Daniel. *Ruth*. Apollos Old Testament Commentary 7B. Nottingham: Apollos; Downers Grove, IL: InterVarsity Press, 2015.
Hays, Richard B. *The Conversion of the Imagination: Paul as Interpreter of Israel's Scripture*. Grand Rapids: Eerdmans, 2005.
———. *Echoes of Scripture in the Gospels*. Waco, TX: Baylor University Press, 2016.
———. *Echoes of Scripture in the Letters of Paul*. New Haven: Yale University Press, 1989.
———. "*Echoes of Scripture in the Letters of Paul*: Abstract." Pages 42–46 in *Paul and the Scriptures of Israel*. Edited by Craig A. Evans and James A. Sanders.

JSNTSup 83. Studies in Scripture in Early Judaism and Christianity 1. Sheffield: JSOT Press, 1993.

Hengel, Martin. "Zur urchristlichen Geschichtsschreibung." Pages 1–104 in *Studien zum Urchristentum (Kleine Schriften VI)*. Wissenschaftliche Untersuchungen zum Neuen Testament 234. Tübingen: Mohr Siebeck, 2008.

Hicks, John Mark. "The Sabbath Controversy in Matthew: An Exegesis of Matthew 12:1–4." *Restoration Quarterly* 27 (1984): 79–91.

Hill, David. *Greek Words and Hebrew Meanings: Studies in the Semantics of Soteriological Terms*. SNTSMS 5. London: Cambridge University Press, 1967.

———. "On the Use and Meaning of Hosea vi. 6 in Matthew's Gospel." *New Testament Studies* 24 (1978): 107–19.

Holladay, William L. *Jeremiah 1: A Commentary on the Book of the Prophet Jeremiah Chapters 1–25*. Hermeneia. Philadelphia: Fortress, 1986.

Hollander, John. *The Figure of Echo: A Mode of Allusion in Milton and After*. Berkeley: University of California Press, 1981.

Hoover, Joseph. "The Wealth of God's Glory: A Response to John Piper's 'Four Problems in Romans 9:22–23.'" *Stone-Campbell Journal* 12 (2009): 47–58.

Horgan, Maurya P. *Pesharim: Qumran Interpretations of Biblical Books*. Catholic Biblical Quarterly Monograph Series 8. Washington, DC: Catholic Biblical Association of America, 1979.

Hossfeld, Frank-Lothar, and Erich Zenger. *Psalms 3: A Commentary on Psalms 101–150*. Hermeneia. Minneapolis: Fortress, 2011.

Hubbard, David A. *Hosea: An Introduction and Commentary*. Tyndale Old Testament Commentaries. Leicester: Inter-Varsity Press, 1989.

Instone-Brewer, David. "Three Weddings and a Divorce: God's Covenant with Israel, Judah and the Church." *TynBul* 47 (1996): 1–25.

Irenaeus of Lyons. *Irenæus Against Heresies*. In vol. 1 of *ANF*. Edited by Alexander Roberts, James Donaldson, and A. Cleveland Coxe. 10 vols. 1885–87.

Jacobson, Rolf A. "Psalm 2: Speaking of Kings." Pages 65–71 in *The Book of Psalms*. By Nancy deClaissé-Walford, Rolf A. Jacobson, and Beth LaNeel Tanner. NICOT. Grand Rapids: Eerdmans, 2014.

Janzen, J. Gerald. *When Prayer Takes Place: Forays into a Biblical World*. Eugene, OR: Wipf & Stock, 2012.

Jewett, Robert. *Romans: A Commentary*. Hermeneia. Minneapolis: Augsburg Fortress, 2007.

Jobes, Karen H. "Got Milk? Septuagint Psalm 33 and the Interpretation of 1 Peter 2:1–3." *Westminster Theological Journal* 63 (2002): 1–14.

Johnson, Luke Timothy. *The Acts of the Apostles*. SP 5. Collegeville, MN: Liturgical Press, 1992.

———. *The First and Second Letters to Timothy: A New Translation with Introduction and Commentary*. AB 35A. New Haven: Yale University Press, 2001.

———. *The Gospel of Luke*. SP 3. Collegeville, MN: Liturgical Press, 1991.

Joosten, Jan. "חסד, 'Benevolence', and ἔλεος, 'Pity': Reflections on Their Lexical Equivalence in the Septuagint." Pages 97–111 in *Collected Studies on the Septuagint: From Language to Interpretation and Beyond*. Forschungen zum Alten Testament 83. Tübingen: Mohr Siebeck, 2012.

Josephus, Flavius. *Flavii Josephi opera*. Edited by Benedictus Niese. 7 vols. Berlin: Weidmannos, 1885–95. Logos Bible Software.

Juel, Donald. "Social Dimensions of Exegesis: The Use of Psalm 16 in Acts 2." *CBQ* 43 (1981): 543–56.

Kaden, David A. "The Methodological Dilemma of Evaluating the Variation Unit in Romans 11:31: A Text Critical Study and a Suggestion about First Century Social History and Scribal Habits." *NovT* 53 (2011): 165–82.

Kaiser, Walter C., Jr. "The Promise to David in Psalm 16 and its Application in Acts 2:25–33 and 13:32–37." *Journal of the Evangelical Theological Society* 23 (1980): 219–29.

———. "The Unfailing Kindnesses Promised to David: Isaiah 55:3." *JSOT* 45 (1989): 91–98.

Keener, Craig S. *Acts: An Exegetical Commentary*. 4 vols. Grand Rapids: Baker Academic, 2012–15.

———. *A Commentary on the Gospel of Matthew*. Grand Rapids: Eerdmans, 1999.

———. *The Gospel of John: A Commentary*. 2 vols. Peabody, MA: Hendrickson, 2003.

———. *Revelation*. NIVAC. Grand Rapids: Zondervan, 2000.

Kelle, Brad E. *Hosea 2: Metaphor and Rhetoric in Historical Perspective*. Academia Biblica 20. Atlanta: Society of Biblical Literature, 2005.

Kepple, Robert J. "The Hope of Israel, the Resurrection of the Dead, and Jesus: A Study of Their Relationship in Acts with Particular Regard to the Understanding of Paul's Trial Defense." *Journal of the Evangelical Theological Society* 20 (1977): 231–41.

Kidner, Derek. *The Message of Hosea: Love to the Loveless*. The Bible Speaks Today. Leicester: Inter-Varsity Press, 1981.

Kittel, D. Rudolf. *Die Psalmen: Übersetzt und erklärt*. Leipzig: Deichert, 1929.

Knight, George W., III. *The Pastoral Epistles: A Commentary on the Greek Text*. NIGTC. Grand Rapids: Eerdmans; Carlisle: Paternoster, 1992.

Koester, Craig R. *Hebrews: A New Translation with Introduction and Commentary*. AB 36. New Haven: Yale University Press, 2001.

Kövecses, Zoltán. *Metaphors of Anger, Pride, and Love: A Lexical Approach to the Structure of Concepts*. Pragmatics and Beyond VII:8. Amsterdam: John Benjamins, 1986.

Kraus, Hans-Joachim. *Psalms 60–150: A Commentary*. Translated by Hilton C. Oswald. Minneapolis: Augsburg Fortress, 1989.

Kristeva, Julia. *Revolution in Poetic Language*. Translated by Margaret Waller. New York: Columbia University Press, 1984.

Kruse, Colin G. *Paul's Letter to the Romans*. The Pillar New Testament Commentary. Grand Rapids: Eerdmans; Nottingham: Apollos, 2012.

Kuyper, Lester J. "Grace and Truth: An Old Testament Description of God, and Its Use in the Johannine Gospel." *Interpretation* 18 (1964): 3–19.

Lakoff, George. *Women, Fire, and Dangerous Things: What Categories Reveal About the Mind*. Chicago: University of Chicago Press, 1987.

Lakoff, George, and Mark Johnson. *Metaphors We Live By*. With a new afterword. Chicago: Chicago University Press, 2003; orig. pub. 1980.

Lane, Nathan. "An Echo of Mercy: A Rereading of the Parable of the Good Samaritan." Pages 74–84 in vol. 2 of *Early Christian Literature and Intertextuality*. Edited by Craig A. Evans and H. Daniel Zacharias. The Library of New Testament Studies 392. London: T&T Clark, 2009.

Lane, William L. *Hebrews 1–8*. WBC 47A. Dallas: Word, 1991.

Langacker, Ronald W. *Theoretical Prerequisites*. Vol. 1 of *Foundations of Cognitive Grammar*. Stanford: Stanford University Press, 1987.

Lincoln, Andrew T. *Ephesians*. WBC 42. Dallas: Word, 1990.

Lofthouse, William F. "*Ḥen* and *Ḥesed* in the Old Testament." *Zeitschrift für die alttestamentliche Wissenschaft* 51 (1933): 29–35.

Longenecker, Richard N. *Biblical Exegesis in the Apostolic Period*. 2nd ed. Grand Rapids: Eerdmans; Vancouver: Regent College, 1975, 1999.

———. *The Epistle to the Romans: A Commentary on the Greek Text*. NIGTC. Grand Rapids: Eerdmans, 2016.

———. *Galatians*. WBC 41. Dallas: Word, 1990.

Luz, Ulrich. *Matthew 21–28: A Commentary*. Translated by James E. Crouch. Hermeneia. Minneapolis: Augsburg Fortress, 2005.

Marshall, I. Howard. *1 Peter*. IVP New Testament Commentary. Downers Grove, IL: InterVarsity Press, 1991.

———. "Acts." Pages 513–606 in *Commentary on the New Testament Use of the Old Testament*. Edited by G. K. Beale and D. A. Carson. Grand Rapids: Baker Academic; Nottingham: Apollos, 2007.

———. *The Acts of the Apostles: An Introduction and Commentary*. TNTC. Leicester: Inter-Varsity Press; Grand Rapids: Eerdmans, 1980.

———. *A Critical and Exegetical Commentary on the Pastoral Epistles*. ICC. Edinburgh: T&T Clark, 1999.

———. *The Gospel of Luke: A Commentary on the Greek Text*. NIGTC. Carlisle: Paternoster; Grand Rapids: Eerdmans, 1978.

Martin, Troy W. *Metaphor and Composition in 1 Peter*. Society of Biblical Literature Dissertation Series 131. Atlanta: Scholars Press, 1992.

Martyn, J. Louis. *Galatians: A New Translation with Introduction and Commentary*. AB 33A. New York: Doubleday, 1997.

Matthews, Victor H. "Family Relationships." *DOTP*, 291–99.

Matthews, Victor H., and Don C. Benjamin. *Social World of Ancient Israel, 1250–587 BCE*. Peabody, MA: Hendrickson, 1993.

Mays, James L. *Psalms*. IBC. Louisville: John Knox, 1994.

McCune, Lorne A. "The Contribution of the Dead Sea Scrolls Toward Understanding the Term *Ḥeseḏ*." MDiv diss., Grace Theological Seminary, 1977.

McKnight, Scot. *1 Peter*. NIVAC. Grand Rapids: Zondervan, 1996.

———. *Galatians*. NIVAC. Grand Rapids: Zondervan, 1995.

McLay, R. Timothy. *The Use of the Septuagint in New Testament Research*. Grand Rapids: Eerdmans, 2003.

McNutt, Paula. *Reconstructing the Society of Ancient Israel*. Library of Ancient Israel. London: Society for Promoting Christian Knowledge; Louisville: Westminster John Knox, 1999.

Megahan, Michael L. "Some Lexemes Associated with the Concept of JOY in Biblical Hebrew: A Cognitive Linguistic Investigation." PhD diss., University of Stellenbosch, 2014.

Meier, John P. *Matthew*. New Testament Message 3. Collegeville, MN: Liturgical Press, 1980.

Meyers, Carol. "The Family in Early Israel." Pages 1–47 in *Families in Ancient Israel*. Edited by Leo G. Perdue, Joseph Blenkinsopp, John J. Collins, and Carol Meyers. The Family, Religion, and Culture. Louisville: Westminster John Knox, 1997.

Michaels, J. Ramsey. *1 Peter*. WBC 49. Waco, TX: Word, 1988.
———. *Revelation*. IVP New Testament Commentary Series. Downers Grove, IL: InterVarsity Press, 1997.
Michel, Otto. *Der Brief an die Römer*. Kritisch-exegetischer Kommentar über das Neue Testament. Göttingen: Vandenhoeck & Ruprecht, 1957.
Mitrović, Branko. "Attribution of Concepts and Problems with Anachronism." *History and Theory* 50 (2011): 303–27.
Montanari, Franco. *The Brill Dictionary of Ancient Greek*. Edited by Madeleine Goh and Chad Schroeder. English ed. Leiden: Brill, 2015.
Moo, Douglas J. *The Letter to the Romans*. 2nd ed. NICNT. Grand Rapids: Eerdmans, 2018.
———. *Romans*. NIVAC. Grand Rapids: Zondervan, 2000.
Morris, Leon. *The Epistle to the Romans*. Grand Rapids: Eerdmans; Leicester: Inter-Varsity Press, 1988.
———. *The Gospel According to Matthew*. Grand Rapids: Eerdmans; Leicester: Apollos, 1992.
———. *Luke: An Introduction and Commentary*. Rev. ed. TNTC. Leicester: Inter-Varsity Press; Grand Rapids: Eerdmans, 1988; orig. pub. 1974.
Motyer, J. Alec. *The Prophecy of Isaiah*. Leicester: Inter-Varsity Press, 1993.
Mounce, Robert H. *The Book of Revelation*. NICNT. Grand Rapids: Eerdmans, 1977.
Mounce, William D. *Pastoral Epistles*. WBC 46. Nashville: Thomas Nelson, 2000.
Moyise, Steve. *Evoking Scripture: Seeing the Old Testament in the New*. London: T&T Clark, 2008.
Munck, Johannes. *The Acts of the Apostles: Introduction, Translation and Notes*. AB 31. Garden City, NY: Doubleday, 1967.
Murphy, Roland E. "*Šaḥat* in the Qumran Literature." *Biblica* 39 (1958): 61–66.
Murray, John. *The Epistle to the Romans: The English Text with Introduction, Exposition and Notes*. 2 vols. NICNT. Grand Rapids: Eerdmans, 1968.
Nelson, Karen. "What About the Women of *Ḥesed*? A Reaction to the Honors Gallery in Sir 44:1–50:24." Pages 152–67 in *Holding Forth the Word of Life: Essays in Honor of Tim Meadowcroft*. Edited by John de Jong and Csilla Saysell. Australian College of Theology Monograph Series. Eugene, OR: Wipf & Stock, 2020.
Newsom, Carol A. "Shirot ʿOlat HaShabbat." Pages 173–402 in *Qumran Cave 4.VI: Poetical and Liturgical Texts, Part 1*. Edited by Esther Eshel et al. DJD XI. Oxford: Clarendon, 1998.
———. *Songs of the Sabbath Sacrifice: A Critical Edition*. Harvard Semitic Studies 27. Atlanta: Scholars Press, 1985.
Nolland, John. *The Gospel of Matthew: A Commentary on the Greek Text*. NIGTC. Grand Rapids: Eerdmans; Bletchley: Paternoster, 2005.
———. *Luke 1–9:20*. WBC 35A. Dallas: Word, 1989.
———. *Luke 9:21–18:34*. WBC 35B. Dallas: Word, 1993.
Osborne, Grant R. *Revelation*. Baker Exegetical Commentary on the New Testament. Grand Rapids: Baker Academic, 2002.
Oswalt, John N. *The Book of Isaiah: Chapters 40–66*. NICOT. Grand Rapids: Eerdmans, 1998.
———. "God." *DOTWPW*, 246–59.
———. *Isaiah*. NIVAC. Grand Rapids: Zondervan, 2003.

Ottenheijm, Eric. "The Shared Meal—A Therapeutical Device: The Function and Meaning of Hos 6:6 in Matt 9:10–13." *NovT* 53 (2011): 1–21.

Pao, David W. "Old Testament in the Gospels." *DJG*, 631–41.

Park, Hyung Dae. *Finding Herem? A Study of Luke-Acts in the Light of Herem*. The Library of New Testament Studies 357. London: T&T Clark, 2007.

Parker, Benjamin H., and Martin G. Abegg, trans. *The Book of Ben Sira*. B VII Verso; B XXI Verso; D II Recto. https://www.bensira.org.

Pattemore, Stephen. *The People of God in the Apocalypse: Discourse, Structure and Exegesis*. SNTSMS 128. Cambridge: Cambridge University Press, 2004.

Perdue, Leo G. "The Household, Old Testament Theology, and Contemporary Hermeneutics." Pages 223–57 in *Families in Ancient Israel*. Edited by Leo G. Perdue, Joseph Blenkinsopp, John J. Collins, and Carol Meyers. The Family, Religion, and Culture. Louisville: Westminster John Knox, 1997.

Pervo, Richard I. *Acts: A Commentary*. Hermeneia. Minneapolis: Augsburg Fortress, 2009.

Plato. Plato. "Euthyphro." Pages 87–99 in *Concepts: Core Readings*. Edited by Eric Margolis and Stephen Laurence. Cambridge: MIT Press, 1999.

Poirier, John C. "The Case for Italics in Bible Translation." *Stone-Campbell Journal* 16 (2013): 207–16.

Porter, Stanley E. "Allusions and Echoes." Pages 29–40 in *As It is Written: Studying Paul's Use of Scripture*. Edited by Stanley E. Porter and Christopher D. Stanley. SBL Symposium Series 50. Atlanta: Society of Biblical Literature, 2008.

———. "Paul and His Bible: His Education and Access to the Scriptures of Israel." Pages 97–124 in *As It is Written: Studying Paul's Use of Scripture*. Edited by Stanley E. Porter and Christopher D. Stanley. SBL Symposium Series 50. Atlanta: SBL, 2008.

———. *Sacred Tradition in the New Testament: Tracing Old Testament Themes in the Gospels and Epistles*. Grand Rapids: Baker Academic, 2016.

Potterie, Ignace de la. "Χάρις Paulinienne et Χάρις Johannique." Pages 256–82 in *Jesus und Paulus: Festschrift für Werner Georg Kümmel zum 70. Geburtstag*. Edited by E. Earle Ellis and Erich Grässer. Göttingen: Vandenhoeck & Ruprecht, 1975.

Propp, William H. C. *Exodus 19–40: A New Translation with Introduction and Commentary*. AB 2A. New York: Doubleday, 2006.

Przybylski, Benno. *Righteousness in Matthew and His World of Thought*. SNTSMS 41. Cambridge: Cambridge University Press, 1980.

Qimron, Elisha, and James H. Charlesworth. "Rule of the Community." *Pages 1–51* in *Rule of the Community and Related Documents*. Vol. 1 of *The Dead Sea Scrolls: Hebrew, Aramaic, and Greek Texts with English Translations*. Edited by James H. Charlesworth. Tübingen: Mohr Siebeck; Louisville: Westminster John Knox, 1994.

Quinn, Jerome D. *The Letter to Titus: A New Translation with Notes and Commentary and An Introduction to Titus, I and II Timothy, the Pastoral Epistles*. AB 35. New York: Doubleday, 1990.

Quintilian. *Institutio oratorio*. Recorded and translated in H. E. Butler. 4 vols. LCL. London: William Heinemann; New York: G. P. Putnam's Sons, 1922.

Rad, Gerhard von. *The Theology of Israel's Prophetic Traditions*. Vol. 2 of *Old Testament Theology*. Translated by D. M. G. Stalker. London: SCM, 1975; orig. pub. 1965.

Rae, Murray. “Response: Reading as Formation.” Pages 258–62 in *Ears That Hear: Explorations in Theological Interpretation of the Bible*. Edited by Joel B. Green and Tim Meadowcroft. Sheffield: Sheffield Phoenix, 2013.

Redditt, Paul L. “Hasideans.” *ABD* 3:66.

Reymond, Eric, trans. *The Book of Ben Sira*. Masada II. https://www.bensira.org.

Riemer, Nick. *Introducing Semantics*. Cambridge Introductions to Language and Linguistics. Cambridge: Cambridge University Press, 2010.

Ringgren, Helmer. “Luke’s Use of the Old Testament.” *Harvard Theological Review* 79 (1986): 227–35.

Roberts, J. J. M. “Hosea and the Sacrificial Cultus.” *Restoration Quarterly* 15 (1972): 15–26.

Rosch, Eleanor H. “Principles of Categorization.” Pages 27–48 in *Cognition and Categorization*. Edited by Eleanor Rosch and Barbara B. Lloyd. Hillsdale, NJ: Laurence Erlbaum Associates, 1978.

Rosch, Eleanor H., and Carolyn B. Mervis. “Family Resemblances: Studies in the Internal Structure of Categories.” *Cognitive Psychology* 7 (1975): 573–605.

Routledge, Robin. “*Ḥesed* as Obligation: A Re-examination.” *TynBul* 46 (1995): 179–96.

Sakenfeld, Katharine Doob. *Faithfulness in Action: Loyalty in Biblical Perspective*. Eugene, OR: Wipf & Stock, 2001. Previously published by Augsburg Fortress, 1985.

———. “Love (Old Testament).” *ABD* 4:375–81.

———. *The Meaning of Hesed in the Hebrew Bible: A New Inquiry*. Eugene, OR: Wipf & Stock, 1978.

———. *Ruth*. IBC. Louisville: John Knox, 1999.

Schaefer, Konrad. *Psalms*. Berit Olam. Collegeville, MN: Liturgical Press, 2001.

Schipper, Jeremy. *Ruth: A New Translation with Introduction and Commentary*. Anchor Yale Bible 7D. New Haven: Yale University Press, 2016.

Schreiner, Thomas R. *1, 2 Peter, Jude*. New American Commentary 37. Nashville: Broadman & Holman, 2003.

Schutter, William L. *Hermeneutic and Composition in I Peter*. Wissenschaftliche Untersuchungen zum Neuen Testament 2.30. Tübingen: J. C. B. Mohr (Paul Siebeck), 1989.

Senior, Donald P. “1 Peter.” In *1 Peter; Jude and 2 Peter*. Edited by Daniel J. Harrington. Collegeville, MN: Liturgical Press, 2003.

Shade, W. Robert, III and Bruce J. Nicholls. *Acts*. Asia Bible Commentary Series. Singapore: Asia Theological Association, 2007.

Shead, Stephen L. *Radical Frame Semantics and Biblical Hebrew: Exploring Lexical Semantics*. Biblical Interpretation Series 108. Leiden: Brill, 2011.

Sheppard, A. R. R. “Pagan Cults of Angels in Roman Asia Minor.” *Talanta* 12–13 (1980–81): 77–101.

Siebeneck, Robert T. “May Their Bones Return to Life! Sirach’s ‘Praise to the Fathers.’” *CBQ* 21 (1959): 411–28.

Silva, Moisés. *Biblical Words and Their Meaning: An Introduction to Lexical Semantics*. Grand Rapids: Zondervan, 1983.

Smalley, Stephen S. *The Revelation to John: A Commentary on the Greek Text of the Apocalypse*. Downers Grove, IL: InterVarsity Press, 2005.

Smith, Gary V. *Hosea, Amos, Micah*. NIVAC. Grand Rapids: Zondervan, 2001.

Snaith, Norman H. *The Distinctive Ideas of the Old Testament*. London: Epworth, 1944.

Stegemann, Hartmut, and Eileen Schuller, eds., with translation of texts by Carol Newsom. *Qumran Cave 1.III: 1QHodayot[a] with Incorporation of 1QHodayot[b] and 4QHodayot[a–f]*. DJD XL. Oxford: Clarendon, 2009.
Stenger, William R. "Paul the Jew." *DPL*, 503–11.
Steudel, Annette. "408. 4QApocryphon of Moses[c]?" Pages 298–315 in *Qumran Cave 4.XXVI: Cryptic Texts; Miscellanea, Part 1*. Edited by Stephen J. Pfann et al. DJD XXXVI. Oxford: Clarendon, 2000.
Stoebe, Hans Joachim. "Gottes hingebende Güte und Treue." ThD diss., Westfälischen Wilhelmsuniversität, 1950.
———. "חֶסֶד *ḥesed*." *TLOT* 2:449–64.
Strack, Hermann L., and G. Stemberger. *Introduction to the Talmud and Midrash*. Translated by Markus Bockmuehl. Minneapolis: Fortress, 1992.
Strugnell, John, and Daniel J. Harrington. "Instruction." Pages 1–504 in *Qumran Cave 4.XXIV: Sapiential Texts, Part 2, 4QInstruction (Mûsār Lĕ Mēvîn): 4Q415 ff.* Edited by John Strugnell, Daniel J. Harrington, and Torleif Elgvin. DJD XXXIV. Oxford: Clarendon, 1999.
Stuart, Douglas. *Hosea—Jonah*. WBC 31. Waco, TX: Word, 1987.
Sweeney, Marvin A. *Micah, Nahum, Habakkuk, Zephaniah, Haggai, Zechariah, Malachi*. Vol. 1 of *The Twelve Prophets*. Berit Olam. Collegeville, MN: Liturgical Press, 2000.
Sweet, John. *Revelation*. SCM Pelican Commentaries. London: SCM, 1979.
Swete, Henry Barclay. *The Apocalypse of St John: The Greek Text with Introduction Notes and Indices*. 2nd ed. London: Macmillan, 1907.
Tan, Kim Huat. "Community, Kingdom and Cross: Jesus' View of Covenant." Pages 122–55 in *The God of Covenant: Biblical, Theological and Contemporary Perspectives*. Edited by Jamie A. Grant and Alistair I. Wilson. Leicester: Inter-Varsity Press, 2005.
Tanner, Beth. "Psalm 86: Hear My Prayer." Pages *659–63 in The Book of Psalms*. Edited by Nancy deClaissé-Walford, Rolf A. Jacobson, and Beth LaNeel Tanner. NICOT. Grand Rapids: Eerdmans, 2014.
Targum Jonathan; Targum of Chronicles; Targum of Psalms. Comprehensive Aramaic Lexicon Project. Cincinnati: Jewish Institute of Religion, Hebrew Union College. https://cal.huc.edu/targumbrowse.html
Tate, Marvin E. *Psalms 51–100*. WBC 20. Nashville: Thomas Nelson, 1990.
Taylor, John R. *Cognitive Grammar*. Oxford Textbooks in Linguistics. Oxford: Oxford University Press, 2002.
———. *Linguistic Categorization*. 3rd ed. Oxford Textbooks in Linguistics. Oxford: Oxford University Press, 2003.
Towner, Philip H. *The Letters to Timothy and Titus*. NICNT. Grand Rapids: Eerdmans, 2006.
Trebilco, Paul R. "Jewish Communities in Asia Minor." *DNTB*, 562–69.
———. "What Shall We Call Each Other? Part Two: The Issue of Self-Designation in the Johannine Letters and Revelation." *TynBul* 54 (2003): 51–73.
Trebilco, Paul R., and Simon Rae. *1 Timothy*. Asia Bible Commentary Series. Singapore: Asia Theological Association, 2006.
Trull, Gregory V. "An Exegesis of Psalm 16:10." *BSac* 161 (2004): 304–21.
———. "Peter's Interpretation of Psalm 16:8–11 in Acts 2:25–32." *BSac* 161 (2004): 432–48.

———. "Views on Peter's Use of Psalm 16:8–11 in Acts 2:25–32." *BSac* 161 (2004): 194–214.

Tsumura, David Toshio. *The First Book of Samuel*. NICOT. Grand Rapids: Eerdmans, 2007.

Turner, David L. *Matthew*. Baker Exegetical Commentary on the New Testament. Grand Rapids: Baker Academic, 2008.

Van der Merwe, Christo H. J. "The Challenge of Better Understanding Discourse Particles: The Case of לָכֵן." *Journal of Northwest Semitic Languages* 40 (2014): 127–57.

———. "A Cognitive Linguistic Perspective on הִנֵּה in the Pentateuch, Joshua, Judges, and Ruth." *Hebrew Studies* 48 (2007): 101–21.

Wagner, J. Ross. "The Christ, Servant of Jew and Gentile: A Fresh Approach to Romans 15:8–9." *Journal of Biblical Literature* 116 (1997): 473–85.

Wakefield, Andrew H. *Where to Live: The Hermeneutical Significance of Paul's Citations from Scripture in Galatians 3:1–14*. Academia Biblica 14. Leiden: Brill, 2003.

Waltke, Bruce K. "A Canonical Approach to the Psalms." Pages 3–18 in *Tradition and Testament: Essays in Honor of Charles Lee Feinberg*. Edited by John S. Feinberg and Paul D. Feinberg. Chicago: Moody, 1981.

———. "Micah." Pages 591–764 in vol. 2 of *The Minor Prophets: An Exegetical and Expository Commentary*. Edited by Thomas Edward McComiskey. Grand Rapids: Baker, 1993.

Waltke, Bruce K., and M. O'Connor. *An Introduction to Biblical Hebrew Syntax*. Winona Lake, IN: Eisenbrauns, 1990.

Watts, John D. W. *Isaiah 1–33*. WBC 24. Waco, TX: Word, 1985.

———. *Isaiah 34–66*. Rev. ed. WBC 25. Nashville: Thomas Nelson, 2005.

Weinfeld, Moshe, and David Seely. "Barkhi Nafshi." Pages 255–334 in *Qumran Cave 4.XX: Poetical and Liturgical Texts, Part 2*. Edited by Esther G. Chazon et al. DJD XXIX. Oxford: Clarendon, 1999.

Weiser, Alfons. *Die Apostelgeschichte*. 2 vols. Ökumenischer Taschenbuch-Kommentar zum Neuen Testament. Gütersloh: Gerd Mohn, 1981–85.

Wilkins, Michael J. *Matthew*. NIVAC. Grand Rapids: Zondervan, 2004.

Williamson, Hugh G. M. *Ezra, Nehemiah*. WBC 16. Waco, TX: Word, 1985.

———. "'The Sure Mercies of David': Subjective or Objective Genitive?" *Journal of Semitic Studies* 23 (1978): 31–49.

Wittgenstein, Ludwig. *Philosophical Investigations: The German Text, with a Revised English Translation*. Translated by G. E. M. Anscombe. 3rd ed. Oxford: Blackwell, 2001.

Wolde, Ellen van. *Reframing Biblical Studies: When Language and Text Meet Culture, Cognition, and Context*. Winona Lake, IN: Eisenbrauns, 2009.

Wolff, Hans Walter. *Hosea: A Commentary on the Book of the Prophet Hosea*. Hermeneia. Philadelphia: Fortress, 1974.

Wright, Benjamin G. *No Small Difference: Sirach's Relationship to its Hebrew Parent Text*. Septuagint and Cognate Studies 26. Atlanta: Scholars Press, 1989.

Wright, G. Ernest. "The Lawsuit of God: A Form-Critical Study of Deuteronomy 32." Pages 26–67 in *Israel's Prophetic Heritage: Essays in Honor of James Muilenburg*. Edited by Bernhard W. Anderson and Walter Harrelson. The Preacher's Library. London: SCM, 1962.

Wright, N. T. *The Climax of the Covenant: Christ and the Law in Pauline Theology*. Edinburgh: T&T Clark, 1991.

———. "The Letter to the Romans: Introduction, Commentary, and Reflections." *NIB* 10:393–770.
———. *Paul and the Faithfulness of God.* 2 vols. London: Society for Promoting Christian Knowledge, 2013.
Yri, Kjell Magne. *My Father Taught Me How to Cry, but Now I Have Forgotten: The Semantics of Religious Concepts with an Emphasis on Meaning, Interpretation, and Translatability*. Acta Humaniora. Oslo: Scandanavian University Press, 1998.
Zimmerli, Walther. *Studien zur alttestamentlichen Theologie und Prophetie*. Theologische Bücherei Altes Testament 51. Munich: Kaiser, 1974.
Zobel, H.–J. "חֶסֶד *ḥeseḏ*." *TDOT* 5:44–64.

SUBJECT INDEX

Abraham, 20, 31, 89n72, 92, 104, 114, 147
  Abrahamic covenant, 83, 92n87, 95, 101, 103n18, 105, 112, 118, 143n48, 172
  Abraham's offspring, 89, 92, 94, 130, 147, 149, 150, 172, 173, 185
  promises to Abraham and offspring (Luke), 103–5, 109, 112, 114, 118, 147, 149, 173, 185
  promises to Abraham and offspring (Paul), 82–83, 89, 89n72, 92, 93, 96–98, 173, 185
acceptance, 75n74, 76, 79, 83, 117, 118
agriculture and nature, imagery from, 36, 36n48, 37, 41, 43, 66, 74, 95, 99, 123–25, 123n23
aid, 19n4, 40, 67, 101, 103, 116, 172, 176, 190
allusions and echoes, criteria for, 9, 10, 83, 102n15, 103n22, 106n44, 130, 180–81
  recurrence, 9, 83, 122, 181
  thematic coherence, 9, 66, 70, 83, 137, 181
  volume, 9, 66, 76, 87n54, 102, 156, 181
appeals, 21, 23, 26–28, 42, 43, 96, 129, 134, 142, 171
  See also pleas
article of transaction, 16–17, 22–26, 38–39, 41–44, 91, 92, 94, 108–11, 114, 169–70
Asidaioi ("Hasideans"), 53–54, 186–87
assistance, 23, 35, 109, 111n53, 112, 114–15, 184–86
  See also aid; help
attributes, 13, 26, 43, 59, 88–89, 127n44, 175
  See also YHWH / the Lord / God: attribute formula for

baptism, 115n66, 146, 149, 153, 178, 183, 191
belief, 97, 146–47, 149, 153, 172, 174, 176, 178, 183, 191
believers, 79, 89–90, 93–94, 122, 125n27, 131–32, 134, 154, 185, 187
blessing, 24–25, 76, 88, 93, 95, 98, 109, 172, 185, 186
  from YHWH / the Lord / God, 51, 89, 90, 92n86, 154
  toward YHWH / the Lord / God, 49, 53, 102, 110, 112, 120, 126, 128, 134, 167, 170
blood
  as a judgment, 161–64, 162n58
  of a lamb / the Lamb, 157n19, 163n63 (*see also* deliverance: by the blood of a lamb)
  of the new covenant, 143n48
  relations, 19, 19n4
  shed, 63, 97, 156n8, 162–66

categorization, 8, 11–18, 188
  fuzzy category boundaries, 12, 23, 48, 87, 91, 177, 188
  levels of, 13, 14, 16, 22
  subcategories, 16–18, 22–34, 39–42, 47–52, 111, 169–74, 181n3, 188–89

Categorization, Intertextual, 7, 18, 179, 188
change
behavioral, 171, 183–84
circumstantial, 25, 41
in salvation history, 149, 151–54, 171, 176–77
semantic, 14–18, 235
characteristic, 22–23, 26–30, 35, 37, 39, 42–44, 57, 60, 93, 169–71
See also YHWH / the Lord / God: characteristic of; YHWH / the Lord / God: characteristics of
Christians, 119, 131n60, 132, 132n65, 133, 133n74, 135, 150, 166
in Asia Minor, 126, 128, 130, 132, 133, 171, 177
Gentile, 89, 97n98, 97n102, 100, 131–32, 154, 157n16, 176, 186, 203
Jewish, 72, 96, 97n98, 97n102, 132, 154, 157n16, 176, 186
circumcision, 80, 82–83, 87, 88, 90, 93–96, 99, 100n3, 109–10, 173
commitment, 5, 19, 26, 53, 58, 75, 113, 144, 167, 187
amid trials, 167, 187, 191
ongoing, 42, 98, 114, 153, 190
See also covenant: commitment; endurance: enduring commitment
compassion, 57, 84, 94, 100, 103, 132, 134, 228
as a manifestation of *eleos*, 93, 111, 113, 116, 118, 122, 132, 171, 176, 181
as a manifestation of *ḥsd*, 24, 28, 33–34, 41, 121, 122, 129–30, 134
rḥm, 89, 121–22, 130, 134, 147, 177, 230, 231
rḥmym, 26, 30, 37–39, 45, 57, 88, 102, 121, 230
conceptualization, 3n11, 4n13, 7–8, 12–16, 18, 118, 184, 188
concept corresponding to *ḥesed*, 2–4, 8–11, 179–90
word-concept correspondence, 3–4, 7n2, 14n43, 18
consignment, 86–87, 94
consistency, 3–4, 55, 57, 74, 97, 130, 134, 182, 191
constancy, 12, 42, 123, 128n46, 133
continuity, 8, 40–41, 43, 149–51, 153–54, 176–78
See also scriptural tradition: continuity with
contrast with the wicked, 35, 37, 37n52, 49, 74, 130n50, 160n43
corruption (*diaphthora*), 138–40, 142, 145–49, 153, 172, 174, 180, 182, 183
covenant, 20, 42, 44, 106, 118, 130, 154, 170
associations with *ḥsd/ḥsyd*, 40, 44, 48, 90, 101, 103, 117, 143, 178
breaking, 1, 34, 37, 41, 66–67, 69, 72, 108 (*see also* covenant: fitting judgment or punishment for breaking)
bryt, 23, 24, 44, 44n68, 143n47, 147n60
for those who come and hear, 131, 142–44, 147, 153, 172n4, 178
commitment, 39, 44, 102n15, 153
community, 44, 46, 116–18, 181
devotion, 72, 77, 106, 114, 155, 166, 167, 177 (*see also* devotion: to covenant relationship)
diathēkē and *diatithēmi*, 101, 130, 143, 143nn47–48
everlasting, 25, 32, 74n65, 130n50, 131, 141–44, 147, 147n60
faithfulness, 59, 116, 117
fidelity, 45, 156, 186n8
fitting judgment or punishment for breaking, 29, 63, 63n5, 74n69, 162–67, 174
holy, 101, 105, 110, 114, 143n48
keeping, 20, 23–25, 37, 41, 69, 76, 103, 113–14, 118, 152, 187
loyalty, 43, 59, 83, 130, 189
new, 91n83, 132, 143n48, 184, 191 (*see also* blood: of the new covenant)
obedience, 63–64, 67, 69, 73, 77
promises, 96, 98, 112, 118, 132, 153, 176–78, 187
relationships, 1, 17, 25, 36, 43, 63, 64, 72, 74, 76–78, 117, 176, 184, 186, 187, 190 (*see also* devotion: to covenant relationship; YHWH / the Lord / God: relationship with: covenant relationship with)

renewal, 75, 112, 112n57, 117, 129, 132, 153
Sinai/Horeb, 108, 112n57, 114, 130
See also Abraham: Abrahamic covenant; covenant people, YHWH / the Lord / God's; David, son of Jesse: Davidic covenant; Israel and descendants: covenant with; YHWH / the Lord / God: covenant partners
covenant people, YHWH / the Lord / God's, 45–51, 54, 96–98, 108, 113, 123, 128, 132, 153, 166–67, 170–71, 174
belonging to, 60, 76, 77, 84, 93, 97–98, 116–18, 131–32, 176–77, 186, 187
current/new generation of, 143, 149, 153, 172, 177, 185, 187
and *eleos*, 76, 98, 112, 116–17, 121–22, 129–32, 182, 186
and *ḥsd*, 27–28, 34, 36, 37, 41, 76, 98, 116, 121–22, 129, 154, 182, 186, 191
reconstitution of, 131–32, 131n60, 176, 187
redefinition of, 69, 77, 116–18, 186
regeneration of, 132, 135, 171, 181, 186–87
responsibilities of, 20, 44, 70, 116–17, 133–35, 184–85
credo. *See* YHWH / the Lord / God: attribute formula for
crown imagery, 36, 53, 102, 123, 123n21, 125, 133, 140n22

darkness, 70, 106, 112, 117n81, 123n19, 131n54, 140, 171
David, son of Jesse, 35, 43, 73, 91, 96, 139, 172, 174, 178
Davidic covenant, 32, 96, 101, 118, 143–48, 151–54, 172, 174, 177, 180, 182
dynasty of, 87n53, 139, 141, 144, 151, 152, 199n17
faithful *ḥsdym/hosia* of, 29–33, 131, 141–44, 147–49, 152–53, 171, 177, 180, 182, 185
house of, 105, 110, 113–14, 131, 143n48, 151, 154, 170, 187
and *ḥsd/hosia*, 1, 24, 31, 81, 96, 104, 113, 131, 140–41, 187
and *ḥsyd/hosios*, 138–41, 145–46, 148–49, 152–54, 174, 180, 182
offspring of, 35, 96, 97n103, 104, 141, 150
promises to David and offspring, 33, 81, 96, 98, 113–14, 118, 136, 143, 151–52, 185
raising up David's offspring, 97n103, 105, 110, 114, 139n17, 143n48, 144, 150, 151n74, 153, 177
Dead Sea Scrolls, 44–45, 52–53, 88n65, 139n20, 141n32, 181n3, 186n8, 189, 235–41, 235nn1–2
deliverance, 49, 53, 122–23, 178, 187
by the blood of a lamb, 157n19, 158, 167
from death, 96n93, 120, 139n18, 140n21, 151, 159n34
from dire straits, 1n2, 111n53
from Egypt and its plagues, 157n19, 158
from enemies, 91, 92, 95, 110, 112, 144, 163–64n63, 170
as a manifestation of *ḥsd*, 25, 27, 28, 41, 96, 140n21, 151, 167, 170
demonstrations, specific, 22–23, 30–33, 35, 42, 43, 110, 147–48, 151, 169–72, 177
devotion, 5, 30, 43, 50, 60, 63, 116, 190
to covenant relationship, 47–50, 52, 77, 154, 156, 159, 166, 169, 173–74, 177, 187, 190
devoted people, 50–52, 60, 136, 166, 190
See also YHWH / the Lord / God: devotion of; YHWH / the Lord / God: devotion to
discipleship, the widening call to, 67n30, 69–71, 74, 76, 85, 95, 98, 173, 176, 186
dislocation, 25, 132, 170
disobedience, 86–87, 86n47, 89–90, 93–94, 130
disposition to act, 23, 26, 39, 42, 44, 129
distress, 25, 28, 28n23, 41, 59, 170, 183
potential death, 28, 41
domain, 14–15, 14nn42–43, 18n59, 57, 57n14, 61n29, 136, 155n2, 189
of *ḥesed* (ancient Israelite interpersonal relationships), 17, 19–21, 43, 179, 184, 188, 190

echoes. *See* allusions and echoes, criteria for
eleaō, 57n14, 83, 83nn27–28, 87, 189
elect exiles, 122, 125–26, 128–34, 171, 186
eleēmōn, 27n19, 62n2, 86, 160n40, 189, 228
eleēmosynē, 35, 36, 189, 227
eleeō, 58, 83–84, 86–87, 93, 121–22, 130, 132, 134, 177, 188–89, 231–32
eleos
  abundance of, 56, 112, 122, 126, 128–34, 171, 175, 181, 183, 186–87
  greatness of, 101, 106, 110, 126, 170, 186
  people of, 69, 76–77, 176, 186–87
  polyeleos or *poly eleos*, 27, 55, 57, 84–86, 90, 103, 108, 121, 130, 134, 227
  See also YHWH / the Lord / God: as agent of *eleos*; YHWH / the Lord / God: *eleos* affections (*splanchna eleous*) of; YHWH / the Lord / God: as possessor of *eleos*
Elizabeth and her neighbors/relatives, 101, 106, 109, 110, 170
emotion, 39, 41, 44, 57–58, 105n28
endurance, 84–85, 94, 133–34
  enduring commitment, 129, 132–34, 177, 179, 183–84
  enduring devotion, 166, 179
  enduring *eleos* or *hosia*, 112, 118, 134, 171, 175, 182–83, 185, 191
  enduring *ḥsd*, 28, 37, 40, 46, 56, 82, 94, 134, 150–51, 154, 183, 191 (*see also* thanksgiving: liturgy)
  enduring throne, 25, 31, 41, 151, 151n72, 152, 170
enemies, 87, 92, 95, 105, 110, 112, 117, 144, 170
  See also deliverance: from enemies
enthronement, 21, 21n20, 131, 131n56, 139, 151, 151n72, 152
entity, 22–23, 33–35, 37, 39, 42–44, 66–70, 93–94, 109, 169, 172–73, 181n3
events reported in the New Testament, 97, 98, 109, 112, 116, 146, 150, 175, 182, 191
exile, 36n50, 42, 43, 123, 125n28, 125n30, 132n65
exodus tradition, 28, 85, 104, 106n42, 158, 158n26, 161n48, 163, 167, 167n79, 178
  themes, 84, 106n42, 157–58, 159n31, 160, 161, 164n63

faithfulness, 5, 29, 38, 114n65, 188, 190
  and *alētheia*, 55, 57, 80, 82–83, 87, 88, 92–93, 95–98, 103–4, 119, 180
  and *alēthinos*, 55, 108, 156nn8–9, 158, 159, 163, 166
  faithful conduct, 25, 27, 33n45, 41, 60, 114, 117, 133, 166
  faithful people, 24, 35, 37, 43, 48, 50, 52, 90, 165, 167, 184
  faithful remnant, 112n57, 123
  ḥsd wʾmt, 24n8, 26, 35, 45, 45n69, 55, 82n20, 98, 108, 175n9
  ʾmt with *ḥsd*, 24, 26–27, 33–37, 40, 45, 63, 82–83, 92, 96–97, 103–4, 119, 131, 159, 180
  ʾmwnh (or translation), 27, 30, 37, 38, 66, 82n23, 103, 113, 151n73, 161
  pistis, 62, 65–66, 115n68
  See also YHWH / the Lord / God: faithfulness of
favor (*ḥn*), 38, 55–56, 55–56n3, 90n80
  See also grace (*charis*)
fidelity, 45, 73, 73n58, 156, 187
forgiveness of sins, 1, 42, 92, 105, 108–10, 112, 129, 144, 147, 171, 174, 178
  See also Jesus: and forgiveness of sins

gathering of God's people, 39, 85, 121–23, 121n9, 129–30
generations, 53, 151
  through multiple, 25, 101–3, 109, 112, 114, 118, 180, 183, 187, 191
  to the thousandth generation, 103, 115, 140n27, 170
Gentiles/nations, 81–82, 96, 98, 147, 153, 171–73, 176, 182–83
  and the circumcision, 80, 82, 83, 93, 95, 96, 173
  Jews and Gentiles, 83, 85–87, 89, 94–99, 101, 118, 132, 135, 149, 154, 176–77, 186, 187

responses of the nations, 80–82, 92, 96–97, 99, 123, 143, 147, 160–61, 164, 167–68
See also Christians: Gentile; YHWH / the Lord / God: glorification of
gezerâ šawâ, 137, 137n6, 153
giving, 82–83, 90n80, 92, 104, 142–43, 147–48, 153, 171, 177
gifts, 39, 44, 127n44, 136, 149, 182
not giving, 138–40, 145–46, 148, 153, 174, 180
See also marriage imagery: betrothal metaphor
gladness, 49, 145, 159, 174
glory, 37, 70, 85, 87, 94, 123, 145, 171, 184, 186
crown/garland of, 123, 123n21, 125, 127n43, 133
doxa, 10, 84, 87, 123, 126, 127, 127nn42–44, 133, 135, 228
doxa/ḥsd of all flesh, 37, 40, 123–29, 133–34, 158, 171, 183, 187
as a withering flower, 36, 42, 124, 129, 131, 180–81
doxazō, 80, 87, 93, 125n30, 126, 127, 127n44, 165n69
goodness, 5, 28, 31, 37, 47, 60, 85, 117n82, 138, 142n36
good conduct, 25, 27, 41, 115n67
good deeds, 28n22, 31
good news, 125, 125n30, 126n33, 133, 147, 153
good things, 76, 112, 123, 178
gospel, 83, 93, 97, 125, 126n34, 152n87, 183
See also goodness: good news
grace (*charis*), 46n74, 55–57, 55n1, 55–56n3, 90n80, 189, 228
See also favor (*ḥn*)
guidance, 110, 112, 171

ḥāsîd, 1, 2, 47n4, 48, 53–54
health, 14, 67
divine physician, 67, 71, 183, 185
healing, 68, 68n33, 69, 71, 71n46, 185, 191
medical imagery, 67, 71, 173
help, 19, 26, 34–35, 43, 70, 71, 92, 107, 119, 185
See also YHWH / the Lord / God: help of
holiness, 50, 59–60, 101, 112, 132, 151, 154, 165
hagioi ("saints"), 92–93, 156n8, 161n48, 164, 166n74, 185
hagios, 51, 58–59, 136, 155, 156, 156n8, 162n53, 165, 178, 190
"holy" as a translation for *hosios*, 1, 51, 58, 136, 155, 156, 165, 169, 187, 190
QDWŠ, *qdwš*, *qdš*, 51, 58, 136
See also covenant: holy; YHWH / the Lord / God: holiness of
hope, 39, 97, 143n49, 145–46, 150, 151, 153, 167, 174, 180–82, 228
living, 119, 121, 126, 128, 129, 134, 175, 181, 191
and waiting, 27n21, 87, 120, 125, 133, 134
hosios
ho hosios, 150–52, 156, 156n9, 162–64, 162n52, 174, 178, 181–82
(hoti) monos hosios, 155n2, 156, 158, 161, 164–67, 174, 187
See also YHWH / the Lord / God: as *hosios*; YHWH / the Lord / God: *hosios* of
ḥsd (noun)
abundance of, 26, 28, 31, 39, 40, 45, 84, 129, 159, 166–67, 186 (see also *ḥsd* [noun]: *rb ḥsd*; *ḥsd* [noun]: *rb ḥsd w'mt*; *ḥsd* [noun]: *rwb ḥsd*)
attributive forms/uses of, 45
Figurative *Ḥsd*, 18, 23, 34, 36–37, 42, 43, 63
great (*gdl*), 28, 39, 40, 120, 129n49, 134, 160n41, 227
men of / people of, 43, 46, 132, 182, 182n4, 187n10
and parallel terms, 24n8, 29, 29n26, 45, 45n70, 66, 81–83, 180
Personified *Ḥsd*, 23, 34–36, 42, 43
plural construct forms, 29, 30, 32–33, 42, 45n72
plural forms/uses, 23, 29, 30, 32, 39, 42, 44–45, 46n75 (see also *ḥsd* [noun]:

ḥsd (noun) (*continued*)
plural construct forms; David, son of Jesse: faithful *ḥsdym/hosia* of)
rb ḥsd, 27, 40, 56, 86, 90, 103, 105, 120, 121, 128, 130, 134, 180, 227
rb ḥsd w'mt, 55, 108
rwb ḥsd, 45
ḥsd/eleos, the keeping of, 23, 24, 31
and keeping YHWH / the Lord / God's commandments, 20, 24, 44, 84n33, 103, 108, 113–14, 140n27
by YHWH / the Lord / God, 20, 24, 33n45, 41, 103, 108, 112–14, 140n27, 165n69
ḥsyd
parallels to, 48–49, 53–54, 116n72, 140
plural forms/uses of, 48–54, 87, 116, 140–41, 150, 153, 174, 176, 186–87
See also YHWH / the Lord / God: as *ḥsyd*; YHWH / the Lord / God: *ḥsyd/ym* of
hypocrisy, 62, 65, 68–69, 75–76, 94, 173, 183

infancy narrative, Luke's, 100, 101, 106, 108, 114, 118
inheritance, 70, 73, 74, 94, 109, 111, 112n58, 116, 132
imperishable, undefiled, and unfading, 121, 126, 128–29, 134, 171, 175, 187, 191
kept in heaven, 121–22, 187, 191
intertextuality, 7–11, 7n2, 16, 18, 188
Israel and descendants
ancestors of, 1, 26, 46, 105, 110, 114, 166–67, 169–70, 184 (*see also* Israel and descendants: promises spoken to ancestors of)
choice of, 51, 98, 132
covenant with, 20n17, 36n48, 97, 98, 102n15, 112n57, 130–32, 142, 144, 147, 153
disobedience/hardening of, 86–87, 89, 94
house of, 103–4, 113–14, 145, 161
and *ḥsd/eleos*, 1, 24, 26–31, 41, 103, 110, 112–14, 118, 161, 170–73, 184
prayer for the salvation of, 94, 95, 99, 171
promises spoken to ancestors of, 92, 103, 105, 109, 112–14, 139, 142, 146, 149, 182
promises to, 97, 98, 113, 114, 130–32, 142–44, 147, 150, 152, 153
See also YHWH / the Lord / God: relationship with: Israel and descendants
Israel of God, 88, 89, 89n71, 89n73, 93, 95, 98–99, 172, 186

Jacob and his line/offspring, 31, 33, 82–84, 85n44, 89, 104n23, 110n50, 122n13, 130
promises to, 82–83, 92, 96–97, 104
Jerusalem, 31, 32, 59, 85, 87, 107, 111, 113, 122n18, 125, 145, 172
Jesus Christ (the Messiah), 131, 152, 176
being "in Christ," 78n1, 89, 95, 133, 185, 187, 191
birth and infancy of, 100–101, 106, 108, 109, 112, 118, 171
burial of, 145, 146, 151n76, 174
critique of the religious leaders, 62, 65–66, 68–69, 75–77, 115n68, 173, 184–85
crucifixion of, 76, 88, 93–95, 98, 145, 152, 173, 175, 182
death of, 9, 126, 138–39, 141, 142, 144–49, 151, 172, 174, 180, 183
as a descendant of Abraham, 89, 93–94
as a descendant of David, 96, 98, 140–41, 144–46, 148, 150–53, 172, 174, 177, 178
disciples of, 67–69, 71–75, 71nn41–42, 73n64, 115n67, 117n82, 127, 173
and *eleos*, 67, 68, 68n33, 71, 77, 120, 173, 176, 183, 186, 187
exaltation of, 146, 151, 174, 181, 187
execution of, 151n76, 172
and forgiveness of sins, 76, 146, 172, 185, 191
incarnation of, 180, 181, 187
life of, 3, 9, 80n9
as Lord and Christ, 109, 120, 125, 126, 128, 134, 139, 145, 152
as Lord of the Sabbath, 68, 70, 72, 72n55, 77, 173

as the Lord's *hosios* / devoted party, 140, 142, 145–46, 149, 151–53, 178, 183, 185
ministry of, 71, 72, 77, 138n14, 176, 179, 181, 183
raised by God, 96, 139, 142, 144–51, 144n53, 172, 174, 177, 180, 182–86
redeeming work of, 132
reign of, 144, 144n53, 162
resurrection of, 9, 121, 126, 129, 131, 134, 141, 149, 172, 181 (*see also* Jesus Christ: raised by God)
resurrection of, as fulfillment of predictions and promises, 139, 142, 144, 146, 151, 153, 178, 180, 187
return of, 166
revelation of, 127n44
as a servant of the circumcision, 83, 87, 90, 93, 96
sonship of, 112, 115n66, 151n74, 152
and the stump/root/shoot of Jesse, 97, 97n103, 110n50, 123, 183
suffering of, 123, 126n33
and the sunrise, 105, 110, 183
trial/s of, 143n48, 151n76
triumph/victory of, 95, 96, 138n14, 185
Jewish heritage, 46, 54, 65, 77, 79, 115, 117, 127, 150–51, 157, 186
Jews, 53–54, 75, 77, 96, 131n59, 133n74, 150n67, 152n87, 153
See also Christians: Jewish; Gentiles/nations: Jews and Gentiles
John the Baptist, prophet of the Most High, 106, 110, 112
joy, 51, 138
See also rejoicing
Judah/Judea, 11n23, 32, 33, 37, 53, 63, 66, 69, 72, 85, 111n51, 125, 125n28
judgment, 57, 60, 61, 120, 125, 134, 162, 163, 190
judgments, 53, 66, 125, 129, 163, 165, 167, 174, 185, 187
See also covenant: fitting judgment or punishment for breaking; YHWH / the Lord / God: faithful and righteous judgments of
justice, 20, 33, 37, 49, 62, 65–66, 68, 74, 75, 79, 120
injustice, 57
justification (*dikaioō*), 146, 146n59, 149, 172, 174, 178, 185, 191

kingdom of heaven, 70–75, 73n61
See also YHWH / the Lord / God: kingdom of; movement, the early Christian: new kingdom movement
kinship, 17, 19–20, 31, 43, 133n82, 187, 190
knowledge, linguistic or encyclopaedic, 13–14, 17

Lamb, 162n56, 164n64, 165n66, 167, 178
redeeming work of, 167, 178
song of, 157, 157n19, 163, 163n63, 164n64
See also blood: of a lamb / the Lamb; deliverance: by the blood of a lamb
law, 73n65
appearance of meticulous keeping, 69, 76, 173, 183
genuine observance of, 62, 70–74, 73n61, 111, 176, 183
Jesus's understanding/interpretation of, 62, 70, 72–73, 73n61, 77, 117, 176, 183–85
of Moses, 75, 146, 149, 150, 174, 185
observing legal minutiae of, 62, 65, 68, 70, 72, 75, 77, 176, 185
"weighty" (priority) matters of, 62, 64, 65, 68–70, 72–73, 75, 77, 172–73, 176, 180–81, 185
Law, 69n36, 72–73, 80, 150n68
Decalogue, 71–72, 189
Torah, 32, 53, 73n57
leaders, religious, 71, 72, 74–76, 172, 183, 185–87, 191
Pharisees, 54, 62, 65, 67–69, 71–72, 74–77, 79, 115, 173, 176
scribes, 62, 65, 68, 74n69, 75, 127n41
life, 21, 37, 120, 142, 142n36, 182
eternal, 74, 111, 112n58, 116, 120, 144
opposed to death, 120, 138n13, 153, 178
paths/ways of, 52, 74n69, 112, 138, 139, 140n27, 145–46, 149, 174
See also preservation of life
light, 106, 106n40, 110, 123n19, 131n54, 171
love, 5, 49, 84, 94, 115, 123, 133, 176, 184
agapē/agapaō, 5, 38, 55–56, 56n5, 115, 115nn67–68, 119, 127n40, 189

love (*continued*)
ʾhb, 38, 56, 56n5, 115n67
ʾhbh, 29, 38–40, 45, 56, 127n40
ʾhbt ḥsd, 45, 45n72
of neighbor, 111, 112n58, 115, 117, 172, 185
of YHWH/God, 24, 44, 103, 108, 111, 112n58, 113–15, 160n43, 165n69, 185
loyalty, 2, 5, 29–30, 32–33, 36n48, 43, 90, 127, 166, 168, 184, 188–91
amid trials, 127, 143n48, 168, 184
See also covenant: loyalty
LXX, influence of, 44
on New Testament language, 3–4, 56, 57, 60–61, 126–27, 155, 156, 175, 177, 189–90
on New Testament writing, 100–101, 136–37, 150n63

marriage imagery, 20, 20n17, 72, 162n56
betrothal metaphor, 20, 29, 36, 36n49, 63, 66
Mary, 102, 109–10, 112, 117, 173
mercy, 38, 83n28, 86n47, 94–95, 121, 132, 134, 171, 172n3, 177
and *eleos*, 57, 62, 73, 77, 78, 98, 101, 103, 114, 116, 118, 134, 169, 187, 189–90
ḥnn ("have mercy / be gracious"), 38, 53, 58, 73, 84, 86–87, 89, 177, 189, 231
Messiah, 73n61, 110n50, 131, 131n56, 139, 141, 141n34, 152n80, 152n83, 178, 183
anointed one (*mšyḥ*), 81, 91, 96, 96n93, 97, 104, 123n21, 152, 152n86, 187
coming/visitation of, 73n61, 105, 110, 112–14, 118, 152, 154, 171, 176, 178, 182, 185
messianic interpretation of texts, 96, 97, 97n101, 101, 110n50, 139, 141, 143n49, 151–53, 152n79
servant-messianic figure, 103n21, 110, 112, 130, 152
See also Jesus Christ (the Messiah)
metalepsis, 8–10
metaphor, 14n43, 15, 18, 35, 36, 36n49, 71, 124n25, 132n65, 139n16, 194
metaphorical expression, 67
metaphorical extension, 15–16
See also health: medical imagery; marriage imagery: betrothal metaphor; vessels (*skeuos*): and the pottery metaphor
metonymy, 30
metonymic extension, 15, 18, 42
monosemy, 16–18, 188
morality, 53, 57, 60, 155n2
Moses, 84, 108–9, 112
as servant of God, 158, 163
songs of, 131, 157, 158, 163
See also law: of Moses
motivation, 39, 43, 77, 91n83, 129–31, 134, 177, 181, 187
movement, the early Christian, 108
new kingdom movement, 72–73, 77, 143n48, 176, 182
origin amongst Jews, 101, 118, 153, 177
pressures and opposition, 123n24, 133, 133n74, 135, 166
mutuality, 21, 25, 33, 41, 43, 103, 114, 127, 134, 177, 184, 189
mutual aid, 19n4, 116, 172, 176, 190
mutual obligations, 1, 1n3, 19, 32, 114
mutual rights and responsibilities, 19–20, 90n79, 142

nature, imagery from. *See* agriculture and nature, imagery from
need, 3n10, 27, 29, 35, 37, 41, 57–58, 70–71, 74, 171–73, 183–85
barrenness, 33, 106, 110, 112, 117, 121, 170, 176, 183, 186
dire, 1n2, 71, 111n53, 114n63, 176, 180, 182, 185
essential, 1n2, 17n58, 25–26, 43, 111n53, 176–77
hunger and thirst, 69–71, 71n41, 73, 74, 76, 109, 112, 117, 147, 186
lowliness, 109, 109n48, 112, 117, 171, 186
meeting, 25, 32, 43, 70, 74–75, 77, 111, 115n70, 116, 119, 176–77, 185–87
the neglected or vulnerable, 117n84, 158
recognition of, 43, 67, 69, 71, 74, 111, 173, 185
the rejected, 117, 118, 129, 186

sickness, 69, 71, 73, 74
situational powerlessness, 25–26, 125, 182, 185
weakness, 79, 111n53, 117n84
weariness, 73, 125
of a wounded man (the Devoted Samaritan parable), 107, 110–11, 111nn51–53, 113, 114n64, 115–17, 115n71, 170, 172, 176, 185
See also sinfulness
neglect, 32, 62, 64–66, 68–69, 71–74, 77, 172–73, 183–85
neighborliness, 100, 115, 115nn70–71, 117, 117n80, 172, 177, 181, 185, 186
being/becoming a neighbor, 107, 110–11, 113, 115, 116n75, 172, 180, 185

obligations, 184
covenant, 20, 114, 154, 185
fulfilling, 46, 72, 73, 76, 113, 185
outwardly meticulous observance of, 77, 173, 183
pretentious observance of, 77, 187
oppression, 165, 166
overcomers, 167, 185, 187
those who have conquered the beast (etc.), 157, 161, 163, 165, 166

participants, semantic, 16, 22
party, devoted, 47–50, 52, 145–46, 148–49, 153, 164–67, 174, 178, 183, 219n40
patients, unexpected, 69, 77, 112, 117, 176
patriarchs and their descendants, 24, 31, 41, 80, 87, 139, 143, 148, 170, 172
Paul's speech in Acts, 137, 139–42, 146–47, 149–53, 150nn67–68, 180
peace, 88–89, 93, 112, 119, 132n65, 147, 171, 172n3, 186
peoples, 81–82, 92, 92n86, 96–97, 122, 143n46
perception, lack of, 74n69, 176
misunderstanding, 67–69, 74
perishability and imperishability, 37, 66, 123–24, 125n26, 126, 128–29, 131, 133, 134, 181, 187
persecution, 28, 133n77, 147, 149, 174
Peter's speech in Acts, 137, 138, 138n14, 140, 141n34, 145–46, 149–53, 180
pit (*šḥt*), 138–40, 139n20, 140nn21–22, 141n34, 145, 149, 153
pity, 24, 38n57, 57–58, 73, 119, 177, 189
plagues, 156, 157, 160n39, 161, 161n48
pleas, 21, 27, 39, 85n40, 116n73, 142
polysemy, 16–18
power, 19, 20n15, 84, 97, 121, 133n77, 162, 184, 199n17, 219n40
imbalance, 21, 29–30, 43, 189
impermanent, perceived and/or political power, 20, 125, 133
the powerful (rich, proud, rulers), 109, 109n48, 112, 171
situational, 1, 24–26, 29, 38, 43, 70, 111n53, 169, 182, 185–86
practice ("doing") of *ḥsd/eleos*
"do *ḥsd* (with)", 26, 43, 79, 91, 104–6, 114, 120, 134, 184, 190–91 (*see also* practice of *ḥsd/eleos*: *ʿśh ḥsd [ʿm]*)
"do [*poieō*] *eleos* (with)", 69–73, 75, 77, 101, 104, 105, 109–17, 120, 170, 175, 176, 183, 186 (*see also* practice of *ḥsd/eleos*: Samaritan man who did *eleos*)
Samaritan man who did *eleos*, 107, 111, 111n53, 113–18, 116n75, 170–72, 176, 183, 185, 186
ʿśh ḥsd (ʿm), 20, 24, 30–31, 33, 38–40, 45, 81, 91, 104–7, 120, 170
praise, 51, 126, 158n20, 159, 160, 165, 166, 171, 174, 176, 178
response to *ḥsd* or *eleos*, 25, 29, 43, 80–82, 92, 94–99, 168
response of *ḥsydym* or *hosioi*, 49–50, 52, 59n24
prayers, (answered), 24, 27, 28, 31, 41, 87, 94, 159n31, 164n65, 185
presence and absence, 33–34, 43, 50, 73, 85, 173
See also YHWH / the Lord / God: presence of
preservation of life, 25, 27, 41, 141, 149, 167
after or from death, 139, 149, 172, 182
priests/priesthood, 48, 49n10, 54, 54n24, 59, 63, 72, 73, 73n63, 73n65, 116n72, 123n19, 156
priest and/or Levite (Devoted Samaritan parable), 111, 111nn52–53, 113, 115, 116, 117n82, 172, 176, 186

proactivity or reactivity, 143, 143n41, 148, 150, 151n76, 153, 178, 183, 186
promises, 21n19, 25, 80, 103, 115, 130, 130n50, 132, 133, 151n74, 171–72
  and fulfillment, 41, 96, 98, 112, 139, 142–44, 146, 147, 150–53, 170, 173, 177–78, 180, 183–86
  remembered, 100, 113–14, 118, 176–78, 181
  See also Abraham: promises to Abraham and offspring; covenant: promises; David, son of Jesse: promises to David and offspring; Israel and descendants: promises spoken to ancestors of; Israel and descendants: promises to; remembrance
Prophets, 33, 34, 72–73, 80, 150n68, 158
protection, 1n2, 19, 34–36, 41, 49, 138, 145, 159
prototypes, 13–18, 16n57, 188
  prototypical features or behavior, 13, 16, 18, 24, 40, 43–44, 52, 56, 90, 180–81
  prototypical scenarios and exemplars, 13–15, 17, 23, 25–26, 28–29, 32, 34–36, 44, 48, 50, 52, 119
  prototypical subcategories or domains, 13, 14, 23, 41, 43, 48

Qumran community, 44, 117n81, 189, 236n8

range, semantic, 60, 190
receptivity, 47–48, 71, 71n42, 74, 89, 149, 153, 153n90, 178, 182–84
recipients, 25, 27, 41, 43–45, 89n71, 165, 171, 176, 182
reciprocity, 1, 21, 25–26, 38, 41, 43, 72, 113–16, 118, 186, 189
  See also relationships: reciprocal
redemption, 27, 41, 106, 110, 112, 129, 170, 184, 186
  See also Jesus Christ: redeeming work of; Lamb: redeeming work of
regeneration, 90, 91n83, 120–21, 125n27, 128–34, 130n52, 175, 181, 186, 187
  anagennaō, 121, 124, 126, 128, 130–31
rejoicing, 97, 146, 152n86, 172n4, 174, 176, 178
  in response to *ḥsd/eleos*, 25, 86, 109, 110, 112, 128, 170, 173
relationships, 19–21, 28–29, 31, 57, 156, 170–72, 176, 179, 190
  mutual, 21, 32, 103, 144, 177, 184–85
  reciprocal, 21, 114, 118
  relational claims, 38
  trusting, 1, 19, 25, 31, 37n52
  See also covenant: relationships; YHWH / the Lord / God: relationship with
remembrance, 27, 30–32, 41, 43, 100–101, 105, 114, 118, 170, 172, 176–77, 181
  not remembering, 24, 131, 166–67
  remembering *ḥsd/eleos*, 101, 103–4, 109, 112–14, 118, 161, 166–67, 175, 180, 184
remnant, 84–87, 112n57, 123, 132, 133, 240n17
repayment (according to works), 90, 163, 163n61, 166, 187
repentance, 28, 67n30, 71n44, 86n49, 152, 187, 191
reputation, 23n7, 26–28, 28n22, 40, 43, 144
requests, 24–26, 38, 40, 41, 43, 107, 109, 129, 167, 170, 217n38
resemblance, 9, 13, 57, 90, 103, 119, 128, 130, 133n82, 172
  family resemblances, 12, 16–17
resonance, 2–3, 3n9, 8, 9n11, 11n23, 56, 105, 120, 122, 185
responsibility, 1n2, 17n58, 33, 43, 52, 90n79, 116
restoration, 76, 87n53, 89, 114n63, 130, 130n50, 142, 144, 176, 191
resurrection from death, 121, 138–39, 140n27, 141, 142, 149, 151, 172, 180
  falling asleep (euphemism) and being raised, 139, 139n16, 142, 144–49, 150n65, 151, 172, 174, 180, 182–83, 185–86
reversal of circumstances, 109, 109n48, 112, 117

reward, 59n24, 71n42, 74, 74n69, 76, 115n67, 123, 125, 166
righteousness, 5, 37, 74–76, 79, 110, 112, 120, 123, 161, 163, 185
  dikaios, 60, 61, 74, 74n66, 74n69, 156, 156n9, 159–66, 160n38, 165n69, 228
  dikaiosynē, 35, 56n6, 58, 58n18, 74, 74n66, 74n69, 106–7, 146n59, 161, 227
  genuine versus pretentious righteousness, 74n69, 75–77, 183, 185, 186, 191
  rewards of, 71n42, 74, 74n69, 76
  righteous ones, 53, 59n24, 71, 71n42, 74–76, 94, 110, 112, 170
  ṣdqh, *ṣdq*, or *ṣdyq*, 33, 37, 53, 56n6, 74, 127n42, 160, 165, 165n69, 230, 235n1
  uprightness, 33n45, 48, 50, 52, 59, 110, 159
rule of new creation, 88, 89, 89n71, 93, 95, 98, 99, 173, 176, 182
rulers, 20–21, 53, 109, 109n48, 122n18, 125, 143
  kings in general, 21, 21n20, 24–25, 31, 34–35, 41, 81, 143n41, 172
  princes, 125
  specified kings, 21, 31–32, 43, 74, 91, 96, 104, 131, 141, 143, 152 (*see also* David, son of Jesse; Jesus Christ: as a descendant of David)

Sabbath and its observance, 68, 68n32, 70–73, 73–74n65, 77, 146, 150n68, 173, 176, 183
sacrifice, 33, 48, 62–64, 66–68, 70–72, 74–77, 173, 176, 185
  sacrificial system, 63–64
salvation, 74, 84, 94, 97, 109, 111, 133, 160–61, 167
  and *eleos*, 69, 81, 87, 90, 91, 96, 104–5, 110, 112, 114, 128–29, 134, 170, 184–86
  history, 130, 149–51, 175, 178
  horn of, 105, 110, 114, 139n17, 143n48
  and *ḥsd*, 25, 27–28, 35–36, 41, 70, 81, 91–92, 96, 103–5, 113, 129, 151, 159–61, 170, 191
  to the Jew first and also to the Greek, 97, 99, 176
  prepared to be revealed in the last time, 121, 126, 128, 175
  salvific act/event, 35, 95, 114n63, 116, 160, 178, 186
  yšʿ (noun), *yšʿ* (verb), *yšwʿh*, and/or *tšwʿh*, 27, 35, 92, 103–4, 113, 151, 160, 230, 232
Savior, 109, 185
  for Israel, 150, 152, 187
schema, 15
  schematic uses, 33, 42, 43, 68n34 (*see also* entity)
script. *See* prototypes: prototypical scenarios and exemplars
Septuagint. *See* LXX, influence of
sinfulness, 78
  iniquity, 104n26, 108–9, 112
  mercy for sinners, 78, 95, 98, 177, 189
  sin, 104n26, 108–9, 112, 121, 127n40, 158n20, 163 (*see also* forgiveness of sins; Jesus Christ: and forgiveness of sins)
  sinners, 48, 67, 69, 71, 74–76, 115, 173, 176, 185–87 (*see also* sinfulness: mercy for sinners)
  transgression, 63, 104n26, 108, 112, 127n40
solidarity, 30, 116, 126n33, 127, 129, 134–35, 166, 177, 184, 187, 189
sonship, 44–45, 97, 112, 115, 115n66, 117, 151, 151n72, 151n74, 152
suffering, 57, 123, 133, 135, 165–67, 174, 177, 178, 184, 185, 191
  trials, 127n44, 132, 178 (*see also* commitment: amid trials; loyalty: amid trials)
  See also Jesus Christ: suffering of
superiority, 1n2, 40, 82, 92, 94, 97, 166, 169

tax collectors, 67, 67n26, 69–71, 76, 173, 176, 183, 185–87
temple, 28, 33, 36n50, 42, 51, 59, 60, 73, 161n46, 162n56
thanksgiving, 28–29, 41, 43, 49–50, 76, 89n67, 92
  liturgy (“his *ḥsd* is forever”), 27, 28, 40, 41, 43, 46, 56n10, 187

tradition, scriptural, 55, 79, 98, 101, 157
as authoritative, 11, 72, 77, 99, 181
continuity with, 11, 17, 74, 114, 118, 130, 134, 170–73, 175–76, 178–79, 181–83
developments within, 17, 22, 41–43, 175, 176, 179, 182, 186
fulfillment of Scripture, 93, 95, 98, 113, 125, 145, 150, 153, 173, 175, 180, 182–83
scriptural endorsement, 123, 138, 139, 150
transactions between two parties, 16–17, 24–26, 30, 33, 40, 43, 114, 169
transformation, 3n9, 125, 128, 174, 181, 182, 184, 191
transumption, 8, 10, 18, 143, 144, 166, 184, 188
triumph, 81, 120, 134, 167
trust, 28, 31, 35, 37, 37n52, 39, 59, 89, 122

vessels (*skeuos*), 84, 85, 85n39, 87, 125n26
of *eleos and orgē*, 83n28, 84–85, 87, 87n53, 89, 93–95, 93n88, 98, 171, 184, 186
and the pottery metaphor, 84–85, 87, 87n53, 93
victory, 81, 91–92, 95, 96, 104, 160, 165, 174, 178, 185
visitation, 105, 105n29, 110, 112, 123n19, 170, 184, 186

women, 117n84
of *eleos*, 102, 106, 109, 110, 112, 117, 170, 176, 183, 186, 187
of *ḥsd*, 1, 24, 31, 33, 46
worship, 43, 108, 112, 178
of the nations, 158, 164, 165, 167–68, 186
true nature of, 64, 72, 77

YHWH / the Lord / God
as agent of *eleos*, 93, 94, 98, 109, 110, 112, 170, 171, 173, 183, 186
as agent of *hosia*, 147, 148, 172, 177
as agent of *ḥsd*, 24, 30, 31, 33, 40, 91–92, 94, 108, 147, 148, 172–73, 186
anger of, 33, 50, 84, 92, 95, 103n17 (*see also* vessels [*skeuos*]: of *eleos* and *orgē*; YHWH / the Lord / God: wrath of)
attribute formula for, 26–28, 55, 61, 86, 102–7, 112, 121, 128–30, 150, 175, 180–81
belonging to, 52, 59 (*see also* covenant people, YHWH / the Lord / God's: belonging to)
call of, 85–87, 89, 93–94, 93n89, 98, 171, 175, 182, 186
character of, 36n49, 132, 165, 174
characteristic of, 26–29, 57, 92, 108–10, 119, 128, 129, 134, 171, 182
characteristics of, 26, 50, 52, 66, 108
choices of, 98, 112
covenant partners of, 24, 31, 41, 170
covenant people of (*see* covenant people, YHWH / the Lord / God's)
delight/desire of, 33–34, 40, 62–64, 66–72, 74–77, 85, 92, 152, 172, 187
as devoted party, 49–51, 156, 156n9, 158–67, 174, 178, 181–84, 186–87
devotion of, 106, 165–68, 177–79, 183, 184, 187
devotion to, 54, 134–35, 165, 205n24
eleos affections (*splanchna eleous*) of, 101, 105, 105n28, 106, 109
faithful and righteous judgments of, 61, 155, 156n9, 163–68, 165n69, 178, 181–82, 184
faithfulness of, 82, 92, 97, 103–4, 113, 116, 160, 165n69, 187
as Father of the Lord Jesus Christ, 126, 128, 131, 134
fear of, 37, 56, 102–3, 112, 158, 160, 164, 165, 167–68, 171
intergenerational, 101–2, 109, 187
glorification of, 80n8, 83, 94, 168, 173, 183
the Lord's name, 158, 164, 165, 165n9
for the sake of *eleos*, 78, 80, 83, 87, 90, 93, 95, 98–99, 172, 180–82, 186
greatness of, 160
help of, 28, 109, 129, 134, 165, 177
holiness of, 122n17, 130n52, 132n63, 133, 155n2, 165, 167
as the Holy One or the Lord God of Israel, 51, 110, 112, 113, 169–71

as *hosios*, 156nn8–9, 164–68, 174, 183–87
hosios of, 138, 139, 139n15, 148, 152–54, 174, 178, 183–85, 187
as *ḥsyd*, 47–49, 47n4, 51, 81, 159–60, 160nn40–41, 165–68, 186
ḥsyd/ym of, 49–50, 81, 87, 138–41, 145, 148, 150–51, 153, 160n41, 167
interventions of, 28, 41, 50, 128, 178, 187
as King (of the nations), 158, 160, 160n38, 160n41, 164
kingdom of, 67n30, 71n40, 74, 162, 166, 185
as the Lord God the Almighty, 156, 156n9, 162–67, 162n56, 164nn63–64, 174, 181, 184, 187
opposition to YHWH's ways, 35, 49, 52, 84n33, 174n7
as perceiver, 29n27, 33, 34, 40, 63–64, 66–70, 77, 108, 147, 172–73
as possessive party, 47–53, 138–41, 145–46, 148–51, 153, 167, 174, 178, 180, 182, 184–85
as possessor of *eleos*, 90, 109, 110, 112, 128, 171, 175, 182, 183
as possessor of *ḥsd*, 25–29, 31, 35, 37, 40, 92, 94, 108, 186
as potential patient of *ḥsd*, 24 (neg.), 27, 29–30
presence of, 35, 109, 127n42, 129, 138
as proactive party, 143, 148, 183, 186
relationship with, 35, 36n49, 42, 47, 128–29, 134, 145–46, 164, 171, 177, 190
covenant relationship with, 20, 41, 48–52, 63, 95–98, 156, 170, 172, 175, 186, 191
Israel and descendants, 1, 29–30, 36–37, 64, 92, 129, 131–32, 150, 171, 173, 187
as justification for *ḥsd*, 25, 27, 31, 35, 37, 40
as relational context for *ḥsd*, 24, 27, 29–31, 34–37, 41, 147, 170, 172, 173
righteous acts of, 158, 164–65
righteous and faithful ways of, 156n9, 158–59, 160n38, 164–65
righteousness of, 156n9, 160, 162, 164, 165, 165n69
servant of, 91, 101–3, 109, 112, 139n17, 140, 173, 186
unique and incomparable nature of, 133, 156n9, 164–67, 166n72, 178, 183–87
will of, 76, 84, 93–94, 98, 150, 171, 182
word of, 35, 113, 116, 124–25, 125n27, 133, 134, 153, 178
works/deeds of, 50, 52, 159–61, 160n39, 165, 174
great, 158, 164–65
wonderful, 158, 160, 164–67, 166n72, 184, 187
wrath of, 33, 84–85, 84n33, 87n53, 95, 121, 161

Zechariah, 105–6, 109–10, 139n17
Zion, 50–53, 59, 122, 123n18, 123n21, 131, 131n55, 143n46, 152n86

www.ingramcontent.com/pod-product-compliance
Lightning Source LLC
Chambersburg PA
CBHW060552080526
44585CB00013B/531
9781646022427